HOW TO THINK LOGICALLY

HOW TO THINK LOGICALLY

Second Edition

GARY SEAY

Medgar Evers College, City University of New York

SUSANA NUCCETELLI

St. Cloud State University

Boston   Columbus   Indianapolis   New York   San Francisco   Upper Saddle River
Amsterdam   Cape Town   Dubai   London   Madrid   Milan   Munich   Paris   Montreal   Toronto
Delhi   Mexico City   Sao Paulo   Sydney   Hong Kong   Seoul   Singapore   Taipei   Tokyo

Editorial Director: Craig Campanella
Editor in Chief: Dickson Musslewhite
Executive Editor: Ashley Dodge
Editorial Project Manager: Kate Fernandes
Director of Marketing: Brandy Dawson
Senior Marketing Manager: Laura Lee Manley
Project Manager: Shelly Kupperman
Production Manager: Susan Hannahs
Senior Art Director: Jayne Conte

Cover Designer: Suzanne Behnke
Cover Art: Thinkstock
Full-Service Project Management: George Jacob, Integra Software Services, Ltd.
Composition: Integra Software Services, Ltd
Printer/Binder: RR Donnelley
Cover Printer: RR Donnelley
Text Font: 9.75/13, NexusMix

Credits and acknowledgments borrowed from other sources and reproduced, with permission, in this textbook appear on the appropriate page within the text.

Many of the designations by manufacturers and seller to distinguish their products are claimed as trademarks. Where those designations appear in this book, and the publisher was aware of a trademark claim, the designations have been printed in initial caps or all caps.

Library of Congress Cataloging-in-Publication Data
Seay, Gary.
    How to think logically / Gary Seay, Susana Nuccetelli.—2nd ed.
        p. cm.
    Includes index.
    ISBN-13: 978-0-205-15498-2
    ISBN-10: 0-205-15498-0
    1. Logic—Textbooks.   I. Nuccetelli, Susana.   II. Title.
    BC108.S34 2012
    160—dc22

                                        2011014099

ISBN 10:   0-205-15498-0
ISBN 13: 978-0-205-15498-2

brief contents

detailed contents

This is a book intended for introductory courses in logic and critical thinking, but its scope is broadly focused to include some issues in philosophy as well as treatments of induction, informal fallacies, and both propositional and traditional syllogistic logic. Its aim throughout, however, is to broach these topics in a way that will be accessible to beginners in college-level work. *How to Think Logically* is a user-friendly text designed for students who have never encountered philosophy before, and for whom a systematic approach to analytical thinking may be an unfamiliar exercise. The writing style is simple and direct, with jargon kept to a minimum. Symbolism is also kept simple. Scattered through the text are special-emphasis boxes in which important points are summarized to help students focus on crucial distinctions and fundamental ideas. The book's fourteen chapters unfold in a way that undergraduates will find understandable and easy to follow. Even so, the book maintains a punctilious regard for the principles of logic. At no point does it compromise rigor.

How to Think Logically is a guide to the analysis, reconstruction, and evaluation of arguments. It is designed to help students learn to distinguish good reasoning from bad. The book is divided into four parts. The first is devoted to argument recognition and the building blocks of argument. Chapter 1 introduces argument analysis, focusing on argument recognition and the difference between formal and informal approaches to inference. Chapter 2 offers a closer look at the language from which arguments are constructed and examines such topics as logical strength, linguistic merit, rhetorical power, types of sentences, uses of language, and definition. Chapter 3 considers epistemic aspects of the statements that are the components of an inference. It explains the assumption that when speakers are sincere and competent, what they state is what they believe, so that the epistemic virtues and vices of belief may also affect statements. Part II is devoted to the analysis of deductive and inductive arguments, distinguishing under each of these two general classifications several different types of argument that students should be able to recognize. It also includes discussions of the principles of charity and faithfulness, extended arguments, enthymemes, and normative arguments of four different kinds. In Part III, students are shown how some very basic confusions in thinking may lead to defective reasoning, and they learn to spot twenty of the most common informal fallacies. Part IV, which comprises Chapters 11 through 14, offers a feature many instructors will want: a detailed treatment of some common elementary procedures for determining validity in propositional logic—including a simplified approach to proofs—and traditional syllogistic logic. Here students will be able to go well beyond the intuitive procedures learned in Chapter 5.

Each of the book's four parts is a self-contained unit. The topics are presented in a way that permits instructors to teach the chapters in different sequences and combinations, according to the needs of their courses. For example, an instructor in a critical thinking course could simply assign Chapters 1 through 10. But in a course geared more to deductive logic, Chapters 1, 4, 5, and 6 and then 11 through 14 might serve best. Other instructors might want to do some of both critical thinking and deductive logic, for which the best strategy might be to assign Chapter 1 and then either 4 through 12, or 4 through 10 plus 13 and 14.

How to Think Logically, in this new second-edition format, includes a number of improvements, thanks to the helpful suggestions of anonymous reviewers selected by Pearson and of philosophers we know who are using the book:

- Chapter 1 has been reworked to present a better introduction to argument, the central topic of the book. The treatment of non-arguments now includes entries for explanations, conditionals, and fictional discourse.

- A more concise treatment of definition now follows discussions of figurative meaning and indirect use of language in Chapter 2. Also added to this chapter is an expanded treatment of sentence types, including speech acts, in connection with the discussion of uses of language, providing a more nuanced and timely treatment of this topic.

- The discussions of contradiction and consistency in Chapter 3 have been rewritten for greater clarity.

- The section on evaluative reasoning in Chapter 4 has been expanded into a much-improved discussion of moral, legal, prudential, and aesthetic norms and arguments.

- Many new examples, of varying degrees of difficulty, have been incorporated in the book's account of informal fallacies. First-edition examples have been brought up to date.

- Exercise sections in all chapters have been greatly expanded. Many new exercises have been added, so that students can now get more practice in applying what they're learning. As a result, instructors will now have a larger selection of exercises from which to choose in assigning homework or in engaging students in class discussions.

- The program of the book has been simplified so that it does much better, and more economically, what instructors need it to do: namely, serve as a text for teaching students how to develop critical-reasoning skills. The 'Philosopher's Corner' features of the first edition have been taken out, following the consensus of reviewers, who said that they almost never had time in a fifteen-week semester to use them if they were teaching the logic, too. In this new edition, references to philosophical theories have been minimized and woven into topics of informal logic. In this way, the overall length of the book has been kept about the same as in the first edition, and the price of the book has been kept low.

But many features of the earlier edition have been retained here. There are abundant pedagogical aids in the book, including not only more exercises, but also study questions and lists of key words. At the end of each chapter are a chapter summary and a writing project. And in the back of the book is a detailed glossary of important terms.

We wish to thank our editor at Pearson Education, Nancy Roberts, and Kate Fernandes, the project manager for this book. Special thanks are due also to Pearson editor-in-chief Dickson Musslewhite, who provided judicious guidance at crucial points in bringing out this new edition. We are also grateful for the criticisms of the philosophers selected as anonymous reviewers by Pearson. Their sometimes barbed but always trenchant observations about the first edition have helped us to make this a much better textbook.

Support for Instructors and Students

MySearchLab.com is an online tool that offers a wealth of resources to help student learning and comprehension, including practice quizzes, primary source readings and more. Please contact your Pearson representative for more information or visit www.MySearchLab.com

Instructor's Manual with Tests (0-205-15534-0) for each chapter in the text, this valuable resource provides a detailed outline, list of objectives, and discussion questions. In addition, test questions in multiple-choice, true/false, fill-in-the-blank, and short answer formats are available for each chapter; the answers are page referenced to the text. For easy access, this manual is available at www.pearsonhighered.com/irc.

PowerPoint Presentation Slides for How to Think Logically (0-205-15538-3): These PowerPoint Slides help instructors convey logic principles in a clear and engaging way. For easy access, they are available at www.pearsonhighered.com/irc.

GARY SEAY has taught formal and informal logic since 1979 at the City University of New York, where he is presently professor of philosophy at Medgar Evers College. His articles on moral philosophy and bioethics have appeared in *The American Philosophical Quarterly, The Journal of Value Inquiry, The Journal of Medicine and Philosophy,* and *The Cambridge Quarterly of Healthcare Ethics,* among other journals. With Susana Nuccetelli, he is editor of *Themes from G. E. Moore: New Essays in Epistemology and Ethics* (Oxford University Press, 2007), *Philosophy of Language: The Central Topics* (Rowman and Littlefield, 2007), and *Latin American Philosophy: An Introduction with Readings* (Prentice Hall, 2004).

SUSANA NUCCETELLI is professor of philosophy at St. Cloud State University in Minnesota. Her essays in epistemology and philosophy of language have appeared in *Analysis, The American Philosophical Quarterly, Metaphilosophy, The Philosophical Forum, Inquiry,* and *The Southern Journal of Philosophy,* among other journals. She is editor of *New Essays in Semantic Externalism and Self-Knowledge* (MIT Press, 2003) and author of *Latin American Thought: Philosophical Problems and Arguments* (Westview Press, 2002). She is co-editor of *The Blackwell Companion to Latin American Philosophy* (Blackwell, 2009) and, with Gary Seay, *Ethical Naturalism: Current Debates* (Cambridge University Press, forthcoming, 2011).

The Building Blocks of Reasoning

What Is Logical Thinking? And Why Should We Care?

After reading this chapter, you'll be able to answer questions about logical thinking, such as

- What is its subject matter?
- How does its approach to reasoning differ from those of neuroscience and psychology?
- Which are the main dimensions of logical thinking?
- How does logical thinking differ from formal logic?
- What is an argument? And how is it distinguished from a non-argument?
- What are the steps in argument analysis?

1.1 The Study of Reasoning

Logical thinking, or informal logic, is a branch of philosophy devoted to the study of reasoning. Although it shares this interest with other philosophical and scientific disciplines, it differs from them in a number of ways. Compare, for example, cognitive psychology and neuroscience. These also study reasoning but are chiefly concerned with the mental and physiological processes underlying it. By contrast, logical thinking focuses on the *outcomes* of such processes: namely, certain logical relations among beliefs and their building blocks that obtain when reasoning is at work. It also focuses on logical relations among statements, which, when speakers are sincere and competent, express the logical relations among their beliefs.

Inference or Argument

As far as logical thinking is concerned, reasoning consists in logical relations. Prominent among them is a relation whereby one or more beliefs are taken to offer support for another. Known as *inference* or *argument*, this relation obtains whenever a thinker entertains one or more beliefs as being *reasons* in support of another belief. Inferences could be strong, weak, or failed. Here is an example of a strong inference:

1 All whales are mammals, and Moby Dick is a whale; *therefore*, Moby Dick is a mammal.

(1) is a strong inference because, if the beliefs offered as reasons ('All whales are mammals,' and 'Moby Dick is a whale') are true, then the belief they are supposed to support ('Moby Dick is a mammal') must also be true. But compare

2 No oranges from Florida are small; *therefore*, no oranges from the United States are small.

In (2) the logical relation of inference between the beliefs is weak, since the reason offered ('No oranges from Florida are small') could be true and the belief it's offered to support ('No oranges from the United States are small') false. But by no means does (2) illustrate the worst-case scenario. In some attempted inferences, a belief or beliefs offered to support another belief might fail to do so. Consider

3 No oranges are apples; *therefore*, all elms are trees.

Since in (3) 'therefore' occurs between the two beliefs, it is clear that 'No oranges are apples' is offered as a reason for 'All elms are trees.' Yet it is not. Although these two beliefs both happen to be true, they do not stand in the relation of inference. Here is another such case of failed inference, this time involving false beliefs:

4 All lawyers are thin; *therefore*, the current pope is Chinese.

Since in (4) the component beliefs have little to do with each other, neither of them actually supports the other. As in (3), the inference fails.

Success and failure in inference are logical thinking's central topic. Let's now look more closely at how it approaches this subject.

1.2 Logic and Reasoning

Dimensions of the Subject

Inference is the most fundamental relation between beliefs or thoughts when reasoning is at work. Logical thinking studies this and other logical relations, with an eye toward

1. Describing patterns of reasoning.
2. Evaluating good- and bad-making features of reasoning.
3. Sanctioning rules for maximizing reasoning's good-making features.

Each of these tasks may be thought of as a dimension of logical thinking. The first describes logical relations, which initially requires identifying common patterns of inference. The second distinguishes good and bad traits in those relations. And the third sanctions rules for adequate reasoning. Rules are *norms* that can help us maximize the good (and minimize the bad) traits of our reasoning. The picture that emerges is as in Box 1.

Understanding these dimensions is crucial to the study of reasoning. Since the third dimension especially bears on how well we perform at reasoning, it has *practical worth* or *cash value*. Its cash value consists in the prescriptions it issues for materially improving our reasoning. But this dimension depends on the other two, because useful prescriptions for adequate reasoning require accurate descriptions of the common logical relations established by reasoning (such as inference). And they require adequate criteria to distinguish good and bad features in those relations.

Formal Logic

What we're calling 'logical thinking' is often known as *informal logic*. This discipline shares with another branch of philosophy, *formal logic*, its interest in inference and other logical relations. Informal and formal logic differ, however, in their scope and methods. Formal logic is also known as *symbolic logic*. It develops its own formal languages for the purpose of

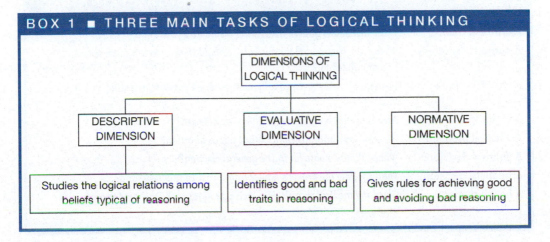

BOX 1 ■ THREE MAIN TASKS OF LOGICAL THINKING

DIMENSIONS OF LOGICAL THINKING

DESCRIPTIVE DIMENSION — Studies the logical relations among beliefs typical of reasoning

EVALUATIVE DIMENSION — Identifies good and bad traits in reasoning

NORMATIVE DIMENSION — Gives rules for achieving good and avoiding bad reasoning deducing theorems from formulas accepted as axioms (in ways somewhat like mathematical proofs). Any such system consists of basic symbolic expressions, the initial vocabulary of the formal language, and rules for operations with them. The rules prescribe how to form correct expressions and how to determine which formulas are the logical consequence of other formulas. In formal logic, then, inference is a relation among formulas: one that holds whenever a formula follows from one or more formulas. Formal logic uses a symbolic notation, which may be quite complex. And its formulas need not be translated into a natural language, which is the language of a speech community, such as English, Arabic, or Japanese. As far as formal logic is concerned, inference is a relation among formulas. It need be neither a relation among beliefs nor one among statements. Furthermore, it need not be identified with inferences people actually make in ordinary reasoning.

Informal Logic

In contrast to formal logic, logical thinking is completely focused on the study of logical relations as they occur when ordinary reasoning is at work. Its three dimensions can be shown relevant to reasoning in a variety of common contexts, as when we deliberate about issues such as those in Box 2.

The study of the inferences we make in these and other issues is approached by logical thinking in its three dimensions: once it describes the logical relations underlying particular inferences, it evaluates them and determines whether they conform to rules of good reasoning. Since doing this requires no formal languages, logical thinking is sometimes known as 'informal logic.' Although this discipline may introduce special symbols, it need not do so: it can be conducted entirely in a natural language. Furthermore, in contrast to formal logic, what we're here calling 'logical thinking' approaches the study of inference as a relation among beliefs—or among statements, the linguistic expressions of beliefs.

Why, then, should we care about logical thinking? First, we want to avoid false beliefs and have as many true beliefs as possible, all related in a way that makes logical sense, and logical thinking is instrumental in achieving this goal. Second, for the intellectually curious, learning

---

BOX 2 ■ SOME PRACTICAL USES OF LOGICAL THINKING

A criminal trial:	*Is the defendant guilty? What shall we make of the alibi?*
A domestic question:	*What's the best school for our kids? Should they go to a private school, or a public school?*
A scientific puzzle:	*How to choose between equally supported, yet opposite, scientific theories?*
A philosophical issue:	*Are mind and body the same thing, or different?*
An ethical problem:	*Is euthanasia morally right? What about abortion?*
A political decision:	*Whom should I vote for in the general election?*
A financial decision:	*Shall I follow my broker's advice and invest in this new fund?*
A health matter:	*Given my medical records, is exercise good for me? Do I need more health insurance?*

about the logical relations that take place in reasoning is an activity worthwhile for its own sake. Moreover, it can help us in practical situations where competent reasoning is required, which are exceedingly common. They arise whenever we wish to do well in intellectual tasks such as those listed in Box 2. Each of us has faced them at some point—for example, in attempting to convince someone of a view, in writing on a controversial topic, or simply in deciding between two seemingly well-supported yet incompatible claims. To succeed in meeting these ordinary challenges requires the ability to think logically. In the next section, we'll have a closer look at this important competence.

Exercises

I. Review Questions

1. How does logical thinking differ from scientific disciplines that study reasoning?
2. What is informal logic? And how does it differ from formal logic?
3. What is the main topic of logical thinking?
4. List one feature that logical thinking and formal logic have in common and one about which they differ.
5. What is an inference?
6. Could an inference fail completely? If so, how? If not, why not?
7. What are the different dimensions of logical thinking?
8. Which dimension of logical thinking is relevant to determining reasoning's good- and bad-making traits?
9. Which is the dimension of logical thinking that has "cash value"? And what does this mean?
10. What is a natural language? Give three examples of a natural language.

II. YOUR OWN THINKING LAB

1. Construct two inferences.

2. Construct a strong inference (one in which, if the supporting beliefs are true, the supported belief must be true).

3. Construct a weak inference (one in which the supporting beliefs could be true and the belief they're intended to support false).

4. Construct a blatantly failed inference.

5. Describe a scenario for which logical thinking could help a thinker in everyday life.

6. Describe a scenario for which logical thinking could help with your own studies in college.

7. Suppose someone says, "Thinking logically has no practical worth!" How would you respond?

8. 'Cats are carnivorous animals. No carnivorous animals are vegetarians; therefore, no cat is a vegetarian' is a strong inference. Why?

9. Consider 'All geckos are nocturnal. Therefore, there will be peace in the Middle East next year.' What's the matter with this inference?

10. Consider 'Politicians are all crooks. Therefore, it never snows in the Sahara.' What's the matter with this inference?

1.3 What Arguments Are

In this book, we call 'inference' the relation whereby one or more beliefs are taken to support another belief, and 'argument' the relation whereby one or more statements are offered in support of another statement. When speakers are sincere and competent, they believe what they assert, and their statements express their beliefs. Thus 'inference' and 'argument' may be taken to apply to the same relation. Just as beliefs are the fundamental parts, or building blocks, of inference, so statements are the building blocks from which arguments are constructed. A statement is like a belief, in that it has a truth value, which is a way of saying that it is either true ('No apples are oranges') or false ('The Pope is Chinese').

But not all relations between statements constitute arguments. Suppose someone says:

> 5 Philadelphia is a large city, and Chicago is larger still, but New York is the largest of all.

Although (5) is made up of three simple statements grouped together, it does not amount to an argument, for there is no attempt at presenting a supported claim; that is, the statements are not arranged so that one of them makes a claim for which the others are offered as reasons. Rather, they are just three conjoined statements. By contrast,

> 6 I think, therefore I am.
>
> 7 All lawyers are attorneys. Jack McCoy is a lawyer. Thus Jack McCoy is an attorney.
>
> 8 No chiropractors are surgeons. Only surgeons can legally perform a coronary bypass. Hence, no chiropractors can legally perform a coronary bypass.
>
> 9 A Chevrolet Impala is faster than a bicycle. A Maserati is faster than a Chevrolet Impala. A Japanese bullet train is faster than a Maserati. It follows that a Japanese bullet train is faster than a bicycle.

In each of these examples, a claim is made and at least one other statement is offered in support of that claim. This is the basic feature that all arguments share: every argument must

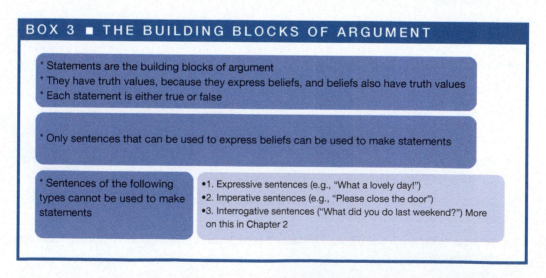

BOX 3 ■ THE BUILDING BLOCKS OF ARGUMENT

* Statements are the building blocks of argument
* They have truth values, because they express beliefs, and beliefs also have truth values
* Each statement is either true or false

* Only sentences that can be used to express beliefs can be used to make statements

* Sentences of the following types cannot be used to make statements
  • 1. Expressive sentences (e.g., "What a lovely day!")
  • 2. Imperative sentences (e.g., "Please close the door")
  • 3. Interrogative sentences ("What did you do last weekend?") More on this in Chapter 2

consist of at least two statements, one that makes a claim of some sort, and one or more others that are offered in support of it. The statement that makes the claim is the conclusion, and that offered to support it is the premise (or premises, if there are more than one).

Now, clearly we are introducing some special terminology here. For in everyday English, 'argument' most often means 'dispute,' a hostile verbal exchange between two or more people. But that is very different from the more technical use of 'argument' in logical thinking, where its meaning is similar to that common in a court of law. In a trial, each attorney is expected to present an argument. This amounts to making a claim (e.g., 'My client is innocent') and then giving some reasons to support it ('He was visiting his mother on the night of the crime'). In doing this, the attorney is not having a dispute with someone in the courtroom; rather, she is making an assertion and offering evidence that supposedly backs it up. This is very much like what we mean by 'argument' in logical thinking. An argument is a group of statements that are intended to make a supported claim. By this definition, then, an argument is not a verbal confrontation between two hostile parties.

Before we look more closely at argument, let's consider Box 4, which summarizes what we already know about this relation among statements.

> ## BOX 4 ■ SECTION SUMMARY
>
> - In logical thinking, the meaning of the term 'argument' is similar to that common in a court of law.
> - For a set of statements to be an argument, one of them must be presented as supported by the other or others.
> - An argument is a logical relation between two or more statements: a conclusion that makes a claim of some sort, and one or more premises that are the reasons offered to support that claim.

Argument Analysis

One essential competence that all logical thinkers must have is the ability to analyze arguments, a technique summarized in Box 5. What, exactly, is required for this competence? It involves knowing

1. How to recognize arguments,
2. How to identify the logical relation between their parts, and
3. How to evaluate arguments.

Recognizing an argument requires identifying the logical relations among the statements that make it up, which is essential to the process of reconstructing an argument. Reconstruction begins by paying close attention to the piece of spoken or written language that might contain an argument. One must read a passage carefully or listen attentively in order to determine whether or not a claim is being made, with reasons offered in support of it. If we have identified a conclusion and at least one premise, we can then be confident that the passage does contain an argument. The next step is to put the parts of the argument into an orderly arrangement, so that the relation between premise/s and conclusion becomes plain.

BOX 5 ■ THE STEPS IN ARGUMENT ANALYSIS

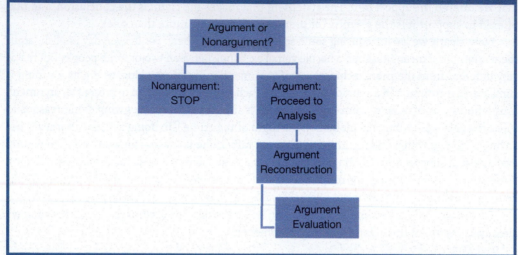

Argument reconstruction is the first step in argument analysis, and argument evaluation is the second. But before argument analysis can get started, we need to determine whether the passage under consideration contains an argument or not. If it does, then we proceed to argument reconstruction: we first make sure that we have identified premises and conclusion correctly. To do that, it's helpful to rewrite these parts of the argument in logical order, placing the conclusion at the end. During argument evaluation, we assess whether the argument's premises do actually succeed in supporting its conclusion, thereby giving good reasons for it. But before we can move ahead to the evaluation of arguments, we must reconstruct them properly. There is, then, one important thing to which we must pay attention before we can go further, and that is the matter of how to distinguish correctly between premises and conclusion.

1.4 Reconstructing Arguments

Identifying Premises and Conclusion

Let's now reconstruct arguments (6) through (9) from the previous section of this chapter. For each argument, we rewrite its premise/s first and the conclusion last, listing each of these statements with a number, which makes it easy to refer to them later if needed. If there are two or more premises, for our purposes here, the order does not matter. It is also customary to introduce, before the conclusion, either a horizontal line or the word 'therefore' to indicate that what comes next is the conclusion. In a reconstructed argument, then, we use the line to signal that a conclusion is being drawn; when you see it, you should think: 'therefore.' Thus reconstructed, (6) through (9) are as follows:

6' 1. I think.
    2. I am.

7' 1. All lawyers are attorneys.
    2. Jack McCoy is a lawyer.
    3. Jack McCoy is an attorney.

8' 1. No chiropractors are surgeons.
    2. Only surgeons can legally perform a coronary bypass.
    3. No chiropractors can legally perform a coronary bypass.

9' 1. A Chevrolet Impala is faster than a bicycle.
    2. A Maserati is faster than a Chevrolet Impala.
    3. A Japanese bullet train is faster than a Maserati.
    4. A Japanese bullet train is faster than a bicycle.

Examples (6'), (7'), (8'), and (9') all have at least one premise, but, as shown here, there may be more—in principle, there is no upper limit to how many premises an argument could have. In all these reconstructed arguments, the premise/s have been listed first and the conclusion last. But 'premise' does not mean 'statement that comes first.' Nor does 'conclusion' mean 'statement that comes last.' Rather, a premise is a reason for an argument's conclusion: its job is to support it. And the conclusion is the claim that is to be supported. Sometimes the conclusion of an unreconstructed argument does come last, but it does not have to: it can come at the beginning of the argument, or in the middle of it, surrounded by premises. The same holds for the premises of unreconstructed arguments: although they sometimes come at the beginning, they don't have to. They can come after the conclusion; or there can be some premises at the beginning, then the conclusion, then more premises. What is essential to a premise is that it is a statement offered in support of some other statement (the conclusion). As we shall see later, sometimes the attempted support succeeds, and other times it fails. But let us now consider some more examples of arguments.

10 Aunt Theresa won't vote in the Republican primary next week, because she is a Democrat, and Democrats can't vote in a Republican primary election.

11 Simon's cell phone will cause an incident at the Metropolitan Museum, since art museums don't allow cell phone use in the galleries, and Simon's is always ringing.

12 It gets lousy gas mileage, so I ought to sell the SUV as soon as possible! After all, it is just too expensive to maintain that vehicle, and besides, it pollutes the atmosphere worse than a regular car.

In each of these arguments, the conclusion is in underlined. As you can see, in both (10) and (11) it comes first, followed by two premises. But in (12), a premise comes first, followed by the conclusion, which is itself followed by two more premises.

Premise and Conclusion Indicators

We have seen that the premises of an argument are sentences offered in support of a certain claim or conclusion. But how can we tell, in any actual argument, which is which? As the examples considered so far demonstrate, when arguments are presented in natural language, the order of premises and conclusion can be scrambled in various ways. So how do we distinguish one from the other? Fortunately, certain words and phrases are often helpful in determining this. These are of two kinds: premise indicators and conclusion indicators. Premise indicators include such expressions as

because	given that	as	for the reason that	follows from
since	assuming that	whereas	inasmuch as	is a consequence of
for	provided that	after all	in that	considering that

When we see one of these expressions, it very often means that a premise is coming next. In other words, one of these (or another synonymous expression) may precede the statements of an argument that are its premises. You can see this in some of the earlier example arguments. Recall

10 Aunt Theresa won't vote in the Republican primary next week, because she is a Democrat, and Democrats can't vote in a Republican primary election.

11 Simon's cell phone will cause an incident at the Metropolitan Museum, since art museums don't allow cell phone use in the galleries, and Simon's is always ringing.

In (10), 'because' is used as a premise indicator; in (11), the premise indicator is 'since.' In (12), 'after all' functions as an indicator of two of its premises:

12 It gets lousy gas mileage, so I ought to sell the SUV as soon as possible! After all, it is just too expensive to maintain that vehicle, and besides, it pollutes the atmosphere worse than a regular car.

We must, however, be careful here. This method is more like a rule of thumb and is not one hundred percent dependable—not all occurrences of these words and phrases actually do indicate that premises are coming next. But many do. How to recognize when they mean this, and when they don't, is a competence acquired with practice, and you'll be getting some of that when you do the exercises in this chapter.

Conclusion indicators also have different degrees of reliability. Here is a list of some conclusion indicators:

therefore	suggests that	from this we can see that	thus
hence	accordingly	we may conclude that	recommends that
so	supports that	we may infer that	for this reason
entails that	consequently	it follows that	as a result

When we see a conclusion indicator, it often means that a conclusion is coming after it. Arguments containing such indicators can be seen in some of the examples in this chapter. In (6), 'therefore' functions as a conclusion indicator, as does 'thus' in (7):

6 I think, *therefore* I am.

7 All lawyers are attorneys. Jack McCoy is a lawyer. *Thus* Jack McCoy is an attorney.

In (8), the conclusion indicator is 'hence'; in (9), it's 'it follows that':

8   No chiropractors are surgeons. Only surgeons can legally perform a coronary bypass. *Hence*, no chiropractors can legally perform a coronary bypass.

9   A Chevrolet Impala is faster than a bicycle. A Maserati is faster than a Chevrolet Impala. A Japanese bullet train is faster than a Maserati. *It follows that* a Japanese bullet train is faster than a bicycle.

Again, you will get more practice in recognizing conclusion indicators when you do the exercises in this chapter. But, as just noted, premise and conclusion indicators are reliable only *for the most part* and not in all cases. What, then, are some cases where these expressions do *not* function as indicators of premises or conclusions? Consider the following:

13 Since he first came to New York in 1979, Max has read *El Diario* every day.

14 Alice took out a health insurance policy on her own, because her employer did not provide a health plan as a part of her employment contract.

In (13) 'since' is not functioning as a premise indicator. Although there are two statements in this sentence, they do not amount to an argument, because neither statement attempts to offer support for the other. Here, 'since' serves merely to introduce a temporal reference: the sentence describes a sequence of actions beginning in the past and continuing for some time. In (14) there are two statements, but it would be a mistake to think of their relation as an argument. Rather, one statement offers an explanation of the other: the last statement serves *to account for* the action described in the first, not to offer support for it. Here is another case in which words that often are premise indicators have some other function:

15 The best way to maintain the peace is to be prepared for war. As a means to peace, disarmament will surely fail.

This is not an argument, because neither statement really attempts to offer support for the other (in fact, they are both saying much the same thing). This should make us suspect that 'for,' in the first statement, and 'as,' in the second, are not serving here as premise indicators at all. This suspicion would be correct—for although both words sometimes serve as premise indicators, neither is doing so in (15).

Again, we must bear in mind that learning how to recognize when words of these kinds are functioning as indicators comes with practice. As with learning to ride a bicycle, one gets better at it by doing it. The more one works at trying to see the distinction and to draw it correctly, the easier it becomes. You'll get some practice at this later, in the exercises.

Arguments with No Premise or Conclusion Indicators

A further problem, however, must be noted at this point: not all arguments have premise or conclusion indicators! Some have none at all. When this happens in an argument, there is simply no other reliable way of identifying premises and conclusion than to ask yourself:

What is the claim being made? (that will be the conclusion) and Which statements are offered in support of the claim that is being made? (those are the premises). Consider this example:

> 16 Crocodiles aren't really dangerous at all. I've seen them on television many times, and they seem very peaceful. And I remember seeing Paul Hogan wrestle one in the movie *Crocodile Dundee*.

This is plainly an argument—a rather bad one—yet it has no indicators of any kind. Even so, we can easily see what its conclusion is: it's the first statement. This is because the first statement is the claim that the other three statements are supposed to support. That the support here seems a bit dim-witted does not change the fact that the last three statements are functioning as premises. It only means that the argument does not really succeed: it gives no good reason to accept the conclusion. In (16), then, we don't really need indicators to be able to recognize premises and conclusion. When arguments do have some indicators of premises and/or the conclusion, that is usually enough to tell you what's what. For arguments that lack such indicators altogether, asking the questions suggested above will be sufficient for this purpose.

Exercises

III. Review Questions

1. What is an argument?
2. What are the parts of an argument?
3. How should the parts of an argument be arranged if one wants to make their logical role clear?
4. How many premises could an argument have?
5. What are premises *for*? What is their purpose with respect to a conclusion?
6. What sense of the word 'argument' is irrelevant to logical thinking?
7. What are the steps in argument analysis?
8. What is involved in reconstructing an argument?
9. Can premises with no indicators be identified? Explain.
10. What should you ask yourself to identify the conclusion of an argument?

IV. The following expressions usually are premise indicators, conclusion indicators, or neither. Identify which is which. *(For exercises marked with a star, answers can be found in the back of the book.)*

SAMPLE ANSWER: 1. 'since' is a premise indicator

1. since	4. if and only if	7. thus	*10. for	*13. accordingly
2. as a result	5. however	*8. perhaps	11. it follows that	14. we may infer
*3. after all	*6. and	9. because	12. given that	15. just in case

V. In the following arguments, put premises in parentheses and underline the conclusion. Mark indicators of premises and conclusion, if any. Use angles '< >' for premise indicators and square brackets '[ ]' for conclusion indicators.

1. SAMPLE: <Since> (all the Dobermans I have known were dangerous) and (my neighbor's new dog, Franz, is a Doberman), [it follows that] <u>Franz is dangerous.</u>

2. Reverend Sharpton has no chance of being elected this time, because his campaign is not well financed, and any politician who is not well financed has no real chance of being elected.

*3. Badgers are native to southern Wisconsin. After all, they are always spotted there.

4. Since all theoretical physicists have studied quadratic equations, no theoretical physicists are dummies at math, for no one who has studied quadratic equations is a dummy at math.

5. Thousands of salamanders have been observed by naturalists and none has ever been found to be warm-blooded. We may conclude that no salamanders are warm-blooded animals.

*6. In the past, every person who ever lived did eventually die. This suggests that all human beings are mortal.

7. Since architects regularly study engineering, Frank Gehry did, for he is an architect.

8. Britney Spears's new CD is her most innovative album so far. It's got the best music of any new pop music CD this year, and all the DJs are playing it on radio stations across the United States. Accordingly, Britney Spears's new CD is sure to win an award this year.

*9. Online education is a great option for working adults in general, regardless of their ethnic background. For one thing, there is a large population of working adults who simply are not in a position to attend a traditional university.

10. Any airline that can successfully pass some of the increases in costs on to its passengers will be able to recover from higher fuel costs. South Airlink Airlines seems able to successfully pass some of the increases in costs on to its passengers. As a result, South Airlink Airlines will remain in business.

11. Jackrabbits can be found in Texas. Jackrabbits are speedy rodents. Hence, some speedy rodents can be found in Texas.

*12. There is evidence that galaxies are flying outward and apart from each other, so the cosmos will grow darker and colder.

13. The Cubans are planning to boycott the conference, so the Venezuelans will boycott it, too.

14. Since Reverend Windfield will preach an extra-long sermon this Sunday, we may therefore expect that some of his congregation will fall asleep.

*15. Captain Binnacle will not desert his sinking ship, for only a cowardly captain would desert a sinking ship, and Captain Binnacle is no coward.

16. A well-known biologist recently admitted having fabricated data on stem-cell experiments. So his claim that he has a cloned dog is probably false.

17. The French minister of culture has announced that France will not restrict American movies. Assuming that film critics are right in questioning the overall quality of American movies, it follows that French movie theaters will soon feature movies of questionable quality.

*18. The University of California at Berkeley is strong in math, for many instructors in its Math Department have published breakthrough papers in the core areas of mathematics.

19. Her Spanish must be good now. She spent a year in Mexico living with a Mexican family, and she took courses at the Autonomous University of Mexico.

*20. No one who knowingly and needlessly endangers his or her life is rational. Thus college students who smoke are not rational, because every college student who smokes is knowingly and unnecessarily endangering his or her life.

21. The next major earthquake that hits California will be more devastating than the great San Francisco earthquake of 1906, because there are many more people in California now than there were then, and the urban concentration along the San Andreas Fault is much greater today.

22. Isaac Newton was one of the greatest physicists of all time. After all, he was the discoverer of the law of gravity.

23. Maestro von Umlaut will not continue in his post as music director of the Philharmonic, since conductors of important orchestras can continue in that post only as long as they deliver great performances, and in the last ten years, von Umlaut has not delivered great performances.

24. Mayor Wilson will have to make a strong campaign for reelection next year. He lost popularity as a result of his position on immigration.

*25. Given that all Athenians are Greeks and that Plato was an Athenian, we may infer that Plato was a Greek.

VI. YOUR OWN THINKING LAB

1. Construct two arguments, one in favor of legalized abortion, the other against it.

2. What's the matter with accepting the two arguments proposed for (1) at once?

3. Construct two arguments: one for the conclusion that God exists, and one for the conclusion that God doesn't exist.

4. Some people argue that the death penalty is morally appropriate as a punishment for murder, but others argue for the opposite view. For which of these two positions might it be appropriate to use as a premise 'Murderers deserve to die'?

5. Construct a strong argument with the premises 'People who commit crimes deserve punishment' and 'The defendant committed a crime,' listing its parts in logical order.

1.5 Arguments and Non-arguments

Explanations

We've seen that an argument can be distinguished from other logical relations among statements chiefly by asking whether it offers some statement(s) in support of a claim. If not, then it's *not* an argument but something else! We've also seen that there are some helpful words and phrases that often point to the presence of an argument, since they could be of help in spotting premises and conclusions. The trouble is, some of these same words and phrases—words like 'because,' 'since,' and 'as a result'—often appear in *explanations*, which many philosophers think are not arguments at all. For our purposes here, we'll assume only that explanations are different enough from arguments that logical thinkers need a reliable way to tell the difference.

Explanations often bear a superficial resemblance to arguments, owing to the fact that each is a type of relation among statements in which one or more of them are supposed to *give reasons* for another statement, which is the claim that's being made. But the reasons are of very different kinds in argument and explanation.

> 1. In arguments, the reasons (premises) are offered to back up a claim (conclusion) that the arguer considers in need of support.
> 2. In explanations, reasons are offered to account for the events or states of affairs described by a claim that the arguer takes to be not in need of support.

Consider these relations among statements:

17 The stock market crashed in 2008 because large banks made reckless home mortgage loans that proved uncollectable, and investors lost confidence in a broad range of securities traded on major stock exchanges.

18 The stock market is not a realistic environment for the small investor, because such investors are unlikely to assume the level of risk that can lead to substantial gains, and market volatility brings the ever-present danger of ruin for those without sizable cash reserves.

Examples (17) and (18) both make use of the word 'because,' which is often a premise indicator. But it has that function in *only one* of these two examples. Can you see which one? It's (18), for (18) features reasons offered in support of the argument's conclusion. In (17), the arguer already accepts that the stock market crashed in 2008 and offers explanatory reasons to account for that event. Notice that in (18), the conclusion comes at the beginning—the claim that 'The stock market is not a realistic environment for the small investor'—and then two other statements offer reasons why we should accept that claim as true. (*Is* the claim true? It may be true. Or maybe not! We need not take a stand on that! We know that it's the conclusion of an argument, because it's offered by the arguer as being supported by the argument's premises.)

By contrast, in (17), the explanation begins with a statement that is accepted by the arguer as a fact: 'The stock market crashed in 2008.' The other two statements serve not to give reasons *why we should accept* the first statement (after all, we don't need to be convinced *that the market crashed in 2008!*), but only reasons *to account for why* that event occurred.

Arguments and explanations, then, could each be thought of as a logical relation between statements. In the case of argument, the relation is between some claim and the statement/s that are supposed to provide reasons for accepting it as true; in the case of explanation, the relation is between a claim that the thinker has already accepted as true and the statement/s that are offered to give an account of why or how it came to be true. In light of this, explanations can be thought of as distinct from arguments, and it's important to be able to tell the difference.

Conditionals

Explanations are not the only logical relation apt to be confused with arguments. Another is that often expressed by 'if ... then ... ' sentences, which are used to make compound statements called 'conditionals.' We'll later discuss them at some length. For our purposes here, it suffices to keep in mind that although they may be *part* of an argument (in fact, this is quite common), conditionals by themselves are not arguments. Let's notice why. Recall that, according to the definition of 'argument' given earlier, there cannot be an argument consisting of fewer than two statements. And the reason for this is easy to see. In any argument, two separate functions are being performed: (1) a claim is being made and (2) some putative support is being offered for that claim. Plainly, this requires that there be at least two *independently asserted* statements. But that's just what we *don't* have in a conditional. Consider

19 If Heinz is a naturalized citizen, then Heinz was not born in this country.

This is a conditional, a compound statement consisting of two simple statements joined by the connective 'if . . . then . . .'. Now, is it asserting that Heinz *is* a naturalized citizen? No! Is it asserting that Heinz *was not* born in this country? No! All it's asserting, as a whole, is *a hypothetical relation between two possibilities*—namely, that *if* Heinz is a naturalized citizen, *then* Heinz was not born in this country. But regarding whether either of these two possibilities *is actually the case*, it says nothing at all. This is typical of conditionals. Compare

20 Heinz is a naturalized citizen; therefore, Heinz was not born in this country.

Example (20) *is* an argument. Here, 'Heinz is a naturalized citizen' is being used as a premise in support of the conclusion that 'Heinz was not born in this country.' The bottom line is,

> Whether some set of statements amounts to an argument or not depends on how they are logically related.

Fictional Discourse

For much the same reason, many other relations among sentences do not amount to arguments. These include not only purely descriptive or expository passages, but also the language of fiction and poetry. The reason for this is that one of our goals as logical thinkers is to evaluate arguments, which in turn will require that we consider whether the argument's conclusion would have to be true if all its premises were true (more on this in Chapter 5). But, strictly speaking, the sentences in a work of fiction are not statements, even those that may seem to represent facts. After all, they are neither true nor false: for example, it is neither true nor false that Oliver Twist lived in London, simply because 'Oliver Twist' doesn't name an actual person but a fictional character invented by Dickens. (It would be preposterous for anyone planning to visit London to look forward to visiting Oliver Twist's house.) Is it true or false that 'Huckleberry Finn is friends with Jim' or that 'Carrie Bradshaw is clever'? It's neither, because Huckleberry Finn and Jim and Carrie Bradshaw are all fictional characters. There are no facts in the real world to make such sentences true or false. Thus, in the language of fiction, as for statement-like sentences in the lyrics of songs and poetry generally, their truth-value seems ambiguous at best. Since such language can't be used to construct assessable arguments, we'll consider any passage of fiction a non-argument.

Exercises

VII. Which of the following passages contain arguments, and which don't?

1. According to a report in the *Daily Times-Gazette*, Senator Smith denied the accusation that he had misused public funds on a trip to Aruba with a French film star. However, he admitted that there was an appearance of wrongdoing, and he vowed not to do it again.

   SAMPLE ANSWER: No argument.

2. Some muskrats are not nocturnal, for naturalists who have studied the habits of these animals have determined that there is evidence of muskrats feeding during the day and sleeping at night.

3. All architectural engineers have studied mathematics. It follows that Judith has studied mathematics, since Judith is an architectural engineer.

*4. Since 1979, Pam has lived in Berlin. She has worked for Deutsche Bank, but now she is looking forward to retirement and has bought a villa in Corsica.

5. Heard melodies are sweet, but those unheard are sweeter; therefore ye soft pipes play on; not to the sensual ear, but, more endeared, pipe to the spirit ditties of no tone . . . (John Keats—from "Ode on a Grecian Urn")

6. I have bought several CDs at the Noble Book Barn, and all have proved defective. One was supposed to be Beyoncé and turned out to be Madonna. Another was missing some tracks. Two others had static that distorted the sound. Therefore, the Noble Book Barn is not a reliable store for CDs.

7. Elena should dump that creep Oscar! After all, Oscar has been nothing but trouble for her. He sneaks around with other women behind her back, and he spends all his money at the racetrack.

8. John is not going to class today, because he is wearing a leather jacket, and he never goes to class wearing that jacket.

9. They all felt that Jane was the sort of woman who needed help. I, on the other hand, saw that she was capable of drawing on inner resources that made her impervious to all adversity.

*10. Although Ed's new BMW will outrun nearly every other car in town, it was not a good idea to buy it, for it costs him a lot to maintain it. And on his meager salary, he will never be able to keep up with the monthly payments on it.

11. If Henderson wins the election, then the balance of power in the legislature will change.

12. Since Vaclav and Bogdan are only fraternal twins, not identical, they don't look exactly alike.

*13. Let me not to the marriage of true minds admit impediments. Love is not love which alters when it alteration finds, or bends with the remover to remove: O no! It is an ever-fixèd mark that looks on tempests and is never shaken. It is the star to every wand'ring bark, whose worth's unknown although his height be taken . . . (William Shakespeare—from Sonnet 116)

14. Companies should incorporate top Latino professionals. For one thing, Latino purchasing power has increased dramatically in the last decade in the United States.

15. To dance beneath the diamond sky with one hand waving free, silhouetted by the sea, circled by the circus sands, with all memory and fate driven deep beneath the waves, let me forget about today until tomorrow! Hey, Mr. Tambourine Man, play a song for me! In the jingle-jangle morning I'll come following you. (Bob Dylan—from "Mr. Tambourine Man")

*16. If judges were strict with criminals, then all offenses would be punished. But some offenses are not punished. So, judges are not strict with criminals.

17. It occurred to me that because twins are genetically identical, their sons are actually half brothers!

*18. Since I went on my first date in high school, more than two hundred species of frogs have disappeared forever.

19. The Mississippi River rises in the lake country of northern Minnesota and flows southward all the way to the Gulf of Mexico. Over the course of this great distance, it divides the eastern watershed of the United States from the western and drains all the rivers for hundreds of miles in both directions in the middle of the continent.

*20. *Superman* cost more than $200 million. Most movies that cost more than $200 million do well. It follows that *Superman* will do well.

21. If Harry Potter is a fictional character, then he cannot vote in England.

22. Tracey will do well on her MEDCAT exams. People who get straight A's in their science courses often do well on MEDCAT exams, and she got straight A's in hers.

23. If hydrogen is the lightest element, then hydrogen is lighter than oxygen.

24. Dolphins are mammals, and whales are mammals, but sharks are a species of fish.

25. The nation's major banks, placing the blame on their own higher costs for borrowed money, raised their prime lending rate yesterday to 13 percent, from 12 percent. The increase sent the prime, the rate charged by banks to their best corporate customers, to its highest level since mid-June.

VIII. In each passage above containing an argument, underline the conclusion and mark the premises with parentheses.

IX. Each of the passages below is either an argument or an explanation. Say which is which.

1. She will soon date someone else. Edgar is never fashionably dressed, and her mother would prefer her having a fashionably dressed boyfriend.

   SAMPLE ANSWER: Argument.

2. Pacifists shouldn't serve in the military. The reason for this is that pacifists believe that all wars are wrong, and the military often engages in wars.

3. Henry always votes in elections, because he believes that it's his duty as a citizen to do so.

*4. Christine is the Green Party nominee for the U.S. Senate, so we can be sure that she cares about the environment.

5. Either matter has always existed in some form, or the universe came into being out of nothing. But since it's inconceivable that something like the universe came into existence out of nothing, it follows that matter must have always existed in some form.

*6. There was a lot of humidity in the atmosphere yesterday, but at dusk a cold air mass moved in from the west. As a result, there were thunderstorms.

7. Senator Smith knew that his chief of staff sent a memo implicating the senator in a sex scandal. After all, the chief of staff was fired the very same day that news of the scandal broke on the *NBC Nightly News*.

8. Man tends to increase at a greater rate than his means of subsistence; consequently, he is occasionally subject to a severe struggle for existence. (Charles Darwin, *The Descent of Man*)

*9. Scotland Yard publicly alleged that a member of the Russian intelligence service was responsible for poisoning a former KGB spy. This suggests that there will be some tense exchanges between Britain's Foreign Office and the Russian Foreign Ministry.

*10. Speculators have been driving up the cost of real-estate downtown. As a result, hardly any middle-class families can afford to live there now.

X. YOUR OWN THINKING LAB

1. Construct an argument of your own with premise and conclusion indicators, marking these as in Exercise V.

2. Construct an argument of your own without premise and conclusion indicators, underlining its conclusion and marking its premises with parentheses.

3. Find an explanation and say why it is not an argument.

4. Construct a conditional of your own and say why it is not an argument.

■ Writing Project

Select a claim you feel very strongly about and write a short essay explaining what you take to be the best reasons for that claim. For further work, keep this essay on file, and go back to it for a critical assessment at the end of this course. By the way, never forget to give full references for your sources of information, if you use any! (Length: about two pages, double-spaced, or as directed by your instructor.)

■ Chapter Summary

Logical or critical thinking: informal logic. It studies *reasoning*, but it is

- Not concerned with brain processes.
- Not concerned with cause–effect explanations.
- Concerned with the logical relations that obtain when reasoning is at work.

Why be logical thinkers?

Two fundamental goals:

- To have true beliefs and avoid false ones.
- To upgrade the set of beliefs we already have by acquiring new true beliefs and avoiding false ones.

Situations where careful reasoning is required:

- Supporting our beliefs
- Acquiring new, supported beliefs
- Persuading others of our beliefs
- Putting various pieces of information together in a way that makes sense
- Deciding between opposite views
- Avoiding common mistakes in reasoning
- Questioning beliefs that may be mistaken, make no sense, or lack adequate evidence

Dimensions of logical thinking:

1. *Descriptive*: it identifies patterns of logical relation such as inference.

2. *Evaluative*: it determines which patterns are good and which are bad.

3. *Normative*: it formulates rules to maximize good reasoning and minimize bad.

> **Statement:** True or false sentence that expresses a thought or belief.
> **Inference:** One or more beliefs taken to support another belief.
> **Argument:** One or more statements taken to support another statement. Arguments express inferences.

Argument analysis: argument reconstruction and argument evaluation.

How to reconstruct an argument:

A. Begin by examining a passage carefully. Distinguish arguments from non-arguments. Keep in mind that, to be an argument at all, a passage must make a claim and offer some reason/s for it. Identify the argument, if any. Once you've done this, move to (b).

B. Identify premise/s and conclusion. Premise and conclusion indicators, if available, can help you here, so you should look for them first; if there are any, they will usually reveal the premise/s and conclusion. But if there aren't any, ask yourself, 'What claim is being made?' The answer will be the argument's conclusion. If there is a claim, then ask yourself, 'What are the reason/s offered for it?' The answer will be the argument's premise/s. Once you have identified premise/s and conclusion, move to (c).

C. List the parts of the argument in order, premise/s first and conclusion last, separated by a horizontal line.

The following are NOT arguments:

- Passages in fictional discourse, such as that of novels, short stories, plays, song lyrics, and poetry.
- Explanations, where some statements are offered to make another statement understandable or to account for its truth.
- Conditionals, which are usually expressed by 'if . . . then . . .' sentences.

■ Key Words

Inference

Informal logic

Formal logic

Argument

Argument analysis

Premise

Conclusion

Premise and conclusion indicators

Statement

Natural language

Conditional

Explanation

Thinking Logically and Speaking One's Mind

In this chapter you'll learn about some matters of concern in logical thinking, and also about some aspects of natural language that can affect arguments. Major topics are

- Rational acceptability and how this depends on logical connections and evidential support.
- The distinction between truth and evidence.
- The irrelevance of linguistic merit and rhetorical power in weighing rational acceptability.
- The role of propositions as the contents of beliefs and statements.
- The uses of language in connection with four basic categories of speech act.
- Four types of sentence and their relation to the basic uses of language.
- How to distinguish between direct and indirect language, and between literal and figurative uses of language.
- Definition as an antidote to unclear language.

2.1 Rational Acceptability

Logical Connectedness

Acceptable thinking requires logical connectedness and the support of reasons. Salient among logical connections is that of argument, which obtains when at least one statement is offered as being supported by others. In argument, the strength of the logical connection between premises and conclusion is proportional to the strength of the argument itself: the more logical connectedness among its parts, the stronger the argument. And since statements are the expressions of beliefs, the same could be said of belief and inference. Consider,

1   That smoking is linked to early lung disease argues against smoking.

(1) contains remarks about the logical relation between premises (that smoking is linked to early lung disease) and a conclusion (which we may paraphrase as 'people should not smoke'). Such remarks point to the feature we are calling 'logical connectedness.' Similarly, logical connectedness is alluded to when we say that a certain statement is a premise, a reason, a conclusion, or follows from another.

Logical connectedness is a matter of degree: some relations among beliefs might have it absolutely, others only in part. In addition, some groups of beliefs may lack it entirely. For example,

2   Florida is on the Gulf of Mexico. Any state on the Gulf of Mexico has mild winters. Therefore, Florida has mild winters.

(2) has a high degree of logical connectedness, since its premises support its conclusion strongly: if they are true, the conclusion has to be true. By contrast, (3) has a low degree of logical connectedness, for it is a weak argument, in the sense that, although its premises are true, its conclusion could be false.

3   Florida has mild winters, and so do Hawaii and Texas; therefore, most U.S. states have mild winters.

Now consider an argument whose premise and conclusion have no logical connectedness at all:

4   Florida is a subtropical state on the Gulf of Mexico; therefore, computers have replaced typewriters.

(2), (3), and (4) illustrate decreasing degrees of logical connectedness. (2) has the highest degree of logical connectedness. Logical thinkers who recognize this, together with the fact that (2)'s premises seem true, cannot reject (2)'s conclusion without a serious failure of reasoning. Logical connectedness partly determines whether an argument is rationally acceptable—that is, whether it counts as acceptable reasoning. Neither (3) nor (4) qualifies as rationally acceptable: (3) lacks a sufficient degree of logical connectedness, and (4) doesn't have it at all. Neither is a model of the sort of reasoning logical thinkers ought to engage in.

Beliefs with a good share of logical connectedness are the kind of reasoning we ought to engage in—provided that they also meet other conditions, such as being based on solid

BOX 1 ■ LOGICAL CONNECTEDNESS AND INFERENCE

- The rational acceptability of an argument depends on its logical connectedness, and also on whether any premise in need of evidential support in fact has it.
- The logical connectedness of an argument resides in the relation between its premises and conclusion. Any deficiency in logical connectedness would undermine an argument's rational acceptability.

reasons or evidence. Acceptable arguments are crucial to our ability to think logically. Furthermore, when an argument is used to persuade (e.g., to convince an audience or win a debate), any deficiency in rational acceptability would make it vulnerable to objections.

Evidential Support

The rational acceptability of many beliefs depends on evidence, which is information obtained from observation, whether one's own or that of reliable sources. Beliefs of that sort are *empirical* and are supported when the total evidence points to their being true. The 'total evidence' for a belief includes all relevant information available to the thinker at a time: evidence *for* the belief, and also evidence *against* it. Thus the total evidence for a belief requires careful consideration of any information pointing to its being false, as well as information pointing to its being true. The total evidence, then, is the result of "factoring in" partial evidence of both kinds. When a belief is empirical, the upshot of considering the total evidence is one of the following:

	Scenario		Evidential-Support Status
I	Most of the relevant evidence points to a belief's being true.	→	The belief is *supported* by the evidence
II	Most of the relevant evidence points to a belief's being false.	→	The belief is *undermined* by the evidence
III	The evidence is "split," equally pointing to a belief's being true and to its being false.	→	The belief is *not supported* by the evidence

Only beliefs that fall within category (I) may be said to be 'supported by the evidence.'

Note that although both logical connectedness and evidential support are needed for rational acceptability, they are independent of each other. After all, any piece of reasoning could have one without having the other. For example,

5 Anyone who breaks a mirror will have seven years' bad luck. Today I broke a mirror. Therefore, I'll have seven years' bad luck.

(5) has logical connectedness, since if its premises are true, its conclusion is also true. Yet we now know that the evidence does not support one of the premises: that anyone who breaks a

mirror will have seven years' bad luck. As a result, (5) falls short of being a rationally acceptable argument.

> When engaging in reasoning, at all times
> ■ Maximize the logical connectedness among beliefs.
> ■ Favor beliefs supported by the evidence.

Truth and Evidence

What matters for the evidential support of a belief is not that it is true, but rather that the total evidence available to the thinker points to its being true. This allows for a range of combinations. To begin with, a false belief could be supported by the evidence. Consider

6   The earth does not revolve.

For people in the Middle Ages, this belief was supported by the evidence. As far as they could tell, the belief was true (all information then available pointed to its being true). Yet (6) was false, and those people were therefore in error. At the same time, a true belief could fail to be supported by the evidence, as was (7) before the twentieth century, when there was not enough evidence pointing to the existence of atoms.

7   There are atoms.

Truth and evidence, then, are different concepts that must not be confused. Truth concerns how things are. A belief is true if and only if things actually are as represented by it. Evidence involves the information about how things are that is available to thinkers—which could turn out to be misleading or even false. Of the two, it is only evidence that bears on rational acceptability. This does not undermine the importance of truth, however, which is arguably desirable for its own sake, given that humans seem to be, by nature, intellectually curious beings.

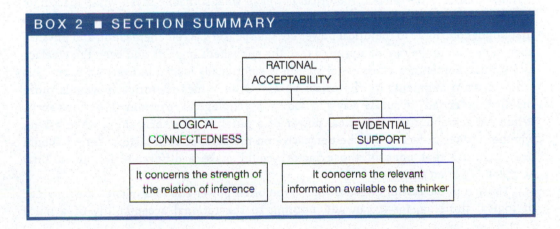

BOX 2 ■ SECTION SUMMARY

RATIONAL ACCEPTABILITY

LOGICAL CONNECTEDNESS

EVIDENTIAL SUPPORT

It concerns the strength of the relation of inference

It concerns the relevant information available to the thinker

2.2 Beyond Rational Acceptability

Linguistic Merit

The features so far identified as making up the rational acceptability of beliefs may also be present in statements. Thought and language are parallel at least in these respects:

> When speakers are sincere and competent,
> - their statements express what they believe, and
> - their arguments express the inferences they make.

Statements may have a number of other features besides rational acceptability. Prominent among them is linguistic merit, which results from a combination of grammatical, syntactical, and stylistic factors such as concision, adequate vocabulary, and compliance with the rules of language. Linguistic merit is a quality of either written or spoken language and is no doubt desirable to have. For one thing, it contributes to the appreciation of expressions on aesthetic grounds. But it is also fundamental to our understanding of what is being said. When an inference is put into words, some degree of linguistic merit is required, since we need to be able to understand what's being said. Beyond this threshold of understanding, however, linguistic merit can make no difference to rational acceptability. Some statements may lack linguistic merit while being rationally acceptable, for example, by being poorly expressed but making a strong argument with premises supported by the evidence. Other statements may have high linguistic merit and be rationally unacceptable. That would be the case of statements that are well expressed but nonetheless deficient in either logical connectedness, evidential support, or both.

Rhetorical Power

Another desirable feature of statements quite independent of rational acceptability is rhetorical power, a feature of persuasive communication. Both linguistic and nonlinguistic factors may contribute to rhetorical power; for example, emotionally charged words and certain tones of voice can add rhetorical power to what someone says—while inaccurate pronunciation or grammar could undermine such power. Among nonlinguistic factors that might contribute to rhetorical power are the speaker's accent, demeanor, and physical appearance, or, in the case of a printed text, the publisher's imprint, and even the typeface and format. Sometimes a passage or speech is emotionally loaded in overt ways, and this emotionalism augments its rhetorical power. Other times rhetorical power is more insidiously "coded" in subtle ways, to arouse psychological reactions of various sorts. When we ask about the rhetorical power of a putative inference, then, we're asking whether it does in fact tend to be persuasive on the basis of such factors. Yet we should bear in mind that none of those factors could make a difference to the rational acceptability of an inference.

Thus, as in the case of linguistic merit, rhetorical power also falls outside the province of logical thinking, for it can add nothing to the rational acceptability of a piece of reasoning. It is a feature of any communication that succeeds in convincing the target audience—though sometimes not by strictly rational means. Some reasoning that lacks rational acceptability might in fact have a lot of rhetorical power: for example, when it is presented by a skillful speaker who knows how to "sell" an idea. On the other hand, thinking that has rational acceptability might in fact lack rhetorical power: for example, reasoning that is too complex and difficult to follow may be rejected by some audiences. This suggests that rational acceptability and rhetorical power are independent. One could exist without the other.

The upshot for the logical thinker is:

> Be aware that although it may be nice to persuade an audience of the beliefs you have, you want to do it in the right way: that is, a way that has rational acceptability.

Rhetoric vs. Logical Thinking

A good rhetorician, either in writing or in speech, is one adept at convincing others. The best rhetoric is simply that which is most successful in convincing—in winning an audience over. That might well, in some cases, include appeals to emotion and other factors that have no bearing at all on rational acceptability, for they can neither enhance nor undermine logical connectedness and evidential support. The political orator whose stem-winding speech arouses feelings of patriotism and nationalism in support of a foreign war, and the defense attorney who plants the defendant's aged mother in the courtroom audience during a closing argument, may succeed in convincing audiences. But, in either case, we might well doubt that the audience has a good reason to be convinced.

It is not logical thinking but rhetoric that studies the art of persuasion. This discipline focuses on the development of various techniques that can enhance rhetorical power. By contrast, logical thinking focuses on rational acceptability, which is the criterion of adequate reasoning—the sort that *ought* to persuade us. We must always keep an eye on the warning signs of weak and misleading reasoning, so that we can avoid the snares laid by unscrupulous or careless persuaders.

Exercises

I. Review Questions

1. In what does rational acceptability consist?
2. How is logical connectedness related to the strength of an inference?
3. What does evidence have to do with rational acceptability? What is the "total evidence" for a belief?
4. How does truth differ from evidence?
5. Is rhetorical power relevant to thinking logically? And what about linguistic merit? Explain.
6. Some statements can have rhetorical power without having rational acceptability, and vice versa. What does this show about the relation between rhetorical power and rational acceptability?

II. Determine whether the following statements bear on logical connectedness, evidential support, linguistic merit, rhetorical power, or a combination of some of these.

1. The Declaration of Independence has just the right words and makes claims that are backed up by reasons.

    SAMPLE ANSWER: linguistic merit and logical connectedness

2. The observation points to the truth of Galileo's law of falling bodies.

*3. The speaker was well dressed and spoke with the right voice and gestures.

4. The fossil record favors neither evolution nor creation.

*5. The fossil record favors evolution.

6. He is a lousy speaker, in that he always uses ungrammatical language. Besides, he is insecure. On top of it, he never looks at you when he speaks.

7. The belief that some mammals are whales is strongly supported by the belief that all whales are mammals. If the latter is true, the former must be true.

*8. It makes no sense to think that Ellen is an ophthalmologist but not an eye doctor. From the fact that she is an ophthalmologist, it follows that she is an eye doctor. After all, "ophthalmologist" means "eye doctor."

9. After seeing him so devastated, I became totally convinced of his story.

*10. The ideas were poorly phrased, in a heavily accented language. Almost a dialect.

*11. Had you been in court this morning, you'd have been persuaded by the prosecutor's stern attitude.

*12. That the butler has an alibi offers some support to the conclusion that he did not do it. But couldn't that conclusion be false even if he does have an alibi?

13. The conclusion that someone is a male sibling follows necessarily from the premise that he is a brother.

14. Magellan's voyage provided empirical data that proved that the Earth is not flat. If the Earth were flat, Magellan's ship couldn't have circumnavigated it. From this, we cannot but conclude that the Earth is not flat.

*15. She couldn't have found better words to make her point succinctly.

III. Each characteristic on the left falls under one of the four standards on the right. Pair them accordingly.

1. Being prolix in language

    SAMPLE ANSWER: Linguistic merit

*2. Having good manners

3. Being concise

*4. Finding fingerprints at the scene of a crime   A. Logical connectedness

5. Persuading the audience   B. Evidential support

*6. Following from some premises

7. Citing the report of a reliable witness

*8. Having a direct visual experience

9. Being inferred from other beliefs

*10. Being strongly inferred from other beliefs

11. Failing to be inferred from other beliefs

*12. Having nervous mannerisms in speech

C. Linguistic merit

D. Rhetorical power

IV. **Determine whether the logical connectedness in each of the following arguments is strong, weak, or failed. Use these criteria: If the conclusion must be true if the premises are true, the connection is strong; if the conclusion is somewhat supported by the premises but it could be false even if the premises are true, the connection is weak; and if premises and conclusion are not related at all, the connection is failed.**

1. Columbus was married. Therefore, Columbus wasn't single.

   SAMPLE ANSWER: Strong logical connectedness

2. Pierre is French. Therefore, he is European.

*3. The Yucatán ruins are well preserved. Therefore, Yucatán is worth visiting.

4. Triangles have three internal angles. Isosceles triangles are triangles. Therefore, cats are feline.

5. My dog, Fido, barks. Therefore, all dogs bark.

*6. She is the string quartet's first violinist. Therefore, she is a musician.

7. The house is now finished. Therefore, a tennis match is going on.

8. A loud sound broke the calm of night. Therefore, there was some thunder.

*9. No candies are nutritious. Therefore, nutritious things are not delicious.

10. We visit only cities that have mild weather. Last year we visited Miami and San Diego. Therefore, these cities have mild weather.

V. **Determine whether each of the following scenarios is possible or impossible. For each one that is impossible, explain why.**

1. A group of statements that is logically connected and it isn't.

   SAMPLE ANSWER: Impossible. This scenario makes two opposite claims at once.

2. A statement for which the evidence is split: half supports it, the other half undermines it.

*3. A rationally acceptable group of statements that conflicts with the available evidence.

4. A rationally acceptable group of statements that has logical connectedness.

5. A rationally acceptable group of statements without rhetorical power.

*6. A rhetorically powerful group of statements that has linguistic merit.

7. A group of statements that has logical connectedness and evidential support but lacks rational acceptability.

*8. A poorly phrased passage that has linguistic merit.

9. A rationally unacceptable inference that lacks rhetorical power.

*10. An unpersuasive speech that has rhetorical power.

11. A speech that has neither linguistic merit nor rhetorical power.

12. A passage that is neither rationally acceptable nor rhetorically powerful.

*13. A passage that has rhetorical power.

14. A false statement that is supported by the evidence.

*15. A true statement that is unsupported by the evidence.

VI. YOUR OWN THINKING LAB

1. Provide a statement that is supported by the current total evidence.

2. Provide an example of a statement that is false but was once supported by the total evidence.

3. Provide an example of a statement that is true but was once unsupported by the total evidence.

4. Provide an example of a statement that has been undermined by the scientific evidence available today.

5. Suppose you believe that there is a party in the street, but, unknown to you, your belief is false. Provide a scenario in which that belief would nonetheless be supported by the evidence.

2.3 From Mind to Language

Propositions

We've already seen that inference is the logical relation that obtains whenever at least one belief is taken to support another, and that it can also be conceived as a logical relation that obtains whenever one or more statements are offered in support of another. When thus considered, inference is often called "argument." Any argument, then, is the linguistic expression of an inference. As *beliefs* are the parts that make up inferences, so *statements* are the parts that make up arguments.

Now, what, exactly, are statements? Roughly, they are the standard way to express one's beliefs by means of language, provided one is sincere and competent. Consider

8   Snow is white.

When someone accepts (8) in thought, that thinker entertains the belief that snow is white. The standard way to express this belief would be to say that snow is white. Whether as a belief in the mind, or put into words in a statement, (8) has the content

9   That snow is white.

(9) represents snow as being in a certain way (white). This content is complete, in the sense that it represents a state of affairs, and if snow is as represented, then (9) is true—and if not, (9) is false. Contents of this sort are called 'propositions.' They are true when things are as represented by them and false when they are not. Since any belief or statement has a proposition as its content, it also has one or the other of two truth values:

> Any belief or statement is either true or false.

This is clearly illustrated by (9), whose truth value is determined by applying the following rule: (9) is true if and only if snow is white, and it is false otherwise. For the content of each belief or statement we are considering, we may formulate its truth conditions in the same manner.

Thus propositions may be said to have truth conditions, which are the conditions that have to be met for a proposition to be true. Compare *concepts*, which are also contents but have no truth conditions. For example,

10 Snow.

By contrast with (9), (10) is incomplete, in the sense that it is neither true nor false. Its truth value cannot be determined because (10) lacks truth conditions: what would be the conditions that (10) has to meet in order to be true? No truth-condition rule similar to that in Box 3 can be offered for isolated concepts, which accordingly have no truth values (i.e., they are neither true nor false). Although isolated concepts can be considered proposition parts, they do not count as propositions.

Note also that when different statements have one and the same information content, they all express the same proposition. Since in any such case the statements would represent the same state of affairs, they would have the same truth conditions. For example, Spanish and French translations of (8) above would be different statements, because the sentences used to make these then would be different—namely,

11 La nieve es blanca.

12 La neige est blanche.

Yet (8), (11), and (12) have the same content, thus expressing the same proposition, (9) above.

Uses of Language

By using language we perform *speech acts*, which are the things we can do simply by uttering (saying or writing) certain words: accepting or rejecting propositions, asking questions, making promises and requests, expressing our feelings, greeting, apologizing, voting, and many more. Speech acts can be classified according to how we intend our utterances to be

> **BOX 3 ■ TRUTH CONDITIONS**
> A proposition is true if and only if things are as represented by it, and it's false otherwise.

understood by an audience. We use language primarily to (A) represent the facts, (B) get the audience to do something, (C) express our own mental world, or (D) show our commitment to bringing about certain states of affairs. Accordingly, our expressions fall primarily within the four categories below, each comprising many speech acts.

A. INFORMATIVES: claiming, asserting, affirming, reporting, stating, denying, announcing, identifying, informing, predicting, answering, describing, and so on. Example: the speech act of claiming that the defendant was involved in the crime.
B. DIRECTIVES: prescribing, asking, advising, admonishing, entreating, begging, dismissing, excusing, forbidding, permitting, instructing, ordering, requesting, requiring, suggesting, urging, warning, and so on. Example: the speech act of prescribing that we should respect our parents.
C. EXPRESSIVES: lamenting, regretting, apologizing, congratulating, greeting, thanking, accepting, rejecting, objecting, cheering, and so on. Example: the speech act of apologizing for having been rude.
D. COMMISSIVES: promising, adjourning, calling to order, bequeathing, baptizing, guaranteeing, inviting, volunteering, naming, and so on. Example: the speech act of naming one's cat 'Felix.'

Informatives are utterances aimed at reporting how things are. For example, a statement that a thing has (or doesn't have) a quality ('Snow is white'); or that it is related to another thing in a certain way ('Snow is softer than ice'). Directives are utterances aimed at eliciting an audience's response, whether an answer (13) or an action (14).

13 How long is the line?

14 Pass me the salt!

Prohibitions are requests to refrain from doing something, so they qualify as directives—for example,

15 No pets allowed.

As illustrated by (16), expressives are aimed at communicating a speaker's psychological world, which includes attitudes (hopes, fears, desires, etc.) and feelings (of regret, thankfulness, acceptance, rejection, exasperation, annoyance, etc.)

16 Good heavens!

Commissives convey the speaker's intent that the utterance itself bring about a state of affairs, such as promising (17), adjourning, agreeing, and bequeathing.

17 At American Telecom, we guarantee you, our customers, unlimited free local calls.

BOX 4 ■ THE USES OF LANGUAGE

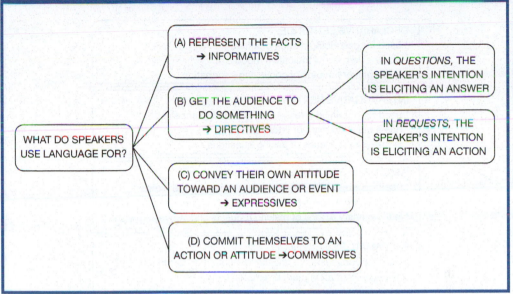

Utterances can bring about such states of affairs, provided, of course, that some conditions are met: for my words to count as bequeathing you my Ferrari, I must, to begin with, own a Ferrari!

Finally, note that only informative expressions ('Snow is white') have straightforward truth conditions: they are true if things are as represented by them and false otherwise. For the most part, expressions of the other types don't have truth conditions, though they do have more idiosyncratic conditions that must be met if the expressions are to succeed. The bottom line: as illustrated by examples (13) through (17), it makes no sense to say that directives, expressives, or commissives are true (or false).

Types of Sentence

A sentence falls under one or another of four types depending on its grammatical form. Natural languages allow for constructing sentences of many different grammatical forms, which could be grouped into the basic types listed in Box 5 below.

Sentences in the indicative mood are declarative ('Snow is white'). Although these sentences are the primary vehicle for the informative use of language, they are sometimes the means for directives ('Passengers are advised not to leave their luggage unattended'), commissives (17 above), and even expressives ('I hope the rope is strong enough'). Imperative sentences are the principal means for requests (15 above) and wishes ('Have fun'); interrogative sentences for questions (13 above); and exclamatory sentences for expressives (16 above). The latter sentences can be used, however, for emphatic requests (14) and assertions ('The king is dead!'). Some sentence types relate better to certain uses of language, even when, except for interrogative sentences, there are no one-to-one relations. Here is a summary of their relations:

BOX 5 ■ BASIC SENTENCE TYPES

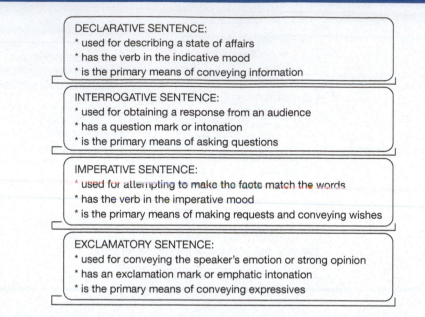

DECLARATIVE SENTENCE:
* used for describing a state of affairs
* has the verb in the indicative mood
* is the primary means of conveying information

INTERROGATIVE SENTENCE:
* used for obtaining a response from an audience
* has a question mark or intonation
* is the primary means of asking questions

IMPERATIVE SENTENCE:
* used for attempting to make the facts match the words
* has the verb in the imperative mood
* is the primary means of making requests and conveying wishes

EXCLAMATORY SENTENCE:
* used for conveying the speaker's emotion or strong opinion
* has an exclamation mark or emphatic intonation
* is the primary means of conveying expressives

BOX 6 ■ LINKING SENTENCE TYPES AND USES OF LANGUAGE

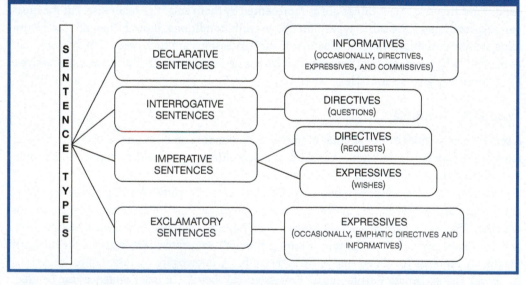

SENTENCE TYPES

DECLARATIVE SENTENCES → INFORMATIVES (OCCASIONALLY, DIRECTIVES, EXPRESSIVES, AND COMMISSIVES)

INTERROGATIVE SENTENCES → DIRECTIVES (QUESTIONS)

IMPERATIVE SENTENCES → DIRECTIVES (REQUESTS) / EXPRESSIVES (WISHES)

EXCLAMATORY SENTENCES → EXPRESSIVES (OCCASIONALLY, EMPHATIC DIRECTIVES AND INFORMATIVES)

2.4 Indirect Use and Figurative Language

As far as logical thinking is concerned, any linguistic phenomenon that may obscure important logical relations among statements, and the beliefs expressed by them, is not welcome. Here we'll study some such phenomena:

- **Figurative language:** A linguistic expression may be used figuratively to mean something different from what it means when it is taken at face value.
- **Indirect use:** A speech act may be performed by way of a different speech act.

These phenomena thrive in natural language, contributing to its richness. Although they could not be avoided altogether in informal logic, which is mostly conducted in natural language, we must follow these rules:

When doing informal logic,

1. Be tolerant about indirect and/or nonliteral uses of language.
2. If possible, recast
   - indirect expressions as direct.
   - nonliteral expressions as literal.

Indirect Use

In order to understand indirect uses of language, we need a closer look at some specific speech acts. Indirect use occurs when a speech act of one type is performed by means of a speech act of another type. Let's recast (14) above as

14′ Can you pass me the salt?

The *direct* speech act performed by an utterance of (14′) is that of asking a question about whether the audience is capable of passing the salt to the speaker. Yet in most situations, that utterance would not be interpreted as asking a question, but instead as requesting that the salt be passed to the speaker. A similar indirect speech act is performed by an utterance of

18 What would human life be without art?

Psychologists researching the relationship between humans and art may very well utter (18) to ask a question. If so, that would be the *direct* speech act thus performed. But (18) could be uttered to assert that art is necessary for human life. In that case, it would perform the indirect speech act of asserting. The possibility of such indirect speech acts makes the links between sentence types and speech-act types more complex. But the links in Box 6 hold whenever language is used directly.

A related question arises when we consider fictional language, which is the language of novels, poems, song lyrics, and the like. As we've seen in Chapter 1, fictional sentences may appear to convey information, but they fall short of making statements. For our purposes here, they are instead manifestations of the expressive use of language.

Figurative Meaning

Sometimes expressions are used with meanings that differ from those they ordinarily have. When that happens, the expressions have *figurative* or *nonliteral* meanings. An expression has nonfigurative or literal meaning just in case its meaning is the result of the standard meanings of each of its parts, together with the way those meanings are combined in the expression. (Combination is important: plainly, 'Mary helps Hercules' doesn't mean the same as 'Hercules helps Mary,' even when each part in the two expressions has the same standard meaning.) Metaphors constitute a common type of figurative meaning. For example,

19 You are a donkey.

The literal meaning of 'donkey' includes elements such as being a domestic *Equus asinus*, often employed as a beast of burden. A person saying (19) to a donkey is using the sentence with its literal meaning. But (19) might be used figuratively to mean that a certain person is obstinate—or unable to understand, say, a theorem. Since here 'donkey' doesn't have its literal meaning, (19) is used figuratively. Similarly, in the context of peace talks, (20) has figurative meaning:

20 The Palestinian and Israeli negotiators have reached a plateau.

In argument reconstruction, whenever possible, recast premises and conclusions in such a way that they feature only declarative sentences, direct speech acts, and literal (nonfigurative) meanings. Suppose someone argues, 'Your current investment strategy is real estate. Are you nuts? An investment strategy is bad if it yields losses for the last five years, and real estate has yielded losses for the last five years.' Here the conclusion ('Are you nuts?') must be recast so that it performs the direct act of stating that the audience's current investment strategy is bad. The conclusion cannot say this by way of asking whether the audience is nuts. Also, the figurative 'being nuts' needs to be replaced with words that can be interpreted literally. Thus reconstructed, the argument is

1. Your current investment strategy is real estate.
2. If an investment strategy yields losses for the last five years, it's a bad strategy.
3. Real estate has yielded losses for the last five years.
4. Your current investment strategy is a bad strategy.

Exercises

VII. Review Questions

1. What is a statement? And what is a proposition?
2. Different statements could express the same proposition. Provide some examples.
3. What are speech acts?
4. Name two characteristics of each sentence type.
5. How are the uses of language related to the sentence types?
6. Which sentence type is commonly associated with the informative use of language? Explain.
7. What are the main categories of uses of language? Provide two examples of each.
8. What is figurative meaning? Provide two examples of your own.
9. Could a speech act be performed by way of another speech act? Explain.
10. Why doesn't informal logic welcome indirect use and figurative meaning?

VIII. Identify the type of speech act that each of the following sentences could be used to perform directly (informative, directive, expressive, or commissive):

1. At first, America was not called "America."

   SAMPLE ANSWER: Informative

2. Home buyers are recommended to be prudent when requesting a mortgage.

*3. How wonderful!

4. I promise to arrive to be there on time.

*5. Whether you like it or not, you must move on with your life.

6. One after another, they all signed up.

*7. Each person has some natural talents.

8. We must go to bed early tonight.

9. No parking at any time.

*10. Let's hope that Boris's problems will be over soon.

11. Evolution vs. creation is an endless debate.

*12. Try a little bit harder.

13. There is life on Mars.

14. Who is telling the story?

*15. What an odd statement to make!

16. Why was Jane traveling alone?

17. That animal is a beaver.

*18. Passengers are advised not to leave their luggage unattended.

19. This is amazing!

*20. We hereby bequeath you our up-state mansion.

IX. Determine which of the following sentences is declarative, interrogative, imperative, or exclamatory:

1. Fido is a dog.

   SAMPLE ANSWER: Declarative

2. Snow isn't white.

3. God exists.

*4. Please shut the door.

5. What time is it?

6. Good Lord!

*7. Winter days are short.

8. Some dentists have clean teeth.

9. Not all cars need gas.

*10. What is your favorite dish?

11. How is John?

12. Today is Monday.

*13. The Amazon forest is being depleted.

14. The moon was a ghostly galleon, tossed upon cloudy seas.

15. Keep your promise.

*16. Oh, my gosh!

17. What are you up to?

18. Make it short.

*19. I have a headache.

20. There is life after death.

X. **For each of the following, identify (A) its sentence type and the (B) direct and (C) indirect speech acts that it could be used to perform. Tip: To answer (C), imagine a context where the sentence could perform a speech act other than that directly associated with it. Be aware that, although we list one possible indirect speech act in the sample answer, more are also possible. Be imaginative!**

1. Isn't it crazy to think that there is no life after death?

   SAMPLE ANSWER: (A) interrogative; (B) asking a question (directive); (C) rejecting that there is no life after death (informative).

2. Can Jill play tennis with that old racket?

*3. When are you going to stop making fun of poor Harry?

4. Gosh, the bank account is empty!

*5. The dog bites!

6. It is a sunny day.

*7. Is he really sleeping?

8. That's not funny.

9. What are you doing in the dark?

*10. Tomorrow is another day.

XI. **For each sentence below, interpret it (A) literally and (B) figuratively.**

1. This room is a pigsty.

   SAMPLE ANSWER: A) This room is used to house pigs. B) This room is dirty.

2. He is Hercules.

*3. Those players are robots.

4. A rose grows in this garden.

5. No parrots allowed here.

*6. We are approaching a volcano.

7. That's the sticking point.

8. We are Romeo and Juliet.

*9. Jim wears two hats.

10. I am not Bill Gates.

11. They went the extra mile.

*12. That city is an anthill.

13. She is a saint.

14. My heart told me that she was the one for me.

*15. He's toast.

XII. The following arguments contain either figurative language or indirect speech acts. First identify which contains which. Then, provide versions of the arguments containing neither figurative language nor indirect speech acts (some flexibility allowed here).

1. Being trailed by a stalker is a scary experience. But Margaret Borgia is a detective, and detectives are tough cookies. Thus she can handle the stalker who's now following her.

   SAMPLE ANSWER. Figurative language. Recast: Detectives can handle scary experiences.

*2. Abe is in no position to recommend that our president should be fired. In order to make such a recommendation, you have to be a person in authority. And who is Abe?

3. According to a recent survey, many high school dropouts go down the drain. The Jones twins are local high school dropouts. So we may expect to read about them soon in the crime section of the *Star News*.

4. Although Twitter's hacker avoided jail, he is a dead duck because now he has a bad reputation.

*5. There is good evidence that Tracy and her friends leaked a video of a U.S. helicopter attack to a blog. Whenever there is such evidence, pressing criminal charges is our duty. Can we press criminal charges now?

6. From a coach's perspective, potential professional players are crops that need to ripen. Since Ali is a potential professional player, his coach will be patient to get the best out of him.

*7. For teenagers, flip-flops are hot. So we may expect to see many such fashionable items in our summer camp for high school students this year.

8. Since it doesn't matter to me, it is up to you whether you attend the party or not.

9. People do not eat peas with their fingers. Therefore, you should not eat peas with your fingers.

10. Relations between the United States and Eastern Europe began to thaw twenty years ago. Poland is an Eastern European country. Thus, in the last twenty years, relations between the United States and Poland have improved considerably.

1. For three sentences of your own, identify which (A) direct and (B) indirect speech acts it could be used to perform.

    SAMPLE ANSWER: Isn't it time to go to bed?

    A.   Direct speech act of asking whether it's time to go to bed (directive)

    B.   Indirect speech act of informing someone that it's time to go to bed (informative)

2. Provide three sentences of your own that could be interpreted first literally, and then figuratively. Give both interpretations.

    SAMPLE ANSWER: Words are cheap. Literally, 'Words don't cost anything.' Figuratively, 'It's easier to talk than to act or prove.'

3. Construct or find a short dialogue that uses some words literally and others figuratively. Identify its figurative and indirect uses of language.

4. Make a list of six common figurative expressions that you believe are overused.

2.5 Definition: An Antidote to Unclear Language

The logical relations that obtain when reasoning is at work can be obscured by nonliteral and indirect uses of language. But we may often be able to minimize obscurity, and sometimes eliminate it completely, by resorting to definitions, which may be used to either clarify or revise the meaning of linguistic expressions. Of interest here are three kinds of definition: reportive, ostensive, and contextual. But first, let's consider the structure of definitions generally.

Reconstructing Definitions

Before we can evaluate a definition, it's best to reconstruct it first, so that we may grasp what is being defined and what provides the definition. This requires distinguishing the two sides of a definition: the *definiendum* (that which is to be defined) and the *definiens* (that which provides the definition). In reconstructing a definition, its *definiendum* is listed first, on the left-hand side, and its *definiens* last, on the right-hand side. We'll adopt the practice of placing the symbol '=df.' (which reads 'equal by definition') between *definiedum* and *definiens* in any reconstructed definition. For example,

21 Puppy   =df.   Young dog

22 Triangle =df.   Plane figure with exactly three internal angles

22 Cube   =df.   Three-dimensional object with six sides, all of which are flat and square

The expression listed on the left-hand side of each definition is its *definiendum*, that on the right-hand side its *definiens*. Everyday definitions are phrased in many different ways—as can be seen in the following familiar ways of defining 'lawyer' as synonymous with 'attorney':

24   To be an attorney is to be a lawyer.

24'   To say that a person is an attorney is to say that the person is a lawyer.

24''   'Attorney' means 'lawyer.'

A succinct reconstruction of any of these reads, 'Attorney =df. Lawyer,' where 'attorney' is the *definiendum* and 'lawyer' the *definiens*.

Reportive Definitions

(21) through (24) are definitions that purport to give the everyday meaning of a word or of some larger linguistic expression. Definitions of this sort are commonly found in dictionaries and translation manuals. To be adequate, the two sides of a reportive definition must have exactly the same meaning:

> A reportive definition is adequate if and only if its two sides are synonymous or meaning equivalent (i.e., they mean the same). Otherwise, it is inadequate.

Among the defects that would make a reportive definition inadequate are being too broad, too narrow, or too broad and too narrow. For example,

25 Sister   =df.   Female person

(25) is too broad because its *definiens* picks out females who are not sisters (e.g., a woman with no siblings). As a result, its two sides are different in meaning.

26 Sister   =df.   Adult female sibling

(26) is too narrow because the *definiens* leaves out sisters who have not reached adulthood.

27 Sister   =df.   Adult sibling

(27) is too broad and too narrow because the *definiens* both picks out some brothers and leaves out sisters who are not adults. Clearly, a *male* adult sibling is not a sister, and a two-year-old sister is not an *adult* sibling. So (27)'s two sides fail to have the same meaning.

Testing Reportive Definitions

When a reportive definition is inadequate, counterexample is the method to show it. A single counterexample would do this. A counterexample to (25) is a female person who is not a sibling; to (26), a sister who is not an adult; and to (27), a male adult who is a sibling or a non-adult sister.

A reportive definition that doesn't have counterexamples is adequate. When presented with a definition, we can use a thought experiment to determine whether it has a counterexample. If we try this method with (21) through (24) above, we soon discover that it's simply not possible that, for example, someone could be an attorney without being a lawyer or a sister without being a female sibling. In any possible world where someone is an attorney, that person *is* a lawyer, and if she is a sister, then she *is* also a female sibling. Since counterexamples to these definitions seem impossible, we must conclude that the definitions are adequate.

> ## BOX 7 ■ COUNTEREXAMPLES AND REPORTIVE DEFINITIONS
>
> - A counterexample to a reportive definition is a case that satisfies one of its sides without satisfying the other.
> - In the absence of counterexamples to it, a reportive definition is adequate.
> - The principle underlying the method of counterexample is: Adequate until proven inadequate!
> - A reportive definition is inadequate just in case there is at least one counterexample to it.

In his dialogue *Laches*, the Greek philosopher Plato (428–347 BCE) has a general of that name proposing a definition of 'courage' that we'll now test for adequacy.

28 Courage   =df.   Moving forward in battle.

(28) is adequate provided there is no case that satisfies one side without satisfying the other. A counterexample to it could be a real-life case or a thought experiment, which is a possible scenario entertained only in thought (see Box 7). To be a counterexample to (28), the scenario should make credible that someone might be courageous without moving forward in battle—or that someone might move forward in battle without being courageous. Here is one such thought experiment: the case of a fighter who moves backward in battle as a strategy (say, to confuse the enemy and counteract more forcefully). Since any such case is possible (and even actual!), the actions of this imaginary fighter satisfy (28)'s *definiendum*, but not its *definiens*, thus amounting to a counterexample to Laches' definition.

When running a thought experiment, we must follow some rules. First, the described scenario must be logically coherent, otherwise it wouldn't qualify as a logically *possible* world. Furthermore, the scenario must be thoroughly described in the same language, without changing the meanings of the words. In addition, we must be competent users of the words employed in describing the scenario: we must have no reason to suspect that our views about their meanings are atypical, in the sense of departing from the ordinary conception of them.

> ## BOX 8 ■ POSSIBLE SCENARIOS AND REPORTIVE DEFINITIONS
>
> A reportive definition is adequate if and only if there is no possible scenario in which something satisfies one of its sides without satisfying the other.
>
> - A reportive definition is adequate just in case there are no counterexamples to it.
> - A counterexample to a reportive definition is a possible scenario in which the words apply on one of its sides, but not on the other.
> - To serve its purpose, the scenario must be coherent and be described without changes in the meaning of the words.

Ostensive and Contextual Definitions

Not all definitions of the meaning of expressions purport to offer a *definiens* that is synonymous with the *definiendum*. Among those that don't are ostensive and contextual definitions, to which we now turn. The *definiens* of an ostensive definition offers some examples of things paradigmatically falling under its *definiendum*—for instance,

> 29 To be a socialist country is to have the socioeconomic system at work in Cuba.

> 30 A metropolis is a city as large as London, São Paulo, or Tokyo.

A *contextual definition* presents in its *definiens* another expression or context in which neither the *definiendum* nor a strict synonym of it occurs. For example, in logic the connective 'unless' is sometimes defined by equivalence with 'either . . . or . . . ' in this way:

> 31 'P unless Q' is equivalent to 'either P or Q.'

Here the *definiens* is logically equivalent to the *definiendum*, in the sense that they both relate 'P' and 'Q' through the same logical relation. But the two sides of the definition are not equivalent in meaning.

Exercises

XIV. Review Questions

1. What is a definition?
2. Name the two parts of a definition and explain their roles.
3. Provide two reportive definitions, and explain in each case why it counts as such.
4. What are ostensive and contextual definitions? Illustrate your answer with examples.
5. Can reportive definitions be inadequate? If so, how? If not, why not?
6. How do reportive, ostensive, and contextual definitions differ? Support your answer with examples.

XV. Reconstruct the following definitions, marking the *definiendum* with a single underline and the *definiens* with a double underline. Make each definition as succinct as possible.

1. In English, an oculist is an eye doctor.

   SAMPLE ANSWER: In English, an oculist is an eye doctor.

   Oculist =df. Eye doctor

2. 'Anger' means the same as 'being inclined to exhibit anger behavior.'

*3. A small elephant is an elephant that is smaller than most elephants.

4. To say, 'An event caused another event,' is to say, 'If the first event had not happened, then the second event would not have happened.'

*5. A creature counts as a human being if and only if it is a featherless biped.

6. By 'glue,' English speakers mean an adhesive substance used to join two surfaces.

*7. A horse is a beast of burden with a flowing mane.

8. To name incorrectly is to misname.

9. What makes you timid or fearful is something that intimidates you.

10. An electronic apparatus for the production and control of sound is a synthesizer.

XVI. **Determine whether the following definitions are reportive, contextual, or ostensive.**

1. Pandas are those animals that we saw in the last cage at the Washington zoo.

   SAMPLE ANSWER: Ostensive

2. 'x is the brother of y' is identical to 'x is a male sibling of y.'

*3. 'All dogs are canines' means 'It is not the case that some dogs are not canines.'

4. To be a woman is to be a female human being.

*5. Bachelor = unmarried man.

6. Chilis are the peppers that you ate at Garza's Rio Grande Restaurant.

*7. 'Some are philosophers' means 'There are philosophers.'

8. 'Hunter' means 'person who hunts.'

*9. Cricket is that sport which is popular in the West Indies.

10. 'P if and only if Q' means 'If P, then Q, and if Q, then P.'

XVII. **For each of the following reportive definitions, indicate whether it is too broad, too narrow, or both.**

1. A human arm is a human limb.

   SAMPLE ANSWER: Too broad

2. To be human is to be an animal.

*3. 'Bachelor' is meaning-equivalent to 'unmarried human being who is sexually neurotic.'

4. A paint stripper is a solvent of paint used for removing bright paint.

*5. A lawyer is an attorney specialized in litigation.

6. Tiger =df. Striped animal.

*7. Lemon =df. natural fruit with yellow peel and vitamin C that grows in Florida.

8. A duck is an aquatic bird that lives in the Great Lakes.

*9. A human being is a creature with lungs.

10. Capitalism is a way of life in the developed world.

XVIII. **Show the inadequacy of the definitions in the above exercise by offering a counterexample to each of them. (Tip: you'd need an example that satisfies one side of the definition without satisfying the other.)**

1. A human arm is a human limb.

   SAMPLE ANSWER: A human leg, which is a limb that is not an arm.

XIX. Redefine the expressions listed in Exercise XVII in a way that avoids the objections of being too broad, too narrow, or too broad *and* too narrow. If that's not possible, explain why.

1. A human arm is a human limb.

   SAMPLE ANSWER: A human arm is an upper-body limb of humans normally attached to the body at the shoulders and ending in a hand.

XX. YOUR OWN THINKING LAB

1. Use the method of counterexample to show the inadequacy of the following definitions:
   A. Morally right action =df. Action that obeys the laws of the state.
   B. Being hungry =df. Saying that one desires food.
   C. Guilty person =df. Someone who has been convicted of a crime.

2. Explain why thought experiments would support the adequacy of the following definitions:
   A. Mother =df. Female parent.
   B. Tennis player =df. One who plays tennis.
   C. Rectangle =df. Plane figure with four straight sides forming four right angles.

Writing Project

University campuses are often seen as prime recruiting grounds by zealots of various descriptions—some political, some religious, some ideological, or other types. They are trying to win converts to their fervently held beliefs. Write a long email (about 300 words) to an imaginary friend, reporting about one such rhetorically skillful speaker you've seen in action recently (this may be either a real-life or an imaginary case). First describe the speech and its context in detail, then assess it critically in light of what you've learned about rational acceptability and warn your friend of the dangers of uncritical acceptance of these speakers' messages.

■ Chapter Summary

Standards for rationally acceptable beliefs:

1. That they have logical connectedness, which is a quality of beliefs that stand in an adequate logical relation such as inference. It comes in degrees.
2. That if they are empirical, they have evidential support, which is provided by information based on observation.

Evidence: the information pointing to a belief's being true. A belief is true if and only if its content corresponds to the facts. Evidence and truth are independent.

Linguistic merit: a quality of either written or oral language resulting from a combination of grammatical, syntactical, and stylistic factors such as concision, adequate vocabulary, and compliance with the rules of grammar.

Rhetorical power: the power to persuade.

Parallel between statements and beliefs: when speakers are sincere and the circumstances are normal, their statements express their beliefs.

Propositions: the contents of statements and beliefs. Since each proposition is either true or false, each statement is either true or false.

Direct links between sentence types and uses of language:

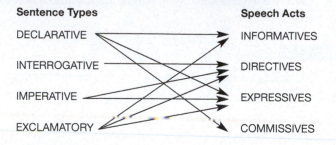

Speech acts: The things we do simply by using language (informing, apologizing, greeting, objecting, promising, recommending, etc.). There are four types of speech acts:

Informatives (language used to convey information)
Directives (language used to get the audience to do something)
Expressives (language used to express the speaker's psychological states)
Commissives (language used to bring about a state of affairs)

Figurative meaning: when an expression isn't used with its customary meaning, as in metaphor and irony.

Definition: the standard means to clarify or revise the meaning of an expression. It has two sides: what is to be defined (*definiendum*), and what does the defining (*definiens*). There are three types of meaning definition:

Reportive definition: its *definiens* is synonymous with its *definiendum*. It's tested by counterexample.
Ostensive definition: its *definiens* points to cases to which the *definiendum* applies.
Contextual definition: its *definiens* offers a replacement of the *definiendum*.

■ Key Words

Evidence
Truth conditions
Proposition
Declarative sentence
Speech act

Indirect speech act
Figurative language
Reportive definition
Ostensive definition
Contextual definition

CHAPTER 3

The Virtues of Belief

This chapter looks more closely at beliefs, the building blocks of inference. In connection with this, you'll learn about such topics as

- Belief, disbelief, and nonbelief.
- Some virtues of belief that are to be cultivated: accuracy, truth, reasonableness, consistency, conservatism, and revisability.
- Some vices of belief that are to be avoided: inaccuracy, falsity, unreasonableness, inconsistency, dogmatism, and relativism.
- The difference between empirical belief and conceptual belief.
- The notions of self-contradiction, contradiction, and logically possible world.
- The "supervirtue" of rationality and the "supervice" of irrationality.

3.1 Belief, Disbelief, and Nonbelief

Beliefs and disbeliefs are two types of psychological attitudes people may have when they are engaged in accepting what they think is true and rejecting what's false. We'll call these was states of mind 'cognitive attitudes' (from the Latin, 'cognoscere,' which means 'to know'). Nonbeliefs represent the lack of either of these two attitudes. A belief is the cognitive attitude of accepting a proposition, which is an information content representing states of affairs. Consider, for example, the proposition expressed by

1   Dogs are carnivorous.

Anyone who believes (1) has the psychological attitude of accepting that dogs are carnivorous. That person takes (1) to be true. If asked whether (1) is true, under normal circumstances, she would assent. Assuming she's sincere and competent, she could voice her belief by stating (1), or many other sentences such as

2   It is true that dogs are carnivorous.

3   It is the case that dogs are carnivorous.

(1), (2), and (3) may be used to express the same content: namely, the proposition that dogs are carnivorous.

Supposing we use 'S' to stand for a speaker (or person), 'P' for a proposition, and 'believing that P' for the psychological attitude of accepting that P, we can define belief in this way:

BOX 1 ■ BELIEF

S has a belief that P just in case S accepts that P. Assuming that the circumstances are normal and S is sincere, if asked,

- 'Is P true?' S would assent.
- 'What do you make of P?' S would assert sentences such as 'P,' 'P is true,' and 'It is the case that P.'

Note that the definition of belief in Box 1 invokes normal circumstances and the speaker's sincerity. In their absence, it may be that what a person S says is not what she believes. Because there are deceivers (whose words misrepresent the beliefs they actually have) and self-deceivers (who deny the beliefs they actually have), we must assume the speaker's sincerity when we draw a parallel between what she says and what she believes. And because S might, out of coercion, delusion, or other impairment, say something she doesn't in fact believe, we must assume normal circumstances, which include the speaker's being competent—that is, not mentally compromised, threatened, or impaired in any way.

But what about those who simply don't believe a certain proposition, such as (1) above? They may have either a disbelief or a nonbelief. A disbelief about (1) may be expressed by sentences such as (4) through (6):

4   Dogs are not carnivorous.

5   It is false that dogs are carnivorous.

6   It is not the case that dogs are carnivorous.

Under normal circumstances, a person who sincerely says any of these disbelieves (1), which amounts to having the psychological attitude of rejecting (1). If asked whether (1) is true, she would dissent. And to voice her disbelief, she would deny (1)—for example, by asserting (4). We may now summarize the concept of disbelief in this way:

BOX 2 ■ DISBELIEF

S has a disbelief that P just in case S rejects that P. Assuming that the circumstances are normal and S is sincere, if asked,

- 'Is P true?' S would dissent.
- 'What do you make of P?' S would deny that P is true by uttering sentences such as 'P is false,' 'Not P,' and 'It is not the case that P.'

What about those who neither believe nor disbelieve (1)? They have the attitude of *nonbelief* about (1). Under normal circumstances, they would neither accept nor reject it. If asked whether that content is true, they might shrug, giving no sign of assent or dissent. Box 3 summarizes all these reactions.

BOX 3 ■ NONBELIEF

S has a nonbelief that P just in case S neither accepts, nor rejects, that P. Assuming that the circumstances are normal and S is sincere, if asked

- 'Is P true?' S would neither assent nor dissent.
- 'What do you make of P?' S would suspend judgment.

Nonbelieving that P, then, amounts to lacking any belief or disbelief about P. The corresponding psychological attitude is that of *suspending judgment* about P. We should bear in mind that whenever we are considering whether to accept or reject a proposition—for example, that dogs are carnivorous—there is also the option of nonbelief, which amounts to withholding belief about a proposition. Thinking logically can help in developing the most adequate attitude toward a proposition, whether that be accepting it, rejecting it, or suspending judgment about it. Deciding which is the correct attitude matters, since our beliefs are the building blocks of our reasoning. Here the rule is that, to keep the whole edifice sound, one must use high-quality building blocks and do regular maintenance. But how are we to tell which building blocks of reasoning are high-quality and which aren't? That's the topic of our next section.

BOX 4 ■ SECTION SUMMARY

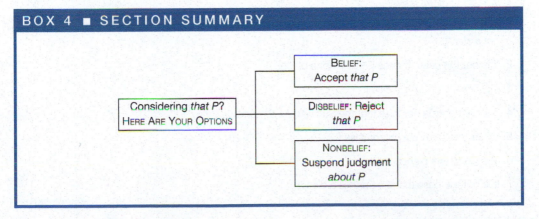

Exercises

I. Review Questions

1. What is a belief? And what do we call the content of a belief?
2. What is the difference between a disbelief and a nonbelief?
3. Is nonbelief a kind of belief? If yes, why? If not, why not?
4. Think of two scenarios of your own where a person has a nonbelief.
5. Is disbelief a kind of belief? If yes, why? If not, why not?
6. In what does suspending judgment consist?
7. Why must the thinker's sincerity be assumed in order to take her statements to express her beliefs?
8. Why must the thinker's competence be assumed in order to take her statements to express her beliefs?

II. For each of the following, indicate whether it expresses a belief, a disbelief, or a nonbelief.

1. I accept that the Earth revolves.

   SAMPLE ANSWER: Belief

2. I reject that the Pope is in Rome.

*3. I neither accept nor reject that God exists.

4. I think that it is false that cats are feline.

*5. In my opinion, it is the case that Newton was smart.

6. I'm convinced that it is not the case that the Moon is bigger than the Earth.

*7. I suspend judgment about whether there is life after death.

8. I neither accept nor reject the belief that there are UFOs.

*9. I'm sure that Barack Obama is tall.

10. In my view, no zealots can be trusted.

III. Report the belief, disbelief, or nonbelief expressed by each of the statements below. Avoid reporting a disbelief as a belief with a negation inside the *that*-clause.

1. The Earth is not a star.

   SAMPLE ANSWER: The disbelief that the Earth is a star. [Avoid reporting this as "the belief that the Earth is *not* a star."]

2. It is not the case that the Earth is not a planet.

3. It is false that Earth is a star.

*4. It is neither true nor false that the Sun will rise tomorrow.

5. Either the Earth is a star or it isn't.

*6. The Earth is a planet.

7. It is not the case that the Earth is a planet.

*8. It is neither true nor false that galaxies are flying outward.

9. Triangles are not figures.

*10. I am thinking.

11. I am not thinking.

*12. Is there life after death? I cannot say.

13. UFOs do not exist.

*14. I'm agnostic about whether humans are the product of evolution or divine creation.

15. If Pluto orbits the Sun, then it is a planet.

IV. YOUR OWN THINKING LAB

*1. Explain why normal circumstances are a needed assumption in exercises (II) and (III) above.

2. Provide two examples of belief.

3. Recast your examples as examples of disbelief.

4. Provide two examples of nonbeliefs.

5. Recast your examples of nonbelief as examples of belief.

*6. Suppose you were considering the proposition that there is life after death. What cognitive attitudes are your options? Report those attitudes.

3.2 Beliefs' Virtues and Vices

Among the traits or features of beliefs, some contribute to good reasoning and others to bad. We may think of the good-making features as virtues, and of the bad-making ones as vices. Prominent among the former is the supervirtue of rationality, and among the latter, the supervice of irrationality. Why are these so significant? Because rationality marks the limits of acceptable reasoning. Irrational beliefs are beyond that limit. In their case, the aims of reasoning are, as we'll see, no longer achievable. In this section, we take up some virtues and vices of belief, leaving rationality and irrationality for the next section. The features of beliefs in our agenda now are those listed in Box 5.

BOX 5 ■ BELIEF'S VIRTUES AND VICES

Virtues	Vices
Accuracy	Inaccuracy
Truth	Falsity
Reasonableness	Unreasonableness
Consistency	Inconsistency
Conservatism	Dogmatism
Revisability	Relativism

First, note that since logical thinkers wish to avoid beliefs with bad-making features, someone might think that it is advisable to avoid beliefs altogether. For if we didn't have any beliefs at all, we wouldn't have any beliefs with bad-making features! But this advice is self-defeating, for it is not possible to avoid having beliefs. The very claim that logical thinkers are better off without beliefs itself expresses a belief, assuming that those who make it are sincere and competent. As logical thinkers, we must have some beliefs, so our aim should be simply to have as many beliefs with good-making features, and as few with bad-making features, as possible. Our aim, in other words, is that of maximizing the virtues and minimizing the vices of beliefs. To say that a belief has a virtue is to praise it—while to say it has a vice is to criticize it. Let's now take up each of the virtues and vices of beliefs.

3.3 Accuracy and Truth

Accuracy and Inaccuracy

To have an acceptable degree of accuracy, a belief must either represent, or get close to representing, the facts. In the former case, the belief is true—in the latter, merely approximately true or close to being true. The following belief represents things as they actually are, and it is therefore true:

7   Brasilia is the capital of Brazil.

True beliefs have the highest degree of accuracy. On the other hand, false beliefs have the highest degree of inaccuracy, simply because they neither represent, nor get close to representing, things as they actually are. For example,

8   Rio is the capital of Brazil.

Any belief that denies (8), which is false, would be true. Thus, that Rio is not the capital of Brazil, and that it is not the case that Rio is the capital of Brazil, are both true—and therefore have maximal accuracy. To determine this, we use the rule in Box 6.

Truth and Falsity

As logical thinkers, we should believe what is true and disbelieve what is false. But it is often difficult to tell which beliefs are true and which are false. Thus sometimes we end up mistakenly believing what is false—as when people in the Middle Ages believed that

9   The Sun revolves around the Earth.

They were, of course, later shown to be mistaken: (9) was always false, and therefore inaccurate. For (9) not only fails to represent the facts truly, but (most crucially) never even got close at all to

---

BOX 6 ■ ACCURACY AND INACCURACY

When a belief is true, it has maximal accuracy; and when it is false, it has maximal inaccuracy.

representing them as they are. A belief can be more or less accurate depending on how close it is to representing the facts as they are—that is, to getting them right. But some beliefs could be accurate without being true. For example,

10 France is hexagonal.

11 Lord Raglan won the Battle of Alma.[1]

(10) is roughly accurate, but not accurate enough to count as strictly true (not good enough for a cartographer!). Similarly, (11) is accurate, but should we say it's true? Well, it's approximately true. In fact, the battle was won by the British army, not just by its commander. Yet it's not clearly wrong to say that "Lord Raglan won it." These examples suggest that accuracy and inaccuracy are a matter of degree: some beliefs are closer to (or father from) representing the facts than others are. Some beliefs are thus more accurate (or inaccurate) than others. Yet truth and falsity are not a matter of degree at all: each belief is either true or false. It makes no sense to say of a belief that it is 'more true' or 'less true' (or 'false') than another belief. A belief is either true or it isn't. At the same time, both accuracy and truth are virtues that either a single belief or a set of beliefs may have (likewise for the vices of inaccuracy and falsity).

In the case of (12) and other beliefs that are vague, it is unclear whether they are true or false, and also unclear whether they are accurate or inaccurate.

12 Queen Latifah is young.

Caution is likewise needed for statements that express evaluations such as (13). It is controversial among philosophers whether evaluative statements are capable of being true or false. Some such statements seem plainly true ("Hitler was evil"), others less clearly true than

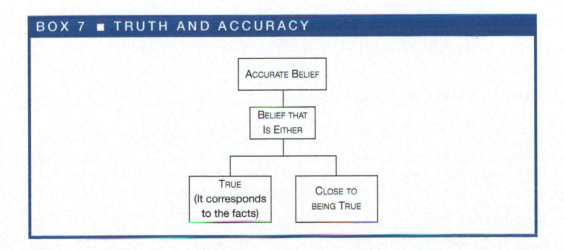

BOX 7 ■ TRUTH AND ACCURACY

ACCURATE BELIEF

BELIEF THAT IS EITHER

TRUE (It corresponds to the facts)

CLOSE TO BEING TRUE

---

[1]For more on puzzling examples of this sort, see J. L. Austin, 'Performative-Constatif' (*La Philosophie Analytique, Cahiers de Royaumont*, 1962).

expressive of endorsement or attitudes of approval ("Frank Sinatra's music is great"). Likewise in judgments of taste such as

    13 Ford Mustangs are better looking than Chevrolet Corvettes.

In cases of this sort, we'll adopt the convention of simply indicating that they are statements of value (more on this in Chapter 4).

3.4 Reasonableness

Beliefs that may fall short of being true, and even accurate, could still be reasonable. How is this possible? To answer that question, let us consider the virtue of reasonableness and the vice of unreasonableness, which, like accuracy and inaccuracy, are features that either a single belief or a set of beliefs can have, and which come in degrees: some beliefs are more reasonable (or unreasonable) than others. Their, degree of reasonableness depends on how much support of the adequate type they possess.

> A belief is reasonable if and only if it has adequate support. Otherwise, it is unreasonable.

Beliefs of different types are supported in different ways. Thus how a belief might attain reasonableness would vary according to its type. Since we'll consider here only two kinds of beliefs, empirical and conceptual, we'll abstain, for the time being, from judging the reasonableness of other types of beliefs: for example, of beliefs that are value judgments such as (13) above.

Two Kinds of Reasonableness

What's required for a belief to be reasonable varies according to what sort of belief it is. Consider

    14 Fido is barking.

    15 Dogs bark.

(14) and (15) can be supported only by observation and are therefore empirical beliefs ('empirical' means *observational*). The kind of support needed for beliefs of this sort to be reasonable differs from that of nonobservational beliefs. Among the latter are conceptual beliefs, which may be supported by reasoning alone. For example,

    16 $7 + 5 = 12$

    17 A brother is a male sibling.

The grounds for (16) and (17) are conceptual: it is sufficient to understand the concepts involved to realize that each of these beliefs is true. The truth of (16) is clear to anyone who has mastered the numbers and the concept of addition—as is the truth of (17) to anyone who has mastered the concepts, 'brother' and 'male sibling.' Thus (16) and (17) are both reasonable, since each is supported by adequate reasoning alone.

> A conceptual belief is reasonable if and only if all that's needed to realize that the belief is true is to master the concepts involved.

A reasonable conceptual belief, then, is one whose truth goes without saying once we understand the content of the belief.

By contrast, (14) and (15) are not eligible for this kind of support: they require the support of observation or evidence. In which circumstances would (14) or (15) be unreasonable? Suppose that someone believes falsely that her dog, Fido, is barking now. That is, she believes (14) even though she knows that Fido has been mute for many years. When challenged, she engages in what is plainly a case of wishful thinking: her desire that Fido could bark somehow makes her believe that the dog is barking. In this scenario, (14) would be unreasonable, simply because it's an empirical belief and the rule is

> To be reasonable, empirical, beliefs must be supported either by evidence or by inference from evidence.

As we saw in Chapter 2, evidence is the outcome of observation, which is provided by the sensory experiences of seeing, hearing, touching, tasting, and/or smelling. Thus if as a result of seeing Fido's barking behavior and hearing him barking one comes to believe (14), then that sensory experience itself would count as evidence for (14), thus rendering it reasonable to believe (in the absence of evidence to the contrary). Trustworthy testimony also counts as evidence, since we may consider it vicarious observation. Being supported by the evidence, then, is all that's usually needed for a belief like (14) to be reasonable.

On the other hand, for beliefs such as (15) to be reasonable, inference from evidence is required. After all, (15) amounts to

15' All dogs bark.

This belief is supported by the evidence *and* by other beliefs based on the available evidence. The evidence consists in the observation that many dogs bark, from which one can infer that all dogs bark. That is, one would need more than simply the firsthand evidence from observing some barking dogs to support (15'). After all, it is impossible to observe *all* barking dogs. What else, apart from evidence, is contributing to its support? Other beliefs are required, such as

18 A great number of dogs have been observed.

19 They all barked.

BOX 8 ■ TWO KINDS OF REASONABLE BELIEF

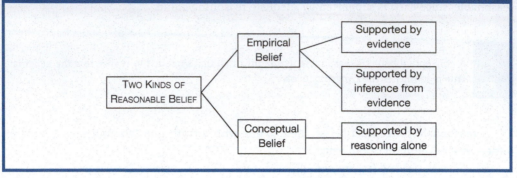

On the basis of (18) and (19), it is reasonable to think that dogs bark. But if (15) is supported by (18) and (19), then the relation among these is that of inference: (15) is inferred from (18) and (19).

For empirical beliefs, then, evidence and inference from evidence are the two standard routes to reasonableness. For conceptual beliefs, the route is reasoning alone. Empirical and conceptual beliefs that lack the adequate kind of support would suffer from a substantial degree of unreasonableness. Yet keep in mind that, for beliefs of other types, the criteria of reasonableness may be different.

3.5 Consistency

Accuracy, truth, and reasonableness are virtues a single belief may have. Consistency, on the other hand, is a virtue that *only* a set of beliefs, two or more of them, can have—and likewise for the vice of inconsistency. But what does 'consistency' mean?

Defining 'Consistency' and 'Inconsistency'

A good place to start for a definition of 'consistency' is 'inconsistency,' since a set of beliefs is *consistent* just in case it is not inconsistent. So, let's begin with 'inconsistency,' defined thus:

> A set of beliefs is *inconsistent* if and only if its members *could not all be true at once.*

Consider (20) and (21),

20 Dorothy Maloney is a senator.

21 Dorothy Maloney is a jogger.

These could both be true at the same time: Dorothy Maloney could be both a senator and a jogger. But suppose we add the belief that

22 Dorothy Maloney is not a public official.

(20), (21), and (22) make up an inconsistent set, since it is impossible for all its members to be true at the same time: clearly, no one could be a senator while at the same time failing to be a public official. We may now say that

> A set of beliefs is *consistent* if and only if its members could all be true at once.

To say that some beliefs are consistent is to say that they are logically compatible. Compatible beliefs need not in fact be true: it is sufficient that they *could* all be true at once. Beliefs that are actually false could make up a perfectly consistent or compatible set if they could all be true in some possible scenario.

Logically Possible Propositions

Consider, for example, a set made up of

23 Arnold Schwarzenegger is a medical doctor.

24 Pigs fly.

(23) and (24) could both be true at once in some logically possible scenario or world. Our world, which we'll call the 'actual world,' is just one among many worlds that are logically possible—where a world is logically possible if it does not involve any contradiction. Logically impossible worlds make no sense and are therefore unthinkable. We can also say that a proposition is logically possible when it meets the condition in Box 9.

BOX 9 ■ LOGICALLY POSSIBLE PROPOSITION

A proposition is logically possible if and only if it involves no contradiction.

Logically Impossible Propositions

Propositions that are not thinkable at all are logically impossible, necessarily false, or absurd, as illustrated by each of the following:

25 All pigs are mammals, but some pigs are not mammals.

26 Arnold Schwarzenegger is a medical doctor and he isn't.

27 Arnold Schwarzenegger is a married bachelor.

Propositions of this sort are *self-contradictions*.

BOX 10 ■ SELF-CONTRADICTION

- A proposition is self-contradictory if and only if it is necessarily false or logically impossible.
- A self-contradictory proposition is false all by itself in every possible world, not just in the actual world.

(25), (26), and (27) illustrate self-contradictions: each is logically impossible or necessarily false, owing to its having self-contradictory concepts or logical words. A quick inspection of (25) and (26) shows that there is no possible world in which either one could be true, simply because they have, respectively, these logical forms:

25' *All* such-and-such are so-and-so, but *some* such-and-such are *not* so-and-so.

26' X *has* a certain feature and *does not have* it.

(25') and (26') exhibit arrangements of logical words (in italics) that make it impossible for any proposition with either of these arrangements to be true. Each is therefore logically self-contradictory. On the other hand, (27) is conceptually self-contradictory: given the concepts involved, there is no possible world where (27) could be true. No one could literally be a *married bachelor*, just as no *triangle* could have *four internal angles*. Any proposition with such contents would be absurd or nonsensical and therefore unthinkable, since it would be impossible to comprehend its content.

It is not only individual propositions that could be logically impossible: entire *sets* of propositions could be. That would be the case in any inconsistent set. Inconsistency occurs in either of these two cases: the set has some propositions that are logically incompatible or contradictory among themselves, or the set has at least one self-contradictory proposition. The propositions that Dorothy Maloney is a senator and that she is not a public official illustrate the first case of inconsistency, that of a set containing contradictory propositions. By the definitions of inconsistency and contradiction, any set consisting of contradictory propositions is inconsistent.

> Any two propositions are contradictory just in case they cannot have the same truth value: if one is true, the other must be false, and vice versa.

Consistency and Possible Worlds

Let's now reconsider the following set:

23 Arnold Schwarzenegger is a medical doctor.

24 Pigs fly.

These propositions, though actually false, are nonetheless consistent. For there are possible worlds (i.e., scenarios involving no contradiction) where they could be compatible. In those possible worlds, they are both true at the same time: for example, a world where Arnold Schwarzenegger never became a movie star but became a medical doctor instead, and where pigs were anatomically equipped to overcome the force of gravity so that they could fly.

In light of these considerations, 'consistent' and 'inconsistent' may be recast as the following:

A set of beliefs is consistent if and only if
- There is a logically possible world where its members could all be true at once.

A set of beliefs is inconsistent if and only if
- There is no logically possible world where its members could be all true at once.

Consistency in Logical Thinking

Given the above definitions, no set of contradictory beliefs is eligible for consistency. Inconsistency, or failure of consistency, amounts to a serious flaw, since it offends against our intuitive sense of what is logically possible and, to that extent, thinkable at all. Inconsistent beliefs are to be avoided completely. Whenever a set of beliefs is found to be inconsistent, logical thinkers must first ask whether it can be made consistent, and if it can, then they must take the necessary steps to make it so. How? By revising it in a way that eliminates the source of inconsistency. Recall our inconsistent set:

20 Dorothy Maloney is a senator.

21 Dorothy Maloney is a jogger.

22 Dorothy Maloney is not a public official.

To remove the inconsistency here requires that either (20) or (22) be abandoned.

Note, however, that although consistency is a virtue, it is not a guide to accuracy or even to reasonableness. Beliefs that could all be true in some possible scenario might, as we have seen, in fact be false and even quite preposterous in our actual world. Another thing to notice is that, like truth and falsity, neither consistency nor inconsistency comes in degrees. No set of beliefs can be 'sort of consistent': it's either consistent or inconsistent. We'll now turn to conservatism, a virtue of beliefs closely related to consistency.

BOX 11 ■ CONSISTENCY AND LOGICAL THINKING

A salient feature of logical thinkers is that they reflect upon their beliefs (or the statements they make) and try to make them consistent.

3.6 Conservatism and Revisability

Conservatism without Dogmatism

Conservatism or familiarity is a virtue that our beliefs have insofar as they are consistent with other beliefs of ours. That is, beliefs have this virtue if they fit in with the beliefs we presently have. Suppose that in a circus performance we observe that

28 A person inside a box was cut in two halves, later emerging unharmed.

Shall we accept (28)? Although (28) appears based on observational evidence, it's inconsistent with beliefs we already have, such as that

29 No one who has been cut in two halves could emerge unharmed.

Conservatism recommends that we reject (28) and that we take it to report nothing more than a clever illusionist's trick. The more outlandish a belief is, the less conservative it is.

Yet conservatism has to be balanced with revisability, to which we'll turn below. Otherwise, conservatism could lead to accepting only what is consistent with what we already believe, whether the evidence supports it or not—which would be not only unreasonable, but dogmatic.

Dogmatism is the vice that some revisable beliefs have when they are held immune to revision. Those who have beliefs with a significant share of this vice are dogmatists. Dogmatism conflicts with revisability, a virtue that boils down to the open-mindedness needed for the accuracy, reasonableness, and consistency of our beliefs. For our beliefs to have any of these virtues, they must be revised often in light of new evidence and further reasoning.

Revisability without Extreme Relativism

Revisability is the virtue that beliefs have insofar as they are open to change. It comes in degrees, as do accuracy and reasonableness. But, unlike them, revisability has an upper limit: too much revisability may lead to extreme relativism, the vice of thinking that everything is a matter of opinion. This makes sense only when beliefs are taken to be 'true for' a group of people—rather than 'true period.' With the qualification 'true for,' the relativist can say that, for example, the belief that the Earth doesn't move was *true for* people in antiquity. At the same time, it is not *true for* us. And there is no contradiction here.

Thus, given extreme relativism, some contradictory beliefs could all be equally true at the same time. But this clashes with some common intuitions. One is that

> A belief is true *if and only if* it corresponds to the facts.

Plainly, it is false that the Earth didn't move in antiquity. That belief did not correspond to the facts then, just as it doesn't correspond to the facts now. Moreover, given relativism, 'true' is actually 'true for . . . ,' where the dots could be filled in with 'culture,' 'social group,' 'historical period,' or whatever is the preference of the relativists. This leads to the relativists' acceptance of at least some contradictions, since opposite beliefs may be 'true for,' for example, different cultures. But a strong view in the West since antiquity is that contradiction makes dialogue among logical thinkers impossible.

BOX 12 ■ CONSERVATISM VS. ACCURACY

Logical thinkers must not be *too* strict about conservatism, for sometimes beliefs that seem *not* to be conservative turn out to be accurate—or even true!

How much revisability, then, counts as a virtue? In fact, this varies according to belief type. Consider mathematical and logical beliefs such as

30 6 is the square root of 36.

31 Either Lincoln is dead or he isn't.

These may perhaps be counted as needing very little of that virtue at all. And similarly for

32 Lawyers are attorneys.

Other beliefs of these types, which are all supported by reasoning alone, may also be only marginally revisable. They will typically have the highest degree of conservatism and the lowest degree of revisability.

On the other hand, consider empirical and memory beliefs such as

33 The John Hancock Building is Chicago's tallest building.

34 I visited the John Hancock Building in 1996.

These have a great share of revisability. (33), an empirical belief, can be revised in light of evidence (it is in fact false), as can (34), which could be nothing more than a false memory. Beliefs of either type change in light of evidence, provided that they are not held dogmatically.

> If we allow our beliefs to be changed too easily and too frequently, we may end up thinking that contradictory beliefs could all be true at once—or that 'true' just means 'true for.' This is the vice of extreme relativism.

3.7 Rationality vs. Irrationality

Rationality is the supervirtue characteristic of all beliefs within the limits of reasoning, while irrationality is the supervice characteristic of all beliefs beyond that limit. Although a person's actions may also be said to be rational in some cases and irrational in others, here we shall consider these features only insofar as they apply to beliefs. Rational belief requires the conditions listed here.

Condition (1) limits the range of beliefs to which (2) and (3) apply: not all beliefs, but just the beliefs a thinker is presently and consciously considering. Typically, as thinkers

---

BOX 13 ■ RATIONAL BELIEF

A thinker's belief is rational only if the thinker

1. Has it presently and consciously in his mind,
2. Could provide evidence or reasons for it, and
3. Is not aware of the belief's failing any of the virtues discussed above.

we have many beliefs, but only some of them are the focus of conscious attention at any given time. Since the vast majority of them are, so to speak, in the back of our minds, then given condition (1), those beliefs can be neither rational nor irrational. Current conscious beliefs, on the other hand, must be either rational or irrational, depending on whether or not they satisfy conditions (2) and (3). Given (2), the rationality of beliefs requires that the thinker be able to account for them. Given (3), rationality requires that the thinker not be aware of her beliefs' failing in accuracy, truth, reasonableness, consistency, conservatism, and/or revisability. Suppose a thinker is currently, consciously entertaining these beliefs:

35 My neighbor Sally Chang died and was resuscitated.

36 No person can die and be resuscitated.

37 (35) and (36) are not consistent.

We may further suppose that the thinker is not only aware of her beliefs' lack of consistency, but does nothing to revise them to restore consistency. Thus her beliefs are irrational. Similarly, they would be irrational if, once challenged, the thinker could produce no reason whatsoever for having those beliefs. Derivatively, the thinker herself may in both cases be said to be irrational.

BOX 14 ■ RATIONAL VS IRRATIONAL BELIEF

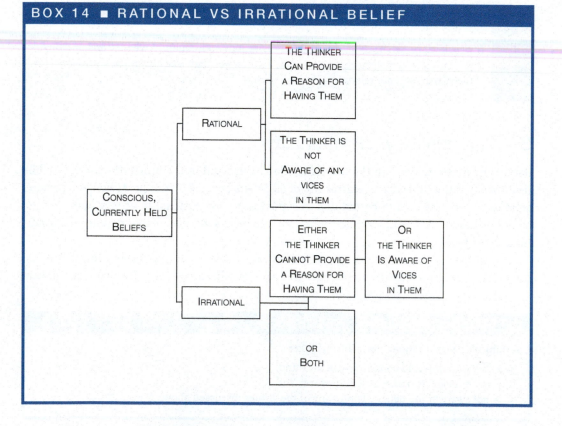

Exercises

V. Review Questions

1. When is a belief accurate? How is truth related to accuracy?
2. Why does belief type matter for reasonableness?
3. Does consistency come in degrees? Explain.
4. When are beliefs consistent? How is consistency related to truth and possible worlds?
5. When is a belief revisable? How is revisability related to conservatism?
6. What is dogmatism? Give a reason why it should be avoided.
7. What is relativism? Give a reason why it should be avoided.
8. How does the relativist understand truth?

VI. Some of the following statements qualify as accurate or inaccurate. Others are vague or evaluative. Indicate which is which.

1. *David Copperfield* is Dickens's finest novel.

   SAMPLE ANSWER: Evaluative statement

2. 1,000 grains of sand make up a heap.

*3. New York City is the capital of the United States.

4. New York City is located in the state of New York.

*5. A five-foot-ten person is tall.

6. To be a dog is to be a reptile.

*7. Hip-hop is better than jazz.

8. Everybody likes Picasso's paintings.

9. Killing animals for food is wrong.

*10. Wikileaks published secret government documents.

11. The Vikings were the first Europeans to visit North America.

12. All members of the Texas legislature are space aliens from another galaxy.

*13. High blood pressure is a dangerous medical condition.

14. The Amazon River is located in Russia.

*15. Slavery is unjust.

VII. Determine which of the statements listed in (VI) above are empirical and which aren't (answers to 3, 5, 7, 10, 13, and 15 in the back of the book).

1. *David Copperfield* is Dickens's finest novel.

   SAMPLE ANSWER: Not an empirical statement

VIII. The following statements are all accurate, but none is actually true. Explain for each one why that is.

1. Magellan circumnavigated the Earth.

   SAMPLE ANSWER: Not true, because Magellan was killed halfway through the voyage, but he is credited with the circumnavigation of the Earth.

*2. Prince Charles is the future king of Great Britain.

3. The United States won World War II.

*4. The Vikings discovered America.

*5. Russia was the first country to orbit the Earth.

6. Argentina invented the ball-point pen.

*7. Italy is a boot.

IX. The following sets of statements express either consistent or inconsistent beliefs. First, say which is which, and then, for any inconsistent set, indicate whether it has contradictory beliefs, at least one necessarily false belief, or both. (Tip: Remember that the actual world is one among many logically possible worlds that matter for consistency.)

1. {The fetus is a person and abortion is wrong. Convicts on death row are also persons, but capital punishment is not wrong.}

   SAMPLE ANSWER: Consistent. By modifying 'person' with 'innocent' in the first case and 'guilty' in the second, any appearance of contradictory beliefs is eliminated.

2. {God exists. There is no deity.}

*3. {All students in Philosophy 101 are juniors. Some students in Philosophy 101 are freshmen.}

4. {All bachelors are married men. No bachelor is married.}

*5. {Helen is a sister. The Earth is a waterless planet.}

6. {The present king of France is bald. Triangles have four internal angles.}

*7. {The Earth is flat. The Earth is not flat.}

8. {New York City is the capital of the United States. New York City is in the state of New York. Snow is white.}

*9. {Some people don't like Picasso's paintings. Everybody likes Picasso's paintings.}

10. {No young dog is a puppy. Some young dogs are puppies.}

*11. {It is false that there is a number that is the largest number. Bachelors are unmarried men.}

12. {Lincoln was not assassinated. Homicide is legal in the United States.}

*13. {Bert was once in Romania. Bert was never in Romania.}

14. {In some countries, abortion is illegal. But in those countries, execution is legal.}

*15. {2+2≠4. Sisters are male siblings.}

X. **For each of the following statements, determine whether its content is empirical, conceptual, or other. For statements that are 'other,' explain why they are in this category. (Hint: In each case, ask yourself, which sort of reasons would matter to determining whether the belief is true? Reasoning alone? Empirical evidence? Or matters of value?)**

1. Abraham Lincoln was assassinated.

   SAMPLE ANSWER: Empirical

2. 'Sister' means 'female sibling.'

*3. 5 + 7 = 12

4. Madonna is taller than Lady Gaga.

*5. If Everest is taller than Aconcagua, then Aconcagua is not taller than Everest.

6. Some mushrooms are tasty.

*7. Poverty is inhumane.

*8. There is no life on Mars.

9. Jazz is intolerable.

10. There are UFOs.

*11. Cookies are delicious.

12. A straight line is the shortest path between two points.

*13. Earth is the center of the universe.

14. Some forms of nonwestern medicine are worth considering.

*15. There is life after death.

XI. **Given the state of our knowledge today, each of the following is either conservative or nonconservative. Indicate which is which.**

1. We are all aliens from another planet.

   SAMPLE ANSWER: Nonconservative

2. 2 + 2 = 4

*3. The Earth will stop rotating tomorrow.

4. All pigeons are robots in disguise.

*5. If a figure is a rectangle, then it is not a circle.

6. Puppies are young dogs.

*7. Whales are fish.

8. The Earth is flat.

*9. Chickens can't fly long distances.

10. The lines of your palm contain information about your future.

*11. There are no witches.

12. Water is H_2O.

*13. Sarah Palin is a Democrat.

14. Alabama is a southern state.

*15. There are out-of-body experiences.

XII. Determine whether the following combinations of propositions are rational or irrational:

1. I know that a bachelor can't be married. Yet I'm a married bachelor.

   SAMPLE ANSWER: Irrational

2. I'm aware that Jane was childless in 1989, but now she has four grandchildren!

*3. I do believe that elephants are extinct and that they aren't extinct.

4. In my view, God does not exist—and neither do angels.

*5. Although there are no good reasons for believing that the end of the universe is coming, I believe it is.

6. I believe that all cats are felines and that some cats are not felines. Furthermore, I believe that these beliefs are contradictory.

*7. As a zoologist, I have no doubts that cats are felines and that all felines are mammals. I'm not aware of these beliefs being defective.

8. I have never seen muskrats. Moreover, I have never acquired any information whatsoever about them. As far as I'm concerned, they are rodents.

*9. There is no evidence that there is an afterlife. Yet I prefer to believe that there is.

10. I believe that Mario and Lucille have a romantic relationship. Yes, Brian says that they do, but he is not a reliable source of information about who is dating whom. But I learned about their relationship from a trustworthy source.

XIII. Your Own Thinking Lab

1. Give three examples of irrational belief.

2. Explain why your examples for (1) above are irrational. What would be required to make them rational?

3. Provide a scenario in which a thinker is a dogmatist.

4. Provide a scenario in which a thinker is a relativist.

5. Write three sets of inconsistent beliefs.

6. Protagoras of Abdera (Greek, c. 490–421 B.C.E.) argued that "man [i.e., human beings] is the measure of all things—of things that are, that they are, and of things that are not, that they are not. As a thing appears to a man, so it is." How does this amount to a relativist position? What sort of objections might be brought against it?

■ Writing Project

Choose one of the following two projects and write a short composition:

1. A nonsense essay, where you describe three logically impossible scenarios, and then explain why they are logically impossible.

2. Consider the passage below, from Lewis Carroll's *Alice in Wonderland*.

> "I can't believe that!" said Alice.
>
> "Can't you?" the Queen said in a pitying tone. "Try again: draw a long breath, and shut your eyes."
>
> Alice laughed. "There's no use trying," she said: "one *can't* believe impossible things."
>
> "I dare say you haven't had much practice," said the Queen. "When I was your age I always did it for half-an-hour a day. Why, sometimes, I've believed as many as six impossible things before breakfast."

Write a short essay where you explain Alice's refusal's to believe impossible things. You may invoke the virtue of conservatism, explaining what it is and how it sometimes leads to refusing to believe things that one "sees."

■ Chapter Summary

Belief: a psychological attitude of accepting a proposition.

Disbelief: a psychological attitude of rejecting a proposition.

Nonbelief: the lack of a psychological attitude of accepting or rejecting a proposition.

Virtue: a good-making trait.

Vice: a bad-making trait.

Accuracy: a belief's virtue of being either true or close to being true. Related vice: inaccuracy. A matter of degree.

Truth: a belief's virtue of representing the facts as they are. Related vice: falsity. *Not* a matter of degree.

Reasonableness: for an empirical belief, the virtue of being supported by evidence, or inference from evidence; for a conceptual belief, that of being based on good reasons. Related vice: unreasonableness. A matter of degree.

Consistency: virtue of a *set* of beliefs insofar as they could all be true at once. Related vice: inconsistency. *Not* a matter of degree.

Conservatism: a belief's virtue of being compatible with other beliefs we already have. Related vice: dogmatism. A matter of degree.

Revisability: a belief's virtue of being held open to change. Related vice: extreme relativism. A matter of degree.

Rationality: a supervirtue a belief has insofar as is currently and consciously held by the thinker, who has some reason to support it and is not aware of the belief's having any of the listed vices. Related supervice: irrationality. When a belief is irrational, that's a compelling reason to reject it.

■ Key Words

Belief	Contradiction
Disbelief	Self-contradiction
Nonbelief	Conservatism
Accuracy	Dogmatism
Truth	Extreme relativism
Reasonableness	Revisability
Consistency	Rationality

Part II

Reason and Argument

CHAPTER 4

Tips for Argument Analysis

This chapter considers some techniques for argument reconstruction. Here you'll learn about

- The roles of faithfulness and charity in reconstructing arguments.
- Arguments that have missing premises.
- Recognizing extended arguments and their component parts.
- The distinction between deduction and induction.
- Normative reasoning
- Normative arguments and missing normative premises.

4.1 A Principled Way of Reconstructing Arguments

That we endorse a certain claim, or reject it, is never the primary aim of argument analysis. Rather, its aim is to decide whether a certain claim should be accepted or rejected on the basis of the premises (reasons) offered for it. But this requires that we first get clear about two requirements of correct argument reconstruction. One is *faithfulness*, the other *charity*—that point to the concerns listed in Box 1.

Faithfulness

Being faithful to the arguer's intention is crucial to argument reconstruction. To meet this requirement, we must observe the principle of faithfulness in interpretation, which recommends that we strive to put ourselves in the shoes of the arguer. That is, we must try to represent her argument exactly as she intends it. Failing that, we're not dealing with the actual argument under discussion, but some other one we have made up!

Charity

Another crucial requirement of argument analysis is that we make the argument as strong as possible. That is, we must observe a second principle, that of charity in interpretation, which recommends that we reconstruct an argument in the way that maximizes the truth of its parts and the strength of their logical relation. We must, in other words, try to give "the benefit of the doubt" to the arguer, and take her argument to be as strong as possible. Maximizing truth requires that we interpret an argument's premises and conclusion in a way so that they come out true, or at least close to true. And maximizing the strength of an argument requires that we interpret the relation of inference among its premises and conclusion in a way that is as strong as possible. In an argument where that relation is strongest of all, if its premises are true, its conclusion must also be. But, as we shall see, not all arguments can be interpreted as consisting in a relation of that sort. For a summary of the two requirements for adequate reconstruction of arguments, see Box 2.

When Faithfulness and Charity Conflict

Although faithfulness and charity are both indispensable to argument analysis and are in most cases compatible, these two principles do, nevertheless, sometimes come into conflict. This happens when maximizing the one implies minimizing the other. Let's consider some examples, beginning with one where faithfulness and charity get along well. Someone argues

1   House rules do not allow dogs in the lobby, but dogs are there. So there has been a breach of house rules.

BOX 2 ■ FAITHFULNESS AND CHARITY

In reconstructing an argument, keep in mind:

- **The principle of faithfulness**
  - ✓ It recommends that we try to set out as carefully as possible exactly what the arguer meant to say.
- **The principle of charity**
  - ✓ It recommends that we take the argument seriously, giving it the benefit of the doubt and maximizing the truth and logical connectedness of its parts.

The second premise may be recast as 'Dogs are in the lobby,' which could be interpreted in two ways: it is either referring to (a) all members of the species dog or (b) just some members of that species. Which one should we choose? Charity and faithfulness both suggest that we choose (b), since otherwise the premise would be false and also say something that doesn't capture the arguer's intentions (and our interpretation would then fail on both charity and faithfulness). Reconstructed without these shortcomings, (1) reads

2 1. House rules do not allow dogs in the lobby.
   2. Some dogs are in the lobby.
   3. There has been a breach of house rules.

Here charity and faithfulness don't clash. But let's consider an argument where the two principles do seem to pull in opposite directions:

3 The following two reasons absolutely prove that witches do not exist: (1) there is no evidence that they exist, and (2) to invoke witches doesn't really explain anything.

Here faithfulness pulls us toward interpreting this argument as one in which the conclusion is supposed to follow with necessity from the premises. That's precisely what "absolutely prove" amounts to. Under that interpretation, however, the argument fails: it is plainly false that its conclusion follows necessarily from its premises, since the premises could be true (as in fact they are in this case) and the conclusion false.

On the other hand, charity pulls us toward reading (3) as making the more modest claim that its conclusion is a reasonable one on the basis of the argument's premises. Under this interpretation, the argument may be recast as

3' The following two reasons make it likely that witches do not exist: (1) there is no evidence that witches exist, and (2) to invoke witches doesn't really explain anything.

We have now maximized the argument's strength, since although (3')'s premises could be true and its conclusion false, the former give good reasons for the latter: the conclusion is likely to be true if the argument's premises are true. Instead of failing, (3') turns out to provide support for its conclusion. But maximizing charity, in this case, comes at the price of minimizing faithfulness: (3') simply isn't what the arguer seems to have had in mind in proposing (3)! Yet since faithfulness always carries the greater weight, here we should stick to our first reading of (3), which is the one that maximizes faithfulness.

You can't simply change what the arguer had in mind in order to make an argument as strong as possible. The price of doing that is to end up analyzing an argument that is altogether different from the one actually proposed.

Compare the argument

4   Contemporary biologists believe that there are microorganisms. From this, it follows necessarily that there are microorganisms.

If we focus on (4)'s premise and conclusion, they both seem plainly true. But here again, once we prioritize faithfulness in reconstructing (4), we must also say that the argument fails simply because its conclusion, though reasonable, does not follow necessarily from its premise. After all, although the possibility that all biologists have got it wrong about microorganisms might be an exceedingly remote one, it is still a possibility. On the other hand, if we prioritize charity in our reconstruction of (4), its premise would be taken as merely providing a reason for its conclusion—and the argument would therefore consist in a weaker relation, such as

4'   Contemporary biologists believe that there are microorganisms. This supports the conclusion that there are microorganisms.

But should we recast (4) as (4')? No, for recall that when the two principles come apart in reconstructing an argument, the rule is: always prioritize faithfulness. In other words, faithfulness is more stringent than charity. The rationale for this rule is in Box 3.

Finally, we should point out that failure to take account of faithfulness and charity in reconstructing arguments can lead to a serious error in reasoning, the 'Straw Man argument,' which we'll discuss in Chapter 10.

4.2 Missing Premises

Charity and faithfulness sometimes require that any missing (but implicit) premise be restored. Recall one of the arguments discussed in Chapter 1,

5   I think, therefore I am.

To make this argument as strong as possible without compromising the arguer's intentions, we must add a missing premise, something to the effect that 'anything that thinks exists.' With this extra premise, the inference is much stronger, for the argument could then be reconstructed as

5' 1. I think.
    2. Anything that thinks exists.   ←   Missing premise
    3. I exist.

It is now such that if its premises are true, its conclusion has to be true. Here is another argument with a missing premise:

6 1. Mary is my sister.
   2. Mary has a sibling.

(6) is a strong inference, since if its premise is true, its conclusion must be true. Yet a connection between the premise and the conclusion is left implicit. A version of (6) that makes that connection explicit would read

7 1. Mary is my sister.
   2. Anyone who is a sister has a sibling.   ←   Missing premise
   3. Mary has a sibling.

4.3 Extended Arguments

Sometimes the conclusion of an argument serves as a premise of another argument. In such a case, we may speak of an extended argument. Here is an extended argument that has as its starting point our previous argument (5):

8 1. I think.
   2. Anything that thinks exists.
   3. I exist.
   4. If I exist, then there is at least one thing (rather than nothing).
   5. There is at least one thing (rather than nothing).

When you are presented with an extended argument, bear in mind that

- You may in fact be presented with two or more arguments linked together.
- The conclusion of the first may be a premise of the second, intended to support some further conclusion . . . and so on.
- Any conclusion that itself fails to be supported by the premises of an extended argument cannot succeed in supporting further conclusions of that argument.

In (8) we have in fact two arguments: one offers two premises to support the first conclusion, statement 3, and the other takes statement 3 as a premise, adds premise 4, and draws the argument's second conclusion, statement 5. Since (8) has more than one conclusion, it is an extended argument. The reconstruction and evaluation of extended arguments proceed according to the principles of faithfulness and charity recommended above.

Exercises

I. Review Questions

1. What are the two main requirements of argument reconstruction?
2. In what respects do the principles of charity and faithfulness differ?
3. Why are charity and faithfulness important in argument analysis?
4. What should the logical thinker do in a case where charity and faithfulness come apart?
5. What is a missing premise?
6. What is an extended argument?
7. In reconstructing an argument, what should one do if there is a missing premise?
8. In reconstructing an argument, charity requires which of the following: to make that argument as strong as possible, to try to capture the author's intentions, or to suspend judgment?

II. Each of the following arguments has a missing premise. Identify that premise. (Some flexibility in wording is allowed.)

1. On paydays Jack rarely goes home before 11:00 p.m.; therefore, he will not be home tonight until 11:00 p.m., at the earliest.

   SAMPLE ANSWER: Today is payday.

2. Buzz will probably not major in one of the sciences, because his grades in mathematics have always been rather low.

*3. Rolf is European, for he was born in Germany.

4. Probably Michael is not a heavy drinker. After all, he is an athlete.

5. If the papers find out, she won't be promoted. So, if the papers find out, she'll feel miserable.

*6. According to the Federal Reserve Board, there will soon be a trend among U.S. banks to raise their prime interest rates. Thus probably U.S. banks will be raising their prime interest rates in the near future.

7. Since she moved to this town, Pam has frequently gone to the doctor. Hence, she is seriously ill.

8. The Bible says that God exists. Thus God exists.

*9. Either she is telling the truth or she is committing perjury. We must conclude that she is committing perjury.

10. If she has a truck, then she can move herself out. Therefore, she can move herself out.

11. No dolphins are fish. Therefore, no dolphins are creatures with gills.

*12. Tony is Canadian. Thus he is used to cold weather.

13. Emily did not come for lunch. For had she come, the maid would have noticed it.

14. Isosceles triangles have three internal angles. After all, they are triangles!

*15. According to a survey, more than 90 percent of cell phone users cannot get through the day without using their phone. Thus Jane cannot get through the day without using hers.

16. Socrates is human. Therefore, Socrates is mortal.

*17. Since creation science is a religious theory, creation science should not be taught in biology courses in public schools.

18. The Earth is a planet and has carbon-based life. This suggests that Mars has carbon-based life.

19. My cousin has good vision, for people who don't wear eyeglasses have good vision.

*20. Canaries are birds and have feathers. Thus pelicans probably have feathers.

21. People who move from city to city frequently have a rough time establishing relationships. Thus Marcello has a rough time establishing relationships.

22. Beatrice might have bone disease. After all, experts have found that exposure to cigarette smoke makes the probability of bone disease three times more likely.

23. Fuel costs are rising. This will deliver a boost to sales of fuel-efficient cars.

*24. Scientists are interpreting the dark areas shown by the Mars probe as dry lake beds. Therefore, there might have been life on Mars at some time.

25. Consuming foods rich in folic acid cuts the risk of dementia. So Grandpa has a lower risk of dementia than others his age.

III. Underline the conclusions of the following arguments, and determine which arguments are simple and which extended.

1. Since I'm happy to be alive, my mother did the right thing in not having an abortion when she was pregnant with the fetus that became me. It follows that I must oppose abortion.

   SAMPLE ANSWER: Since I'm happy to be alive, <u>my mother did the right thing in not having an abortion when she was pregnant with the fetus that became me.</u> It follows that <u>I must oppose abortion.</u> Extended argument.

2. Teens who sleep only a few hours a day often report psychological problems. Tom is a teenager who sleeps about two hours a day. As a result, he is likely to report psychological problems.

*3. No real vegetarian eats meat. Alicia is a real vegetarian. Thus she doesn't eat meat. Hence, there is no point in taking her to Tony Roma's Steak House.

4. Tonight I'll be working extra hours. Whenever I work extra hours, I'm home late. It follows that tonight I'll be home late. All days when I'm home late are days when I don't see my kids. Thus I won't see my kids today.

*5. If the ocean is rough here, there will be no swimming. If there is no swimming, tourists will go to another beach. Thus if the ocean is rough here, tourists will go to another beach.

6. Fluffy is a feline, for cats are felines and Fluffy is a cat. Since felines are carnivorous, Fluffy is carnivorous.

*7. No Democrat votes for Republicans. Since Keisha voted for Republicans, she is not a Democrat. Thus she won't be invited to Jamal's party, for only Democrats are invited to his party.

8. If we go by car, it will take us four hours but we'll save money. If we fly to that location, we'll spend more money, and it will take us a little more than three hours, from the time we leave the house until we arrive at the hotel. This suggests that we should go by car.

*9. To understand most web pages, you have to read them. To read them requires a good amount of time. Thus to understand web pages requires a good amount of time. Since I don't have any time, I keep away from the web, and as a result, I miss some news.

10. If whether the fetus is a person is controversial, then whether abortion is morally permissible is also controversial. It is in fact controversial whether fetuses count as persons. Therefore, whether abortion is morally permissible is controversial.

*11. Because Jerome is an atheist and Cynthia's mother does not like him, it follows that Jerome will not be invited to the family picnic next month. We may also infer that Jerome will come to see Cynthia only when her mother is not around.

12. Actor Owen Wilson must have done something wrong in his movie *You, Me and Dupree*. After all, there is a document posted on a website claiming that the "rip-off with *Dupree* was uncool."

*13. Professor Veebelfetzer will surely be expelled from the Academy of Sciences. For he admits using false data in his famous experiment on rat intelligence. As a result, his name will also be removed from the list of those invited to the academy's annual banquet next fall.

14. The electronics industry is growing twice as fast in Japan as in the United States. For this reason, Japanese-made computer screens will probably take over the American market. Thus some American electronics companies will go out of business. It also follows that Americans will be able to buy less expensive computer screens.

*15. Since books help to develop comprehension skills, web pages do that too. After all, in both cases one must read carefully to understand what is presented.

IV. **For each of the following arguments, determine whether it is (A) simple; (B) extended, with at most two conclusions; or (C) extended, with more than two conclusions.**

1. A reliable study shows that soda drinkers have weaker bones. Therefore, soda is bad for the bones.

SAMPLE ANSWER: Simple.

2. Central High School must have a good science department, since many of its graduates every year go on to study science in college and several members of the graduating class this year have won science scholarships. So Ms. Gomez must be a good science teacher, since she teaches in the science department at Central High School.

3. Because Wolfinger spent his entire paycheck at the racetrack, therefore we can expect that his wife will berate him fiercely when he gets home. It also follows that his mother-in-law will not speak to him for at least a month.

*4. Since Wittgenstein authored two path-breaking books, he is rightly considered one of the most important twentieth-century philosophers. Thus any educated person today should know about Wittgenstein's works. Accordingly, any college survey of twentieth-century philosophy should include some discussion of them.

5. There is evidence that people exposed to radiation tend to develop thyroid disease in greater numbers than those not exposed to it. This suggests that radiation exposure increases the risk of thyroid disease.

6. Many members of his party oppose the prime minister's position on the Middle East. Therefore it's doubtful that the party will continue to support him. So we may expect that he will not remain as prime minister.

*7. Since the Venezuelans and the Cubans are hostile to the Organization of American States, therefore the Bolivians are hostile too. So they will be ineffectively represented at the O.A.S. In consequence, some voices from Latin America will be ignored at this forum and the O.A.S. will not solve the region's problems.

8. Because of last summer's infestation of gypsy moths in New York, we must conclude that the same pestilence will return this summer. It also follows that the infestation may reach at least New Jersey and Connecticut.

9. "Our new cars offer distinctive styling and outstanding fuel economy," said the vice president for sales and marketing. Now, a vice president is usually a responsible person unlikely to make false claims. Therefore, probably his company's new cars do offer distinctive styling and outstanding fuel economy.

*10. Spies work for secret intelligence services. Now we have irrefutable evidence that Ken is a spy. It follows that he works for a secret intelligence service. So we should pass this information to the press without delay.

V. YOUR OWN THINKING LAB

1. Use the following argument in an extended argument of your own: 'If I get a good review, I'll be promoted. Therefore, if I get a good review, I'll have a better salary.'

2. State the missing premise in (1).

3. Provide two arguments of your own with missing premises and then identify each missing premise.

4. Write an argument with a missing premise for this conclusion: 'I have a right to an education.'

4.4 Types of Reason

Deductive vs. Inductive Reasons

We have seen that an argument consists of a conclusion that makes a claim of some sort and one or more premises intended as support for that conclusion. But there are two different ways such support can be offered, depending on whether the premises aim at guaranteeing the truth of the conclusion, or at simply providing some reasons for it. A rough distinction between these two might be to say that the former amounts to a conclusive relation, the latter a nonconclusive relation. But we can now be more precise and say that a conclusive relation between certain premises and a claim is the mark of a *deductive* argument, a nonconclusive relation that of an *inductive* argument. All arguments exemplify either the one or the other of these two relations.

A deductive argument is one in which the conclusion is supposed to follow necessarily from the premises. The following illustrate such arguments:

9 1. If today is Monday, then we have logic class.
2. Today is Monday.
3. We have logic class.

10 1 All dogs bark.
　 2. Fido is a dog.
　 3. Fido barks.

11 1. Today is cloudy and warm.
　 2. Today is cloudy.

In each of these, if the premises are all true, the conclusion must be true too (it cannot be false). So they are all plainly deductive. Now compare

12 1. Most university students have studied plane geometry.
　 2. Some students in this class have studied plane geometry.

13 1.Many cats are docile.
　 2. Felix is a cat.
　 3. Felix is docile.

Both (12) and (13) illustrate arguments where the premises provide at most nonconclusive reasons: they both fall short of guaranteeing the truth of the conclusions they're offered to support. In each, the conclusion could be false even if the premises are true. Thus we count such arguments as inductive.

In argument analysis, it's useful to keep in mind the distinctions represented in Box 5. We must always decide whether a given argument is deductive or inductive, since the standards of evaluation vary accordingly. Many arguments are defective if evaluated as deductive but quite good if evaluated as inductive. When in doubt, what should we do? Simply ask yourself: Are the premises presented as *guaranteeing* the conclusion? If so, then the argument is best considered deductive and should be analyzed by deductive standards. Or, are the premises presented as merely providing *some* reason for the conclusion, which might still be false even if all the premises are true? If so, then the argument is best considered inductive and should be analyzed by inductive standards. Just *what* these standards are, in the case of either deduction or induction, is the topic of the next two chapters.

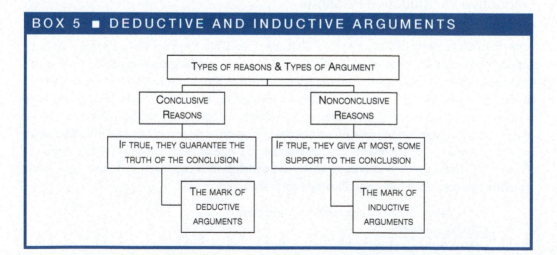

BOX 5 ■ DEDUCTIVE AND INDUCTIVE ARGUMENTS

TYPES OF REASONS & TYPES OF ARGUMENT

CONCLUSIVE REASONS — NONCONCLUSIVE REASONS

IF TRUE, THEY GUARANTEE THE TRUTH OF THE CONCLUSION — IF TRUE, THEY GIVE AT MOST, SOME SUPPORT TO THE CONCLUSION

THE MARK OF DEDUCTIVE ARGUMENTS — THE MARK OF INDUCTIVE ARGUMENTS

Exercises

VI. Review Questions

1. What is a conclusive reason? Contrast it with a nonconclusive reason.
2. Define 'deductive argument.'
3. Define 'inductive argument.'
4. Could a deductive argument with true premises have a false conclusion? Explain.
5. Could an inductive argument with true premises have a false conclusion? Explain.

VII. Read each of the following arguments carefully, adding any missing premise if needed, and then determine whether it is deductive or inductive.

1. The defendant is not guilty. After all, his mother says he wasn't at the scene of the crime.

   SAMPLE ANSWER: Inductive

2. Soledad O'Brien is either a TV news anchor or a newspaper reporter. Since she is not a newspaper reporter, it follows that she is a TV news anchor.

*3. Pigeons fly. Sparrows fly. Even ducks fly. It follows that all birds fly.

4. The Wisconsin Badgers will win this season because they have trained hard. In the past, when they trained hard, they usually won.

5. If whales are mammals, then they are not fish. Hence, whales are not fish, since they are mammals.

*6. Joe will fail Philosophy 100, because he never goes to class, and most students who don't go to class fail.

7. Gold expands under heat. Aluminum expands under heat. Copper expands under heat. It follows that all metals expand under heat.

*8. All metals expand under heat. Gold is a metal. So, gold expands under heat.

9. George will have lung problems, because a high percentage of smokers develop lung problems, and he is a smoker.

*10. Lawyers are attorneys. Rumpole is a lawyer. Therefore, Rumpole is an attorney.

11. Cats are furry animals. It follows that all pets are furry animals.

*12. Coffee is a common beverage and contains caffeine. Tea is a common beverage and contains caffeine. Coca-cola is a common beverage and contains caffeine. In sum, all common beverages contain caffeine.

13. Some mothers are married. Gwen is a mother. Therefore, she is married.

14. No bankers are jokers. Harriet is a banker. Therefore, she is not a joker.

*15. Harriet drives a Mercedes-Benz. After all, she is a banker and many bankers will drive nothing but a Mercedes-Benz.

16. The reality show's winner will either meet the president or he will meet the vice president. It is not the case that he'll meet the vice president. Therefore, he'll meet the president.

17. Today I met someone in an Internet chat room. But there is no chance that we could have a successful long-term relationship, for no people who meet in internet chat rooms can have successful long-term relationships.

*18. Some Texans are tall. Billy Bob is a Texan. Therefore, Billy Bob is tall.

19. No sharks are friendly. Hammerheads are sharks. Therefore, no hammerheads are friendly.

*20. Columbus was either Spanish or Italian. He was not Spanish. Therefore, he was Italian.

21. Lady Gaga has no problems. She is a famous singer, and no famous singer has problems.

22. All famous politicians are celebrities. Some governors are famous politicians; therefore, some governors are celebrities.

*23. Some comedians are Canadians. Mike Meyers is a comedian. So Mike Meyers is probably a Canadian.

24. Lake Michigan most likely carries commercial shipping, since it's one of the Great Lakes, and the other Great Lakes carry commercial shipping.

*25. No hip-hop artist is a fan of harmonica music. Since Zoltan is a fan of harmonica music, it follows that he is not a hip-hop artist.

VIII. **All the arguments below have missing premises and may be counted as either deductive or inductive, *depending on what missing premises are put in*. For each argument, provide the missing premise that would make it (a) deductive, or (b) inductive. Some flexibility in wording is allowed!**

1. People waste a huge amount of time surfing the web. It follows that the web is not such a great invention.

   SAMPLE ANSWER:

   1a: No invention that allows people to waste a huge amount of time is great.

   1b: Many inventions that allow people to waste a huge amount of time are not great.

2. Ellen is a sophisticated artist, hence she listens to jazz.

3. Digsby was fired. After all, he had been spending all day surfing the web.

4. Latino purchasing power is approaching billions of dollars in the United States. Therefore, there will be better employment opportunities for talented Latinos.

5. Air Canada is an airline. Therefore, Air Canada charges a baggage fee to passengers who check bags.

6. The British red squirrel is a rodent. Consequently, the British red squirrel is an endangered species.

7. The galaxies are flying outward. This suggests that the Milky Way Galaxy will spin apart.

8. Mount Everest is a tall mountain. Therefore, Mount Everest is difficult to climb.

9. President Calvin Coolidge was a fiscal conservative. So he was not a gambler.

10. The NAFTA treaty regulates North American commercial relations. Therefore, the NAFTA treaty is unpopular with opponents of free trade.

1. Consider the claim 'Ray has at least one sibling.' Write two arguments for it, one deductive (i.e., providing conclusive reasons) and the other inductive (i.e., providing nonconclusive reasons).

2. Write an argument with a missing premise, and then identify that premise.

3. Consider the claim 'There is life after death.' Write an argument for it and another one against it. Discuss whether these arguments are conclusive or nonconclusive.

4.5 Norm and Argument

What Is a Normative Argument?

We've seen that *all* arguments fall into either one of the other of two classes: they're either deductive or inductive. From a different perspective, both deductive and inductive arguments could be classified as being either *normative* or *non-normative*. The examples we've discussed in this book up to now have nearly all been made up entirely of statements that assert or deny some facts (or putative facts) about the world, such as 'Toronto is the largest city in Ontario,' 'Mercury is heavier than water,' and 'Jerry Seinfeld is a comedian.' Statements of this sort fall under the category of non-normative. But some other expressions go beyond facts to *assess* individuals, actions, and things, or to say what an individual ought to do (or ought not to do) or how things should be (or not be). For example, 'You ought to keep your promises,' 'Reggae music is cool,' 'Hitler was evil,' and 'Elena deserves credit for her hard work.'

Expressions of this latter type are used to make normative judgments, which figure in a sort of reasoning that we'll call *normative reasoning*. When we make a normative judgment and offer reasons intended to support it, the result is a *normative argument*. These are arguments for the conclusion that something has a certain value, such as being good or bad, right or wrong, just or unjust, beautiful or ugly, and the like. Also, arguments for the conclusion that something is permissible (may be done), obligatory (ought to be done), or forbidden (should not be done) may be classified as being normative arguments. Consider

14 1. One ought to obey one's parents.
2. My parents told me not to go to the party on Friday night.
3. I ought not to go the party on Friday night.

The conclusion of (14) is a normative judgment, since it represents a certain action (going to the party on Friday night) as being forbidden. By doing so, it directs or guides the arguer's behavior in a certain way—namely, *away from* the Friday-night party. That the conclusion is a normative judgment here is sufficient to make argument (14) normative. In addition, (14)'s premise 1 belongs to the category of general normative judgments, sometimes also called 'principles,' because they state rules that are supposed to apply not just to one person, but to anyone. We may distinguish between normative judgments that express a generalization or rule and those—like (14)'s conclusion—that are particular sentences used to make claims about individual persons, things, events, and so on. The distinctions we have in mind here are summarized in Box 6.

BOX 6 ■ NORMATIVE JUDGMENTS

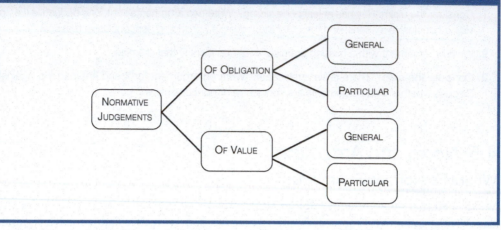

Judgments of obligation involve concepts such as right and wrong, and duty (what we're obligated to do or forbear from doing, what we're permitted to do or forbidden to do). For example,

15 You ought not to deceive your friends.

16 Spreading that malicious rumor about Anderson was wrong.

Judgments of value, or simply *evaluative* judgments, are about the value of actions or things (whether they are good or bad, just or unjust, etc.). For example,

17 Honest people make good co-workers.

18 The desert of southern Utah is beautiful.

(15) and (17) are *general:* they purport to apply to a set of individuals or things. (16) and (18) are *particular:* they purport to apply to a single individual or thing.

Of concern here are certain general and particular normative judgments about matters of taste, the law, prudence, and morality. We'll classify them accordingly as aesthetic, legal, prudential, or moral judgments. Whenever any such normative judgment is the conclusion of an argument, we'll say that the argument itself is aesthetic, legal, prudential, or moral, as the case may be. A normative judgment is aesthetic just in case it expresses an evaluation or norm involving a matter of taste such as that some piece of art is beautiful or ugly, a dish is tasty or inedible, or that we ought to admire good music. Aesthetic judgments could be either particular ('Beyoncé's recordings are superior art,' 'Frank Lloyd Wright's designs are overrated,' 'The Parliament buildings in Ottawa are a majestic sight') or general ('White socks don't go well with black shoes,' 'You ought to watch *Law and Order*').

The conclusion of a legal argument features a normative judgment involving a legal matter: something that's said to be a duty or obligation according to the law, or to be permitted to do or forbidden to do by statute—for example, that drivers ought not to tear up a parking ticket or are permitted to turn right on red (except in New York City!) and that adults have a duty to file an income tax return. Legal normative judgments could have a conditional form, as in 'If a person is called for jury service, that person must show up,' and 'When a person is sworn as a witness in court, that person is obligated to tell the truth.'

The conclusion of a prudential argument makes a claim about what it would be in your own self-interest to do, such as 'You ought to be especially nice to your rich Aunt Gertrude,' 'It's not in your interest to antagonize your boss,' 'People should look out for themselves first!' and 'Don't cheat your business associates if you don't want them to cheat you.'

The conclusion of a moral argument is a moral judgment. Judgments of this sort make a claim about what is good or bad, just or unjust, and what ought (or ought not) to be done, not because it's sanctioned by the law, but because, as the case may be, it deserves praise or blame— for example, 'Lying is wrong,' 'You ought to help the earthquake survivors,' 'Matthew's behavior was dishonest,' and 'The firefighters showed great courage on 9/11.'

The upshot, then, is that when normative judgments of any of these four types occur in the conclusion of an argument, the argument is itself normative. And it's by paying attention to the type of normative judgment in the conclusion that we tell *which* type of normative argument it is: aesthetic, legal, prudential, or moral.

Missing Normative Premises

Earlier in this chapter, we saw that when arguments are presented in everyday language, they sometimes have missing premises that need to be restored if the argument is to be reconstructed in a way that respects the principles of faithfulness and charity. One especially common way in which important premises may be left out is a pattern that sometimes occurs in normative arguments. In fact, such arguments often have normative judgments, not only in their conclusions, but also in at least one premise, and it's that premise that is sometimes left out.

What we shall call *normative general premises*, such as 'Keeping promises is right,' 'Slavery is unjust,' or 'One ought to obey the law,' are judgments that may seem to the arguer too obvious to need repeating, and so they may get left out. Here are some examples of normative arguments in which the normative general premises are in place. As you read them, try imagining what they'd sound like with that crucial premise left out.

19 Legal argument:
   1. Driving faster than 55 miles per hour on the Taconic Parkway
      is forbidden by law.   ←   NORMATIVE GENERAL PREMISE
   2. Yesterday I drove faster than 55 miles per hour on the Taconic Parkway.
   3. Yesterday I did what I ought not to do, according to the law.

20 Aesthetic argument:
   1. Music that consists of only a random collection of honks, bleats,
      and screeches is worthless noise.   ←   NORMATIVE GENERAL PREMISE
   2. Professor Murgatroyd's 'Second Symphony' consists of only a random collection
      of honks, bleats, and screeches.
   3. Professor Murgatroyd's 'Second Symphony' is worthless noise.

BOX 7 ■ NORMATIVE ARGUMENTS WITH MISSING PREMISES

- Normative arguments often leave out general normative reasons.
- Such reasons must be made explicit in argument analysis.
- The bottom line is that a careful logical thinker will want to be sure that <u>all</u> of an argument's premises are in place, since only in that way can a fair assessment be made of the argument's conclusiveness or nonconclusiveness.

21 Prudential argument:
1. You ought to do whatever would best serve
    your own self-interest. ←   NORMATIVE GENERAL PREMISE
2. Agreeing with your boss whenever possible would best serve your own self-interest.
3. You ought to agree with your boss whenever possible.

22 Moral argument:
1. Lying is wrong.   ←   NORMATIVE GENERAL PREMISE
2. Failing to report income on your tax return is lying.
3. Failing to report income on your tax return is wrong.

Normative arguments are properly reconstructed only when their normative premises are made explicit, as they are here (together with whatever other reasons are given in the argument's premises). Now, the point to be noticed is that normative arguments of the sort one is likely to meet in everyday life very often fail to include among their premises the relevant normative general principles—since such premises are often taken for granted, as in

20' Professor Murgatroyd's ' Second Symphony' consists of only a random collection of honks, bleats, and screeches; thus Professor Murgatroyd's 'Second Symphony' is worthless noise.

21' Agreeing with your boss whenever possible would best serve your own self-interest, so you ought to agree with your boss whenever possible.

In (20'), 'Music that consists of only a random collection of honks, bleats, and screeches is worthless noise' is the missing premise. What's left out is the normative general premise that purports to say what worthlessness in music is. In (21') the missing premise is 'You ought to do whatever would best serve your own self-interest'—again, a normative general premise, in this case holding that serving one's self-interest is a sufficient reason to justify an action (something we might take for granted as being *too obvious* to need stating—but is it *true?*).

Exercises

X. Review Questions

1. What is a normative argument?
2. When a normative argument has a missing premise, what sort of premise is likely to be left out?
3. What is a normative general premise?

4. How do prudential arguments differ from moral arguments?

5. What is an aesthetic argument?

6. What's the difference between a normative judgment of obligation and a normative judgment of value?

XI. **Some of the following arguments are normative, and some are non-normative. Indicate which is which.**

1. The Internet gives a huge opportunity to waste time web surfing while at work. It follows that the Internet is not such a great invention.

   SAMPLE ANSWER: Normative

2. Plain and simple: the European Union did the right thing. For funding for stem-cell research should not be banned when so many lives could be saved and so much suffering with debilitating illnesses could be stopped.

*3. You oppose abortion. Therefore, you probably oppose the deaths of children by way of "collateral damage" in war.

4. If cell technology develops, then people afflicted by certain illnesses could be cured, which is clearly good. Thus any restriction on stem cell research ought to be avoided.

*5. The challenge for us is reducing the impact of greenhouse gas emissions on the climate. After all, we've already agreed that we want to preserve ecodiversity.

6. If we are serious about helping the developing world, new kinds of energy are needed. Since we do want to help the developing world, it follows that new kinds of energy are needed.

*7. We should either save money or the environment. Attempts to save the environment cannot succeed, scientists say. Therefore, we should save money.

8. If you care about switching to a new laptop, you also care about fast Internet access. But fast Internet access doesn't matter to you. So you shouldn't waste your money on a new laptop.

*9. One liter of seawater can contain more than twenty thousand different types of bacteria, according to an international project attempting to catalog all ocean life. As a result, microbial biodiversity is now considered much greater than previously thought.

10. It's clear that unless we can control carbon-dioxide emissions, we'll run into climate change sooner than expected. But we cannot control carbon-dioxide emissions. It follows that sooner than expected, we'll run into climate change.

*11. You must sign up! We won't judge you. If you don't wish to risk your own safety in the future, you should be one of us.

12. Taxpayers' money should not be used to help build more laboratories to carry out tests on animals for medical research. After all, many taxpayers are against such research.

*13. The first commercial trip around the Moon for "space tourists" will cost an estimated $100 million. So each space tourist will have to pay a great deal of money.

14. A recent survey reveals that while 75 percent of people think it is rude to use a cell phone during dinner, only 9 percent of respondents said it was unreasonable to do so on a train. Therefore, although it is rude to use a cell phone during dinner, it is permissible to use it on a train.

*15. Whenever a species is in the news, that species is at risk of disappearing. Thus polar bears and hippos might disappear, since they have recently been in the news.

16. Anabolic-substance users deserve to be suspended from athletic competition. So Natalia ought to be banned from competition at next year's Olympics, since she is an anabolic-substance user.

*17. Actor Ben Stiller must have made some mistake in his movie *Meet the Parents*. After all, there is a document posted on a website claiming that the "comedy scenes with Stiller and De Niro were not successful."

18. Orville is the Liberal Party nominee for chief of dog catchers, so he will be running for office in the next election. From this we can also conclude that Orville is not indifferent to politics.

*19. Because Messina is running against Foley, and Messina is a popular candidate, therefore Foley will spend more money for campaign advertising next year.

20. Los Angeles and Mexico City are places where there is a lively mix of cultures and also a lot of wealth. Such places tend to be good places to live. It follows that both Los Angeles and Mexico City are good places to live.

XII. The following arguments are either moral, aesthetic, prudential, legal, or a combination of some of these. In each case, indicate which is which.

1. Thelonious Monk's music is great jazz, as it has subtle harmonic phrasing and tonal complexity that distinguish it from all other jazz.

   SAMPLE ANSWER: Aesthetic

2. It is in your self-interest to succeed in college. Besides, that's what you promised to your parents. It follows that you must try to succeed in college.

3. Senator Jones favors legalizing embryonic stem-cell research. Embryonic stem-cell research is immoral. Therefore, Senator Jones favors immoral legislation.

*4. Julia Roberts's performances are well crafted. Comparing hers with those of other Hollywood actresses today, we must acknowledge that hers are the best and that she deserves an award.

5. Benito Mussolini had many of his opponents shot. So he was an evil man.

*6. Wal-Mart uses partially hydrogenated oil in its food products, and these oils are a health hazard. Furthermore, it has questionable labor practices. It follows that I ought not to buy at Wal-Mart.

7. A woman has a right to choose on the question of abortion. Our laws require that those who favor women's rights speak up. Furthermore, their views can improve our society. Therefore, we should speak up on this question.

8. Five-year-old Tyler must get his vaccinations. After all, he needs to start school with the other children, and the law requires children to be inoculated if they're going to attend school.

*9. Since you're going to smoke, you must step outside the restaurant.

*10. I know my boss has been breaking the law with his illegal stock trading. But since nothing could be gained by reporting this, I should keep quiet about it.

11. In light of the legal right to freedom of speech in the United States, defamation laws cannot be used to stifle neo-Nazi comments on the Internet. Some blogs make neo-Nazi comments on the

Internet. Therefore, defamation laws cannot be used to stifle those blogs' comments on the Internet.

12. World champion cyclist Landis was found to violate the regulations of the Tour de France by using a banned steroid substance in the race. Thus what he did was both illegal and wrong.

*13. Recently, polar bears and hippos were added to the list of threatened species. This suggests that we should take the necessary steps to protect them. It is good for its own sake and, in the long run, can only benefit us.

14. Since consumers are wrestling with higher interest rates and other increased household costs on a monthly basis, in order to stay competitive in the present market we should adopt new sales strategies.

*15. We should all support the Municipal Museum of Art, because it contributes toward making our city a more beautiful place to live. And by contributing to the quality of life in our city, it thereby also raises our property values.

16. It is now apparent that key scientists who advised the World Health Organization to stockpile vaccines for the expected swine flu pandemic had financial ties with pharmaceutical companies that stood to profit from this policy. So these scientists did what they must have known was wrong.

*17. Small private colleges are not doing well in the present economic environment. Therefore, they must downsize if they are going to stay in business.

18. Any winner of the Gershwin Prize in Music must have created great popular music. Sir Paul McCartney was honored recently with the Gershwin Prize. So, no doubt about it: he has created great popular music.

19. According to a new federal law, small banks that enter into mergers with other small banks qualify for government stimulus money. Thus First Investors Trust and the Squeedunk National Bank should consider merging for their own sake. As a result, they would also have a rightful claim on stimulus money.

*20. People who pursue higher education stand to benefit over the long term by their college training and broad exposure to the arts and sciences, but they are also better able to contribute to the improvement of their communities. So Ignacio ought to go ahead with his plans for college. He owes it to himself and also to his fellow citizens.

XIII. Each of following arguments has at least one missing normative premise. Identify that premise or premises. (Some flexibility in wording is allowed.)

1. Voluntary euthanasia reduces suffering. Thus voluntary euthanasia is ethically justified

   SAMPLE ANSWER: Whatever reduces suffering is ethically justified.

2. Cambodian dictator Pol Pot brought misery and death to millions of people. Therefore what Pol Pot did was wrong.

*3. The new Hearst Building was designed by Sir Norman Foster; therefore, the Hearst Building is beautiful.

4. It's better to be safe than sorry. You are playing games that are not safe. Therefore, you should stop playing those games.

5. Mendoza & Co. are honest brokers. After all, their dealings with me have always been fair.

*6. On the R train, it would take you twenty minutes to travel the same distance that now takes you forty minutes on the local bus. Thus you are better off taking the R train.

7. That witness is committing perjury. Therefore, he should be prosecuted.

8. Cookies are full of sugar. As a result, they are not good for you.

*9. Sandy deals poorly with her financial problems. Thus she ought to get married.

10. Having a college degree will improve your earning potential, so you should finish your degree.

11. Spreading false rumors about one's competitors is a form of lying; therefore, spreading false rumors about one's competitors is wrong.

*12. Celine Dion's songs are the best. After all, her songs are always hits.

13. Since the ocean is rough today, swimming is not a smart idea.

14. SUVs pollute the atmosphere worse than cars, so they are bad for the health of Americans.

*15. Jason ought to report for active duty in Afghanistan. After all, Jason is a member of the Army Reserve, and his commanding officer ordered all the soldiers in his unit to report for active duty in Afghanistan.

16. Since *The Jerry Gordon Show* is watched by millions, it follows that it's great television.

17. Everybody knows that Frank betrayed his friends, so Frank is a reprehensible character.

*18. Capital punishment is the appropriate punishment for murder. Therefore, capital punishment is ethically justified.

19. A former president is a big fan of Raymond Chandler's novels. So Raymond Chandler's novels are great literature.

*20. You ought to pay that traffic ticket right away. After all, that's the law.

XIV. YOUR OWN THINKING LAB

1. Write an argument with a missing normative premise, and then identify the type of normative sentence that it exemplifies.

2. Suppose you're in the checkout line at the supermarket. The cashier asks you, "Paper or plastic?" What sort of normative reasons could be relevant in answering this question? Discuss.

3. Oskar Schindler was a German industrialist in the 1940s and a member of the Nazi Party, but he helped many Jews escape the death camps. Now, clearly Schindler was disloyal to his superiors. But do we want to say he behaved *badly*? We don't want to say that! Can you see what the problem is here? What kind of word is 'disloyal'? Write a short paper in which you discuss this.

■ Writing Project

Consider the claim 'Killing another human being is always wrong.' Write a short essay (about three pages, double-spaced) offering at least one argument for the claim and one against it. Then discuss which judgments in your arguments are normative.

■ Chapter Summary

Principle of faithfulness: At all times, try to reconstruct an argument in a way that captures the arguer's intentions—that is, premises and conclusion should say just what the arguer intends them to say.

Principle of charity: At all times, make the argument as strong as possible—maximize the truth of premises and conclusion, and the strength of the relation between them.

Rule for balancing faithfulness and charity: When there is a conflict between these two, faithfulness takes priority.

Missing premise: Implicit premise that must be made explicit in reconstructing an argument.

Extended argument: An argument with more than one conclusion.

Deductive argument: Its premises are offered as guaranteeing the conclusion.

Inductive argument: Its premises are offered as providing some support for its conclusion.

Normative judgment: Judgment to the effect that something has a certain value, or is permissible, obligatory, or forbidden.

Normative argument: An argument with a normative judgment as its conclusion. It could be aesthetic, legal, moral, or prudential.

Aesthetic judgment: It concerns evaluations or norms involving matters of taste.

Legal judgment: It concerns evaluations or norms involving what's permitted or obligatory or forbidden by law.

Moral judgment: It concerns evaluations or norms about what is ultimately good or bad, right or wrong—not because it's sanctioned by the law, but because it *deserves* praise or blame.

Prudential judgment: It concerns evaluations or norms about what is in one's own self-interest.

■ Key Words

Principle of charity	Normative argument
Principle of faithfulness	Prudential judgment
Missing premise	Aesthetic judgment
Extended argument	Moral judgment
Inductive argument	Legal judgment
Deductive argument	

Evaluating Deductive Arguments

In this chapter, you'll look more closely at deductive reasoning, focusing first on the concept of validity and then on related topics, including

- The difference between valid and invalid arguments.
- Some alternative ways of talking about validity.
- The relation between validity and argument form.
- How to represent propositional and categorical argument forms.
- Soundness as an evaluative standard.
- Deductive cogency as an evaluative standard.
- The practical implications (or 'cash value') of validity, soundness, and cogency.

5.1 Validity

Sometimes people use 'valid' to mean 'true' or 'reasonable' and 'invalid' to mean 'false' or 'unreasonable.' But these are *not* what 'valid' and 'invalid' mean in logical thinking. A deductive argument is valid if and only if its premises necessitate or entail its conclusion, where 'entailment' is defined as in Box 1.

As we've seen, a deductive argument is one in which the conclusion is supposed to follow necessarily from the premises—so that if the premises were all true, the conclusion would be, too. Since a valid argument's premises, if true, determine that the conclusion is true, valid arguments can also be said to be truth-preserving. Any argument that fails to be truth-preserving would be one whose premises could be true and its conclusion false at once. Such an argument is, by definition, invalid: its premises do not entail its conclusion. Note that we're introducing here some different expressions that all mean the same thing. To say that an argument is valid is equivalent to saying that its premises entail its conclusion. And both of these are equivalent to saying that the argument is truth-preserving, and that its conclusion follows necessarily from its premise or premises. The upshot of all this is:

> In a valid argument, it makes no logical sense to accept the premises and reject the conclusion.

Once you accept a valid argument's premises, were you to reject its conclusion (i.e., think that it is false), that would be contradictory or nonsensical. Contradictory statements cannot have the same truth value: if one is true, the other must be false. Consider this valid argument:

1 If the Ohio River is in North America, then it is not in Europe. The Ohio River is in North America; therefore it is not in Europe.

You cannot accept both that *if the Ohio River is in North America, then it is not in Europe* and also that *it is in North America* and at the same time reject that *the Ohio River is not in Europe.* That would be contradictory, thus making no logical sense.

Validity is one of the standards used to evaluate deductive arguments. Whether an argument is valid or not is never a matter of degree, but instead one of *all or nothing.* An argument cannot be 'sort of valid.' It's either valid or it's not. Furthermore, there is a simple test to determine the validity of an argument. As you read it, ask yourself, 'Could the conclusion be false with all the premises true at once?' If so, the argument flunks the test: it's invalid. But if not, then you may accept it as valid. Let's consider some examples. Suppose we ventured to predict what next summer in Baltimore will be like. We might say,

---

BOX 1 ■ ENTAILMENT

There is entailment in an argument if and only if the truth of the argument's premises guarantees the truth of its conclusion—in the sense that, if the premises are all true, the conclusion cannot be false. Such an argument is *valid* and truth-preserving.

2 Next summer there will be some hot days in Baltimore. After all, according to Baltimore's records for the last 100 years, nearly all summers have included some hot days.

Or imagine that we want to decide what to expect on our European vacation. We might reason,

3 Yves is a Parisian and speaks French. The same is true of Odette, Mathilde, Marie, Maurice, Gilles, Pierre, Jacques, and Jean-Louis. So, all Parisians speak French.

Now clearly in both arguments the conclusion could be false and the premises true. Although the likelihood of that may seem exceedingly remote, it is possible. Both arguments are therefore invalid. In claiming that false conclusions are 'possible,' we have in mind logical possibility. Whether (2) and (3) would be likely to have true premises and false conclusion in our actual world, with things being as they are, is beside the point. Rather, if there is some scenario, 'possible' in the sense that it implies no internal contradiction, in which these arguments' premises could be true and their conclusions false at once, then the arguments are invalid.

At the same time, notice another thing: whether an argument is valid or not is entirely a matter of whether its conclusion follows necessarily from its premises. The *actual* truth or falsity of premises and conclusion in isolation is mostly irrelevant to an argument's validity. What matters is whether the premises could be true and the conclusion false at once, because that would determine the invalidity of the argument. Thus, a valid argument could have one or more false premises and a true conclusion, as in

4 1. All dogs are fish.
   2. All fish are mammals.
   3. All dogs are mammals.

Or it could be made up entirely of false statements, as in

5 1. All Democrats are vegetarians.
   2. All vegetarians are Republicans.
   3. All Democrats are Republicans.

Validity is best thought of as a kind of *relation* between premises and conclusion in an argument, where the *actual truth or falsity* of the component statements is largely irrelevant. What matters is: do the premises necessitate the conclusion? If so, it's valid. If not, it's invalid.

BOX 2 ■ VALID VS. INVALID ARGUMENTS

1. Arguments may be divided into two groups: those that are valid and those that are invalid.
2. Only valid arguments are truth-preserving: If their premises are true, then it is not possible for their conclusion to be false.
3. Only in a valid argument do the premises entail the conclusion.
4. A logical thinker who accepts the premises of a valid argument cannot reject its conclusion without contradiction. But this doesn't happen in the case of an invalid argument.

Valid Arguments and Argument Form

An argument form is the type of logical mold or pattern that each argument exemplifies. Often the same argument form is the underlying pattern of many actual arguments. To show the form of an argument, it is customary to replace some words in it by "place holders" or symbols such as capital letters, keeping only the words that have a logical function. For example, in (4) we could replace 'dogs' by 'A,' 'fish' by 'B,' and 'mammals' by 'C,' representing its argument form as:

4' 1. All A are B
   2. All B are C
   3. All A are C

(4') is a valid argument form, because any argument with this underlying form would be valid: if its premises were true, its conclusion would have to be true. Argument (5) above also exemplifies this form—as does

6 1. All laptops are computers.
   2. All computers are electronic devices.
   3. All laptops are electronic devices.

Since (4) above likewise exemplifies argument form (4'), which is valid, therefore (4) is valid—quite independent of the fact that its premises are false. For an argument to be valid, it is of no importance whether it has all false premises, as in the case of (4), or a false conclusion with at least one false premises as in (7) or even all false statements as in (5).

7 1. All professional soccer players are athletes.
   2. All athletes are college students.
   3. All professional soccer players are college students.

Since these arguments exemplify a valid argument form, they are valid. Their form is such that any argument with true premises exemplifying it must have a true conclusion.

> ### Validity and Argument Form
>
> In any argument exemplifying a valid form, there is a relationship of entailment between premises and conclusion. If the argument's premises are true, its conclusion cannot be false. Validity consists in this relationship, and nothing more. The fact that an argument might have one or more false premises is of no importance for its validity, which is entirely a matter of argument form.

Invalidity is also a matter of argument form: an argument form is invalid if and only if an argument with that form *could* have true premises and a false conclusion. But 'could' here means 'logically possible,' which leaves open the possibility that a given invalid argument may have true premises and a true conclusion. For instance,

BOX 3 ■ INVALIDITY AND COUNTEREXAMPLE

- A **counterexample** to prove the invalidity of a given argument is another argument exemplifying the same form but with true premises and a false conclusion.
- To find a counterexample may require imagining a scenario that is "possible" in the sense that it *involves no internal contradiction*. The actual world is only one among many such possible scenarios called "possible worlds."

8   1. All BMWs are motor vehicles.
    2. Some motorcycles are motor vehicles.
    3. Some motorcycles are BMWs.

(8)'s conclusion is true (indeed, all three statements are true), but the argument is invalid because it exemplifies an invalid argument form—namely,

8'   1. All A are B
     2. Some C are B
     3. Some C are A

Any argument that exemplifies this argument form lacks entailment, for its conclusion does not follow necessarily from its premises. To prove that an argument form is invalid, logical thinkers use the method of *counterexample*: they try think of an argument with true premises and a false conclusion that has exactly that same argument form. For example, a counterexample that shows the invalidity of (8') above is the following:

9   1. All frying pans are cookware.
    2. Some cookie cutters are cookware.
    3. Some cookie cutters are frying pans.

(9) has the exact same form, but with true premises and a false conclusion. The method of counterexample can be used to prove the invalidity not only of certain argument forms, but also of the actual arguments that have those forms. Thus (9) is a counterexample to (8) above. That is, (9) is an example that proves (8)'s invalidity, because it shows that it is possible to have an argument with exactly the same argument form but with true premises and a false conclusion. And that shows that, in (8), the premises *do not* necessitate the conclusion.

'Validity' as a Technical Word

As we have been using the words 'valid' and 'invalid' here, there is no such thing as a "valid statement" or an "invalid statement." Though these expressions are sometimes heard in everyday language, 'valid' and 'invalid' are technical words in logic that cannot be applied to a single statement, but only to a relation between statements—namely, the relation called *argument*. 'Valid' can apply only to an argument whose premises necessitate or entail its conclusion, 'invalid' only to one whose premises fail to do this. Only some relations among statements, then, may be valid or invalid. Thus these technical words apply only to arguments, not to individual statements.

Now, notice a further point: because validity is very demanding, some arguments that count as invalid by this standard may yet be okay by a less demanding one. Some arguments in which the conclusion fails to follow with necessity from the premises may yet be arguments in which it follows with probability. That is, some arguments in which the premises fall short of guaranteeing the conclusion may nevertheless make it likely. And many of these arguments may be very useful to us—for example, if they support certain generalizations about the workings of nature or of human societies. Recall *inductive* arguments: although their premises might provide some reasons for the conclusion, they would never entail it. According to this definition, all inductive arguments fail to meet the standard of validity. But the premises of some such arguments may yet provide strong reasons for believing their conclusions, even when they fall short of entailing them. We'll examine this type of argument at length in Chapter 6.

At the same time, it makes no sense to say that an argument is "true" or "false." *Statements* and *beliefs* can be true or false. But arguments can't have a truth value! As with 'validity' and 'invalidity,' 'true' and 'false' are used here in a technical sense, which should not be confused with the everyday senses of those words. Keep in mind, then, that in logical thinking,

Statements are

- either true or false,
- but neither valid nor invalid.

Arguments are

- neither true nor false,
- but either valid or invalid.

Exercises

I. Review Questions

1. When is an argument invalid? When is an argument valid?
2. What is entailment? How is entailment related to validity?
3. What does it mean to say that 'validity' is a technical term?
4. What does it mean to say that a valid argument is 'truth-preserving'?
5. What is an argument form? And how does an argument differ from an argument form?
6. Could an argument be an instance of more than one argument form? If so, how? If not, why not?
7. Could different arguments be instances of the same argument form? If so, how? If not, why not?
8. Define validity and invalidity in terms of argument form.

II. Determine whether the following arguments are valid or invalid.

Tip: For each argument, ask yourself: could all the premises be true with the conclusion false? If so, the argument is invalid. Otherwise, it is valid.

1. No successful movie stars are poor. Queen Latifah is a successful movie star. It follows that Queen Latifah is not poor.

2. New York, Toronto, Denver, Boston, Chicago, Minneapolis, Pittsburgh, Montreal, and Detroit are all big cities in North America, and all of these cities have snow in winter. We may infer that all big North American cities have snow in winter.

3. Since Mr. and Mrs. Gunderson are Republicans, their son Mark must be a Republican, too.

*4. All squares are polygons; for all squares are rectangles, and all rectangles are polygons.

5. All whales are fish, and some whales are members of the Conservative Party. Thus some fish are members of the Conservative Party.

6. Isaac Newton wrote a book called *Principia Mathematica*. Alfred North Whitehead and Bertrand Russell wrote a book called *Principia Mathematica*. Hence, Russell, Whitehead, and Newton were co-authors.

*7. No people who wear wool sweaters are cold. So Uncle Thorvald is never cold, because he always wears a wool sweater.

8. Since beavers are nocturnal, we may infer that badgers, weasels, and wolverines are, too, for all of these animals are small, fur-bearing mammals found in the upper Midwest.

9. Seven-year-old Jason has contracted chicken pox. This occurred only a week after his three younger sisters, Gwendolyn, Samantha, and Hermione, were stricken with chicken pox. Consequently, Jason caught the chicken pox from his sisters.

*10. Bart Simpson cannot run for governor of California because Bart Simpson is a cartoon character, and no cartoon characters are citizens of California. Only citizens of California are eligible to run for governor of California.

11. For as long as records have been kept, every winter there has been some rain in Vancouver. Therefore, next winter there will be some rain in Vancouver.

12. Since Venus Williams and Serena Williams are star tennis players, and Venus and Serena are sisters, we may infer that at least two members of the Williams family are athletes; for all tennis stars are athletes.

*13. Since this is a freshman-level course, it is an easy course, for all freshman-level courses are easy.

14. It is unlikely that Joe will be a senator. Most senators are people who win public debates, and so far Joe has lost every one.

15. If my computer keeps crashing, then it must have picked up a virus somehow. Therefore, it must have a virus, because it keeps crashing!

*16. The Washington Redskins is a football team that has thousands of enthusiastic fans. The same is true of the Denver Broncos, the New York Jets, the Minnesota Vikings, and the Dallas Cowboys. It follows that all American professional football teams have thousands of fans.

17. Since no health-conscious people are sedentary couch potatoes, no marathon runners are sedentary couch potatoes, for all marathon runners are health-conscious people.

18. The value of stocks is now falling every day. Whenever this happens, stocks are not a good investment. Thus stocks are not a good investment now.

*19. For us, the options tonight are either to watch a movie at home or go out for dinner. We won't watch a movie at home. Thus we'll go out for dinner.

20. Sally is always happy, because she is a singer, and many singers are always happy.

21. Nat is not a spy. All spies have espionage training, and he has never had such training.

*22. JJ's won't get the support of the Chamber of Commerce, for the Chamber of Commerce usually supports only local firms, and JJ's is from out of state.

23. The Ethiopian city of Addis Ababa is a center of African culture. All cities that are centers of African culture are large cities. Hence, Addis Ababa is a large city.

24. Either Syria will stop supporting Lebanon or it wants a war with Israel. But clearly Syria does not want a war with Israel, so Syria will stop supporting Lebanon.

*25. Many undergraduates in the United States receive some form of financial aid. Since Jane is a college undergraduate, she has financial aid.

26. An inspector at a Sony computer factory found that, out of the many computers she inspected, none had defects. She concluded: 'At this factory, no computer is defective.'

27. Since it's a Friday, Atkins will not be home until late tonight. Most Fridays, Atkins makes a stop at Miller's Bar and Grill on the way home for a beer or two and never leaves Miller's before 11:00 p.m.

*28. Simon Peterson is a cardinal. Since no cardinals are Protestants, Peterson is not a Protestant.

29. Most people who have a tooth extracted without an anesthetic are in pain. I'll have one extracted without an anesthetic later today. Therefore, I'll be in pain.

30. Mr. Abernathy must be at least sixty-five years old, since no one can be receiving Social Security payments unless he is sixty-five years old or older, and Mr. Abernathy gets a Social Security check in the mail every month.

III. For each of the above arguments that are valid, construct an argument of your own that follows the same pattern. In this exercise, premises need not be true.

IV. Determine whether the following types of argument are logically possible or impossible. For each that's logically possible, give an example.

1. A valid argument whose premises are true and conclusion false.

    SAMPLE ANSWER: Logically impossible.

2. An invalid argument whose premises are true and conclusion false.

*3. An invalid argument whose premises are true and conclusion true.

4. An invalid argument form that cannot have true premises and a false conclusion.

*5. A valid argument whose premises are false and conclusion false.

6. A valid argument whose premises are false and conclusion true.

7. An invalid argument whose premises are false and conclusion false.

*8. An argument that is more or less valid.

V. Your Own Thinking Lab

Consider each of the following claims as a *conclusion*, and construct two arguments to support it, one valid, the other invalid. (For the purposes of this exercise, premises need not be true.)

1. Joan is married.

2. Oranges are nutritious.

3. The Dodgers play well.

4. Laptops are not easy to break.

5. Sharks have gills.

6. Derek Jeter is wealthy.

7. Pelicans fly.

8. Iron expands when heated.

Propositional Argument Forms

As we have seen, another way to refer to valid arguments is as arguments that are truth-preserving. This is the same as saying that if their premises are true, then their conclusions must also be true—or, equivalently, that the truth of their premises guarantees the truth of their conclusions. Being truth-preserving is a characteristic a valid argument has in virtue of the form or pattern it exemplifies. Some arguments have the characteristic of being truth-preserving because the statements that constitute their premises and conclusion are connected in certain ways, forming distinctive patterns of relationship that transfer the truth of the premises (if they are true) to the arguments' conclusions. Other arguments have it because within the statements that constitute their premises and conclusions there are some expressions, usually called *terms*, that bear certain relationships to each other that make the arguments' conclusions true if the premises are true. Arguments of the former type are *propositional*, those of the latter *categorical*.

We'll examine each type in more detail later, but before we go on, it's important to be clear about what we mean by 'proposition.' Recall that a proposition is the *content* of a belief or statement, which has a truth value: it is either true or false. Let's now consider some propositional arguments—that is, those for which being truth-preserving hinges on relations between the propositions that constitute their premises and conclusions. For example,

10 1. If my cell phone is ringing, then someone is trying to call me.
    2. My cell phone is ringing.
    3. Someone is trying to call me.

(10) is a valid argument because of the relation among the propositions that make it up. Its premise 1 features two simple propositions connected by 'if … then … ,' and its premise 2 asserts the first of those two simple propositions. After replacing each simple proposition in this argument with capital letters used as symbols, keeping the logical connection, if … then … , (10)'s argument form becomes apparent. It is

10' 1. If M, then C
   2. M
   ——
   3. C

In (10'), M stands for 'My cell phone is ringing' and C for 'Someone is trying to call me.' (10') is not an argument but an *argument form* showing a certain relation between premises and conclusion that is known as *modus ponens*. Any argument with this form exemplifies a *modus ponens*. For example,

11 1. If thought requires a brain, then brainless creatures cannot think.
   2. Thought requires a brain.
   ——
   3. Brainless creatures cannot think.

Let's now consider other propositional argument forms. This argument has the logical form *modus tollens*:

12 1. If there is growth, then the economy is recovering.
   2. But the economy is not recovering.
   ——
   3. There is no growth

This is revealed by symbolizing it as

12' 1. If G, then E
   2. Not E
   ——
   3. Not G

Box 4 offers a short list of some valid propositional argument forms, which we'll revisit in Chapter 12. For now, let's illustrate the other forms in Box 4.

13 1. If inland temperatures increase, then crops are damaged.
   2. If crops are damaged, then we all suffer.
   ——
   3. If inland temperatures increase, then we all suffer.

BOX 4 ■ SOME VALID PROPOSITIONAL ARGUMENT FORMS

Modus Ponens
If *P*, then *Q*

P
——
Q

Modus Tollens
If *P*, then *Q*

Not *Q*
——
Not *P*

Hypothetical Syllogism
If *P*, then *Q*

If *Q*, then *R*
——
If *P*, then *R*

Disjunctive Syllogism (1)
Either *P* or *Q*

Not *P*
——
Q

Contraposition
If *P*, then *Q*
——
If not *Q*, then not *P*

Disjunctive Syllogism (2)
Either *P* or *Q*

Not *Q*
——
P

(13) is an instance of a hypothetical syllogism, for it has the form

13' 1. If I, then C
    2. If C, then A
    3. If I, then A

And, as you can prove for yourself, (14) and (15) below illustrate the two versions of *disjunctive syllogism* in Box 4, while (16) illustrates *contraposition*:

14 1. Either American Dennis Tito or South African Mark Shuttleworth was the first space tourist.
    2. South African Mark Shuttleworth was not the first space tourist.
    3. American Dennis Tito was the first space tourist.

15 1. Either American Dennis Tito or South African Mark Shuttleworth was the first space tourist.
    2. American Dennis Tito was not the first space tourist.
    3. South African Mark Shuttleworth was the first space tourist.

16 1. If Persia was a mighty kingdom, then Lydia was a mighty kingdom.
    2. If Lydia was not a mighty kingdom, then Persia was not a mighty kingdom.

All these arguments are substitution instances (or simply, instances) of one or another of the argument forms in Box 4, which are all valid. This means that in any argument that is an instance of one of these forms, there is entailment, no matter what actual statements the symbols stand for. That is, no actual arguments of the forms listed in Box 4 above could have true premises and a false conclusion. There are many such forms, but again, we'll examine this topic at greater length in Chapter 12.

> SUGGESTION: In this section, there are a number of valid argument forms. For quick reference and to gain familiarity, construct a card with these forms. Write down on one side those where validity hinges on relations among propositions, and on the other side those where validity hinges on relations among terms.

Categorical Argument Forms

Many arguments are clearly valid, even though they don't fit into any form of propositional logic. Consider

17 1. All dentists have clean teeth.
    2. Dr. Chang is a dentist.
    3. Dr. Chang has clean teeth.

(17) is plainly valid, for if its premises are true, then its conclusion must be true. Now suppose we replace its parts by letter symbols, treating the argument as if it were an instance of an argument form in propositional logic. We would then get this form:

17' 1. D
    2. C
    3. E

But (17') is an invalid form, since there are counterexamples to it: that is, arguments of the same form with true premises and a false conclusion. Here is one,

18 1. Whales are mammals.
    2. California is the most populous state in the United States.
    3. The Earth is flat

So to take (17), a valid argument, to have an invalid argument form such as (17') would be incorrect. What's needed is a different system, one where letter symbols do not stand for propositions. In other words, (17') is too coarse-grained to serve as the correct argument form of (17), where the entailment hinges on relations among certain expressions *within the propositions* that make up that argument, rather than on relations among the propositions themselves that constitute premises and conclusion. In (17) the entailment depends on relations among terms such as 'all,' 'Dr. Chang,' 'dentist' and 'clean teeth.'

A more fine-grained representation is needed for arguments such as (17). We shall represent their forms by adopting the following conventions:

> 1. Use 'to be' in present tense as the main verb in each premise and conclusion.
> 2. Make explicit any logical expressions, such as 'all,' 'some,' and 'no.'
> 3. Replace expressions such as 'dentist' and 'clean teeth' with capital letters.
> 4. Replace expressions for specific things or individuals, such as 'Dr. Chang,' 'Fido,' 'I,' and 'that chair' with lowercase letters.

In this language, the logical form of (17) is similar to that of

19 1. All soda companies are businesses that prosper.
    2. Pepsi is a soda company.
    3. Pepsi is a business that prospers.

(19)'s argument form is

19' 1. All A are B.
    2. c is an A.
    3. c is a B

In (19'), 'A' stand for the term 'soda companies,' 'B' for 'businesses that prosper,' and 'c' for 'Pepsi.' We can also represent in this language arguments such as

20 1. All ophthalmologists are doctors.
    2. Some ophthalmologists are short.
    3. Some doctors are short.

(20) is a plainly valid argument: it is a substitution instance of a valid categorical argument form.

Another instance of the same form is

21 1. All red squirrels are rodents.
    2. Some red squirrels are wild animals.
    3. Some rodents are wild animals.

The argument form of both (20) and (21) is,

20' 1. All A are B
     2. Some A are C
     3. Some B are C

Here 'A' stand for 'red squirrels' (or 'ophthalmologists'), 'B' for 'rodents' (or 'doctors'), and 'C' for 'wild animals' (or 'short').

Let's now recall a point made at the beginning of this section: that another way to understand validity is to say that whether an argument is valid or not is simply a matter of whether it has a valid form.

Consider

22 1. No Peloponnesians are Euboeans.
    2. All Spartans are Peloponnesians.
    3. No Spartans are Euboeans.

Even someone who knew nothing at all about Greek geography could nevertheless see that the argument is valid, because it is an instance of the valid form number 3 in Box 5. No argument with this form could have true premises and a false conclusion. Similarly, the following argument is valid even though its premises are false. Why? Simply because it has valid form number 3 in Box 5.

BOX 5 ■ SOME VALID CATEGORICAL ARGUMENT FORMS

1	2
All A are B	Some A are B
No B are C	All A are C
No C are A	Some C are B
3	**4**
No A are B	All A are B
All C are A	All C are A
No C are B	All C are B
5	**6**
All A are B	All A are B
All B are C	Some A are not C
All A are C	Some B are not C

23 1. All apples are oranges.
  2. All bananas are apples.
  3. All bananas are oranges.

Validity, then, is entirely a matter of argument form. The same could be said for the other examples above. This brings us to another important point: for each form that is valid, all of the arguments that have it will be valid. Similarly, for each invalid form, all of the arguments that have it will be invalid.

Propositional or Categorical?

- When you see certain connections between propositions, such as 'Either . . . or . . . ' and 'If . . . then . . . ,' the argument is probably better reconstructed as propositional.
- On the other hand, when you see in the premises certain words indicating quantity, such as 'All,' 'No,' and 'Some,' the argument is probably better reconstructed as categorical.

The Cash Value of Validity

Logical thinking has goals, such as learning, understanding, and solving problems. Each of these requires argument analysis and sometimes refutation, the process by which a given argument is shown to fail. But, far from being among logical thinking's primary goals, refutation is a result of argument analysis unavoidable in some cases. Achieving logical thinking's primary goals greatly depends on charitable and faithful reconstruction of arguments. For those that are deductive, charity recommends making them as strong as possible, maximizing the truth of their premises and conclusion and the validity of their forms—while faithfulness recommends trying to capture the arguer's intentions. In all of this, logical thinkers strive to capture the form of an argument correctly, adding missing premises when needed. Once they have properly reconstructed an argument, they then move on to evaluate it, keeping in mind rules such as

---

- Do not criticize/accept an argument by focusing solely on its conclusion.
- Direct each objection to the argument form, or to a clearly identifiable premise.
- Use the evaluative criteria offered here.
- Do not make unsubstantial criticisms, such as 'that is a matter of opinion.'

Any challenge to validity is a challenge to the argument form. If the premises of an argument with a certain form could be true and its conclusion false, then the argument is invalid because it has an invalid form. Yet finding an argument invalid is not a conclusive reason to reject it, since it could still be a good inductive argument (more on this in Chapter 6). Once an argument is found valid, logical thinkers should then check whether its premises are true, a topic we'll take up later in this chapter.

The *cash value* of standards for argument evaluation, such as validity, is simply their *practical impact*: knowing whether an argument meets them or not determines the attitude we should have about its conclusion on the basis of its premises. Validity has this cash value: when an argument meets this standard, its form is valid—and if we know this, then we know that its conclusion cannot be false if all its premises are true. Therefore, asserting that argument's premises and denying its conclusion at the same time would be a contradiction. For example,

24   1. If Felix is a cat, then he is a feline.
     2. Felix is a cat.
     3. Felix is a feline

Since argument (24) is valid, we cannot accept its premises and deny its conclusion without falling into contradiction. For if an argument is valid, then if you assert (or accept) the argument's premises, you must logically assert its conclusion. Asserting (24)'s premises and denying its conclusion would amount to saying something like this:

25   If Felix is a cat, then he is a feline. And Felix is a cat. But he is not a feline.

Clearly, these three statements cannot all be true at once. (25) should be rejected, since its three statements are a logically impossible set: there is no possible world where all its members could be true.

What about the cash value of invalidity? It is this:

> If you know that an argument is invalid, you know that its premises could all be true and its conclusion false at once.

Note, however, that

> If *all* you know about an argument is that it is invalid, then you *don't know* that its premises are in fact true and its conclusion in fact false.

You know only that such a scenario could be the case: the argument form makes that possible (something that could not happen with a valid argument form). As discussed above, in all cases of invalidity, arguments fail to be truth-preserving—so that then any arrangement of truth values in premises and conclusion would be logically possible.

Exercises

VI. Review Questions

1. What does it mean to say that an argument's form is propositional?
2. What does it mean to say that an argument's form is categorical?
3. What's the convention for representing propositional argument forms?
4. What's the convention for representing categorical argument forms?

5. Is finding that an argument is invalid a reason to reject it? If yes, why? If not, why not?

6. What does the expression 'cash value,' as used above, mean?

7. What's the cash value of validity?

8. What's the cash value of invalidity?

VII. All of the arguments below are propositional. For each, give the underlying argument form. The symbols suggested below loosely correspond to the first letter of an important word in each proposition.

1. If Vatican City is not a part of Italy, then it is an independent state. Vatican City is not a part of Italy; thus Vatican City is an independent state. (V, I)

   SAMPLE ANSWER: If not V, then I

   Not V
   ―――――
   I

2. If we do intend to meet the challenges of the twenty-first century, new kinds of energy must be found. Since we do intend to meet such challenges, new kinds of energy must be found. (W, E)

*3. Either Carolyn went to the movies last weekend or she went to the beach. Since she did not go to the movies last weekend, it follows that she went to the beach. (M, B)

4. If Samantha bought the house, then she was able to get a mortgage. But she was not able to get a mortgage. Therefore, Samantha did not buy the house. (H, M)

*5. Either the United States will sell wheat to China or the United States will have a wheat surplus this year. But the United States will not sell wheat to China. Therefore, the United States will have a wheat surplus this year. (C, S)

6. If Dorothy takes the job with General Electric, then she will be moving to California next month. Therefore, if Dorothy will not be moving to California next month, then she will not take the job with General Electric. (G, C)

*7. If Air France has regularly scheduled flights to Mumbai, then Mumbai must be a populous city. Now, in fact Air France does have regularly scheduled flights to Mumbai. It follows that Mumbai is a populous city. (M, C)

8. If the president favors regulation of the oil industry, then he believes in restricting the autonomy of private enterprise. And if he believes in restricting the autonomy of private enterprise, then he is a liberal. Accordingly, if the president favors regulation of the oil industry, then he is a liberal. (P, R, L)

VIII. All of the arguments below are categorical. For each, give the underlying argument form. As before, the symbols suggested below loosely correspond to the first letter of an important word or phrase in each proposition.

1. Javier is a successful business executive, for all successful business executives are cautious investors, and Javier is a cautious investor. (j, B. C)

   SAMPLE ANSWER: All B are C

   j is C
   ―――――
   j is B

*2. Alaska is a large state in the United States. No large state in the United States is densely populated. Thus, Alaska is not densely populated. (a, L, D)

3. All rattlesnakes are snakes. No snakes are friendly pets. Therefore, no rattlesnakes are friendly pets. (R, S, P)

4. Some mathematicians are logicians. No logicians are space travelers. Thus some mathematicians are not space travelers. (M, L, T)

*5. All Afghans are peace-loving people. Some peace-loving people are French. Therefore, some Afghans are French. (A, P, F)

6. All residents of the Vatican are religious believers. No religious believer is an atheist. Therefore, no resident of the Vatican is an atheist. (V, B, A)

7. Kate is not a tourist. All Niagara Falls visitors are tourists. It follows that Kate is not a Niagara Falls visitor. (k, T, V)

*8. No Marine Corps drill instructors are sympathetic friends. So Sergeant Osberg is not a sympathetic friend, since he is a Marine Corps drill instructor. (I, F, o)

IX. For each of the following arguments, determine whether it is propositional or categorical.

1. All living creatures need liquid water. My cat is a living creature. Thus my cat needs liquid water.

SAMPLE ANSWER: Categorical argument

2. There is no extraterrestrial intelligence. After all, if there were extraterrestrial intelligence, we should have evidence of it by now. But we don't have it.

*3. No desert is humid. The Atacama is a desert. Therefore, the Atacama is not humid.

4. Doctors are exposed to agents that cause ailments. Jane is a doctor. Hence, she is exposed to agents that cause ailments.

*5. If the Orinoco crocodile is a rodent, then the Chinese alligator is a rodent. But the Chinese alligator is not a rodent. Therefore, the Orinoco crocodile is not a rodent.

6. Euripides enjoyed tragedy. After all, all fifth-century Greeks enjoyed tragedy, and Euripides was a fifth-century Greek.

*7. All hibernating mammals slow their breathing in the winter. Since all black bears are hibernating mammals, therefore all black bears slow their breathing in the winter.

8. If one has poor health, one goes to the doctor. If one goes to the doctor, one spends money. Thus, if one has poor health, one spends money.

*9. Chris will take summer courses this year, because either he takes them or he'll wait until next fall for graduation, and he won't wait that long.

10. All diesel engines produce exhaust gases. All school buses have diesel engines. Thus all school buses produce exhaust gases.

*11. The universe can act as a magnifying lens, since if relativity theory is correct, the universe can act as a magnifying lens. And relativity theory is correct.

12. All people who drink a glass of warm milk before bedtime are sound sleepers. Given that Beth always drinks a glass of warm milk before bedtime, she is a sound sleeper.

*13. All chameleons are lizards that change their color. All lizards that change their color are scary creatures. So all chameleons are scary creatures.

14. If crocodiles wallow in mud holes, then they are rarely killed by predators. Crocodiles do wallow in mud holes. Thus they are rarely killed by predators.

*15. No Ohio farmer grows papayas, for no northern farmer grows papayas, and Ohio farmers are northern farmers.

X. The arguments below are either propositional or categorical. Indicate which is which and give the argument form.

1. If the defendant's car was used in the robbery, then the car was at the scene of the crime. But it was not at the scene of the crime. Thus the defendant's car was not used in the robbery. (D, C)

SAMPLE ANSWER: Propositional

If D, then C

Not C

Not D

2. If these snakes are cobras, then they're poisonous. Therefore, if these snakes are not poisonous, then they are not cobras. (C, P)

3. If offenses against the innocent are punished, then we have a fair system of justice. If we have a fair system of justice, then the guilty are treated as they deserve. So if offenses against the innocent are punished, then the guilty are treated as they deserve. (O, J, G)

*4. Since all computers are mechanical devices, no computers are things that can think, for no things that can think are mechanical devices. (C, D, T)

5. Archie doesn't eat chicken, for Archie is a vegan, and if he is a vegan, then he doesn't eat chicken. (A, C)

*6. If Mississippi does allow gay marriage, then its laws governing marriage are liberal. In fact, its laws governing marriage are not liberal. So, Mississippi does not allow gay marriage. (M, L)

7. Either doctors favor the new health program or the uninsured suffer. But doctors do not favor the new health program. Hence the uninsured suffer. (N, U)

8. All accountants are good at math. Greg is not an accountant. Therefore, he is not good at math. (A, M, g)

*9. If a flower is an orchid, then it is a tropical flower. Therefore, if it is not a tropical flower, then it is not an orchid. (O, F)

10. Since no tropical country has blizzards and Venezuela is a tropical country, Venezuela doesn't have blizzards. (C, B, v)

*11. All babies are infants. Some babies are good at crawling. Therefore, some infants are good at crawling. (B, I, C)

12. All carrots are vegetables full of vitamin A. All vegetables full of vitamin A are foods good for your eyesight. So carrots are foods good for your eyesight. (C, V, F)

*13. No schoolchildren are college graduates. All college graduates have a college diploma. Therefore, no schoolchildren have a college diploma. (S, G, D)

14. If penguins are birds, then they are likely to have feathers. Since it is the case that penguins are birds, we must conclude that they are likely to have feathers. (B, F)

*15. No planet is a star. Hence, Venus is not a star, since Venus is a planet. (P, S, v)

16. Anne is Mario's wife. Thus Mario is not a bachelor. For if Anne is his wife, then he is not a bachelor. (A, B)

17. No professional gambler is good at saving money. Since Nathan is a professional gambler, we may infer that he is not good at saving money. (G, M, n)

*18. If oxygen is the lightest element, then oxygen is lighter than hydrogen. But oxygen is not lighter than hydrogen. Therefore, oxygen is not the lightest element. (O, H)

19. If Winston Churchill was English, then he was not Brazilian. But if he was not Brazilian, then he was not South American. Thus if Winston Churchill was English, then he was not South American. (E, B, S)

*20. Melissa will either pledge Gamma Phi or she will not join a sorority at all this year. Accordingly, she will not join a sorority at all, since she will not pledge Gamma Phi. (M, J)

XI. For each of the above arguments that is propositional, give the name of its form (answers to 3, 6, 9, 18, and 20 in the back of the book).

SAMPLE ANSWER: 1. *Modus tollens*

XII. Indicate whether the following statements are true or false.

1. A valid argument cannot have a false conclusion.

SAMPLE ANSWER: False

2. A valid argument cannot have a false premise.

*3. A valid argument cannot have true premises and a false conclusion.

4. Invalid arguments always have true premises and false conclusions.

*5. A valid argument could have a counterexample.

6. All valid argument forms are truth-preserving.

*7. An invalid argument could never have a true conclusion.

8. An invalid argument could never have true premises.

*9. If there is entailment in an argument, then that argument is truth-preserving.

10. An invalid argument could have no counterexample.

XIII. **The following categorical arguments are invalid. After symbolizing their forms accordingly, show invalidity in each case with a counterexample. (Tip: Use the same counterexample for arguments exemplifying the same invalid form. When the given argument plainly has true premises and a false conclusion, you can simply point that out in lieu of counterexample.)**

1. All female college students are students. Some students are smokers. Therefore, some female college students are smokers.

   SAMPLE ANSWER: All F are D
   Some D are M
   Some F are M.

   Counterexample: F, D, and M stand for 'fish,' 'animal,' and 'mammal.' [All fish are animals. Some animals are mammals. Thus some fish are mammals.]

2. All giraffes are mute. That animal is mute. Thus that animal is a giraffe.

*3. Most American citizens are permitted to vote in the United States. Michael is not permitted to vote in the United States. So, Michael is not an American citizen.

4. Roses are flowers. Some flowers are daffodils. Thus roses are daffodils.

*5. No SUVs are easy to park. Some SUVs are speedy vehicles. Hence, no speedy vehicles are easy to park.

6. Some days are rainy days. Some days are sunny days. Therefore, some rainy days are sunny days.

*7. Fido is a dog. Some dogs bark. Therefore, Fido barks.

8. Most Mexicans speak Spanish. Some non-Mexicans speak Spanish. Therefore, some non-Mexicans are Mexicans.

9. All intellectuals support stem-cell research. Barbra Streisand supports stem-cell research. Therefore, Barbra Streisand is an intellectual.

10. No desktop computer is light. My computer is not light. Hence, my computer is not a desktop.

XIV. YOUR OWN THINKING LAB

1. Explain in your own words the relation between 'invalidity' and 'counterexample.'

2. Explain in your own words the claim that validity is a matter of argument form.

3. Give two arguments of your own for each of the following valid argument forms: *modus ponens*, *modus tollens*, hypothetical syllogism, disjunctive syllogism, and contraposition.

4. Give a counterexample to the following argument: Horses are domestic animals. Dobbin is a domestic animal. Therefore, Dobbin is a horse.

5. For each of the following argument forms, construct an argument with true premises on a topic of your choice that illustrates that form:

   1. All A are B
      All B are C
      All A are C

2. All A are B

   Some A are not C

   Some B are not C

3. No As are Bs

   All C are A

   No C are B

4. All A are B

   Some A are C

   Some B are C

5. All A are B

   c is not a B

   c is not an A

6. All A are B

   c is an A

   c is a B

6. For each of the following argument forms, construct an argument with true premises on a topic of your choice that illustrates that form: *modus ponens, modus tollens,* contraposition, hypothetical syllogism, and disjunctive syllogism.

5.2 Soundness

Must we then always accept the conclusions of valid arguments? No, for there may still be something wrong with them (as is clear in some of the examples above). To evaluate an argument, validity is the first criterion we use, but not the only one. After we have decided that an argument is valid, we must also determine whether it is sound, bearing in mind that

> An argument is sound if and only if it is valid and all of its premises are true.

Thus consider some arguments given earlier:

22 1. No Peloponnesians are Euboeans.
    2. All Spartans are Peloponnesians.
    3. No Spartans are Euboeans.

4   1. All dogs are fish.
    2. All fish are mammals.
    3. All dogs are mammals.

5   1. All Democrats are vegetarians.
    2. All vegetarians are Republicans.
    3. All Democrats are Republicans.

Argument (22) is sound. But (4) and (5) are unsound. This is because if an argument lacks either validity or true premises (or both), then it is unsound. The problem with (4) and (5) is that their premises are false, thus rendering the arguments unsound, even though, as we have seen, both are valid. Important things to remember are, first, that if *even one* of an argument's premises is false, then the argument is unsound, whether it's valid or not. Second, a premise counts as *true* only if there is no controversy about whether it's true. Third, since validity is a necessary condition of soundness, an argument can also be unsound because its form is invalid. For example,

26 1. Any city that is the capital of a country is a center of political power.
   2. Chicago is a center of political power.
   3. Chicago is the capital of a country.

Here both premises are true, yet the argument is unsound because it is invalid.

Validity and true premises, then, are the necessary conditions for soundness. The question of whether an argument's premises *are in fact* true or false is another matter entirely (which cannot be answered by logic alone). Most such answers belong rather to the sciences, or to the investigations of historians, geographers, and other fact finders. To be sure, a good logical thinker will want to get her facts straight! But this is where she must head for the library or the laboratory and consider the evidence for the premises of arguments that purport to be sound.

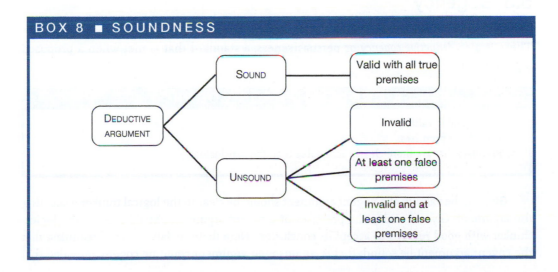

The Cash Value of Soundness

Why, then, is soundness so important? Why is soundness a desirable characteristic in arguments? Because if one is aware of an argument's soundness, then not only is one fully justified in accepting its conclusion, one *has to* accept it! As defined above, all valid arguments are truth-preserving—if their premises are true, their conclusions must be true. If an argument is valid and also *actually has* true premises, it is sound; and that means that the truth of the premises transfers to the conclusion. Thus there is no denying the conclusion of any such argument without *saying something false.*

Soundness has a practical impact or worth because whenever a given deductive argument meets this standard, its conclusion is guaranteed to be true. In fact, the cash value of soundness is twofold:

> When an argument is sound, then
>
> - Given its validity, you can't assert its premises and deny its conclusion without saying something contradictory.
> - Given its validity and its true premises, you can't deny its conclusion without saying something false.

What about unsoundness? What is its cash value for logical thinkers? An unsound argument fails to guarantee the truth of its conclusion. If an argument is valid but unsound, that means that it has at least one false premise. The realization of this is sufficient reason to reject that argument. If an argument is unsound but has all true premises, that means that its argument form is invalid: as we'll see in Chapter 6, some such arguments are better considered inductive and evaluated according to standards other than soundness.

5.3 Cogency

Validity and soundness are not the only standards used to evaluate deductive arguments. There is also *deductive cogency* or persuasiveness, a standard that is met when a proposed argument has

> ### BOX 9 ■ THREE CONDITIONS FOR COGENCY
>
> 1. Recognizable validity.
> 2. Acceptable premises.
> 3. Premises that are more clearly acceptable than the conclusion.

Given 1, the validity of a cogent argument should be clear to the logical thinker evaluating the argument. Given 2 and 3, the premises of a cogent argument should provide the logical thinker with good reasons to accept its conclusion. Note that this falls short of requiring that the cogent argument be sound: that is, an unsound argument could be cogent, provided that the thinker recognizes its validity and takes the premises to provide good reasons for its conclusion, even when, unknown to the thinker, at least one of its premises happens to be false. Consider a thinker who seems to have seen Ingrid at the library and reasons as follows:

27 1. Ingrid is at the library.
    2. If Ingrid is at the library, then she is not at the cafeteria.
    3. Ingrid is not at the cafeteria.

Since he *just saw* Ingrid at the library, he seems to have evidence that premise 1 is true. 2 is also true, since nobody could be in two different places at the same time. From 1 and 2 together, conclusion 3 follows validly by *modus ponens*. So the argument is deductively cogent: it is recognizably valid and has *acceptable* premises that *support the conclusion*. But suppose that in fact, unknown to the thinker, it wasn't Ingrid at all he saw in the library but her identical twin, Greta. In this situation, the argument is unsound—but still perfectly cogent!

On the other hand, there can sometimes be sound arguments that are non-cogent. For having recognizable validity and true premises might not be enough for an argument to be *persuasive*. Consider:

28 1. The Earth is not flat and is not the center of the universe.
    2. The Earth is not the center of the universe

(28) is plainly valid, since if its premise is true, its conclusion cannot be false. Moreover, since its premise is in fact true, the argument is also sound. But anyone who reasonably doubted (28)'s conclusion would not be persuaded to accept it. (28) fails to meet condition 3 above: namely, having a premise that is more clearly acceptable than the conclusion. Imagine this argument being offered in the Middle Ages, when all available evidence pointed to the falsity of its conclusion. Even though people at that time would have rejected premise 1, unknown to them that premise was true—and the argument sound. Thus even sound arguments can fail to be cogent when their premises fail to be more acceptable than the conclusion they are offered to support.

BOX 10 ■ SECTION SUMMARY

A deductive argument meeting the three conditions of cogency in Box 9 is one whose premises give the logical thinker good reasons to accept its conclusion.

The Cash Value of Cogency

Anyone who recognizes the validity of an argument and finds its premises to provide good reasons for its conclusion cannot rationally reject the argument. Such an argument may be said to be 'rationally compelling' (or simply 'compelling'). If the thinker were to reject the argument, that would be irrational: it would make no logical sense. Since argument (28) cannot persuade thinkers to accept its conclusion on the basis of its premises, the argument is not cogent (i.e., not rationally compelling). Logical thinkers should be on guard for such arguments and strive to avoid them altogether. In Chapter 8 we'll discuss a pattern of mistake in arguing that affects the cogency of some valid, and even sound, arguments.

Exercises

XV. Review Questions

1. What does it mean to say that a deductively cogent argument is rationally compelling?
2. Explain the difference between soundness and cogency.
3. Given a certain standard for deductive arguments, it is contradictory to assert the premises of an argument that satisfies it and yet at the same time deny the conclusion. What standard is that?
4. What's the effect of denying the conclusion of sound argument?
5. What's the effect of denying the conclusion of an argument that one recognizes as cogent?
6. Must the conclusion of an invalid argument always be rejected? Explain your answer.

XVI. Which of the following statements are true, and which are false?

1. An unsound argument could have a valid form

   SAMPLE ANSWER: True

*2. A sound argument could have all false premises.

3. A sound argument could have one false premise.

*4. A sound argument could be invalid.

5. An unsound argument could have a true conclusion.

*6. A sound argument could have a false conclusion.

7. A sound argument could have true premises and true conclusion.

*8. A sound argument could have a true conclusion.

XVII. What's the matter with the following arguments? Explain.

1. An argument whose premises entail its conclusion is valid. Hence, one should accept the conclusion of any valid argument.

   SAMPLE ANSWER: Such an argument could be non-cogent, or have false premises and thus be unsound.

*2. Only sound arguments guarantee the truth of their conclusions. Thus entailment and therefore validity are of no importance.

3. Logic books make too much fuss about soundness. After all, unsound arguments may also have true conclusions.

*4. Validity doesn't matter in science, for science values truth, and there is no relation between validity and truth.

XVIII. Indicate whether the following scenarios are logically possible or impossible:

1. An unsound argument where there is entailment

   SAMPLE ANSWER: Logically possible (a valid argument with at least one false premise)

2. An unsound argument with a false conclusion

3. A valid argument where there is no entailment

*4. A sound argument that is not truth-preserving

5. An argument that is an instance of a valid form

*6. An invalid argument with true premises and a false conclusion

7. A sound argument with false premises and a true conclusion

*8. An unsound argument with false premises and a false conclusion

9. A sound argument where there is no entailment

*10. A cogent argument that is not rationally persuasive

11. A cogent argument that is invalid

*12. A cogent argument that is unsound

XIX. YOUR OWN THINKING LAB

1. For any possible arguments in the previous exercise, provide an example of your own.

2. Give two examples of your own to illustrate the following: *modus ponens,* contraposition, and disjunctive syllogism.

3. Explain why your examples above are valid.

4. Explain each of the following claims:
   A. Denying the conclusion of a cogent argument is irrational.
   B. Asserting the premises while denying the conclusion of a valid argument is contradictory.
   C. Some valid arguments might not be cogent.
   D. Some unsound arguments might not be cogent.
   E. Some unsound arguments might be cogent.
   F. A deductively valid argument might yet be clearly unsound.

5. Illustrate each of the statements above with an example, supplying the context when needed.

■ Writing Project

Find two arguments on the issue of immigration policy, one supporting tighter restrictions on undocumented aliens, the other opposing them. The sources, which should be identified in your work, may be blogs or articles from a website, a newspaper, or a magazine. First, reconstruct the arguments as deductive, and then discuss whether they are sound. The simpler the argument, the easier it is to determine whether it is sound. A length of 700 words should be adequate.

■ Chapter Summary

Propositional argument: the relation of inference hinges on relations among the propositions expressed by its premises and conclusion.

Categorical argument: the relation of inference hinges on relations among the terms within its premises and conclusion.

Argument form: the symbolic pattern of the logical relations in an argument.

Counterexample to an argument: another argument of the same form with clearly true premises and a false conclusion. It proves that the original argument has an invalid form.

Substitution instance of an argument form: an actual argument exemplifying that form.

Some valid forms of propositional arguments: *modus ponens, modus tollens,* hypothetical syllogism, disjunctive syllogism, and contraposition.

Validity, soundness, and cogency: standards for evaluating deductive arguments.

VALIDITY

Definition
An argument is valid if and only if it has entailment (its premises necessitate its conclusion).

Cash Value
- It is not possible that the argument's premises are true and its conclusion false.
- The conclusion could be false, if at least one of the premises is false.
- It is contradictory to accept a valid argument's premises and reject its conclusion.

SOUNDNESS

Definition
An argument is sound if and only if it is valid and all its premises are true.

Cash Value
- The argument's conclusion is true: to deny it is to say something false.
- A logical thinker who recognizes an argument as sound must accept its conclusion.

COGENCY

Definition
An argument is cogent if and only if it is recognizably valid and has acceptable premises which are more acceptable than the conclusion they attempt to support.

Cash Value
- Any argument that satisfies these conditions is rationally compelling, in the sense that it would move the thinker to accept its conclusion (provided she accepts its premises and works out the entailment).
- It would be irrational for the thinker to reject the conclusion of that argument.

■ Key Words

Validity	Categorical argument
Entailment	Soundness
Truth-preserving argument	Counterexample
Argument form	Substitution instance
Propositional argument	Cogency

Analyzing Inductive Arguments

This chapter looks more closely at inductive reasoning. Among its topics are:

- The nature of inductive arguments.
- Universal and non-universal generalizations.
- Identifying types of inductive argument: enumerative induction, statistical syllogism,
- causal argument, and analogy.
- Two standards for evaluating inductive arguments: reliability and strength.
- Mill's methods for establishing causal connections between events: agreement and difference, and concomitant variation.

6.1 Reconstructing Inductive Arguments

Since we have already dwelt at some length on deductive arguments, in this chapter we turn to inductive ones, which are crucial to ordinary and scientific reasoning. As we have seen, an argument is either deductive or inductive, depending whether the premises guarantee the truth of the conclusion. If they do, the argument is deductive; if not, it's inductive. There are a number of related tests that may help in recognizing an inductive argument. First, in the case of any such argument, ask yourself

> Could the premises of the argument be asserted and the conclusion denied without logical contradiction?
> - If yes, the argument is inductive.
> - If no, the argument is deductive.

Let's consider some examples—first, a simple deductive argument:

1   Pam is energetic and athletic. Therefore, Pam is athletic.

The first test recommends trying to see what happens when (1)'s premises are asserted and its conclusion denied. The test yields

2   Pam is energetic and athletic. But Pam is not athletic.

(2) is contradictory: there is no logically possible scenario in which the statements that make up (2) could all be true or all false at once. In light of such a result, argument (1) above is deductive. By contrast, consider

3   1. Pam is athletic.
    2. Most of those who are athletic don't eat junk food.
    3. Pam doesn't eat junk food.

Argument (3)'s premises could all be asserted and its conclusion denied without contradiction. After all, there are possible scenarios in which these premises are true and the conclusion false—for example, a scenario in which Pam is athletic, and most athletic people do not eat junk food, but Pam does eat junk food. Thus (3) is inductive. Similarly, (4) and (5) are inductive, given that their premise could be asserted and their conclusion denied without contradiction:

4   1. Many horses are friendly.
    2. Mr. Ed is a horse.
    3. Mr. Ed is friendly.

5   Housing prices will continue to go down, for we are having a recession and usually housing prices go down in recessions.

Compare (4) with (6),

6 1. All horses are friendly.
    2. Mr. Ed is a horse.
    3. Mr. Ed is friendly.

(6) is deductive, since it is not possible to assert its premises and deny its conclusion without contradiction. If we try to do so, we would be saying something contradictory, namely,

7 All horses are friendly. Mr. Ed is a horse. But Mr. Ed is not friendly.

There is no possible scenario where all three statements could be true at once. For if it is true that all horses are friendly and that Mr. Ed is a horse, it must be false that he is not friendly. Notice that in a deductive argument, its conclusion doesn't add any information that was not already in the premises. By contrast, an inductive argument always involves an inferential leap, for its conclusion invariably conveys information that was not given in the premises. Thus its conclusion is not strictly contained in its premises. But this feature makes inductive arguments ideally suited for scientific reasoning in fields such as physics and biology, where scientists often make causal connections or reach general conclusions on the basis of only a sample of observed cases. The observation that a great number of metals expand under heat plays a role in the scientists' conclusion that all metals do so—as does research on the habits of people with lung disease in their concluding that smoking increases the risk of contracting such ailments. But both conclusions add something that was not among the scientists' premises.

Another distinctive feature of inductive arguments is that newly acquired evidence could always make a difference in the degree of support for their conclusions, strengthening it in some cases, weakening it in others. Consider

8 1. 98% of State College students are involved in politics.
    2. Heather is a State College student.
    3. Heather is involved in politics.

Argument (8) is inductive. Its premises, if true, would provide some support for its conclusion. New evidence to the effect that Heather is indifferent to politics, however, could undermine that support. Once that evidence is added, the argument then is

9 1. 98% of State College students are involved in politics.
    2. Heather is a State College student.
    3. Heather never votes.
    4. Heather is involved in politics.

A quick comparison of (8) and (9) shows that in the latter, support for the claim that Heather is involved in politics has been undermined by the addition of premise 3.

The features of inductive arguments so far reviewed suggest that there is no entailment in them: their premises, even in cases where they succeed in supporting their conclusions, could never necessitate them. That is, no inductive argument is truth-preserving. Although an inductive argument may in fact have true premises and a true conclusion, what makes the argument inductive is that an argument of the same form could have true premises and a false conclusion—which, again, is the same as saying that the premises of an inductive argument do not entail its conclusion. Yet, as we shall see in this chapter, the lack of entailment in inductive arguments does not mean that they cannot offer support for their conclusions. In fact, they often make their conclusions probably true, or reasonable to believe, by providing evidence for them, even though their premises always fall short of necessitating their conclusions. This is why it is common to refer to the premises of inductive arguments as 'evidence.' At the same time, since the conclusions of such arguments may be supported but are never completely proved true by the premises, they have the status of conjectures and are often called 'hypotheses.'

Given these features, inductive arguments are *plausibility* arguments. That is, although the evidence that any such argument may provide for its hypothesis never entails that hypothesis, when successful, they can make it plausible. To say that a claim is plausible is to say that it is likely to be true, probably true, or at least reasonable to accept. We shall look closely at the standard for successful induction once we have examined some common types of inductive argument. Before leaving this section, however, it is important that you know the answers to the questions in Box 1.

BOX 1 ■ INDUCTIVE ARGUMENTS

What sort of argument counts as inductive?

- Any argument whose premises may provide evidence for its conclusion or hypothesis but do not guarantee it.

How does one determine whether an argument is inductive or not?

By checking

- whether it would be possible for an argument with the same form to have true premises and a false conclusion.
- whether one can assert its premises and deny its conclusion without contradiction.
- whether the conclusion adds information not contained in the premises.

If in any case the answer is Yes, then the argument is inductive.

6.2 Some Types of Inductive Argument

Enumerative Induction

Of the four types of inductive argument discussed in this chapter, we'll begin with enumerative induction. An enumerative induction always has a universal conclusion to the effect that all things of a certain kind have (or lack) a certain feature. This conclusion is drawn from evidence that some things of that kind have (or lack) that feature. The conclusion of any such argument, often called an 'inductive generalization,' is a *universal generalization:*

> A universal generalization
> - is a statement asserting that all of the members of a certain class have (or don't have) a certain feature.
> - may be expressed by a great number of different patterns of sentence. Some standard patterns are 'All . . . are . . . ,' 'Every . . . is . . . ,' 'No . . . is. . . .'

Consider

> **10** Roses blossom in the summer.

Unless more information is provided here, (10) should be read as saying 'All roses blossom in the summer,' which illustrates the pattern 'All A are B.'

To support (10) with an enumerative induction, we may adopt one or the other of two equivalent strategies. First, offer a single premise to the effect that, for example, many roses have been observed to blossom in the summer. That would be a non-universal generalization:

> A non-universal generalization
> - is a statement asserting that some, perhaps many, of the members of a class have (don't have) a certain feature.
> - may be expressed by a great number of different patterns of sentence. Some standard patterns are 'Most . . . are . . . ,' 'A few . . . are . . . ,' 'Many . . . are . . . ,' 'n percent of . . . are . . . ' (where n percent is less than 100 percent), 'Some . . . are . . . ,' and 'Some . . . are not. . . .'

According to this strategy, the argument would run:

> **11** 1. Many roses have been observed to blossom in the summer.
>   2. All roses blossom in the summer.

Why is conclusion 2 a universal generalization? Because it asserts that *all* things of a certain kind (roses) have a certain feature (blossoming in the summer). Here are other such generalizations common in science and everyday life:

> **12** Every metal expands when heated.
> **13** Any potato has vitamin C.
> **14** Each body falls with constant acceleration.
> **15** All bodies attract each other in proportion to their masses and in inverse proportion to the square of the distance between them.
> **16** No emeralds are blue.
> **17** No seawater quenches thirst.
> **18** No mules are fertile.

Following the above strategy, we could attempt to support these generalizations by enumerative induction. Clearly, scientists could not have observed all metals in order to conclude (12), so the premise for (12) must be a non-universal generalization saying, for example, that many metals so far observed expand when heated. Similar enumerative inductions support the other universal generalizations in our list. Each such enumerative induction would have a premise that would be a non-universal generalization to the effect that things of the relevant kind have (12 through 15) or do not have (16 through 18) a certain feature.

An alternative, yet equivalent, strategy to support these universal generalizations by enumerative induction would have specific statements as premises.

A specific statement is a statement about an *individual* thing or person. For example: 'Benjamin Franklin founded the University of Pennsylvania,' 'That oak is infested,' 'Mary's cap is waterproof,' and 'The UN is in session.'

If we wish to use this strategy to support the conclusion that roses blossom in the summer, our argument may run:

19 1. Rose 1 has been observed to blossom in the summer.
    2. Rose 2 has been observed to blossom in the summer.
    3. Rose 3 has been observed to blossom in the summer. . .
    4. Rose number *n,* has been observed to blossom in the summer.
    5. All roses blossom in the summer.

When *n* is a large number (say, billions) of individual roses, the universal generalization in conclusion 5 would be supported by the argument's premises, each of which is a specific statement about individual roses found to blossom in the summer. This strategy is equivalent to the one used in (11) above, given that (19)'s premises spell out what (11)'s premise summarizes. Similar to (11) is

20 1. Every raven so far observed has been black.
    2. Ravens are black.

Argument (20)'s conclusion is a universal generalization ascribing a certain feature (blackness) to all ravens. Like other inductive arguments, this makes an inferential leap: from a number of ravens having a certain feature, it draws the conclusion that all ravens have that feature. Its premise, if true, supports the claim that a great number of ravens have that feature, but it does not guarantee that all ravens do. After all, nobody can observe all past, present, and future ravens! Argument (20)'s conclusion, then, goes beyond the information given in its premise. Inductions of this sort run along the lines of (21).

21 1. A number, *n,* of A have been observed to be *B*
    2. All A are B

Clearly, any argument with this form could have a true premise and a false conclusion, since it is always possible that some unobserved A lacks the feature of being a B. This could happen even in cases where *n* turns out to be a very large number. Note that if *n* were taken to involve all cases, the argument would be deductive.

Furthermore, notice that (20)'s hypothesis is a universal generalization, namely,

22 All ravens are black.

Therefore a single raven that is observed not to be black would be a counterexample proving (22) false. Similarly, were a single whale observed to be a cold-blooded animal, that would be a counterexample to

23 No whale is a cold-blooded animal.

Here the rule is

> Any exception to the conclusion of an enumerative induction has the status of a counterexample. That is, it proves that conclusion false.

Another familiar use of enumerative induction is to predict the future and to explain the past—as, for example, when someone reasons,

24 1. In the past, most animal species have survived by adaptation.
    2. All animal species will continue to survive by adaptation.

(24)'s conclusion is a universal generalization about future events that naturalists might defend by pointing out that for millions of years in the past many species of animals have survived by adaptation. That premise is a non-universal generalization, which can be based only on cases of species that have been observed to survive by adaptation. At the same time, species found not to have survived by adaptation would be counterexamples, in light of which our naturalists would be forced to drop the universal generalization in the conclusion. The bottom line is this:

> Counterexamples have consequences for scientific laws such as those of physics and biology, which are universal generalizations such as Galileo's law of free fall and Newton's law of gravitation (14 and 15 above). If a counterexample to any such generalization is found, then the scientific theory built on it is in need of revision.

Statistical Syllogism

A statistical syllogism is an inductive argument whereby a certain feature is ascribed to a case or cases on the basis of their being subsumed within a larger class of things, some of which, perhaps many, have the ascribed feature. For example,

25 1. Most surgeons carry malpractice insurance.
    2. Dr. Hagopian is a surgeon.
    3. Dr. Hagopian carries malpractice insurance.

(25) meets our definition of statistical syllogism. It has a non-universal generalization in premise 1 that ascribes a feature to some surgeons, and then it ascribes it also to Dr. Hagopian, on the basis of his being part of the class of surgeons. Its form is

25' 1. Most *A* are *B*
2. *h* is an *A*
3. *h* is a *B*

(25') should not be confused with the following deductive form:

26 1. All *A* are *B*
2. *h* is an *A*
3. *h* is a *B*

In a statistical syllogism, the crucial generalization in its premises must be non-universal, since otherwise the argument would be deductive rather than inductive. So keep in mind that in this sort of argument, there is always one premise that is a non-universal generalization, which may be expressed as

27 n percent of *A* are *B*

To count as inductive, in the argument containing this generalization 'n' has to be a number smaller than '100.' For example,

28 1. 72 percent of *A* are *B*
2. *m* is an *A*
3. *m* is a *B*

Like other inductive arguments, statistical syllogisms are common, both in ordinary and scientific reasoning. Their premises could be put at the service of explaining the past, as in

29 1. Most famous battles involved careful strategy.
2. Trafalgar was a famous battle.
3. Trafalgar involved careful strategy.

Or predicting the future, as in

30 1. 80 percent of police officers have antiterrorism training.
2. Michael will be a police officer.
3. Michael will have antiterrorism training.

The size of the non-universal generalization in a statistical syllogism matters for the argument's reliability: the greater the size, the more reliable the argument (more on this in section 3). For now, let's recall the crucial distinction between universal and non-universal generalizations.

> **BOX 2 ■ UNIVERSAL AND NON-UNIVERSAL GENERALIZATIONS**
>
> 1. A *universal generalization* involves all members of a certain class. It may be expressed by linguistic devices such as 'all' and 'no.'
> 2. A non-universal generalization involves only some members of a certain class. It may be expressed by 'some,' 'most,' 'many,' 'a few,' 'lots of,' 'n percent,' etc.

Causal Argument

It is a matter of well-documented observation that whenever a flame comes in contact with combustible substances, this is invariably followed by a fire. Given that evidence, we may safely conclude that Jim lighting a match this morning near the gas caused the fire that erupted immediately after. Here we reason from an observed effect (the fire) to a possible cause that we may, or may not, have observed (Jim lighting a match this morning near the gas). Parallel causal reasoning is at work when only the effects of an event have been observed and we infer from them their likely cause—as is not uncommon in crime investigations. Other times, facts have been observed pertaining to the cause of an event and these are then used in causal reasoning to predict possible effects, as in recent medical research that has revealed certain genes likely to be responsible for a type of mental illness manifesting as a social pathology. Here the genes appear to be a likely cause, in the sense that their presence is necessary (though not sufficient) for developing the social pathology. After all, not everyone with the genes will develop the illness: other factors, including environmental ones, would also be needed. In the explosion case, Jim's lighting of a match this morning near the gas was sufficient but not necessary for the explosion to occur: in the described circumstances, an action of that sort would invariably cause an explosion, but other types of action could also cause an explosion.

Knowledge of the causal relations between events is instrumentally valuable for us, because the control of nature is essential for human survival and flourishing. From a prudential point of view, we wish to promote those causes that have good effects while preventing those that have bad effects. Knowing that droughts were causally related to failed crops spurred the early development of irrigation systems by engineers, and farmers in antiquity. Similarly, our prospect of learning about causal connections between certain microorganisms and illnesses has triggered medical research that has resulted in our being able to prevent or contain infections and deadly diseases such as malaria and polio. So it is not an exaggeration to say that much of our everyday lives and scientific progress depend greatly on our being able to make causal connections between things and events.

We take some phenomena (things and occurrences of things) to be the effects or results of other phenomena, which are their causes, and reason accordingly, ascribing causal relationships to new phenomena that we encounter. Reasoning about how certain events stand in cause/effect relations with other events takes the form of causal arguments:

> A causal argument makes the claim that two or more things or events are causally related in any of these ways:
>
> 1. Y results from Z.
> 2. Y causes Z.
> 3. Y and Z are the cause or the effect of another thing X.

The reasoning underwriting causal arguments is fundamental to both commonsense and scientific knowledge. It is at work when, if presented with some empirical evidence of state of affairs E, we set out to discover how E came to be. This requires determining which state of affairs C is linked to E—as its sufficient cause, its necessary cause, or its necessary and sufficient cause— for the word 'cause' can be used to mean a number of different relationships. When used to talk about a phenomenon that is always enough to bring about a certain outcome all by itself, it means *sufficient cause*, as illustrated by this causal argument:

32   1. There was a power blackout in my neighborhood yesterday.
     2. My computer malfunctioned yesterday.
     3. Yesterday's blackout was responsible for the malfunctioning of my computer.

In (32), yesterday's blackout is taken to be the sufficient cause of the malfunctioning of the computer—just as overcooking one's dinner is sufficient for spoiling it. But the blackout isn't a necessary cause of the computer malfunctioning, because in the absence of a power blackout, the computer could still malfunction because of some other condition, such as rough handling, obstructed ventilation, and defective parts.

Other times, an event C is the *necessary cause* of another event E, which is to say that E cannot occur in the absence of C. Since *AIDS* cannot occur in the absence of *HIV*, this is the sense of 'cause' at work in the claim that

33 *HIV* causes *AIDS*.

There is also a sense of 'cause' that denotes a condition that is both necessary and sufficient to bring about a certain effect: that would be the case of a cause that's enough all by itself to cause something to happen and also necessary, in the sense that the effect could not have happened without it—as when we say that

34 Having the genome of a cat causes Fluffy the kitten to grow up to be a cat.

Here, having a certain genetic code is both a necessary cause for the animal to be a cat (rather than, say, a monkey) and a sufficient cause, since it will always produce the same result.

Note, however, that causal claims could be a generalization such as (33), or a particular statement such as (34) and the conclusion of (32). But when arguers make particular causal claims, their claims often rest on implicit generalizations. In the case of (32), it's a missing premise that could be reconstructed as being either a universal or a non-universal generalization. If the former, the argument would be deductive; if the latter, inductive. As an inductive argument, it could run this way:

32' 1. Power blackouts are often the cause of computer malfunctions.
     2. There was a power blackout in my neighborhood yesterday.
     3. My computer malfunctioned yesterday.
     4. Yesterday's blackout was responsible for my computer's malfunction.

(32')'s conclusion has the status of a hypothesis, which would be well supported, provided its premises are true. Because, as reconstructed here, (32')'s premises don't guarantee its conclusion, the argument is inductive.

BOX 3 ■ THREE MEANINGS OF 'CAUSE'

1. *Sufficient cause:* C is a sufficient cause of E if and only if C always produces E.
2. *Necessary cause:* C is a necessary cause of E if and only if E cannot occur in the absence of C.
3. *Necessary and sufficient cause:* C is a necessary and sufficient cause of E if and only if C always is the sole cause of E.

The methods of agreement and difference, and of concomitant variation. In his *System of Logic* (1843), John Stuart Mill (1806–1873) made use of ordinary intuitions in an attempt to establish generalizations about cause-and-effect relations. According to those intuitions, whenever something occurs, it is often possible to narrow the range of acceptable hypotheses about its likely cause—or about its effect—by eliminating plainly irrelevant factors until at last we find the hypothesis most likely to be the actual cause (or effect) of the occurrence. Of the five methods to establish generalizations about causal relationships proposed by Mill, we'll here consider two: the so-called *method of agreement and difference* and the *method of concomitant variation.*

The method of agreement and difference   The method of agreement and difference rests on the following basic principles:

1. Agreement: What different occurrences of a certain phenomenon have in common is probably its cause.
2. Difference: Factors that are present only when some observed phenomenon occurs are probably its cause.

Suppose a coach wants to find out why Mick, Jim, and Ted, three of his best players, often perform poorly on Friday afternoons. After collecting some data about what each player does before the game, the coach reasons along these lines:

35 1. Mick, Jim, and Ted have been performing poorly on Friday afternoons.
  2. Going to late parties on Thursday is the one and only thing that all three do when and only when they perform poorly.
  3. Going to late parties on Thursday likely causes their poor game performance.

The coach's reasoning here illustrates 'agreement,' since it runs roughly alone these lines:

36 1. X has occurred several times.
  2. Y is the one and only other thing that precedes all occurrences of X.
  3. Y causes X.

But to make a more precise cause-effect claim, the coach should also use the method of difference: first, he should compare the players' performance when they've been going to late parties and when they haven't, and then, if they perform poorly only in the former cases, he should conclude that that difference also points to late-evening party-going as the likely cause of their poor performance. In fact, although the methods of agreement and difference are independent, they are usually employed jointly for the sake of greater precision.

The method of concomitant variation The method of concomitant variation rests on the following principles:

1. When variations of one sort are highly correlated with variations of another, one is likely to be the cause of the other, or they may both be caused by something else.
2. When variations in one phenomenon are highly correlated with variations in another phenomenon, one of the two is likely to be the cause of the other, or they may both be caused by some third factor.

Suppose now someone asks the coach why being fit matters for the members of a team. He may safely invoke empirical evidence to argue that there is a causal relationship between a player's being fit and his or her performance:

37 1. The more fit the players are, the better their performance.
    2. Probably, being fit causes their better performance, or their better performance causes their being fit, or something else causes both their better performance and their being fit.

The underlying reasoning is roughly

38 1. X varies in a certain way if and only if Y varies in a certain way.
    2. Y causes X, or X causes Y, or some Z causes both X and Y.

Analogy

Analogy is a type of inductive argument whereby a certain conclusion about individuals, qualities, or classes is drawn on the basis of some similarities with other individuals, qualities, or classes. Here is an example of an analogy whose conclusion about a certain vehicle rests on this vehicle having some things in common with other similar vehicles:

39 1. Mary's vehicle, a 2007 SUV, is expensive to run.
    2. Jane's vehicle is a 2007 SUV and is expensive to run.
    3. Simon's vehicle is a 2007 SUV and is expensive to run.
    4. Peter's vehicle is a 2007 SUV.
    5. Peter's vehicle is expensive to run.

In (39), the arguer attempts to make her conclusion reasonable by analogy: Peter's vehicle shares two features with Mary's, Jane's, and Simon's: being a 2007 model and an SUV. This provides some reason to think that it may also have in common a third feature, that of being expensive to run. Let 'm,' 'j,' 's,' and 'p' stand, respectively, for Mary's vehicle, Jane's vehicle, Simon's vehicle, and Peter's vehicle; and A, B, and C for the ascribed features: being a 2007 model, being an SUV, and being expensive to run. Then (39)'s pattern is

39' 1. m is A, B, and C
2. j is A, B, and C
3. s is A, B, and C
4. p is A and B
5. p is C

Any argument along these lines would fall short of being deductive (i.e., of entailing its conclusion). Yet if its premises are true, they might provide good evidence for it. Analogies can make their conclusions plausible, provided that they meet the standards for good inductive arguments discussed below. Among the specific factors that matter for the success of analogies are those presented in Box 4.

Now consider

40 Extensive research on polar bears and hippos has shown that they have a great number of relevant features in common with large animals that live in the wild. These animals are also listed as endangered species. So polar bears and hippos might disappear.

The pattern of reasoning underlying this analogy is

> 1. Polar bears and hippos have a number of relevant things in common with species x, y, and z.
> 2. Species x, y, and z also have feature f (being an endangered species).
> 3. Polar bears and hippos probably have feature f.

If polar bears and hippos do in fact share a number of features with threatened species, and such features are truly relevant to the conclusion of this argument, then (40) can be said to succeed in rendering its conclusion plausible.

BOX 4 ■ ANALOGY

Whether an analogy succeeds or not depends on

1. The number of things and the number of features held to be analogous.

   ■ Greater numbers here would make an analogy stronger.

2. The degree of similarities and dissimilarities among those things.

   ■ More of the former and less of the latter would make an analogy stronger.

3. The relevance of ascribed features to the hypothesis.

   ■ Greater relevance would make an analogy stronger.

4. The boldness of the hypothesis with respect to the evidence.

   ■ Modesty in the hypothesis would make an analogy stronger.

Exercises

I. Review Questions

1. Discuss three features of inductive argument that distinguish them from deductive arguments.
2. What's the problem with asserting the premises of an inductive argument while denying its conclusion?
3. Why are the premises and conclusion of an inductive argument called 'evidence' and 'hypothesis', respectively?
4. What does it mean to say that a hypothesis is 'plausible'?
5. What is an enumerative induction?
6. What's the difference between universal and non-universal generalizations? How can a universal generalization be proved false?
7. Describe the structure of a statistical syllogism.
8. Describe the structure of a causal argument.
9. Why is the word 'cause' ambiguous?
10. Describe the structure of an analogy.

II. Determine whether the following arguments are deductive or inductive.

1. Many whales observed in this region are white mammals. Therefore, any whale in this region is a white mammal.

   SAMPLE ANSWER: Inductive argument

2. Triangles have exactly three internal angles. Rectangles have exactly four internal angles. Therefore, rectangles are not triangles.

*3. If all magnolias have a scent, then the magnolias in the vase have a scent. But they don't. It follows that it isn't true that all magnolias have a scent.

4. Buying a house is a good investment. After all, that's exactly what statistics have shown for the last ten years.

5. All samples of river water so far tested have been polluted. Thus all river water is polluted.

*6. The Crusades were bloody, for most medieval wars were bloody, and the Crusades were medieval wars.

7. Surely the Earth is not flat. If it were flat, then Magellan could not have circumnavigated it. But he did!

8. Jane is a dentist and has clean teeth. Bruce is a dentist and has clean teeth. Therefore, all dentists have clean teeth.

*9. Cars are mechanical devices. No mechanical devices are easy to fix. Thus no car is easy to fix.

10. Many medical doctors care about their patients. Tom is a medical doctor. Thus he cares about his patients.

11. Mary doesn't like being denied a salary increase, for she is a state worker, and no state worker likes that.

*12. To be an ophthalmologist is to be an eye specialist MD. My new neighbors are eye specialist MDs, so they are ophthalmologists.

13. Children riding in school buses always arrive punctually. Jill rides in a school bus. Therefore, Jill always arrives punctually.

14. Carl is divorced. Therefore, Carl was married.

*15. White feathers in pigeons are likely to be an adaptation against predators, for such feathers have been observed to distract falcons and other attackers in the air.

III. For each of the arguments in the previous exercise that is inductive, make it deductive by modifying premises and conclusion as needed. Add premises if necessary.

SAMPLE ANSWER: 1. All whales observed in this region are white mammals.
Therefore, no whale observed in this region has not been a white mammal.

IV. For each of the following inductive arguments, determine whether it is an enumerative induction, an analogy, a statistical syllogism, or a causal argument.

1. Dinosaurs were warm-blooded animals, since the fossil record supports that hypothesis by showing a large number of dinosaurs in heat-conserving poses typical of such animals.

SAMPLE ANSWER: Enumerative induction

*2. Of a group of 250 seventh graders, only those who received fruits rich in zinc performed well in cognitive tasks. Thus zinc may be good for boosting cognitive acuity.

3. People who drink a warm glass of milk before going to bed always sleep well. Therefore, drinking a warm glass of milk before going to bed helps a person sleep well.

4. Infants like baby talk. This is supported by recent experiments on 2,000 infants led by cognitive psychologists at Columbia University.

*5. The earth is a planet with carbon-based life. The three elements required for carbon-based life are carbon, liquid water, and energy. These elements appear to be, or to have been, present in Mars, which is also a planet. This suggests that Mars could have had carbon-based life.

6. 84 percent of the students quit smoking after seeing in health class films of smokers' blackened lungs. Therefore, visually demonstrating how a drug affects one's body is conducive to avoidance of that drug.

7. Like you or me, doctors are human beings. Hence, they are also exposed to ordinary 'wear and tear,' as well as to common agents that cause ailments.

*8. The Orinoco crocodile belongs to the species Crocodylia and is critically endangered. The Chinese alligator belongs to the species Crocodylia and is critically endangered. The Philippine crocodile belongs to the species Crocodylia and is critically endangered. The Nile crocodile belongs to the species Crocodylia. It follows that the Nile crocodile is critically endangered.

*9. Dalinsky's Drugstore is a small business and therefore affected by the current increase in household costs. After all, most small businesses are wrestling with such costs.

10. Appearances are misleading. For example, the landscape looks lifeless in Atacama, a Chilean desert thought to be lifeless until very recently. But satellite images have identified geological formations

there that contain minerals similar to those in the Sahara Desert, where microbes sometimes nestle. Thus, make no mistake: microbes may nestle in the Atacama Desert.

*11. People who have a high percentage of folic acid in their diets also have a lower incidence of Alzheimer's disease. But these are people who generally have more healthy habits. Thus either a high percentage of dietary folic acid causes a lower incidence of Alzheimer's disease, or having healthy habits causes both.

12. During repeated experiments of consumption of high-flavonoid cocoa, researchers measured significant improvements in blood flow and the function of endothelial cells. They concluded that high-flavonoid cocoa may help blood pressure and blood flow.—*New York Times*, "Science Times," February 17, 2004.

13. Smaller, more fuel-efficient vehicles are now quite popular among many college students. My roommate is about to buy a vehicle. I predict that he'll buy a small, fuel-efficient car.

*14. Anyone wishing to be a space tourist will have to pay $100 million. For, according to my records, each space tourist has recently paid $100 million for traveling in space.

15. Russia's Olympic champion Natalya Sadova has been banned for two years after testing positive for an anabolic substance. A great number of athletes who are banned for illegal-substance consumption never regain popular support. Therefore, Natalya Sadova is unlikely to regain popular support.

V. YOUR OWN THINKING LAB

1. Provide the following extended argument: an enumerative induction whose conclusion is a premise in a deductive argument used to draw another conclusion.

2. Explain the reasoning underwriting Mill's methods of agreement and difference and of concomitant variation. Support your explanation with two arguments illustrating each of these methods.

3. Write an inductive generalization and imagine what would be a counterexample to it. Explain how your counterexample would undermine the generalization.

6.3 Evaluating Inductive Arguments

Inductive Reliability

Suppose we try to reconstruct many of the above arguments as if they were deductive, and then proceed to evaluate them according to deductive standards, such as validity, soundness, and cogency. That would plainly conflict with charity and faithfulness, since no such argument could pass that evaluation. But some of the arguments seem to give support for their conclusions provided that their premises are true. This suggests that to assess inductive arguments, we need standards other than deductive ones. Chief among the needed standards is *reliability*, which concerns the form of an inductive argument:

> An inductive argument is <u>reliable</u> if and only if its form is such that, if its premises were true, it would be reasonable to accept its conclusion as true.

When an inductive argument is reliable, it has a form that makes its conclusion *plausible* provided that its premises are true. Consider

41 1. 99 percent of guitar players also play other musical instruments.
    2. Phong is a guitar player.
    ―――――――――――――――――――――――――
    3. Phong also plays other musical instruments.

This inductive argument seems pretty reliable: its form is such that, if its premises were true, its conclusion would be plausible. Compare (42), which is itself less reliable than (41) but more reliable than (43):

42 1. 59 percent of guitar players also play other musical instruments.
    2. Phong is a guitar player.
    ―――――――――――――――――――――――――
    3. Phong also plays other musical instruments.

43 1. 39 percent of guitar players also play other musical instruments.
    2. Phong is a guitar player.
    ―――――――――――――――――――――――――
    3. Phong also plays other musical instruments.

Inductive reliability is, then, a matter of degree. An inductive argument of (44)'s form is more reliable than (45):

44 1. 59 percent of A are B
    2. p is an A
    3. p is a B

45 1. 39 percent of A are B
    2. p is an A
    3. p is a B

The cash value of inductive reliability for logical thinkers can be better appreciated by comparing it to the cash value of deductive validity. Each of these concerns argument form, as well as the support an argument's premises may give its conclusion, provided they are true. In the case of a valid argument, if its premises are true, its conclusion *must* be true. In that of a reliable argument, if its premises are true, its conclusion is likely to be true. As we saw in Chapter 5, a valid deductive argument is truth-preserving. By contrast, a reliable inductive argument is not. Even so, inductive reliability is one of the two desirable features that ordinary and scientific arguments should have.

Inductive Strength

Strength is another desirable feature for inductive arguments; thus we may use it to evaluate such arguments. An inductive argument is strong just in case it meets the conditions listed in Box 5.

BOX 5 ■ STRONG INDUCTIVE ARGUMENT

An inductive argument is strong if and only if
1. It is reliable.
2. It has all true premises.

When an inductive argument is strong, it is reasonable to accept its conclusion. That is, it is reasonable to think that the conclusion is true. We may think of this standard in terms of competition: given the structure of an inductive argument, rival conclusions are always logically possible. Imagine a case where a professor in Biology 100 has just received an email from one of her new students, whose name is Robin Mackenzie. She is trying to decide whether she should begin her reply, 'Dear Mr. Mackenzie' or 'Dear Ms. Mackenzie.' Let's assume that it is true that 80 percent of the students in Biology 100 are women and reason through the steps of this inductive argument:

46   1. 80 percent of the students in Biology 100 are women.
    2. Robin is a student in Biology 100.
    3. Robin is a woman.

Since (46) is an inductive argument, the conclusion, statement 3, may in fact fail to be true, even if both premises are true. After all, a person named 'Robin' could be a man. Even so, given the evidence provided by the premises, it seems that conclusion 3 is more plausible than the other competing hypothesis (i.e., that Robin is a man). But imagine a different scenario: suppose that we knew that 80 percent of the students in Biology 100 were men. Then, among then the competing hypotheses, the conclusion that is most likely to be true on the basis of that information is that Robin is a man. The argument now is

47   1. 80 percent of the students in Biology 100 are men.
    2. Robin is a student in Biology 100.
    3. Robin is a man.

We may alternatively define inductive strength in this way:

> An inductive argument is *strong* if and only if its hypothesis is the one that has the greatest probability of being true on the basis of the evidence.

In the same way that inductive reliability can be contrasted with deductive validity, inductive strength can be contrasted with deductive soundness. For one thing, the latter does not come in degrees, since it depends on validity and truth, neither of which is itself a matter of degree (there's no such thing as a 'sort of true' premise or a 'sort of valid' argument). Hence, just as any given deductive argument is either valid or invalid, so, too, it's either sound or unsound. On the other hand, inductive strength does come in degrees, for it depends in part on reliability, which is a matter of degree. What about the cash value of these standards? When an argument is deductively sound, its conclusion is true—and must be accepted by any logical thinker who recognizes the argument's soundness. But the conclusion of any inductively strong argument can be, at most, probably true—and thus reasonable to accept by a logical thinker who recognizes the argument's strength. For each of the two criteria by which we assess inductive arguments, then, we may summarize its cash value as follows:

> **Inductive Reliability's Cash Value**
>
> ■ If an argument has a good share of reliability, then it would be reasonable to accept its conclusion, provided that its premises are true.
>
> **Inductive Strength's Cash Value**
>
> ■ If an argument has a good share of inductive strength, then it's reasonable to accept its conclusion, since it has a reliable form and its premises are true.

What, then, of inductive arguments that fail by one or the other of these two criteria? No such argument could provide good reasons for their conclusions.

Exercises

VI. Review Questions

1. What are the two standards for evaluating an inductive argument? Define each.
2. Does inductive reliability depend on the form of an argument? What about strength?
3. What question should we ask to determine whether an inductive argument is reliable?
4. Assuming that an inductive argument is reliable, when would it be strong?
5. Does the cash value of deductive validity differ from that of inductive reliability? Explain.
6. What factors are relevant to determining whether an enumerative induction is reliable?
7. What factors are relevant to determining whether an enumerative induction is strong or weak?
8. What factors are relevant to determining whether an analogy is reliable?

VII. Identify whether the arguments below are enumerative inductions, analogies, causal arguments, or statistical syllogisms, and determine which are reliable and which are not. For any argument whose reliability cannot be determined, explain why not.

1. There is consensus among experts that heavy drinking is linked to liver disease. Therefore, heavy drinking leads to liver disease.

   SAMPLE ANSWER: Causal argument, reliable

2. Millions of fish so far observed have all been cold-blooded animals. Thus all fish are cold-blooded animals.

*3. Most South American coffee beans are dark. Brazilian coffee beans are South American coffee beans. Hence, Brazilian coffee beans are dark.

4. Nancy lives downtown and pays a high rent. Bob lives downtown and pays a high rent. Pam pays a high rent. Thus Pam probably lives downtown.

5. 40 percent of college students sleep less than eight hours a day. Peter is a college student. Therefore, Peter sleeps less than eight hours a day.

*6. Every pizza eater I have met liked mozzarella. Thus pizza eaters like mozzarella.

7. Betty's pet is carnivorous, and so are Lois's, Brenda's, and John's. It follows that all pets are carnivorous.

8. Senegal is an African nation and has a forest. Nigeria is an African nation and has a forest. Since Egypt is also an African nation, it probably has a forest.

*9. Caffeine is related to poor memory. All recent studies have shown that people can improve their memory by reducing their daily consumption of caffeinated drinks.

10. Among families that have lived in Spring Valley for more than ten years, nearly 90 percent say they like it there. My family will soon move to Spring Valley. So my family will like it there, too.

11. Since their discovery, microorganisms have been observed to be present in all infections. Thus microorganisms are responsible for infections.

*12. Mike sells junk food, for he owns a fast-food restaurant, and that's what most fast-food restaurants sell.

13. Frank Sinatra sang in a 1950s movie wearing a tuxedo. Sammy Davis Jr., Peter Lawford, and Joey Bishop were all in tuxedos in that movie with Frank, and they made up 90 percent of the male actors cast in it. Since Dean Martin also sang in the same movie, he must have worn a tuxedo.

14. From 1951 to 2001, Sir Richard Doll documented the mortality rate of British male doctors born between 1900 and 1930. 81 percent of nonsmokers lived to at least age seventy, but only 58 percent of smokers lived to that age. Cigarette smoking stood out in Doll's findings as the only major factor distinguishing these two groups of doctors. Thus the shorter survival rate in the second group was a result of smoking.

*15. Chase is a bank and makes home-finance loans. Citibank is a bank and makes home-finance loans. Wells Fargo is a bank and also makes home-finance loans. This suggests that all U.S. banks make home finance loans.

16. After an extensive study involving major research universities, scientists discovered that poison ivy grew there at 2.5 times its normal rate when they pumped carbon dioxide through pipes into a pine forest. Their work suggests that atmospheric carbon dioxide is at least partially responsible for the higher growth rate of poison ivy.

17. I'll be accepted. Let's not forget that 98 percent of applicants with my qualifications get accepted.

*18. Given that Tina Turner is a famous singer and has an insurance policy on her legs, Queen Latifah probably has one, too. After all, she is also a famous singer.

19. 92 percent of computer owners cannot get through a typical day without using their computers. John is a computer owner; thus he probably cannot get through a typical day without using his computer.

20. It'll cool off soon, for these winds from the northeast are bringing a cool front.

*21. Wood can be made to rot by breaking down lignin, the compound that holds plant tissue together. This is in fact what fungus does to lignin. It has been proved that the molecular structure of lignin and construction glues is similar. Therefore, fungus can be used to break construction glues.

22. Most people with low levels of 'good' cholesterol are at risk of heart disease. John has low levels of 'good' cholesterol. Therefore, John is at risk of heart disease.

*23. According to a new study by naturalists, African elephants rarely climb hills. This is because climbing hills is too costly for them in terms of energy.

24. Some people aged between eighteen and forty say that cars have improved their lives. Betty and Miguel are both nineteen years old. Therefore, Betty and Miguel both probably think that cars have improved their lives.

*25. We all have to pay more for manufactured goods. The reason is well known: U.S. producers' prices are pushed up by the price of fuel.

VIII. The following inductive arguments are not reliable. In each, introduce any change needed to make it reliable. Use your imagination!

1. Chickens are birds, and they cannot fly. Ostriches are birds, and they cannot fly. Rheas are birds. Therefore, rheas cannot fly.

   SAMPLE ANSWER: Chickens are heavy birds adapted for ground motion and they cannot fly. Ostriches are heavy birds adapted for ground motion and they cannot fly. Rheas are heavy birds adapted for ground motion. Therefore, rheas cannot fly.

2. A few birds can fly. Sparrows are birds. Therefore, sparrows can fly.

3. Some fictional characters don't exist in real life. Since Cinderella is a fictional character, she doesn't exist in real life.

4. John F. Kennedy International Airport has tight security. Minneapolis/St. Paul is also an international airport. Hence, Minneapolis/St. Paul has tight security.

5. Sodium burns orange. After all, an experiment recently performed has shown that it does.

6. San Francisco is on the coast and it's a diverse, densely populated city in the United States. Miami is on the coast and it's a densely populated U.S. city. Therefore, Miami is diverse.

7. All muscles turn to fat when one stops working out. After all, that's what happened to me last year when I stopped working out due to a small accident.

8. Avoid scorpions: Some such creatures observed in the Arizona desert sting you with poison.

9. Mechanical problems have been found in a few Lockheed L-1011s. The plane I'm now riding in is an L-1011. So the plane I'm now riding in has mechanical problems.

10. Theodore Roosevelt ran for president without the endorsement of a major party and he was defeated. Since Ted Smith is running for president without the endorsement of a major party, he'll be defeated.

IX. Your Own Thinking Lab

1. Select the standard for deductive arguments that is more adequately contrasted with inductive strength, and discuss the cash value of each.

2. Select the standard for deductive arguments that is more adequately contrasted with inductive reliability, and discuss the cash value of each.

3. Propose a strong analogy and a weak analogy. Identify which is which and explain in either case what makes it strong or weak.

■ Writing Project

Find three commonly held superstitious beliefs about the causes of certain phenomena in ordinary life. For example, that a pregnant woman's being frightened by a bat will cause her baby to be "marked." Use those generalizations to construct inductive arguments about specific cases, whether real or imagined. For example, use premises such as 'Mary is pregnant, and she was frightened by bat on Tuesday.' Make the argument inductively reliable, but discuss why it is inductively weak.

■ Chapter Summary

Inductive Argument: Its premises, if true, could at most provide evidence for its conclusion, but could not entail it (since it is logically possible for the premises to be true, and the conclusion false). The conclusion of such an argument always has the status of a hypothesis.

Types of Inductive Argument:

1. **Enumerative induction.** From premises ascribing a feature to a number of things of a certain kind, the argument concludes that *all* things of that kind have that feature.

2. **Statistical syllogism.** The argument ascribes a certain feature to a particular case or class on the basis of its being subsumed within a larger class of things, some of which, perhaps many, are said to have the ascribed feature.

3. **Causal argument.** The argument has one or more premises that are offered to support the hypothesis that a certain event is causally related to another event.

4. **Analogy.** The argument draws a conclusion about an individual or class of individuals on the basis of some similarities that individual or class has with other individuals or classes.

Two of Mill's methods for identifying causes:

1. *Agreement and difference.* What different occurrences of a certain phenomenon have in common is probably its cause, and factors that are present only when some observed phenomenon occurs are probably its cause.

2. *Concomitant variation.* When variations in one phenomenon are highly correlated with those in another, one is likely the cause of the other, or both may be caused by some third factor.

Criteria for inductive argument evaluation:

1. *Reliability.* It concerns argument form and is in this respect comparable to validity for deductive arguments. In a reliable argument, the relation of premises to conclusion is such that if all the premises were true, then it would be reasonable to accept the conclusion.

2. *Strength* requires that the inductive argument be reliable and have all true premises (compare deductive soundness). When an argument is inductively strong, it's reasonable to accept its conclusion.

3. Inductive reliability and strength come in degree.

■ Key Words

Induction	Causal argument
Evidence	Inductive reliability
Hypothesis	Inductive strength
Analogy	Non-universal generalization
Enumerative induction	Universal generalization
Statistical syllogism	Method of agreement and difference
Inductive generalization	Method of concomitant variation

Informal Fallacies

CHAPTER 7

Some Ways an Argument Can Fail

This chapter introduces the notion of fallacy as illustrated in common patterns of defective argument and proposes a way of classifying twenty of the so-called informal fallacies. It then considers how inductive arguments can fail in at least five different ways, each of which illustrates one of the fallacies of the abuse of induction. Here you'll find:

- A classification of twenty informal fallacies.
- Discussion of the fallacy of hasty generalization.
- Discussion of the fallacy of weak analogy.
- Discussion of the fallacy of false cause and three of its common variations.
- Discussion of the fallacy of appeal to ignorance.
- Discussion of the fallacy of appeal to unqualified authority.
- Discussion of arguments that appeal to authority but are not fallacious.

7.1 What Is a Fallacy?

We've seen that arguments sometimes go wrong by failing to meet deductive standards, such as validity and soundness, or inductive ones, such as reliability and strength. We'll now look more closely at other types of defect that arguments may have. We can learn a lot about what good reasoning is by paying close attention to some clear examples of how reasoning can go wrong. Here we begin the study of fallacies, which are recurrent types of mistake in reasoning, affecting especially arguments and other relations among beliefs and concepts. In logical thinking, a fallacy is not simply an erroneous belief or a mistaken opinion—as, for example, when in an ordinary conversation someone speaks of the "fallacy that animals do not feel pain." Rather,

> A *fallacy* is a pattern of failed relation among concepts or beliefs. It affects any reasoning that exemplifies that pattern.

Fallacies are worth studying, not only because arguments that exemplify them fail to support their conclusions, but also because they could be misleading. They may affect an argument in subtle ways, so that it will seem okay when we first read or hear it. But the more we think about it, the more we will come to suspect that something has gone wrong. Fallacies are standardly classified as either formal or informal. A formal fallacy is a type of mistake made in arguments that may appear to be instances of a valid argument form but are in fact invalid in virtue of their form. As there are many types of such mistakes, there are many formal fallacies. They all have in common that they affect only deductive arguments whose forms superficially resemble valid forms of a logical system, such as propositional or categorical logic, but are actually invalid. When one such type of mistake is recurrent, it's usually given a name—we'll discuss some of these in Part IV. The informal fallacies, on the other hand, involve defects that arguments may have in virtue of instantiating some patterns of error in form or content. They may affect either deductive or inductive arguments, in all cases rendering them ill-suited to support their conclusions. For example, an argument committing an informal fallacy may show a pattern of failed relation between premises and conclusion that's not related to any specific argument form. It may also be affected by confusion in expression or content. Since there are many types of informal fallacy, our first step must be to provide some assistance in site navigation by offering a tentative classification.

BOX 1 ■ THE CASH VALUE OF AVOIDING FALLACIES

Logical thinking requires knowing *how to detect and avoid fallacies*—that is, knowing

- how to recognize when someone else's argument commits a fallacy (so as not to be fooled), and
- how to keep one's own arguments from committing them (so that they can support their conclusions).

7.2 Classification of Informal Fallacies

There is more than one way to classify the informal fallacies. But some fallacies are more important than others. In this book, you'll find a fairly standard list, which includes the following.

Fallacies of Failed Induction

1. hasty generalization
2. weak analogy
3. false cause
4. appeal to ignorance
5. appeal to unqualified authority

Fallacies of Presumption

6. begging the question
7. begging the question against
8. complex question
9. false alternatives
10. accident

Fallacies of Unclear Language

11. slippery slope
12. equivocation
13. amphiboly
14. confused predication

Fallacies of Relevance

15. appeal to pity
16. appeal to force
17. appeal to emotion
18. ad hominem
19. beside the point
20. straw man

We'll consider each of these subcategories one by one, looking carefully at each of the informal fallacies grouped under them. Since we've just finished (in Chapter 6) discussing inductive reasoning, let's look first at fallacies that may arise through the abuse of induction.

7.3 When Inductive Arguments Go Wrong

In this chapter, we consider five informal fallacies associated with the misuse of inductive reasoning, grouped as follows:

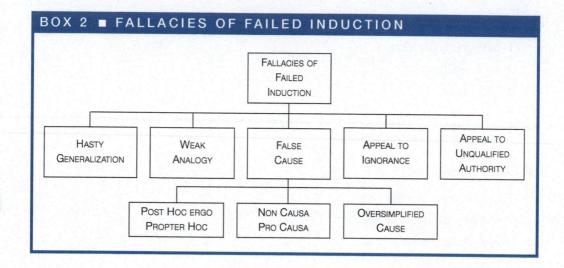

BOX 2 ■ FALLACIES OF FAILED INDUCTION

Hasty Generalization

The fallacy of hasty generalization may affect enumerative induction. Earlier we saw that an enumerative induction typically starts out with premises asserting that certain things have (or lack) some feature, and then draws a general conclusion about all things of that kind, to the effect that they have (or lack) that feature. The conclusion of the argument is a *universal generalization*, such as 'All leopards are carnivorous' and 'No leopard is carnivorous'. Thus an enumerative induction might go like this:

1.
   1. All leopards so far observed have been carnivorous
   2. All leopards are carnivorous

When a representative sample of leopards has been observed to be carnivorous, the conclusion of this inductive argument is well supported. Similarly, if we've observed a representative sample of leopards and found them all to be wild animals, we would be justified in drawing the general conclusion that leopards are wild animals on the basis of those observations. Our inductive argument would be,

2.
   1. Every leopard observed so far has been a wild animal
   2. All leopards are wild animals

But for any such inductive conclusion to be justified, the conditions listed in Box 3 must be met. If either of those two conditions, or both, is unfulfilled, then the argument commits the fallacy of hasty generalization and therefore fails.

> **Hasty generalization** is the mistake of trying to draw a conclusion about *all* things of a certain kind having a certain feature on the basis of having observed too small a sample of the things that allegedly have it, or a sample that is neither comprehensive nor randomly selected.

Suppose a team of naturalists were to observe 500,000 leopards, which all turn out to be wild animals. Yet they were all observed in India, during the first week of August, at a time when these animals were about to eat. The sample seems large enough, and the observers might therefore draw the conclusion that

3   All leopards are wild animals.

But they would be committing a hasty generalization, since leopards are also found in other parts of the world. And they are found at other times of the year, and in other situations. Clearly, the sample lacks comprehensiveness and randomness. In this case, argument (2) would fail to provide a good reason for its conclusion. On the other hand, suppose the naturalists directly observed patterns of wild behavior among leopards in all parts of the world where such animals are found, at different times of the year, and in many different situations. Yet the sample now consists of only thirty-seven leopards. Do the naturalists have better grounds for concluding (3) above? No, because although the comprehensiveness and randomness criteria are now met, the sample is too small. The charge of hasty generalization would similarly apply in this scenario.

It is, however, not only naturalists and other scientists who will need to beware of this sort of blunder. Logical thinkers will want to be on guard for hasty generalization in many everyday situations. Among these is the familiar mistake of stereotyping people. Suppose someone from the Midwest visits California for the first time. He becomes acquainted with three native Californians, and it happens that all three practice yoga. Imagine that, on his return home after his vacation, he tells his friends,

4   All Californians practice yoga.

If challenged, he would offer this argument:

5   1. I met Margaret Evans, who is Californian and practices yoga.
    2. I met Alisa Mendoza, who is Californian and practices yoga.
    3. I met Michael Yoshikawa, who is Californian and practices yoga.
    4. All Californians practice yoga.

The reasoning in (5) is again an instance of hasty generalization. Furthermore, it stereotypes Californians: on the basis of the sample described by the premises, the conclusion is simply unwarranted.

Now imagine a different scenario: suppose that an anthropologist visited California with the intention of studying the folkways of modern Californians. Suppose she went to southern California, northern California, the San Joaquin Valley, the Bay Area, all regions of the state, and met Californians from all walks of life, all social groups, all religions, all ethnic groups—from cities, suburbs, small towns, and rural areas. Suppose she talked to thousands, and suppose she discovered that all of these people practiced yoga! (This is unlikely, but suppose it happened.) Then it would not be a fallacy to draw conclusion 4: assuming the thoroughness and breadth of the study, this conclusion would be a reasonable outcome of a strong enumerative induction.

But notice how different this argument is from the earlier (5) above! A conclusion about all Californians based only on three instances is plainly unreasonable. It is a mockery of enumerative induction, and an offensive stereotype, to boot. To avoid stereotyping, together with the fallacy of hasty generalization that always underlies it, logical thinkers should keep in mind that

> No conclusion about a class or group could gather support from a sample that is either
> - too small, or
> - insufficiently comprehensive and random, or both.

BOX 3 ■ HOW TO AVOID HASTY GENERALIZATION

In evaluating an enumerative induction, keep in mind that it would avoid hasty generalization only if

- The sample on which its conclusion is based is large enough. In examples (1) and (2) above, the arguer has to have observed quite a few leopards.
- The sample is both comprehensive and randomly selected among the target group.
  In (1) and (2), the arguer has to have observed typical leopards, under a variety of different circumstances, from all the regions of the world where leopards are found.

Weak Analogy

Weak analogy is another way an inductive argument could fail to support its conclusion. The underlying pattern of reasoning in analogy is something like this:

6   1. f and j are alike in that both have features n.
      2. f also has feature $n + 1$.
      3. j has also feature $n + 1$.

But whether an argument of this form can succeed depends very much on whether it passes the test outlined in Box 4. If the test shows that $n + 1$ may be features that only f has, then the things thought to be analogous would actually be disanalogous and the argument would commit the fallacy of weak analogy, which we may summarize as follows:

> To succeed, an analogy must make reasonable that the things alleged to be alike in the premises are in fact analogous in ways relevant to its conclusion. Any failure to do so would count as a fallacy of **weak analogy**.

Imagine this scenario: there are two siblings, a boy five years old and his sister, who is thirteen. One evening it's little Johnny's bedtime, and his mother says to him, "Johnny, it's nine o'clock. Time for bed!" But Johnny replies, "You let Susie stay up late." Could Johnny rightfully claim unfair treatment here? His argument may be reconstructed as follows:

7   1. Susie and I are alike in a number of ways.
      2. Susie is not supposed to go to bed at 9:00 p.m.
      3. I'm not supposed to go to bed at 9:00 p.m.

This, however, is a weak analogy, since it takes for granted that Susie's situation and Johnny's are relevantly similar. Yet they are not. Although they live in the same house, attend the same school, and have the same parents, there is a feature relevant to this argument that they don't share: the same age. Johnny is only five years old, while Susie is thirteen. When it comes to staying up late, the mother may reasonably respond: What I allow for a thirteen-year-old differs from what I allow for a five-year-old. In this respect, the two cases are relevantly dissimilar; thus Johnny's argument is too weak an analogy to support its conclusion.

Of course, not all cases of weak analogy are as clear-cut as this, and often there is room for disagreement about whether a certain analogy is a fallacy at all. Some analogies are weak, but others are strong. Still others are borderline cases whose degree of strength or weakness is hard to assess. Moreover, analogy is one of the most common forms of argument in everyday reasoning. It's a form widely used in political rhetoric. Logical thinkers are advised to beware of attempts by politicians to treat certain analogies as obviously strong, when in fact they are debatable. Was the threat from Saddam Hussein's Iraq really analogous to that of Hitler's Germany? Is the Afghan War really analogous to the Vietnam War? When we think logically about current affairs, we will want to do careful research into the facts of the matter before we decide that an analogy is strong or weak. And obviously, this is the kind of argument on which much may depend in real-life decisions. When presented with an argument to the effect that j has feature D because j and f are similar in having some other features A, B, and C in common, and because f also has feature D, we should

Accept the analogy's conclusion only if

- having A, B, and C is relevant to also having D; and
- no available evidence suggests that f and j differ in some important respect relevant to whether or not both have D.

BOX 4 ■ HOW TO AVOID THE FALLACY OF WEAK ANALOGY

In evaluating an argument of (6)'s form, ask these questions:

- How large is number n? And are these n features relevant to the analogy's conclusion? (Here we want to know whether the premises provide an exhaustive account of the features relevant to the claim being made in the analogy's conclusion.)
- Are the things alleged, in the premises, to be alike really alike, in that they all have features n? (Here we want to know whether the similarities alleged in the premises are in fact present.)

False Cause

We saw earlier that a causal argument occurs when, on the basis of having observed two constantly conjoined events, it is inferred that they are causally related to each other or to some other event. Some such arguments can be inductively strong. If little Emily comes down with the chicken pox only a week after her sisters, Penelope and Bernice, had chicken pox, and if Emily has been in contact with Penelope and Bernice during that time, we may reasonably infer that she caught the chicken pox from her sisters. Given what we know about how infectious diseases are transmitted, this inductive conclusion seems supported. But not all causal arguments are strong. When either of the two types of error listed in Box 5 occurs, a fallacy of *false cause* has been committed.

> **False cause** is the mistake of arguing that there is a significant causal connection between two phenomena, when in fact the connection is either minimal or nonexistent.

BOX 5 ■ HOW TO AVOID THE FALLACY OF FALSE CAUSE

Causal arguments can fail in two basic ways:

- The argument concludes that there is a cause–effect connection between two phenomena where there is none at all.
- The argument mistakenly identifies some phenomenon as a sufficient (or determining) cause, when in fact it's only a contributory cause (i.e., one among many) of some observed effect.

Let's consider three different ways the fallacy of false cause may occur. One is:

> *Post hoc ergo propter hoc* ('after this, therefore because of this'):
> The fallacy of concluding that some earlier event is the cause of some later event, when the two are in fact not causally related.

The inclination to commit this fallacy in everyday life rests on the fact that, when we see two events constantly conjoined—so that they are always observed to occur together, first the one, then the other—it may eventually seem natural to assume that the earlier is the cause of the latter. But it is not difficult to imagine cases of precisely this sort where an imputation of causal connection would be absurd. Suppose we saw a bus passing the courthouse in the square just before the clock in the tower struck 9:00 a.m., and we then continued to see the exact same sequence of events day after day. Do we at last want to say that it's the bus's passing the courthouse that *causes* the clock to strike 9:00 a.m.? Of course not! And yet, in our experience, the two events have been constantly conjoined: the clock's striking has always been preceded by the bus's passing.

Clearly it would be preposterous to argue, in that case, that, from the evidence of constant conjunction between the bus's passing and the clock's striking 9:00, it follows that the former causes the latter. But equally absurd arguments are in fact sometimes heard in everyday life. Suppose that Hector and Barbara are not getting along, and one of their friends ventures to explain the source of the problem:

8 1. Hector was born under the sign of Capricorn.
    2. Barbara was born under Pisces.
    3. Capricorns and Pisces are not compatible.
    4. Their recent difficulties are owing to their having incompatible zodiac signs.

Argument (8) fails to support its conclusion, since it claims a causal connection for which the argument gives no good evidence—nor, in this case, should we expect good evidence to be forthcoming. After all, there's no good reason to think that configurations of stars and other celestial events really do affect the courses of our lives, and whatever the cause of this couple's troubles may be, it's probably traceable to something else. Argument (8) is a fallacy of *post hoc ergo propter hoc*, a form of false cause, for it assumes a cause–effect relation between being born on a day when celestial bodies have a certain configuration (which determines a certain zodiac sign) and subsequently growing up to develop certain personality traits. But there is no reason to think that these two sequential events are in fact causally related.

Another way false cause may occur is

> **Non causa pro causa** (roughly, what is not the cause is mistaken for the cause):
> A fallacy in which the error is not an imputation of causality in a temporal sequence of events (as in *post hoc ergo propter hoc*, where an earlier event is wrongly thought to be the cause of a later one), but rather the simple mistake of misidentifying some event contemporaneous with another as its cause, when in reality it's not.

One form of this error occurs when cause and effect are confused. An early nineteenth-century study of British agriculture noted that, of farmers surveyed, all the hard-working and industrious ones owned at least one cow, while all the lazy ones owned no cows. This led the researchers to conclude that productivity could be improved overall and habits of industry encouraged in the lazy farmers by simply giving them each of those farmers a cow!

Now, plainly there is something wrong in this reasoning. But what? It seems to rest on an extended argument along these lines:

9 1. All of the observed industrious farmers are cow owners.
   2. None of the observed lazy farmers is a cow owner.
   3. All and only cow-owning farmers are industrious.
   4. There is a positive correlation between cow-owning and industriousness.
   5. It's cow-owning that causes industrious farmers to be industrious.

If we grant, for the sake of discussion, that the sample of British farmers in the study was large enough, and that it was also comprehensive and randomly selected, then premises 1 and 2 support conclusion 3, and its restatement, conclusion 4. But 5's claim about cause and effect fails to be supported! It's *industriousness* that is probably *the cause of cow-owning*, and not the other way around. By confusing cause with effect, (9) commits *non causa pro causa*.

Finally, there is a version of false cause in which the source of the mistake is something rather different from what we've seen so far:

> **Oversimplified cause:**
> The fallacy of overstating the causal connection between two events that do have some causal link.

Suppose a vice president, campaigning for reelection, says,

10 1. At the beginning of this administration's term, the national economy was sluggish.
2. At the end of this administration's term, the national economy is booming.
3. White House economic policies do have an effect on the nation's economy.
4. The improvement in the economy is due to this administration's policies.

(10) fails to support its conclusion. Let's assume that the premises are true. Even then, the causal relation asserted in premise 3 is merely one of contributory cause—in effect, one causal factor among others—which amounts to a rather weak sense of 'cause.' But 4 grandly asserts as the conclusion something much more than that: namely, that the actions taken by the incumbent administration are a sufficient cause of the improvement in the economy. Now, surely this is an exaggeration. The campaigning vice president commits a fallacy of oversimplified cause by taking full credit for the nation's economic turnaround, thereby overstating the sense in which his administration's policies 'caused' it. Of course, many politicians are quite prepared to take credit for anything good that happens while they're in office. But proving that it was due entirely to their efforts is something else again. The logical thinker should be on guard for this and any of the other versions of false cause as representing different ways in which a causal argument may fail.

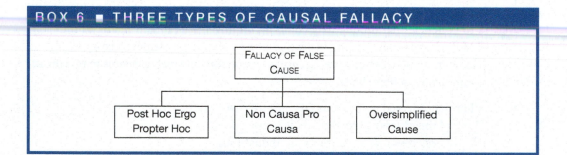

BOX 6 ■ THREE TYPES OF CAUSAL FALLACY

FALLACY OF FALSE CAUSE

Post Hoc Ergo Propter Hoc | Non Causa Pro Causa | Oversimplified Cause

Appeal to Ignorance

Another fallacy of failed induction is the appeal to ignorance (or *ad ignorantiam*): an argument that commits this fallacy concludes either that some statement is true because it has never been proved false, or that it is false because it has never been proved true. More generally,

> The fallacy of **appeal to ignorance** is committed by any argument in which the conclusion that something is (or isn't) the case is supposedly supported by appeal to the lack of evidence to the contrary.

Suppose someone reasons,

11 1. It has never been proved that God doesn't exist.
2. We can confidently assert that God exists.

(11) commits the fallacy of appeal to ignorance, but so does (12):

12 1. It has never been proved that God exists.
2. We can confidently assert that God doesn't exist.

Similarly, a believer in 'extrasensory perception' might argue,

13 1. No one has ever been able to prove that ESP doesn't exist.
2. It's reasonable to believe that there is ESP.

Clearly, the only reason offered by (13) to support its conclusion is the absence of contrary evidence. But from that premise, all that can be supported is that we *don't know what to say* about ESP! The conclusion given—that "it's reasonable to believe that there is ESP"—is far too strong to be supported by such a flimsy premise. Reasoning along similar lines could also be used to demonstrate the failure of (11) and (12).

BOX 7 ■ HOW TO AVOID THE FALLACY OF APPEAL TO IGNORANCE

- An argument whose premises merely invoke *the lack of evidence against* a certain conclusion commits the fallacy of appeal to ignorance. Such premises are bad reasons for the conclusion they attempt to support, and the argument therefore fails.
- Why? Because the mere *lack of negative evidence* does not in itself constitute positive evidence for anything! It justifies nothing more than an attitude of nonbelief (i.e., neutrality) toward the conclusion.

We must, however, add a note of caution. Suppose that the attempt to prove some claim has occasioned rigorous scientific investigation, and that these efforts have repeatedly turned up no evidence in support of the claim. Furthermore, suppose that the claim doesn't serve the purpose of explaining anything. In that case, it is not a fallacy to reject that claim out of hand. Here we have to proceed case by case. Consider the claim,

14 There are witches.

Although there is of course a long history of claims that witches exist, all efforts to prove those claims have so far failed for lack of evidence. Furthermore, the concept of a witch has no serious explanatory function in any scientific theory: the existence of witches doesn't explain anything that happens in the natural world. These considerations suggest that it is not a fallacy to conclude,

15 Probably there are no witches.

Inductive conclusions of this sort are rendered plausible by the absence of reliable empirical evidence after thorough investigation, and must not be confused with the fallacy of appeal to ignorance.

BOX 8 ■ TWO VERSIONS OF THE APPEAL TO IGNORANCE

APPEAL TO
IGNORANCE

| No one has shown that P is false Therefore, P is true. | No one has shown that P is true. Therefore, P is false. |

Appeal to Unqualified Authority

Another fallacy of weak induction that may prevent an argument from supporting its conclusion is the *appeal to unqualified authority,* also known as *ad verecundiam.*

> An argument commits the fallacy of **appeal to unqualified authority** when its premises attempt to support the conclusion by invoking an alleged authority that in fact either has no expertise relevant to the claim that's being made or presents a point of view at odds with the consensus of expert opinion on the topic.

When CNN talk-show host Larry King, the well-known television personality, proclaimed the health benefits of 'Ester-C,' a brand of vitamin C pills, King's many fans might well have been influenced in their beliefs about the nutritional properties of this vitamin supplement. Suppose that a viewer, inspired by King's message, argued,

16 Ester-C will help me to be healthier, because Larry King said so.

(16) is an appeal to unqualified authority. King, though undoubtedly an expert on popular celebrities in entertainment, sports, and politics, has no special expertise in the field of nutrition. He was merely exploiting his own immense popularity by serving as a television pitch man for a product. But note that in this case, it's not King committing the fallacy—it's the TV viewer speaking in (16), who wrongly thinks that the television personality's testimony supports the claim that a regimen of Ester-C pills will be conducive to health. The argument would not have committed this fallacy if she had instead cited a view for which there is consensus among experts on the topic of the commercial in support of the claim. Experts on this topic would be respected nutritionists and biomedical researchers. But whether such real-life experts would actually have shared King's on-camera enthusiasm for the product is not clear.

Now, notice another important point: not all appeals to authority are fallacious. Consider,

17 1. To prevent tooth decay, the American Dental Association recommends daily flossing.
2. Daily flossing is a good way to prevent tooth decay.

Although (17) appeals to an authority, the American Dental Association, in support of its claim about the benefits of daily flossing, it does *not* commit the fallacy under discussion. Since the ADA is a qualified authority on the topic of the conclusion (namely, dental health), that conclusion is supported by (17)'s premise. There are, then, perfectly legitimate uses of appeal to authority. When the expert opinion being cited is that of a person, group, or organization that is truly well informed on the topic of discussion, and therefore in a position to render an authoritative judgment about it, an argument from authority citing that source commits no fallacy. Indeed, *most of what we know* is known on the basis of testimony from sources we trust (certainly most of what we know about science, and *nearly all* of what we know about history, is known in this way). And although this trust is usually justified, it sometimes is not, for even the most respected experts are occasionally wrong. The truth of the conclusions of arguments that appeal to authority, then, is at best probable in some degree, never certain. Since expertise is itself something had by degree (some experts are bigger experts than others), the degree of support provided by premises appealing to authority is never conclusive. Such arguments are plainly inductive.

Even so, it is beyond denying that there are cases of uncontroversially bogus claims made by mountebanks and crackpots who present themselves as 'experts' when they are nothing of the kind. And it is the appeal to the testimony of such pseudo-authorities on behalf of a claim that is perhaps the most egregious form of the fallacy of appeal to unqualified authority. But an equally misleading form of the fallacy occurs when one cites, on behalf of a claim, the testimony of a genuine expert *on one side* of a question disputed among the experts themselves. That is, on a topic on which there is presently no consensus among experts, to treat *only one side's view* as ultimately authoritative by citing it in support of one's conclusion amounts to an appeal to unqualified authority. That Sir Arthur Eddington, an eminent physicist, believed 'paranormal' psychic phenomena deserved to be taken seriously as a topic of research gives us no good reason to believe it too, for Eddington's view on this subject does not represent the consensus of expert opinion among physicists, either in his day or in ours.

Yet another version of this fallacy occurs when we draw a conclusion based on the testimony of sources that are biased by virtue of self-interested involvement in the issue at hand. In a study reported recently in the *New York Times*, researchers attempted to determine whether the use of paper towels or air dryers was more efficient in drying hands quickly. But the research was sponsored by a paper company! Unsurprisingly, the researchers discovered that drying with paper towels was quicker. Now, imagine using that conclusion as the basis of a knowledge claim about the quickest way to dry your hands. It would plainly be an appeal to unqualified authority.

Thus appeals to authority are sometimes open to dispute—and may be fallacious—only when the invoked source is not authoritative on the subject of the claim an argument makes, or when a genuine authority's views are presented as representing expert consensus when in fact they do not. Consider

18 State University Law School is a great place to study law, because Uncle Jack says so.

This appeal would be fallacious unless Uncle Jack is an authority expressing a view well represented among experts on law schools. By contrast, the appeal to authority is not fallacious in

19 Many eminent jurists and law professors hold State University Law School in high regard.
   State University Law School is a great place to study law.

Argument (19) appeals to the view of experts on the topic of the conclusion, which is supported—provided that the premise is true. Since an appeal to authority is often needed for the justification of many claims, it is crucial that we distinguish between legitimate authorities who have expertise relevant to the claim being made and those who don't. The rule is:

> In evaluating an argument of the form, **A says P, therefore P,** check whether A is a genuine authority expressing a view on P that is well represented among the experts on P. If A is not, then the argument fails to support its conclusion and must be rejected.

For example, beliefs about history are more reasonable when based on the writings of reputable professional historians than when proposed by amateur ones. If we want to have well-founded beliefs about the French Revolution, the Ming Dynasty, or the presidency of Theodore Roosevelt, we should look to writers whose books are not "self-published" or published by vanity presses (where the authors pay to get their books into print). We should look for historians who are held in high regard by peers in their fields and whose work has been favorably reviewed. Although none of these criteria *guarantee* expertise, they make it vastly more likely. Similarly, for beliefs about nature, it goes without saying that respected journals in the natural sciences are generally dependable sources of information, unlike supermarket tabloids that describe miracle cures for cancer and 'evidence' of mental telepathy. For scientists, too, being the author of respected, mainstream scholarship and having the favorable regard of fellow scholars are usually the marks of credibility as genuine experts. For logical thinkers, then, an important competence is the ability to tell the difference between real experts and bogus ones, since it is often on that distinction that the difference between legitimate appeals to authority and the fallacy of appeal to unqualified authority turns.

BOX 9 ■ HOW TO AVOID FALLACIOUS APPEALS TO AUTHORITY

To avoid fallacious appeal to authority, keep in mind the way it differs from appeals to authority that aren't fallacious. The difference hinges on whether the authority cited in support of a claim

- does indeed have sufficient expertise in the relevant field; and
- is expressing a view well represented (perhaps the prevailing one) among experts on the topic.

Exercises

I. Review Questions

1. What is a fallacy?
2. What's the point of studying fallacies, as far as logical thinking is concerned?
3. What is the fallacy of hasty generalization?
4. Are all generalizations to be avoided?
5. What is stereotyping? And how is this related to hasty generalization?

6. What is the fallacy of weak analogy?

7. The fallacy of false cause has at least three different forms. Identify the kind of mistake each makes, and explain why they are all mistakes in causal reasoning.

8. What is the fallacy of appeal to ignorance?

9. When a fallacy of appeal to unqualified authority is committed, who commits it? Is it the arguer or the bogus authority?

10. What is the difference between the legitimate use of appeal to authority and the fallacy of appeal to unqualified authority?

II. Each of the following arguments commits one of the fallacies of failed induction discussed in this chapter. Identify the fallacy.

1. I'm an Aquarius, so I love doing lots of projects at once.

   SAMPLE ANSWER: False cause

2. Some people can cure heart disease by meditation. I know because the coach of my son's soccer team told me.

*3. Wage and price controls will not work as a means of controlling the rate of inflation. After all, no economist has ever been able to give conclusive proof that such controls are effective against inflation.

4. Most HIV patients are young. Thus youth causes HIV.

5. Yogi Berra, an Italian American, was one of the greatest baseball players of all time. Other all-time greats of baseball include Joe DiMaggio, Mike Piazza, and Roy Campanella. So, no doubt about it, Italian Americans are great baseball players.

*6. Last week, when Notre Dame won the game, the coach was wearing his green tie. So their victory must have been due to the coach's choice of necktie, since this nearly always happens when he wears that tie.

*7. Foreign wars are good for a nation, just as exercise is good for the body. In the same way that exercise keeps the body fit, foreign wars keep a nation fit as a society.

8. According to recent polls of registered voters, the state of Massachusetts has a large percentage of voters who are political liberals. This suggests that all states have a large percentage of voters who are political liberals.

*9. The chances for stability in the Middle East will continue to improve. Popular singer Britney Spears has recently said that that is what she expects to happen.

10. Dallas and Houston are North American cities, and one can drive from the one to the other in only a few hours. Montreal and Los Angeles are also North American cities. Thus one can drive from Montreal to Los Angeles in only a few hours.

11. Some years ago, after not having seen my best friend from Duckwood High School for several years, we met for lunch and were surprised to find that our clothes and hairstyles were the same! The only possible explanation for this is that we both went to Duckwood High.

*12. Some regular churchgoers believe that taxpayers' dollars should not be used to fund laboratories that carry out tests on animals for medical research. Hence, it is wrong to go on spending taxpayers' dollars for that purpose.

13. I think you're giving up on advanced calculus too easily. Calculus and simple arithmetic are both parts of math. Since you can do simple arithmetic, you can also do advanced calculus.

14. Every rainy day I have a pain in my elbow; so it must be the damp weather we're having that's solely responsible for this pain.

*15. Sandra Day O'Connor, the first woman to serve on the United States Supreme Court, did not do a good job. This suggests that women are not fit to serve as Supreme Court justices.

16. There is no extraterrestrial life. After all, no one has ever found observable data to support the claim that such life exists.

17. The Internet is a great technological advance and is available to many people. Space travel is another great technological advance. Thus space travel is available to many people.

^18. Off-shore oil drilling is an environmental hazard, for there is no conclusive evidence to prove that it is safe.

*19. Several television personalities on the *David Letterman Show* the other night said that they had decided to invest in gold. So, it's probably a good idea to buy gold now.

20. Local radio station KNSR provides lively reporting on local and national news. So probably all local radio stations provide lively reporting on local and national news.

III. Each of the following arguments commits one or two of the fallacies of failed induction discussed in this chapter. Identify the fallacies.

1. There is no evidence linking industrial waste in our rivers with the higher incidence of birth defects in this area. Thus industrial waste in our rivers is not responsible for such defects. So it must be the mothers' carelessness that is responsible for them.

   SAMPLE ANSWER: Appeal to ignorance/false cause

2. The reason why the band U2 hasn't had a hit in the Top 40 for nearly a year is simply that they have been touring for too long, which follows from what a fan of the band told a local TV news reporter today: "U2 toured New Zealand, Australia, Japan, and Hawaii this year. Now they don't have any hit in the Top 40. This failure is no doubt the result of being on the road too long."

*3. Irving Berlin ate beet soup every day, and he lived to be 101. Therefore, regular consumption of beet soup leads to longevity.

4. The attorneys for the prosecution were not able to establish beyond a doubt that Hinckley was sane when he fired at President Reagan. We know this because Hinckley's own lawyers declared that at the end of the trial. So we have no choice but to conclude that he was insane.

*5. Bats not only harbor Ebola virus, but also are the hidden cause of mental illnesses among humans. Each of these long-standing suspicions has been proved true on the *Austin American-Statesman* website by Alicia Smith, professor of ancient Greek at Texas A&M.

6. To achieve something good, we sometimes have to break things. A famous twentieth-century political leader once observed, "In order to make an omelet, it is necessary to break some eggs." So, in exactly the same way, in a revolution to make a better world, some civilian enemies of the revolution will have to be shot."

*7. Drinking and smoking are not harmful for anyone. In fact, they promote longevity. After all, Winston Churchill and Ulysses S. Grant both smoked cigars and drank whiskey every day, and they did not die young.

8. I ought to wait before deciding whether or not to take that job in California, because my friend Mack, who is a professional astrologer, told me to wait.

*9. Bud had a stomachache before he was to take the LSAT exam to qualify for law school. He failed the exam and went on to become a taxi driver. Thus a stomachache caused Bud to become a taxi driver.

10. My grandfather never went to a doctor in his life. He went to a healer who practiced folk medicine. As a result, granddad lived to be ninety-four. So folk remedies always work.

*11. When I'm really hungry, the best thing for me is a double cheeseburger. I know this because the ad for Burger King says, "Double cheeseburger: what you really need when you're really hungry!"

*12. All the stories in the newspaper about Zheng's resignation are false. For one thing, some interested parties tried to prove them true and did not succeed.

13. When Professor Digby began studying philosophy as a young man, he also began losing his hair. The more philosophy he read, the balder he became. After years of study, he was completely bald. We may infer that Digby could have avoided baldness if he hadn't studied philosophy.

14. The top ten biggest earners in music include Aerosmith, Coldplay, and Sir Paul McCartney, and they all play popular music. Since Aerosmith and Coldplay are bands, we may infer that Sir Paul McCartney is a band.

*15. Toyota Corollas are fuel-efficient Japanese cars recently found to have defective accelerators that made them dangerous. Subaru Foresters are also fuel-efficient Japanese cars. So Subaru Foresters are likely to have defective accelerators that make them dangerous. This also suggests that all Japanese-made cars are dangerous.

IV. **For each of the above arguments, explain how it commits one or more fallacies.**

V. **Assuming that the premises of the following arguments are true, determine which commits a fallacy of appeal to unqualified authority and which doesn't.**

1. We must accept that Landis was the best American rider in the last Tour de France, since that's precisely what tour director Jean-Marie Leblanc reported as an opinion shared by all the judges of this important event.

   SAMPLE ANSWER: Not a fallacy

*2. Leonardo DiCaprio is the best American actor this year. We may be sure of this because it is the unanimous decision of the worldwide Leonardo DiCaprio Fan Club.

3. The most recent National Census shows that Latinos are the fastest-growing ethnic group, representing the largest minority in the country. Therefore, Latinos are the fastest-growing ethnic group, representing the largest minority in the country.

*4. There is reason to suspect that Mel Gibson may have been involved in drunk driving, since a spokesman for the sheriff's department confirmed that Gibson has been charged with driving while intoxicated. His bail was set at $5,000.

*5. The Secretary of Defense sees signs of growth in our economy. Thus our economy is recovering.

6. The universe can act as a magnifying lens. One of the best current physical theories, Einstein's, says so.

*7. It is simply false that cell-phone use creates the risk of developing a brain tumor. Five well-established cell-phone companies surveyed this issue extensively, all reaching the same conclusion: no such risk exists. More details on this are available at the companies' web pages.

8. There is nothing wrong with drinking coffee. Many U.S. presidents, including Theodore Roosevelt, are known to have been coffee drinkers.

*9. Although much can be said against diets low in carbohydrates, one thing is decisive: calories from carbohydrates enhance cognitive tasks. After all, that's the shared view among leading nutritionists.

10. Kids should avoid riding in school buses. This conclusion is supported by the remarks of the treasurer of the Parents' Association at the last meeting at Emerson School, who noted that the exhaust gases produced by diesel vehicles harm the children's respiratory systems.

VI. YOUR OWN THINKING LAB

For each the following arguments, first identify the fallacy that it might commit, and then provide premises or a scenario where it does not commit that fallacy.

*1. Every tiger so far observed has been fearless. Therefore, all tigers are fearless.

2. My mother and her circle of friends think that species have evolved. Therefore, species have evolved.

*3. Nobody has ever observed a centaur. Therefore, centaurs do not exist.

4. Ellen and Jose are both college students who vote. Both are also pre-law majors. Jose is also interested in golf. Therefore, Ellen is interested in golf.

■ Writing Project

The language of the media makes frequent use of analogy. Go to the web and Google three articles containing analogies on topics such as 'Saddam and Hitler,' 'Vietnam and Afghanistan,' and 'Recession and the Great Depression' or another analogy of your choice (be sure to check with your instructor on that). Select and summarize the arguments in three of the articles. Use your summaries to write a short essay (about two double-spaced pages) discussing whether the analogies in each are strong or weak analogies. If weak, explain why the analogy fails. Otherwise, explain why you think it should be allowed to stand.

■ Chapter Summary

Fallacy: in the case of argument, a pattern of failed relation between premises and conclusion. It could be:

1. A **formal fallacy,** which is a type of mistake made by arguments that may appear to be instances of a valid argument form but are in fact invalid in virtue of their form.

2. An **informal fallacy,** which is a pattern of failed relation between the premises and conclusion of an argument owing to some defect in expression or content.

BOX 10 ■ INFORMAL FALLACIES

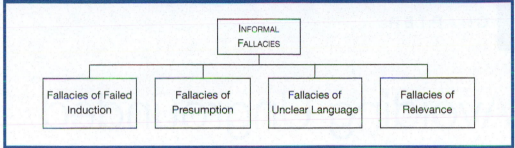

Hasty generalization: Committed by any enumerative induction whose conclusion rests on a sample that is either too small or lacking in comprehensiveness and randomness, or both. Stereotyping people is one form of hasty generalization.

Weak analogy: Committed by any analogy in which the things alleged to be alike are in fact not very much alike in relevant ways. Not all arguments from analogy are fallacious.

False cause: The mistake of concluding that there is a significant causal connection between two events, when in fact there is either a minimal causal connection or none at all. Not all causal arguments are fallacious.

Appeal to ignorance: Committed by any argument whose conclusion rests on nothing more than the absence of evidence to the contrary.

Appeal to unqualified authority: Committed by any argument in which the conclusion is supposedly supported by the say-so of some "authority" who is not really an expert in the relevant field or whose position is at odds with the prevailing consensus of expert opinion. Not all appeals to authority are fallacious.

■ Key Words

Fallacy

Informal fallacy

Weak analogy

False cause

Appeal to ignorance

Appeal to unqualified authority

Post hoc ergo propter hoc

Oversimplified cause

Non causa pro causa

Hasty generalization

Avoiding Ungrounded Assumptions

In this chapter you'll learn about the fallacies of presumption and some related logical and philosophical issues. The topics include

- Circular reasoning: When is it vicious? When is it benign?
- The fallacies of begging the question and begging the question against.
- The concept of *burden of proof*.
- The fallacy of complex question.
- The fallacy of false alternatives.
- The fallacy of accident.

8.1 Fallacies of Presumption

Now we're ready to look at some fallacies that can be grouped together because arguments committing them take for granted something that is in fact debatable. Such arguments rest on presumptions, which are strong assumptions or background beliefs taken for granted. Generally, there is nothing wrong with presumptions: arguments commonly rest on implicit beliefs that create no fallacy of presumption at all. But when an argument takes for granted a belief that is in fact debatable, it commits a fallacy of presumption. The unsupported belief at work in such fallacious arguments may at first seem innocent or even acceptable, though in reality it is neither. The patterns of mistake illustrated by arguments that rest on debatable presumptions include the five types of fallacy listed in Box 1.

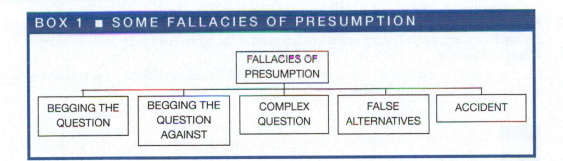

BOX 1 ■ SOME FALLACIES OF PRESUMPTION

FALLACIES OF PRESUMPTION

BEGGING THE QUESTION | BEGGING THE QUESTION AGAINST | COMPLEX QUESTION | FALSE ALTERNATIVES | ACCIDENT

8.2 Begging the Question

In Chapter 5 we saw that the premises of valid arguments could be true yet fall short of counting as persuasive reasons for their conclusion. That would be the case with any sound argument that failed to be cogent. As a result, no such argument can move a rational thinker to accept its conclusion, even when the validity of the argument may be obvious to the thinker. Why? Imagine that we intend to convince you rationally to accept a certain claim—say, that

1 We care about logical thinking.

We offer you this reason as a premise:

2 It is not the case that we don't care about logical thinking.

The argument is

3 1. It is not the case that we don't care about logical thinking.
  2. We care about logical thinking.

(3) is valid, and we may assume that it has a true premise. Yet it lacks cogency, since it doesn't offer reasons that could persuade a logical thinker of the truth of its conclusion if that thinker is skeptical about that very conclusion. Philosophers call this 'circular reasoning.' (3) is affected by a degree of circularity that may be considered 'vicious,' since it would make any argument that has it fail—by contrast with 'benign circularity,' which, as we'll see, is the tolerable degree of circularity that affects many deductive arguments.

(3) is viciously circular because its premise and conclusion have the same content, so that the premise is not more acceptable than the conclusion it is offered to support. It simply amounts to a restatement of that conclusion, as shown by this quick look at the argument's form:

3′ 1. It is not the case that not P
    2. P

Since double negations cancel each other out, (3′) amounts to the patently circular form (3″):

3″ P
    ─
    P

Any argument of this form is valid, and if its premise is true, it's also sound. In (3)'s case, since we do care about logical thinking, the premise is true, and the argument therefore sound. But it is not difficult to see that it is also affected by a kind of circularity that would undermine any argument thus affected. For recall that a premise's job is to support an argument's conclusion. Plainly, P cannot support P, since one is a restatement of the other. For similar reasons, not not P cannot support P.

Any argument exhibiting vicious circularity of this kind commits the fallacy of *begging the question*, also called '*Petitio Principii.*'

- When a valid (or even a sound) argument begs the question, its premises fail to offer compelling reasons for accepting its conclusion.
- Any argument that begs the question fails to be cogent.
- The conclusion of a question-begging argument may in fact be quite acceptable, but this would be for reasons other than those offered by that argument.

Sometimes, however, a failure in cogency due to begging the question is not so easy to detect. Suppose an animal-rights watch group is investigating a complaint about the treatment of animals at the North Carolina Zoo in Raleigh. They interview a worker who argues

4   The treatment of animals in our zoo is humane, given that animals are not treated inhumanely in this zoo.

(4) would fail to persuade the animal-rights watch group simply because it begs the question. Even though the argument is valid, its premise provides no good reason for accepting its conclusion. Since 'being humane' is equivalent to 'not being inhumane,' the premise is just a restatement of the argument's conclusion. Thus it cannot do the job it's supposed to do (namely, support the conclusion). By begging the question in a similar way, the following arguments for and against the existence of God also fail:

5   1. It is not the case that God doesn't exist.
    2. God exists.

6   1. It is not the case that God exists.
    2. God doesn't exist.

Now consider

7 1. Homer wrote the <u>Odyssey</u>.
    2. Homer existed.

It seems that for (7)'s premise to be acceptable, one would have to previously accept the very conclusion the argument attempts to support (namely, that there *actually was* a poet, Homer). As a result, (7) begs the question, thereby failing to offer a reason that could compel logical thinkers to accept its conclusion, even if its premise is true and the argument valid.

Notice that, unlike (3), (5), and (6), the circularity affecting (7) does not depend on argument form, but hinges on the concepts or ideas involved: that Homer wrote the Odyssey presupposes that he existed.

- An argument begs the question if and only if one or more of its premises can be accepted only if the conclusion has already been accepted. Since in any such argument, at least one premise assumes the conclusion, that premise cannot be a reason for accepting that conclusion.
- The argument is said to 'beg,' rather than to support, its 'question' or conclusion.

Begging the question is a failure in the cogency of a deductive argument that amounts to a fallacy arising from viciously circular reasoning, which may hinge on the argument form or the concepts involved. If the premises of a valid argument are found acceptable only because the conclusion has already been accepted, then they cannot do their job of persuading a thinker to accept the conclusion. Thus whenever an argument begs the question, it lacks cogency—the important virtue of valid arguments discussed in Chapter 5. Put another way, the premises of any viciously circular argument are not able to transfer their support to the conclusion. They provide no persuasive reason for the conclusion.

BOX 2 ■ HOW TO AVOID BEGGING THE QUESTION

The bottom line is that given a valid argument with acceptable premises, you must ask yourself whether they are more acceptable than the conclusion they're offered to support. If yes, the argument is cogent. If no, it's question-begging.

Circular Reasoning

All valid arguments have some degree of circularity, since the information in the conclusion of such arguments is always included in the premises. However, not all deductive arguments beg the question. The context of a circular argument, together with the degree of circularity in it, can help to determine whether that argument begs the question. Let's try to clarify this by having a brief look at circular arguments.

As just noted, any valid argument has some degree of circularity, due either to its form, the concepts involved, or both. The following two arguments are affected by circularity hinging on argument form:

8 1. Today it's cloudy and breezy.
   2. Today it's breezy.

9 1. The Pope is in Rome.
   2. The Pope is in Rome.

Clearly, the circularity afflicting these arguments hinges on their forms—which are

8 1. C and B
   2. B

9 1. E
   2. E

Any argument with either of these forms is valid, for if its premise is true, then its conclusion must also be. But in each case the premise is not more acceptable than the conclusion it attempts to support. As a result, no one could come to accept the conclusion on the basis of having worked out the validity of the argument and found the premise acceptable.

Yet circularity may also be conceptual, hinging on the meaning or concepts involved. Consider

10 1. If Kobe Bryant is a basketball player, then he plays basketball.
    2. Kobe Bryant is a basketball player.
    3. Kobe Bryant plays basketball.

11 1. Marianne was once abducted by alien beings from outer space.
    2. There are alien beings from outer space.

In each argument, the premises presuppose the conclusion they are supposed to support, *given the concepts involved*. In (10), no logical thinker who doubts that Kobe Bryant plays basketball could come to accept that on the basis of the argument's premises. In (11), no logical thinker who doubts the existence of alien beings from outer space could be persuaded that there are such beings by the argument's premise. Each argument begs the question, thereby failing to be cogent. As in (8) and (9) above, these arguments too are affected by circularity that renders them fallacious. Whether formal or conceptual, circularity comes in degrees: too much of it causes an argument to beg the question.

Benign Circularity

But circularity does not always make an argument question-begging. Compare

12 1. If the mind is the brain, then the mind is organic matter.
    2. If the mind is organic matter, then it perishes with the body.
    3. If the mind is the brain, then it perishes with the body.

BOX 3 ■ FORMAL AND CONCEPTUAL CIRCULARITY

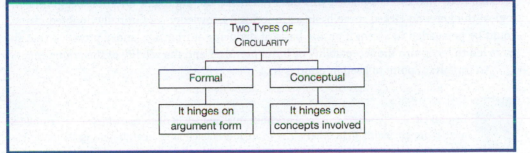

Here the argument form is

12′ 1. If M, then O
2. If O, then B
3. If M, then B

In an argument with this form, there is some formal circularity, since the propositions represented as *M* and *B* appear not only in the conclusion, but also in the premises. Yet (12) does not beg the question, because finding its premises acceptable and recognizing the argument's validity could provide reasons to move logical thinkers to accept its conclusion. Anyone who accepts the argument's premises and works out the entailment thereby possesses a compelling reason to accept its conclusion. By contrast with viciously circular arguments, coming to accept (12)'s conclusion on the basis of its premises amounts to a cognitive achievement.

Let's now compare some conceptually circular arguments such as

13 1. Salsa is music for dancers.
2. Salsa is music for those who dance.

14 1. Andrew is a bachelor.
2. Andrew is unmarried.

15 1. She has drawn an isosceles triangle.
2. She has drawn a triangle.

All three of these arguments are valid: if their premises are true, their conclusions must be true, as well. Yet under ordinary circumstances, each begs the question, for in each case acceptance of its premise requires a previous acceptance of the conclusion. No logical thinker who disputed the conclusion could be compelled to accept it on the basis of the argument's premise and recognition of the argument's validity. But consider

16 1. The Moon orbits the Earth.
2. The Moon is a large celestial body.
3. Any large celestial body that orbits a planet is a satellite.
4. The Moon is a satellite.

Although in (16) there is some conceptual circularity between the concepts 'satellite' and 'large celestial body that orbits a planet,' this does not make the argument question-begging. For a logical thinker who lacked some basic astronomical knowledge and initially doubted claim 4 could be persuaded to accept it on the basis of deducing it from 1, 2, and 3, provided that she were led to recognize the acceptability of those premises and the validity of the argument.

An important point to keep in mind is that

> Logical circularity, whether formal or conceptual, comes in degrees. Some valid arguments have more circularity than others. The more logically circular an argument is, the more its conclusion follows trivially from its premises and is likely to beg the question.

The Burden of Proof

It is not uncommon to find the expression 'burden of proof' in dialectical contexts, which are situations involving deliberation among two or more parties, such as a debate, controversy, or deliberation on a disputed question between opposing sides defending incompatible claims. 'Burden of proof' refers to the obligation to take a turn in offering reasons, which, at any given stage of the deliberation, is on one side or the other (except for the paradoxical situations discussed below). A deliberation commonly follows this pattern: one party, C, makes a claim. The other party, O, replies by raising some objections to it. If these objections are adequate, the burden of proof is now on C, who must get rid of (or 'discharge') it by offering reasons for her claim. If she comes up with a sound or strong argument that outweighs O's argument, the burden of proof then switches to O, who must try to discharge it by offering the appropriate arguments.

It may happen, however, that the reasons on both sides appear equally strong. As a result, there would then be a dialectical impasse, or standoff in the deliberation. No progress can be made until new reasons are offered to resolve the conflict. Except for these situations, however, we may expect that the burden of proof will, at any given stage of a deliberation, be on either the one side or the other. As the deliberation progresses, it will likely switch from the one side to the other more than once, always falling on the participant whose claim is more in need of support.

BOX 4 ■ WHERE IS THE BURDEN OF PROOF?

In the following debate, ⊗ shows the burden of proof and ⊙ an impasse.

1. $\underline{A}$ rejects a claim made by $\underline{B}$, which is a commonly held belief. ⊗ $\underline{A}$
2. $\underline{A}$ defends her rejection with an argument that begs the question against $\underline{B}$. ⊗ $\underline{A}$
3. $\underline{A}$ recasts her argument so that it now seems cogent. ⊗ $\underline{B}$
4. $\underline{B}$ offers an argument that turns out to be clearly invalid. ⊗ $\underline{B}$
5. $\underline{B}$'s argument is modified and now seems as cogent as $\underline{A}$'s. ⊙
6. $\underline{A}$ provides further strong evidence in support of her view. ⊗ $\underline{B}$
7. $\underline{B}$ replies by offering weak evidence for his view. ⊗ $\underline{B}$
8. $\underline{B}$ offers further evidence which is equally strong as $\underline{A}$'s. ⊙

Commonsense beliefs, which are ordinary beliefs based on observation, memory, and inference, enjoy a privileged standing with respect to the burden of proof. Whoever challenges them has, at least initially, the burden of proof. For example, the belief that the Earth has existed for more than five minutes belongs to common sense. If someone challenges it, the burden of proof is on the challenger, who must now offer adequate reasons against that commonsense belief. But that advantage can be overridden by a strong argument if available.

Knowing where the burden of proof is at any given stage of a debate has this cash value:

- If you know that the burden of proof is on you, you know you must discharge it by offering an adequate argument in support of your claim.
- If you know that the burden of proof is on the other side, you can rest until a sound objection to your view has been offered.
- If you know that you are defending a claim that is part of common sense, then you also know that the burden of proof is on any challenger.

Finally, note that some deliberation goes on 'internally'—for example, when a person reflects upon which of two opposite theories is correct. If, in the course of inner deliberation, a thinker is fair-minded, then the burden of proof will tend to shift from one position she is considering to an opposite view, following the same general considerations outlined above.

BOX 5 ■ RATIONAL DELIBERATION

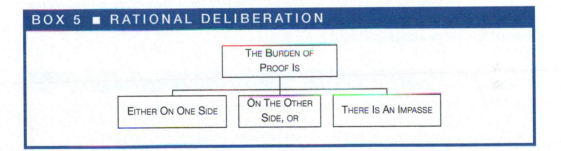

8.3 Begging the Question Against

A common mistake that undermines argument is committed by failing to discharge the burden of proof. Suppose that we assert 'Not P' (i.e., that P is false), but someone else, Melinda, has just offered us some good reason for thinking that P is true.

BOX 6 ■ HOW TO AVOID BEGGING THE QUESTION AGAINST

Don't include any controversial statement among your premises without first offering adequate reasons for it.

The burden of proof is now on us, and we must discharge it by offering an adequate argument against P. The failure to do so—by assuming that P is false, without offering a reason for this—commits the fallacy of *begging the question against* Melinda. For it amounts to implicitly reasoning in either of these viciously circular forms:

17 1. P is false
  2. P is false

Or similarly,

18 1. Not P
  2. Not P

The fallacy of *begging the question against* (your opponent) is often committed in everyday arguments on controversial topics. For example, when someone maintains

19 1. In abortion, the fetus is intentionally killed.
  2. A fetus is an innocent person.
  3. Intentionally killing an innocent person is always murder.
  4. Abortion is always murder.

Although 1 seems unobjectionable, 2 and 3 are controversial premises that cannot be employed unless good reasons have already been offered to back them up. Premise 2 begs the question against the view that a fetus is not a person—a view that can be supported in a number of ways (as most parties to the current popular debate over the morality of abortion now recognize).

Begging the question against can be difficult to detect, for it involves presupposing the truth of premises that, although controversial, are sometimes inadvertently taken for granted. To avoid this fallacy, always abide by the rule in Box 6 above.

BOX 7 ■ SECTION SUMMARY

1. When an argument begs the question, at least one premise assumes the conclusion being argued for.
2. When an argument begs the question against, at least one premise assumes something that is in need of support.

Exercises

I. Review Questions

1. What do all fallacies of presumption have in common?
2. What does it mean for an argument to be 'circular'? Is all circularity bad?
2. Define non-cogency in relation to begging the question.
3. What's wrong with a question begging argument?
4. What is the fallacy of begging the question against? How does it differ from begging the question?
5. Against whom is the question begged in any argument that begs the question against?

6. Could the conclusion of a question-begging argument be true? Explain.

7. What is meant by *burden of proof*? How do commonsense beliefs matter to it?

8. Where is the burden of proof at each stage of a deliberation?

II. Each of the following arguments begs the question. Explain why.

1. Dylan is a brother. Therefore, Dylan has a sibling.

   SAMPLE ANSWER: The logical thinker who rejects the conclusion would reject that Dylan is a brother.

2. Capital punishment is cruel, for it is cruel and unusual punishment. And it's demeaning to the society that inflicts it.

*3. The mind is different from the body. Hence, the mind and the body are not the same.

4. Mount Aconcagua and Mount Whitney are both tall mountains. But Mount Aconcagua is taller than Mount Whitney. Consequently, Mount Whitney is shorter than Mount Aconcagua.

*5. Demons are supernatural beings. Supernatural beings are only fictional. Therefore, demons do not exist.

6. Dorothy is a historian. For, she is a historian and art collector.

*7. Since Aaron is a hunter, he is someone who hunts.

8. The U.S. president and the British prime minister both oppose the treaty. Hence, it's false that both leaders do not oppose the treaty.

*9. If a plane figure is a circle, then it is not a rectangle. Therefore, if the figure is a rectangle, then it is not a circle.

10. The first witness is not trustworthy, since he is not reliable.

III. [*Note: This exercise is somewhat more challenging.*] For each of the above arguments, determine whether the circularity is formal, conceptual, or both.

IV. For each of the following arguments, determine whether it would, under normal circumstances, beg the question, beg the question against, or do both.

1. Whoever is less productive should have lower wages. Women are less productive than men. Hence, women should have lower wages.

   SAMPLE ANSWER: Begs the question against

2. Euthanasia is murder and is wrong. So, euthanasia is wrong.

*3. Fido is a puppy. Therefore, Fido is a young dog.

4. A woman has an absolute right to control her own body. And if a woman has an absolute right to control her own body, then abortion is morally permissible. Therefore, abortion is morally permissible.

*5. Since the Democrats won the '08 presidential election, it is simply false that they didn't win.

6. Derek Jeter has an insurance policy on his cars, for it is not the case that his cars lack such a policy.

*7. The fetus is an unborn baby. Therefore, it is not the case that the fetus is not an unborn baby.

8. Anyone who is an idealist is also a loser. Thus idealists are losers.

9. Vladimir is a bachelor. Therefore, Vladimir is unmarried.

*10. Infanticide is always morally wrong. So, infanticide is never morally right.

11. If there is intelligent life elsewhere in the universe, then life on Earth is not unique. But life on Earth is unique. Hence, there is no intelligent life elsewhere in the universe.

12. The right to life is God's will. Therefore, the right to life is the will of Divine Providence.

*13. Given atheism, God doesn't exist. But it is not the case that He doesn't exist, so atheism is mistaken.

14. Priscilla got a B on her philosophy paper this semester. Therefore, she turned in a philosophy paper this semester.

15. There is life after death. Therefore, there is an afterlife.

*16. Since no person should be denied freedom, and Bruno is a person, it follows that Bruno is entitled to freedom.

17. Magdalene is a sister. Therefore, she is a female.

18. Since capital punishment is murder, capital punishment is wrongful killing.

*19. Northfield is not far from Minneapolis. Thus Northfield is close to Minneapolis.

20. Socialism is an unjust system of government. Unjust systems of government must be abolished. Therefore, socialism must be abolished.

V. Determine whether the following arguments are possible or impossible.

1. An argument that is cogent for a logical thinker but not rationally compelling.

   SAMPLE ANSWER: Impossible

2. A valid argument that is non-cogent.

3. A sound argument that is non-cogent.

*4. A question-begging argument that is not circular.

5. A circular argument that is not fallacious.

*6. A cogent argument that begs the question against.

7. A sound argument that is cogent.

*8. A question-begging argument that is sound.

9. A question-begging argument that is rationally compelling.

*10. The burden of proof being on the side that has offered the most cogent argument.

VI. In the deliberation described below, determine where the burden of proof lies at each stage: if on Carolyn, write 'C'; if on Karl, write 'K'; and if there is a dialectical impasse, write 'I.'

1. C rejects a commonsense belief held by K.

   SAMPLE ANSWER: C

2. C defends her rejection with an argument that begs the question against K.

3. C recasts her argument in a way that makes it clearly unsound.

*4. C offers a new argument that turns out be invalid.

5. C's argument undergoes another recast that makes it cogent.

*6. K advances a valid yet question-begging argument against C.

7. K offers a non-question-begging argument with clearly false premises.

*8. K recasts his argument so that it is now as cogent as C's.

VII. In the following deliberation, either *S* or *O* has the burden of proof. Identify which has it at any given stage in the deliberation, and mark dialectical impasses. Explain your choice.

1. *S* makes a claim that challenges a commonly held belief.

   SAMPLE ANSWER: Burden of proof on S. When commonsense beliefs are at issue, the burden of proof is on the challenger.

2. *S* attempts to support her claim by offering an inductively weak argument.

*3. *S* recasts her argument so that it is now clearly valid but unsound.

4. *S* recasts her argument again so that it is now sound but question-begging.

*5. *S*'s argument undergoes another recast that makes it deductively cogent.

6. *O* responds with a valid argument that begs the question against S.

*7. *O* recasts her argument so that it is now non-question-begging but plainly unsound.

8. *O* recasts her argument once more so that it is now as cogent as S's argument.

VIII. YOUR OWN THINKING LAB

*1. Consider the following argument: "Marriage can be only between two persons of different sexes. Therefore, gay couples cannot be married." What's the matter with this argument?

2. Provide an argument that both begs the question and begs the question against.

3. Provide an argument that begs the question without begging the question against.

4. Provide an argument that begs the question against without begging the question.

*5. Discuss the conditions an argument must meet to be deductively cogent.

*6. An argument that is invalid always falls short of being rationally compelling, but could such an argument be cogent? Must its conclusion be rejected? Explain your answers.

7. Imagine a debate in which two rival claims are equally well supported by observational data. Of the two, one agrees with common sense, the other doesn't. Does this make a difference? Where is the burden of proof? Explain.

8. Discuss what's wrong with an argument that begs the question.

9. Discuss what's wrong with an argument that begs the question against.

*10. Suppose you are engaged in a rational debate. Your opponent has just offered a seemingly adequate argument for a claim that you wish to reject. Where is the burden of proof? What does 'burden of proof' mean?

8.4 Complex Question

Another fallacy of presumption is *complex question*, which is a pattern of mistake in asking a question that can be answered only by yes or no, but which assumes either

1. that there is only one question when there are in fact two or more, each with its own answer, or
2. that some claim is true when in fact it is either false or, at the very least, doubtful.

Whenever this fallacy is committed, the question being asked is unfair because it has an unjustified assumption embedded within it, in one or the other of these two ways. An example of 1 would be a question one can imagine being asked of a presidential candidate:

20 If elected, would you continue the best traditions of your party and promote wasteful spending on welfare programs that only encourage laziness? Yes or no?

Clearly, this is not one question but two. The candidate may indeed want to continue the best traditions of his party but also have no intention of promoting "wasteful spending on welfare programs that only encourage laziness." But the interlocutor is demanding a yes or no on the whole query at once and not allowing him to divide the question.

An example of 2 would be a question that is implicitly critical of the person being queried. A classic case of this is that of a man who's asked,

21 Have you stopped beating your wife?

Here a 'yes' is just as bad as a 'no,' because it seems to follow from this question that the addressee was engaged in wife beating. Questions of this sort are unfair, since the person queried will convict himself with either answer. (Note, however, that context does matter. If a man is actually known to be a wife beater, then posing (21) to him would not commit a fallacy.) Consider another example: Tyler is a high school student who plays in a punk-rock band. He has multiple piercings and tattoos but has never used drugs of any kind. One evening he has a date with Dahlia to go to the movies. But when he arrives to pick her up, he meets her father, who regards him with suspicion and says,

22 Before you take my daughter to the movies, I must ask you this: do you intend to conceal from me your history of marijuana use?

Now, what is the correct answer to this? Obviously, Tyler doesn't want to answer 'yes.' But if he answers 'no,' then that is equally to admit to marijuana use (something he's innocent of). Either answer will convict him. Notice, however, that that is only because the question itself is unfair. It assumes—without any supporting evidence—that the young man has used marijuana!

It's not difficult to see the mistake here. But how is this an *argument*? First, the question asks whether or not Tyler intends to conceal his history of marijuana use. If he does, then he has a history of marijuana use. And if he doesn't, then he also has a history of marijuana use. Assuming that he either does or doesn't, it follows that he has a history of marijuana use. But there is a problem with these premises, since they rest on an assumption that is false—namely, that the person queried (Tyler) does have a history of marijuana use.

Yet not all arguments that commit the complex-question fallacy are intended specifically to trap an individual. Some consist simply in questions phrased so that any answer a respondent gives to them must necessarily endorse an unsupported assumption built into the question itself. Suppose that a politician, in a speech, asks,

23 Does my opponent agree with the president's disastrous economic policy which is now leading our nation to ruin?

Because the question assumes (without anything in the context making it plausible) that the president's economic policy *is* 'disastrous,' and that it *is* 'leading our nation to ruin,' anyone who responds to (23), either in the affirmative or in the negative, will be implicitly endorsing those views! Again, a fallacy of complex question has been committed, in this case by the politician. To a complex question, it seems, any answer is a wrong answer. But that is only because there is something wrong with the question itself. It is phrased so that it assumes something not yet supported.

BOX 8 ■ HOW TO AVOID COMPLEX QUESTION

Beware of any yes/no question presupposing that, if the answer is yes, a questionable proposition P (for which no argument has been offered) follows, and if you answer is no, P also follows.

8.5 False Alternatives

False alternatives is a defect in reasoning that might affect an argument containing a disjunction as premise. A disjunction is a compound proposition with two members or 'disjuncts.' An exclusive disjunction has the form

24 Either P or Q (but not both).

Here P and Q represent propositions standing as exclusive alternatives, because if one is true, the other is false and vice versa. For example,

25 Either the groundhog hibernates during the winter or it continues in a state of animation.

This is an exclusive disjunction, since it presupposes that exactly one of the alternatives is true. By contrast, consider the inclusive disjunction

26 Apples that are either too small or too ripe are discarded.

This has the form

26′   Either *P* or *Q* (or both).

That is, (26) presupposes that any apple that is both too small and too ripe is also discarded. Another thing to notice about these disjunctions is that they present the alternatives as being *exhaustive*—that is, they are the *only* possible alternatives. For example, (25) presupposes that hibernation (or suspended animation) and animation are the only two possible states a groundhog could enter in winter.

> An argument commits the fallacy of **false alternatives** if and only if it offers in its premises a disjunction presenting two extreme alternatives as the only ones possible, when in reality there are one or more others equally plausible.

When an arguer offers a disjunctive premise as presenting exhaustive, exclusive alternatives, we must determine whether this is really so. This involves checking premises of (24)'s form, to be sure that *P* and *Q* exhaust all the alternatives and could not both be true—provided that the disjunction is intended to be exhaustive and exclusive. A fallacy of false alternatives would be committed, for example, by this argument:

27 There are only two possibilities: either our country abandons its involvement in foreign wars or it continues to interfere in other nations' affairs. If it does the former, then it will become neutral like Switzerland, but if it does the latter, it'll get deeper in debt to China. So our country will either become neutral like Switzerland or get deeper in debt to China.

Although this argument is valid, it is also unsound, since its first premise is false in virtue of treating as exhaustive, exclusive alternatives what are in reality only two among plausible scenarios. In fact there are more alternatives than the two expressed in that premise! Much the same problem affects

28 1. Either all U.S. universities will convert their programs entirely into online courses, or they'll all soon go bankrupt.
    2. U.S. universities will not convert their programs entirely to online courses.
    3. They'll all soon go bankrupt.

This argument, too, is plainly valid, but unsound owing to the falsity of premise 1, which causes the argument to commit false alternatives.

Let's consider one more example. Suppose that a political activist is trying to convince us to agree with her. She appeals to our sense of civic duty and says,

29 You must join my party, the only one that offers a solution to the problem of homelessness. For you're either part of the solution or part of the problem.

But these options seem unduly restrictive. Why are *just those* the only choices? Perhaps we are neither part of the problem (since we did not really contribute to causing it) nor part of the solution (since our participation might not make any difference). Or perhaps we are both part of the problem and also (potentially) part of its solution—isn't that equally possible? So, in this example, the activist commits the fallacy of false alternatives. Once all missing premises are stated, her extended argument is:

29′ 1. There is a problem of homelessness.
2. Either you are part of this problem or part of its solution.
3. It is wrong for you to be part of the problem.
4. You must be part of the solution to the problem of homelessness.
5. To be part of the solution to that problem, you must join my party.
6. You must join my party.

Assuming that other premises are true, premise 2 rests on an inaccurate assumption: namely, that our choice is limited to either the one or the other of the two mutually exclusive alternatives offered there—that is, to being either part of the solution or part of the problem. Since that is false, the argument should be rejected on the ground that it commits the fallacy of false alternatives.

Yet not all arguments featuring exhaustive, exclusive disjunctions commit this fallacy, for there are situations that do appear to present us with such a choice. It is plausible to say that citizens of France in 1940 really did have to make a decision between only two mutually exclusive alternatives: either collaborate with the puppet government imposed by Hitler's invading armies, or resist it in some way. And a southerner in the United States in 1961 really did have to choose whether or not to support the integration of schools, churches, and lunch counters—a movement that was then challenging racially discriminatory laws. But most everyday situations are not likely to be as dramatic as these. Therefore, for the most part, one is well advised to be skeptical when someone claims that there is a choice of only two extreme alternatives. (It may be so, but probably not.)

BOX 9 ■ HOW TO AVOID FALSE ALTERNATIVES

In evaluating an argument with a disjunctive premise, check that premise to see if

1. It claims that the two extreme alternatives offered are the only possible ones.
2. The alternatives are assumed to be incompatible.
3. In reality, both (1) and (2) are false.

If these conditions are met, then the argument commits the fallacy of false alternatives.

8.6 Accident

Accident is another fallacy of presumption that can undermine arguments: it is committed when some 'accidental' or exceptional feature of the case at hand is overlooked.

> The **fallacy of accident** is committed by an argument that treats a certain case as falling under a general rule or principle when in fact the case counts as an exception to it.

Suppose someone reasons as follows:

30 1. Dogs are friendly animals.
    2. My Rottweiler, Otto, is a dog.
    3. Otto is a friendly animal.

But suppose it's also true that Otto has recently bitten six of my friends and two hapless bystanders. What, then, shall we say about the above argument? Although it's true in general that "dogs are friendly animals," that rule does not apply to Otto. Thus (30) commits the fallacy of accident. As in other arguments committing this fallacy, here the arguer fails to notice that some principle that is generally true may not be always true, so that he fails to allow for an exception to the rule in a case where an exception is warranted.

Now imagine that Smith invites Adkins to lunch one day. "Come on, let's go to lunch," he says. "We can go to the corner delicatessen, and I'll treat you." Adkins is about to accept but then thinks to himself, "Wait a minute! There's no such thing as a free lunch!" Now, this judgment results from the fallacious reasoning involved in accident. Although part of the problem is that a familiar cliché is being taken too literally, the larger mistake is that some principle that is generally true is being misapplied. Of course, for the most part, it is true that "there's no such thing as a free lunch" (meaning that things ostensibly free of charge ordinarily come with hidden costs we must pay), but if Smith is *inviting* Adkins to lunch, then this is an exception. *Usually* there's no free lunch. But today there is. Adkins is simply being obtuse.

Or again, suppose Jones believes that one should always tell the truth. In general, this is of course a good rule to follow. One day Jones meets his next-door neighbor in the supermarket. She says, "How do you like my new hat?" Jones looks at the hat and thinks to himself, "Always tell the truth, no matter what." So he says, "I think it looks ridiculous," thereby hurting her feelings and contributing slightly toward increasing the unhappiness in the world. Now, wouldn't we say here that Jones is simply being too fanatical about truth telling? Yes, one should usually tell the truth. But surely this was a case in which a small lie was called for! No one would have been treated unfairly or otherwise wronged by doing so, and a small degree of happiness would thereby have been produced. By not recognizing this, Jones has committed a fallacy of accident. He has failed to understand that, although the rule prescribing veracity is in general a good one, there are justifiable exceptions; and here he has not allowed for an exception where an exception was warranted.

Exercises

IX. Review Questions

1. What sort of questions may commit the fallacy of complex question?
2. In which sense may complex questions be considered arguments?
3. Are all questions with presuppositions instances of complex question?

4. How does complex question differ from begging the question? And how do both count as fallacies of presumption?

5. What is the fallacy of accident?

6. Consider: 'All arguments featuring an either/or statement commit the fallacy of false alternatives.' Is this claim true? Explain.

X. The following arguments are instances of complex question, false alternatives, and accident. Determine which is which.

1. Are you still in agreement with the senator's unpatriotic view that tax cuts will help the economy?

   SAMPLE ANSWER: Complex question

2. Jorge plans to apply to the University of Texas, where one can major in biology or in history. But since he cannot stand history, he'll major in biology.

*3. Since people generally survive influenza, you shouldn't worry about your eighty-eight-year-old grandfather's catching it.

4. Have you stopped cheating on your taxes?

5. One can be either a Roman Catholic or a Protestant. But since both religions are too demanding for me, it's clear that there is no religion suitable for me.

*6. I'm sure that Jane avoids eating at night. For she has been losing weight without dieting. And to lose weight, one either diets or avoids eating at night.

7. Professor Wilson almost never gives F's in her classes. So I'm sure I won't get an F this time, even though I've missed all but one of her class sessions and failed all three exams.

8. Midwesterners vacation in either Florida or the Rocky Mountains. The Gustafsons are Midwesterners but don't like the Rocky Mountains. Therefore, the Gustafsons vacation in Florida.

*9. Does the defendant wish to deny his past connections to terrorist organizations?

10. Since successful people usually come from a background of wealth and privilege, and Pele, the soccer player born in a shantytown in Brazil, was a successful person, he must have come from a background of wealth and privilege.

11. How long will we permit taxpayer dollars to be used as a welfare program for rich farmers?

*12. There can be no such thing as the "politics of happiness" for America. For either we'll have a Republican president who'll get us into more wars, or we'll have a Democrat who'll get us into a recession.

*13. People with long-lived parents and grandparents often can expect to be long-lived themselves, so I'll be long-lived. Of course, I've smoked cigarettes, a pack a day, for the last thirty years. But because of my long-lived parents and grandparents, I'm sure I'll live to be at least ninety-five.

14. Is Aunt Betty still wasting her days watching soap operas on television?

*15. Cancer is a deadly disease, so Isabel should resign herself to her breast cancer and simplify her life by refusing treatment for it—even when it was detected early in her case.

XI. The following arguments are instances of begging the question, begging the question against, complex question, false alternatives, or accident. Determine which is which. (Note that in some cases an argument could *both* beg the question and beg the question against.)

1. Jane has to come to work. She may be sick, as she says, but she is needed in the office. Whenever an employee is needed in the office, she must show up.

   SAMPLE ANSWER: Accident

2. Women should not be deployed for military service, because no woman should serve in the military.

3. We've had record hot weather for two weeks. In a heat wave as bad as this, there are only two options: either one spends all day complaining about it, or one shuts up and goes about one's work. So we'll have to go on with our work, since complaining is not an option for us.

*4. Is MacKenzie still forcing his employees to use obsolete technology in his office?

5. Everyone should get some strenuous physical exercise every day, like running a mile before breakfast. So, my Uncle Olaf, who is ninety-seven years old, ought to run a mile every day before breakfast.

*6. To be wealthy, you have to be either a Wall Street financier or a drug dealer. You are wealthy, but you are not a Wall Street financier. It follows that you are a drug dealer.

7. Have they given up yet on casting a short blond actor, Daniel Craig, as James Bond?

8. Sarah had better marry Dombrowsky. For either she marries him or ends up single.

*9. In general, any average person's statistical chance of suffering a gunshot wound is minimal. So I'm not worried about my friend Al, who just joined the police force.

10. Did Melissa manage to get along with Justin?

11. Was he able to stay out of trouble during his last visit?

*12. Murderers don't have a right to life. Since Joe is a murderer, he doesn't have a right to life.

13. Certainly there is life after death, since there are people who have lived previous lives and have memories of those earlier selves long ago.

14. The law clearly states that if citizens fail to pay their taxes, they'll be prosecuted. So my four-year-old cousin Egbert should be prosecuted! After all, I happen to know that he paid no taxes last year.

*15. Do you support Senator Krank's ridiculous school appropriations bill, which would bankrupt our state government?

16. Martial arts are either taekwondo or jujitsu. Yoshizuki is trained in the martial arts, but he doesn't practice taekwondo. Therefore, he practices jujitsu.

*17. It will surely be in the interest of the United States to abolish tariffs on commerce with nations south of the Rio Grande, for free trade with Latin America can only be in the interest of the United States.

18. Do you really want to pass up your chance of a lifetime to invest in Swampwood Estates, Florida's most exclusive and luxurious new residential neighborhood?

19. Were you sober last weekend?

*20. I can say whatever I want about my neighbor, O'Connor. Whether it's true or not, I can say it, and no one can stop me! After all, the First Amendment guarantees freedom of speech in the United States.

21. If there is no substantial economic growth in our country this year, then either there will be disruptive social upheaval or the military will overthrow the government. We're at a point now where there could only be minimal economic growth. Therefore, we can expect a military overthrow of the government to happen soon.

*22. Lakeesha's donation of her prize money to AIDS research was selfless. It follows that her action was not selfish.

23. Either the United States invades Mexico or drugs cartels continue to destabilize Mexican society. Since the United States won't intervene, it follows that drugs cartels continue to destabilize Mexican society.

24. Since media literacy is a proven tool against crime, it could be used to reform convicted murderers.

*25. Abigail has been reporting intractable insomnia since 1999. A warm glass of milk before going to bed should end the problem for her. After all, it helps others to sleep well.

XII. YOUR OWN THINKING LAB

*1. 'If a principle has proved to be generally true or reliable, it's probably true all of the time.' Should we agree with this rule? Explain your answer.

2. Suppose I find in an argument some premise that itself can be accepted only if the conclusion has already been accepted. What's wrong with the argument? Explain the fallacy it commits.

3. Provide two circular arguments, one that begs the question and one that doesn't. What's wrong with those arguments?

*4. Ask a complex question and explain why it is a fallacy.

■ Writing Project

The principle that we should be tolerant of the beliefs and actions of others is highly regarded in our culture. Find at least three examples of current beliefs or actions that you think fall beyond the reach of that principle and write a short essay entitled "Beyond Tolerance." In each case, first construct an argument where that principle is used to contend that some episode (of hate speech, Holocaust denial, terrorism, etc.) should be tolerated. Then explain why the argument fails by showing that it commits the fallacy of accident.

■ Chapter Summary

Fallacies of Presumption: They make an argument fail in virtue of some unwarranted assumption built into its premises. The argument seems OK only when the assumption is made. They include:

1. **Begging the Question.** The argument features at least one premise that itself depends on the conclusion's being true, so that it can be accepted only if one has already accepted the conclusion.

2. **Begging the Question Against.** The *argument* features at least one controversial premise that is assumed to be true but not argued for. Note: when a claim is controversial, an argument that commits this fallacy is no help in discharging the burden of proof.

3. **Complex Question.** The question either has an unsupported assumption built into it or is a conflation of two or more different questions.

4. **False Alternatives.** The argument features a premise with a disjunction, mistakenly taking it to be either exclusive, when in fact both disjuncts could be true, or exhaustive, when in fact there is a third alternative.

5. **Accident.** The argument assumes that some principle generally applicable is applicable also in the anomalous case, when in fact it isn't.

■ Key Words

Presumption	Formal circularity
Begging the question	Conceptual circularity
Begging the question against	Complex question
Burden of proof	False alternatives
Commonsense belief	Accident
Vicious circularity	Benign circularity

CHAPTER 9

From Unclear Language to Unclear Reasoning

This chapter considers some common forms of unclarity in language, and the ways in which they lead to unclarity in reasoning. Its topics will include

- Three types of linguistic unclarity that may lead to fallacies: vagueness, ambiguity, and confused predication.
- The heap paradox.
- The fallacy of slippery slope.
- The fallacy of equivocation.
- The fallacy of amphiboly.
- The fallacy of composition.
- The fallacy of division.

9.1 Unclear Language and Argument Failure

Vagueness, ambiguity, and confused predication are three different sources of unclear language. Each may lead to argument failure, and we shall find, rooted in these defects, several types of informal fallacy as well as a type of puzzling argument. When an expression is vague to a significant degree, it is unclear whether it applies to certain things. For instance, it's unclear whether 'rich' applies to Betty, who has $900,000 in her bank account. She's certainly doing well, but she's not even a millionaire, much less a billionaire! The problem is that 'rich' is a vague word: for some cases, it's not clear what (or who) counts as being 'rich.' By contrast, when an expression is ambiguous to a significant degree, it has more than one meaning and reference, and it is unclear which one is intended by its user. For example, it is unclear whether "challenging arguments" means either *the act of disputing some arguments* or *complex arguments that are difficult to follow.* Roughly, the reference of an expression is what the expression applies to, while its meaning is its content. Consider

1 The sum of 1+1

2 The smallest even number.

Both (1) and (2) may be used to refer to the same thing, since they both apply to the same number—namely, the number 2. Yet (1) and (2) don't have the same content, which is equivalent to saying that they don't have the same meaning, for

MEANING = CONTENT

Since reference and meaning belong to the semantic dimension of a language, vagueness and ambiguity are two different forms of semantic unclarity. Each may undermine an argument by affecting some of the terms or concepts that make up its premises and conclusion.

Confused predication, on the other hand, also amounts to semantic unclarity, but it can arise only at the level of relations between statements in an argument. That is, confused predication is a fallacy involving a certain error committed in using some predicate, or expression that attributes some feature or quality to a thing— for example, 'occupying 60 percent of the surface of the Earth' in the conclusion of this argument:

3 Since oceans occupy 60 percent of the surface of the Earth and the Mediterranean is an ocean, therefore the Mediterranean occupies 60 percent of the surface of the Earth.

While 'occupying 60 percent of the surface of the Earth' might be truly predicated of all oceans taken collectively, it obviously fails to be true of the Mediterranean Sea. The confusion in (3) is a common type of mistake that stems from an erroneous inference involving a predicate (we'll have more to say about predicates later in this chapter).

Linguistic unclarity rooted in any of these phenomena (confused predication, vagueness, or ambiguity) can render an argument fallacious. Yet before we examine common ways in which this may happen, we must ask why such mistakes matter to logical thinking at all.

BOX 1 ■ SOME FALLACIES OF UNCLEAR LANGUAGE AND A PARADOX

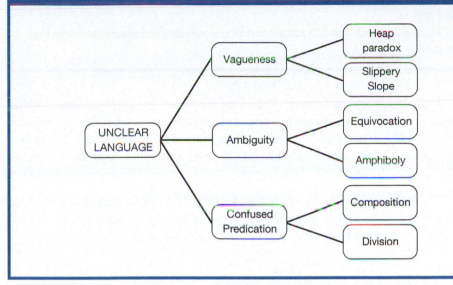

Two millennia ago, Greek philosophers pointed out that unclarity in language is a sign of unclarity in reasoning. Today we'd say much the same. Assuming that speakers are sincere, what they say is what they believe. And since beliefs are the building blocks of their reasoning, it is then quite likely that any unclarity in what they say results from unclarity in how they reason (for more on this topic, see Chapters 2 and 3).

9.2 Semantic Unclarity

Vagueness and ambiguity are forms of semantic unclarity that may affect linguistic expressions of different kinds, as well as the logical relations between them. When an expression is vague, it is unclear whether or not certain cases fall within its reference. When an expression is ambiguous, it is unclear which of its possible meanings is the one intended by the speaker. Suppose someone says

4   She got the cup.

Furthermore, this is said in a room where there are several women, without pointing to anyone in particular. In this context, it is unclear to whom the word 'she' applies. At the same time, the term 'cup' is ambiguous, since it may equally mean and refer to either 'bowl-shaped drinking vessel' or 'sports trophy.' Furthermore, if we assume that it is used to refer to a drinking vessel, it is unclear just how wide the range of its application may be. Does it apply, for example, to coffee mugs? What about beer tankards? These seem borderline cases about which 'cup' neither definitely applies nor definitely fails to apply. Hence, 'cup' is not only ambiguous, but also to some degree vague.

> **BOX 2 ■ VAGUENESS AND AMBIGUITY**
>
> ■ When an expression is vague, there are borderline cases where it is unclear whether the expression applies.
> ■ When an expression is ambiguous, it has more than one meaning and sometimes more than one reference.

Vagueness and ambiguity are, however, also found at a higher level in the statements that make up arguments. Here the worst-case scenario is one where a defect of either type renders an argument misleading. In any such argument, although its conclusion might at first appear acceptable on the basis of the argument's premises, a closer look could show that in fact it's not. The premises actually provide no support for it.

> Logical thinkers should be alert for misleading arguments and try, through careful, case-by-case scrutiny, to unmask fallacies lurking behind vague or ambiguous language.

These two forms of semantic unclarity are unavoidable features of many everyday arguments. Such arguments are, after all, cast in a natural language, which, unlike a formal language, is rich in semantic connotations. For example, suppose that a college instructor, on the day of an examination, receives this phone message on her answering machine:

5   This is Mary. I was at the bank during the test, so I'd like to take the makeup.

Unable to recognize the voice, and aware of several financial institutions as well as a river nearby, the instructor cannot make much of (5). For one thing, of the several students named 'Mary' who missed the exam, it is unclear who the caller in (5) is. Furthermore, of the two meanings of 'bank' possible in (5), either 'financial institution' or 'side of a river,' it is unclear which one is intended. Suppose the student who left the message later sends a note from the local Citibank branch attesting that, on the date of the exam, she, Mary McDonald, had to go there to refinance her mortgage. Putting two and two together, the instructor reasons that

6   Mary McDonald was the student who reported her absence. She can prove she was at the local Citibank branch the day of the exam. Thus she qualifies for the makeup.

No ambiguity remains now: a look at contextual information has eliminated the semantic unclarity in (5) above.

Yet sometimes semantic unclarity bearing on the soundness or strength of an argument persists even after we have engaged in a charitable and faithful reconstruction of the argument. In that case, we must reject the argument on the ground that its premises provide no support for its conclusion, even though they might at first appear to support it. As we shall presently see in detail, each of these two types of semantic unclarity can render an argument misleading.

9.3 Vagueness

Vagueness is at the root of some philosophically interesting puzzling arguments and also of many fallacious ones. Later in this section, we'll examine some cases of each. But first, let's consider a shortcoming common to all arguments affected by vagueness: indeterminacy.

> When either the premise or conclusion of an argument is significantly vague, that statement is indeterminate: neither determinately true nor determinately false. Such indeterminacy undermines the argument as a whole.

This is because, as you may recall, to be deductively sound or inductively strong, an argument must have premises that are determinately true. Without that, it counts as neither. Consider this argument:

7   1. Tall buildings in Chicago are in danger of terrorist attacks.
    2. The 30-story Nussbaum Building in Chicago is a tall building.
    3. The 30-story Nussbaum Building in Chicago is in danger of terrorist attacks.

This argument seems valid, since if its premises are true, its conclusion cannot be false. At the same time, it also seems unsound, for soundness requires determinately true premises, and premise 2 suffers from a significant degree of vagueness: putting aside the problem that tallness is relative, although a 100-story building is clearly tall (even by Chicago standards) and a 2-story building clearly not tall, it is unclear whether a 30-story building is tall in Chicago. No contextual information is available to reduce the vagueness of premise 2, which results from the two facts described in Box 4. The problem is that there is no determinate point or cutoff between tall Chicago buildings and Chicago buildings that are not tall.

When a statement has a vague term applied to a borderline case, that statement is neither determinately true nor determinately false. Try this yourself: run another series with, for example, 'cold,' beginning with the determinately true statement, 'A temperature of zero degrees Fahrenheit is cold,' and continuing to a point where you 'cannot draw the line.' Is it 47 degrees? 48 degrees? 50? Again, any cutoff point in the series would be rather arbitrary.

Keep in mind, however, that vague terms may have non-vague occurrences. Compare

8   The 30-story Nussbaum Building is tall.
9   The 100-story John Hancock Building is tall.
10   The one-story Exxon Station on Route 10 is tall.

While (8) is indeterminate, (9) seems determinately true and (10) determinately false.

BOX 5 ■ SUMMARY OF VAGUENESS

When a term is **vague,**

- It is indeterminate whether it applies or not to certain borderline cases.
- There is no cutoff between the cases to which it determinately applies and those to which it determinately does not.

When a statement is vague, it is neither determinately true nor determinately false.

The Heap Paradox

Every bit as puzzling to us today as it was to the philosophers of ancient Greece who discovered it is the heap paradox, also called 'argument from the heap' or '*sorites*' (from the Greek, *soros*, 'a heap'). The argument begins with obviously true premises, but, because they contain a vague term, ends with an obviously false conclusion:

11   1.   One grain of sand is not a heap.
    2.   If 1 grain of sand is not a heap, then 2 grains of sand are not a heap.
    3.   If 2 grains of sand are not a heap, then 3 grains of sand are not a heap.
    4.   If 3 grains of sand are not a heap, then 4 grains of sand are not a heap.
    5.   If 4 grains of sand are not a heap, then . . .
    6.   A large number (say, a million) grains of sand are not a heap.

Given (11), no matter how many grains of sand there are, they never make up a heap. Something has gone wrong in (11), but since it is difficult to tell what, (11) is a puzzle or paradox. After all, it seems that,

A.   The argument is valid.
B.   Its premises are true.
C.   Its conclusion is false.
D.   But a valid argument can't have true premises and a false conclusion.

Like other heap arguments, (11) then creates a paradox, for D is true by definition of 'valid argument.' Therefore, A, B, and C cannot all be true, but it is difficult to say which of them is false.

A **paradox** is a puzzle without apparent solution involving claims that cannot all be true at once, even though each seems independently true. Standardly, a paradox may be dealt with in one or the other of two ways: it may be solved or it may be dissolved. To solve a paradox, at least one of its claims must be shown false. To dissolve it, it has to be shown that the claims are not really inconsistent.

Until we do either the one or the other, the paradox remains. Since antiquity, the heap paradox has resisted many attempts of both kinds, all of which have turned out to be flawed in one way or another.

Let's now use another vague word, 'child,' to run a simplified heap paradox.

12 1. A 3-year-old is a child.
    2. If a 3-year-old is a child, then a 4-year-old is a child.
    3. If a 4-year-old is a child, then . . .
    4. A 90-year-old is a child.

Again, the argument seems valid, its premises true, and its conclusion false. Premise 2 suggest a chain of premises such as

13 If a 4-year-old is a child, then a 5-year-old is a child.

14 If a 5-year-old is a child, then a 6-year-old is a child.

The series eventually reaches borderline cases such as a 14-year-old or a 15-year-old, about whom to the term 'child' neither clearly applies nor doesn't apply. There is no cutoff point between these and the previous cases, to which the word clearly applies. Or between these and the following case, to which the word clearly doesn't apply:

15 A 110-year-old person is a child.

The unclarity affecting (12), then, is owing to the vagueness of the word 'child.'

More needs to be said about what goes wrong in the heap argument, but on the basis of its puzzling aspects, it has all the marks of a paradox.

The above arguments run into the heap paradox because they feature words such as 'heap' and 'child,' which are affected by vagueness.

The Slippery-Slope Fallacy

By contrast with the heap paradox, we can tell what has gone wrong in arguments that commit the fallacy of concern here:

A **slippery-slope** argument proceeds from a premise about a harmless scenario to one or more premises about apparently similar scenarios that are taken to have unwelcome consequences, either flouting well-accepted rules or leading to disaster. The argument would commit a fallacy just in case there is no good reason to think

- That the scenarios in question are analogous in the way assumed in the argument, or
- That the chain of events envisioned will in fact happen as assumed in the argument.

Thus arguments that commit this fallacy begin with a premise that seems clearly true and move through a continuum of cases to a conclusion that appears to be the unavoidable result of sound reasoning. Yet close scrutiny often shows that it isn't sound. Imagine two arguments on opposite sides of a City Council debate on whether to enact legislation requiring registration of handguns.

16 Council Member Robinson argues, "If we pass a law requiring registration of handguns, that will lead inevitably to other laws requiring registration of all firearms, including hunting weapons. And that will then mean that the government will have a list of all the gun owners. But if the government has such a list, the next inevitable step is the confiscation of all weapons by the government. From this, it is but a small step to dictatorship and the end of freedom."

16' Council Member Richardson replies, "If we fail to pass a law requiring the registration of handguns, these guns will become easier and easier to obtain. And this will mean that criminals and psychopaths of every description will have their pick of dangerous firearms, including assault weapons. If that happens, crime will increase exponentially and our cities will become lawless battlefields. Ultimately, all social order will break down. Armed thugs will run roughshod over the rights of citizens as our nation descends into anarchy."

The thing to notice in this debate is that *both* of these arguments commit the slippery-slope fallacy. They both begin by issuing a warning about an apparently innocent first step and then predict a succession of worsening conditions, leading ultimately to disaster, if the initial step is taken (Robinson) or not taken (Richardson). But is there really any good reason to think that the hopeless slide to catastrophe envisioned in either of these two very different arguments really would happen? Of course, such things could happen. But we're not justified in believing it would on the basis of the "reasons" presented here. Both of these council members are offering arguments that are little more that speculative fearmongering and hype. They plainly commit slippery slope.

In a different variant of the slippery-slope argument, an argument may fail because there is no good reason to think that an assumed similarity between premises actually obtains. Suppose you arrive five minutes late to a wedding without making much of it. The conventional rule is that arriving, say, sixty minutes late to a wedding is a serious breach of etiquette and therefore not acceptable. Someone thinks that your five-minute delay is not acceptable, because allowing it is not significantly different from allowing a sixty-minute delay, which would in effect overthrow that rule altogether. This example of slippery-slope fallacy runs,

17 Whatever justifies arriving five minutes late to a wedding would justify arriving six minutes late, seven minutes late,. . . and even sixty minutes late! Thus accepting a justification for arriving five minutes late would amount to overthrowing an important social convention.

Clearly there is a kind of reasoning by analogy here, since consistency requires that we treat like cases alike, ascribing the same qualities to each pair of relevantly similar cases in the series (six minutes late is not much different from seven minutes late, which is itself not much different from eight minutes late, etc.). But the background assumption seems to be that a sequence of small differences can never amount to a substantial difference between any two points in the sequence. And that's plainly false. Small differences can sometimes add up to a big difference in the end. Furthermore, even in the comparison of two similar cases, it may turn out that some predicates are true of one without being true of the other. For example, on some highways the law stipulates a speed limit of 70 miles per hour. Now, there is no significant difference in speed between 70 miles per hour and 71 miles per hour; but because of the law, driving at 70 miles per hour on those highways is legal, while driving at 71 is technically illegal. So the predicate 'legal' truly applies in one case but not in the other, even though they are otherwise not substantially different. We may conclude that any argument committing the slippery-slope fallacy rests on this false principle: What is true of A is also true of Z, provided there is a series of cases B, C,. . ., Y between A and Z that differ from each other only minimally.

BOX 6 ■ HOW TO AVOID THE SLIPPERY-SLOPE FALLACY

Reject the principle fueling a slippery-slope argument, for that something is true of some given case doesn't guarantee that it's likewise true of any other similar case. Although it is reasonable that similar cases share many predicates, small differences in a *series* of cases can add up to a big difference between the initial case and the one featured in the slippery-slope argument's conclusion. The slippery-slope arguer fails to take this into account.

9.4 Ambiguity

Vagueness must be distinguished from ambiguity. As we have seen, a word or phrase is vague if its reference is indeterminate, so that it is unclear whether or not it applies to a certain case. But ambiguity is a different kind of semantic unclarity that is also apt to cause havoc in arguments, and therefore is equally likely to mislead. A word is ambiguous if it has more than one meaning and a given context makes unclear which meaning is intended.

> When an ambiguous word occurs in an argument's premise, it may be uncertain whether the argument's conclusion is supported by it at all.

Consider this argument:

18 Entertainment Television features news about stars. So, probably many astronomers watch Entertainment Television.

Here 'star' is the ambiguous word occurring in the premise, which as a result provides no support for the argument's conclusion. For the argument to succeed, we would need to know whether the intended meaning of 'star' is 'celestial body seen as a small fixed point of light' or 'celebrity entertainer.' If the former, then, assuming that that's known, the premise would give a reason for the conclusion, provided that the premise is true. But if the latter, then it wouldn't (for in that case the premise and conclusion would be completely unrelated). Yet, as it stands, since in (18) 'stars' is ambiguous and the context leaves the intended meaning unclear, the argument fails to support its conclusion. We'll now look more closely at some types of defective reasoning where arguments are fallacious by virtue of containing ambiguous expressions.

Equivocation

The fallacy of equivocation is always rooted in ambiguous expressions, whether words or phrases, in either an argument's premises or its conclusion.

> **Equivocation** occurs when some crucial expression is used with more than one meaning over the course of an argument—for example, in one place it means one thing, in another something else—and the argument appears to support the conclusion *only as long as one doesn't notice* that there has been this shift in meaning.

Suppose, for instance, that someone argues,

19 1. All laws require a lawmaker.
   2. Galileo's principle of inertia is a law.
   3. Galileo'principle of inertia requires a lawmaker.

Here two different meanings of the word 'law' are conflated. In the first premise, it means 'statute'—a codified public regulation enacted by a legislature or other authority. But in the second premise, it means 'scientific generalization based on observed regularities of nature.' Because the word is being used with two different meanings over the course of the argument, the argument is an instance of the fallacy of equivocation. As such, its premises fail to provide adequate support for the conclusion, and the argument fails. Another argument with the same type of problem is

20 "I read the advertisement for Aqueduct Racetrack. It said, *Aqueduct: if you're out to have a good time, you can't lose.* But I just lost $600 there! My horse came in last! So they're using fraudulent advertising."

Here there is an equivocation on 'you can't lose.' The conclusion, signaled by 'so,' follows only if we take it to mean 'you can't lose your bet,' but really it's intended to mean 'you can't fail to have a good time.' No fraudulent advertising there! Finally, consider this example:

21 The sign at the garage says "Reserved Customers Only," so I guess that means that my Uncle Evinrude, who's constantly cracking jokes and impersonating barnyard animals, would not be welcome.

If 'reserved' is taken to mean 'restrained in words and actions,' then it certainly doesn't apply to Uncle Evinrude. But surely the 'reserved' customers the garage management have in mind are not necessarily the quiet and dignified, but simply those who have made arrangements in advance for a parking space.

Be on guard against expressions rendered ambiguous either by having different meanings in different places in an argument, as in (19) and (20), or by having two or more possible meanings in a single occurrence, as in (18) and (21). Either of these forms of equivocation may make it unclear whether the argument's conclusion follows from the premises. To detect (and avoid) the fallacy of equivocation, follow this rule:

BOX 7 ■ HOW TO AVOID EQUIVOCATION

In evaluating an argument, check thoroughly to be sure that its crucial expressions

- Have unambiguous meaning.
- Have the same meaning in each occurrence in the argument.

Amphiboly

Another form of misleading argument where ambiguity is the source of the problem is the fallacy of amphiboly.

> In **amphiboly**, it's the awkward construction of sentences—the confusing way their words are arranged—that renders them unclear, and so invites drawing the wrong conclusion from them.

We say 'wrong' because the conclusion drawn from an amphibolous premise either doesn't clearly follow from it or doesn't follow from it at all. To see the fallacy at work, consider the following joke, a comedy routine from vaudeville:

22 *Patient:* Doctor, Doctor! My arm hurts in two places! What should I do?
    Doctor: Don't go to those places!

We smile when we read or hear amphibolous sentences like the patient's, where a clumsy word order causes it to have a double meaning. Of course, the sentence by itself is not an argument, but if its ambiguity leads the 'doctor' to draw the wrong conclusion from it, then the dialogue contains an implicit argument. How, then, does that argument commit the fallacy of amphiboly? Plainly, it is defective by virtue of ambiguity caused by word order. The argument runs,

23 1. Your arm hurts in two places.
   2. Pain is to be avoided.

   3. You shouldn't go to those places where your arm hurts.

Assuming that premise 2 is true, even so, since premise 1 is amphibolous, (23) fails to support statement 3. Fortunately for those who want to be alert for this fallacy, there is a distinguishing characteristic that may help in recognizing it: in all cases of amphiboly, the ambiguity can be eliminated by recasting the sentence. For example, in (22), the patient's complaint is not amphibolous if recast as

24 There are two places on my arm that hurt.

Although not all amphibolies are humorous, the amphiboly that makes us laugh is fairly typical of this fallacy. Here is another example:

25 The Chase Manhattan Bank once ran an advertisement that said, *Talk to one of Chase's small business advisers today.* "So," one potential customer wondered, "what is the average height of business advisers at Chase?"

In this argument, the conclusion (signaled by 'so') is phrased as a question, but really it's a sarcastic reaction to the advertisement, better rendered as, 'So Chase bankers who specialize in business loans are all short!' The semantic confusion that generates this miscommunication is in the amphibolous phrase 'small business advisers.' Is it the businesses that are small? Or is it the advisers? Let's look at one more example, this time from Moses Hadas, the distinguished classical scholar. An author who had sent his book to Hadas hoping for a favorable review received Hadas's acerbic reply,

26 I have read your book and much like it.

If, from this sentence, the author had drawn the conclusion, "Therefore, Hadas liked my book!" he would have been too hasty, since it's not clear that that's what Hadas meant. (26) is ambiguous, owing to its grammar: in this case, 'like' could be either a verb expressing Hadas's favorable assessment of the book, or a modifier of 'it.' In the latter case, the statement would have meant, "I have read your book and many other things very similar to it" (i.e., "this work lacks originality!").

The lesson we can take from all of these examples is that we must be on guard for language that carries a double meaning. To detect (and avoid) the fallacy of amphiboly, the rule is to inspect an argument's premises as directed in Box 8. If you find ambiguity caused by awkward grammar, word order, excessive concision, or mere carelessness in the wording of a premise, recast that premise, when possible, in a way that removes the ambiguity. In doing so, be sure to follow the principles of charity and faithfulness for argument reconstruction.

9.5 Confused Predication

We must now turn our attention to two types of informal fallacy that are rooted in a confusion involving predication. First, let's explain terminology. What, exactly, is 'predication'? Consider, for example,

27 Mount Whitney is tall.

Of the two terms in (27), 'tall' and 'Mount Whitney,' only the former is uncontroversially a predicate—in this case, one that attributes the property of being tall to Mount Whitney. Predicates are often used to describe individual entities as being in certain ways. But they may also be used to attribute properties to complex entities such as classes, groups, and wholes. Those entities may involve a class of things (e.g., yellow cars), a collective group (e.g., the Cleveland Orchestra), or a whole made up of parts (e.g., a computer). Classes and collective groups have members, while wholes have parts. Predicates are used to attribute properties and relations to individual things or persons and also to such complex entities. Consider the following:

28 Yellow cars are fashionable.

29 The Cleveland Orchestra is first-rate.

30 My new computer is well designed.

Here *being fashionable*, *being first-rate*, and *being well designed* are the properties attributed by the predicates. There is, of course, nothing wrong with using predicates in these ways to describe individual things or classes, collectives, and wholes. We couldn't do without these types of descriptions.

But sometimes a confusion in predication leads to defects in reasoning that happen when the arguer fails to notice either of these:

1. Some properties that apply to a whole, a class of things, or a collective group, as stated in an argument's premises, do not apply to each part of the whole or to each individual member of the class or group as stated in its conclusion.

2. Conversely, some properties that apply to a part of a whole, or an individual member of a class or a group as stated in an argument's premises, do not apply to the entire whole, class, or group as stated in its conclusion.

Whether it is an individual thing that is said to have a property or a class of things (or a collective group or a whole) matters for clarity in reasoning. When this important distinction is ignored, an argument may, for example, fallaciously attribute a certain property to a class of things in the premises and to a member of that class in the conclusion, as in argument (3) at the beginning of this chapter:

3 Since oceans occupy 60 percent of the surface of the Earth and the Mediterranean is an ocean, therefore the Mediterranean occupies 60 percent of the surface of the Earth.

Let's now look closely at two informal fallacies of confused predication, known as *composition* and *division*.

Composition

Confused predication underlies the informal fallacy known as 'composition.'

Composition rests on the mistake of thinking that, since each of the parts of some whole, or each of the members of a class or group, has a certain property, therefore the whole, class, or group itself also has that same property.

For example, consider this argument:

31 1. Each player for the Chicago Cubs is an excellent player.
2. The Chicago Cubs are an excellent team.

It is very likely that (31)'s premise is true (in baseball, one has to be very good to get into the major leagues). Yet even if each player for the Cubs is excellent, that wouldn't support the claim that the team as a group is excellent. For an excellent team is more than just a collection of excellent individual athletes. It's a team that functions well as a coordinated group. Argument (31), then, is defective, even if the premise and conclusion are both true. Why? Because it commits the fallacy of composition through overlooking the crucial distinction in Box 10.

BOX 10 ■ HOW TO AVOID THE FALLACY OF COMPOSITION

- It is one thing to predicate a property of each individual member of a team, class, and so on, but quite another to predicate it of the team itself. What may be true in the one case might not be so in the other.
- If an argument concludes that a whole itself has a certain property on the basis of its parts each having that property individually, it commits the fallacy of composition and should be rejected.

Similarly, consider

32   1. Each part of a computer consumes very little energy.
     2. A computer consumes very little energy.

Argument (32) falls short of being deductively valid, or even inductively strong. A research-lab supercomputer would make its premise true and its conclusion false. Again, the root of the problem is in thinking that because each of the parts individually has a certain property (namely, that of running with little energy), therefore the whole made up of all of those parts must have it, too. Here's another argument with the same sort of problem:

33   Advertisement: "At Global Gobel Airlines, we've got the best-maintained fleet of planes in the air. We have more than 500 state-of-the-art jets, and each plane is expertly operated. Therefore, our airline is expertly operated."

To predicate the property 'expertly operated' of the airplane is one thing. To predicate that same property *of the airline* is something else. So it doesn't follow that Global Gobel is 'expertly operated' just because each of its planes is. Argument (33) commits the fallacy of composition.
     Bear in mind the advice in Box 10.

Division

Another fallacy of confused predication is division.

Division rests on the mistake of thinking that because the whole has a certain property, therefore each of the parts or members that make it up has that same property.

Unlike composition, division makes the mistake of thinking that what can be truly predicated of the whole can likewise be truly predicated of the parts that make it up. Suppose someone argues,

34   1. The U.S. Congress represents every state in the Union.
     2. Each member of the U.S. Congress represents every state in the Union.

Here the premise is uncontroversially true, but the conclusion is plainly false. What has gone wrong is that a simple principle has been ignored. That a property can be truly predicated of some collective group provides no guarantee that it can also be truly predicated of each member of that group. In (34), someone's being a member of a body that represents every state in the Union is taken to support the conclusion that that person individually represents every state in the Union. And, of course, that does not follow. What is true of the Congress may well not be true of each member of Congress. Thus the argument commits the fallacy of division.

While we're on the subject of Washington, here is another argument that commits the fallacy of division:

35 1. <u>The taxicabs in Washington, D.C., are numerous.</u>
      2. Each taxicab in Washington, D.C., is numerous.

(35) makes an inferential move from a predicate being true of a class of things (i.e., Washington taxicabs) in the premise, to that predicate's being true of each individual Washington taxi in the conclusion. Thus this is an instance of division. It is only classes of things that can (collectively) be numerous. Individuals can't be, so the conclusion in (35) is just nonsense! As we've seen, the fact that some collective entity has an attribute does not provide a good reason to conclude that the same attribute can rightly be ascribed to any part of it. Let's look at one more argument:

36 The annual National Spelling Bee contest has grown popular over the years, partly as a result of the Academy Award–nominated documentary *Spellbound*. Therefore, the fourteen-year-old girl from Ohio who has won the spelling bee has grown popular over the years.

Again, the problem is that a property rightly attributed to a complex whole is being wrongly attributed to the part. In this case, the complex whole is the National Spelling Bee, and the part is the current winner of the contest, the girl from Ohio. The property in question is that of having 'grown popular over the years.' From the fact that that is true of the spelling bee, it doesn't follow that it's true of the girl. A fallacy of division has been committed.

Logical thinkers, then, should beware of the informal fallacies that can arise through confusion in predication and be able to distinguish the two different types of confusion that underlie division, on the one hand, and composition, on the other. To detect and avoid these fallacies, follow the rules in Boxes 11 and 12.

BOX 11 ■ HOW TO AVOID THE FALLACY OF DIVISION

In evaluating an argument, ask whether it concludes that each part of a whole has a certain property on the basis of the whole's having that property. If it does, the argument commits the fallacy of division and should be rejected.

BOX 12 ■ SUMMARY OF CONFUSED PREDICATION

In evaluating an argument, check whether

- It concludes that each part of a whole has a certain property because the whole has that property, or
- It concludes that a whole itself has a certain property because each of its parts has that property individually.

If either of these is the case, then the argument commits one of the fallacies of confused predication and must therefore be rejected.

Exercises

I. Review Questions

1. What is the difference between meaning and reference?
2. Explain the difference between vagueness and ambiguity.
3. What is a predicate? Provide examples of sentences, identifying their predicates.
4. What is the heap argument? And why is it a paradox?
5. Explain what a slippery-slope fallacy is. Why should such arguments be rejected?
6. What is the fallacy of equivocation?
7. Name three sources of confusion that might lead to the fallacy of amphiboly.
8. Why are composition and division fallacies of confused predication?

II. Some of the following are plainly vague and some are not. Determine which is which.

1. Hot day

    SAMPLE ANSWER: Plainly vague

2. Young

*3. Equilateral triangle

4. Leopard

*5. Bachelor

6. U.S. District Attorney

*7. Poor

8. Populous

*9. Parallel lines

10. Odd number

11. The United Nations

*12. Person

13. Human being

14. Gold

*15. Bald

III. For each of the above terms that are plainly vague, show its vagueness by constructing a heap paradox involving that term.

IV. For each of the following expressions, show that it can be used ambiguously by constructing a sentence where the expression could have different meanings. If necessary, provide a context.

1. Sub

   SAMPLE ANSWER: 'My recent experience with subs has been a disaster.' In one context, 'sub' may mean a type of naval vessel; in another, a type of sandwich; in still another, a substitute worker.

2. Snake in the grass   6. Desert

3. Fraternity   7. Pirate

4. Siren   9. Honey

5. Birthday   10. Plateau

V. The following are instances of the heap paradox, slippery slope, equivocation, amphiboly, composition, or division. For each argument, indicate which of these it exemplifies.

1. The one who testified against Tony Soprano was a rat. A rat is a rodent of the genus *Rattus*. It follows that the one who testified against Tony Soprano was a rodent of the genus *Rattus*.

   SAMPLE ANSWER: Equivocation

2. Donors to the Philharmonic's fund-raising campaign have given the orchestra millions of dollars this year. My neighbor Mrs. Martinez was one of those donors. We may infer that Mrs. Martinez gave the orchestra millions of dollars.

*3. Phil is taking six courses this semester, and they're all three-credit courses. But each course is easy, so Phil will have an easy semester.

4. Leon Kass, a prominent bioethicist, argues for a ban or moratorium on human cloning. Permitting such cloning, he insists, can only lead to abuse. "Today, cloned blastocysts for research; tomorrow, cloned blastocysts for baby-making"—*New York Times*, February 17, 2004.

5. Perhaps you think that twelve is an even number? Well, I can prove that it is odd. Consider my uncle Horace. He was born with five toes on one foot and seven toes on the other, which gives him twelve toes. Now, I'm sure you'll agree that twelve toes is an odd number of toes for a man. Therefore, twelve is an odd number.

6. If we continue to permit abortion, then we'll soon be allowing euthanasia on demand. This line of reasoning leads straight to justifying mass exterminations of any 'unwanted' people. At last we'll be led to death camps and outright genocide. Therefore, abortion should not be permitted.

*7. Sue says: "The Department of Traffic Control announced last month that in Boston a pedestrian is hit by a car once every thirty-seven minutes." Sam replies: "Wow! That guy must be in bad shape!"

8. The manager told me she would lose no time in looking at my résumé. So I'm sure she will read it immediately.

9. Young people are independent minded. Ryan Seacrest is young, so he is independent minded.

*10. Some people think that all citizens should have to carry national identity cards, just as people do in most other countries. But it's clear that this is a bad idea. Once we begin registering our identities with the government, that can lead only to more government control over individual lives. Eventually, all our precious freedoms will be gone, and we'll have a dictatorship.

11. The Rolling Stones were at their best in the first half of the year. It follows that their guitarist Keith Richards was at his best in the first half of the year.

12. If a man has one hair on his head, he is bald, isn't he? Suppose he has two hairs: he is also bald. This seems to suggest that a man with one million hairs on his head is also bald.

*13. The Brooklyn Bridge is made up entirely of atoms. Science has proved that atoms are invisible. Therefore, the Brooklyn Bridge is invisible.

14. Mother says Uncle Ryan is a couch potato. Since potatoes are vegetables, it follows that Uncle Ryan is a vegetable.

15. Dissenters must be suppressed at once, to ensure that they do not undermine presidential authority. One dissenter today means millions of dissenters tomorrow. If even a single person is allowed to dissent, this will be the first step that will lead ultimately to anarchy.

16. Private universities are not particularly expensive. For they are charging about $48,000 per year for tuition plus room and board. If that's expensive, then $47,999 is expensive, too. But if $47,999 is expensive, then $47,998 is expensive. It follows that any amount, even $1, is expensive.

*17. You can eat that chocolate chip cookie if you want, but I say you're asking for trouble. Next you'll be eating ice cream, then hot fudge sundaes. Soon it'll be double cheeseburgers, fried chicken, and layer cakes! Stroke and a heart attack are waiting for you, without a doubt.

18. The chemical designation for common table salt is sodium chloride (NaCl). Salt is a compound of sodium and chlorine. And since salt is, of course, edible and not at all poisonous, it follows that sodium and chlorine are each edible and not at all poisonous.

19. A "cybersquatter" misused a web address containing Tom Cruise's name, which must be returned to the actor, since the arbitrators have determined that the actor owns it.

*20. Ice cream is enjoyable. Beer is enjoyable, too. Therefore, ice cream and beer for lunch would be enjoyable.

21. Colleges should not consider cheerleading a competitive sport, for that will lead to their having to consider tai chi a competitive sport. That will lead to considering hotdog eating, stilt walking, and many other activities as competitive sports. The concept of sport would then lose its meaning.

22. In the ancient world, Persia was a mighty kingdom. But Croesus, the Greek king, also ruled a mighty kingdom in Lydia. When Croesus asked the Delphic Oracle for advice, she told him, "If Croesus crossed the river Halys (i.e., invaded Persia) he would destroy a mighty kingdom." Croesus was delighted with this news and concluded that he should immediately invade Persia, which he did. As a result, Lydia was destroyed.

23. Some who read the *New York Times* headline 'ON DRUGS, BUSH AIMS FOR A MEETING OF THE MINDS AT LEAST,' concluded that the president was on drugs!

*24. Residents of San Francisco come from every country in the world. Ms. Solomon is a resident of San Francisco. It follows that Ms. Solomon comes from every country in the world.

25. A candidate for Congress introduces himself as follows: "My name is Henry G. Honest, and I believe you should vote for me. I'm the only candidate in this election who can truly call himself honest."

26. Announcement in church bulletin: "For those of you who have children and may not know it, there is a nursery available in the parish hall during worship services." Thus it seems that some members of the church have children and don't know it!

*27. The average American family has 2.5 cars. The Johnsons are an average American family. Therefore, the Johnsons have 2.5 cars.

28. Taxpayers' dollars are dollars. There is nothing wrong with using dollars to buy myself a trip to Europe. Thus there is nothing wrong with using taxpayers' dollars to buy myself a trip to Europe.

29. Only cardinals can vote to elect the Pope. The St. Louis Cardinals will play in the World Series this year. Therefore, some voters to elect the Pope will play in the World Series this year.

*30. An online news source recently ran the headline "Slain Preacher's Wife to Testify at Murder Trial." We may infer that a dead person will give testimony in court!

31. A one-year-old is young. Since adding one year more doesn't make a difference, we must conclude that an eighty-six-year-old is young.

32. One way to lose weight would be to fast: that is, to give up eating certain foods for a while. Of course, you would not have to give up everything—some foods you could continue to eat. But what foods? Well, foods appropriate to a fast, I suppose. McDonald's and Burger King are well known fast-food restaurants. Therefore, if I want to lose weight, I should eat only at McDonald's or Burger King.

*33. After seeing this newspaper item—"The current pastor of Old South Church, now 333 years old, is the Rev. James W. Crawford"—I concluded, "Funny, he doesn't look a day over fifty!"

34. Since flying is more expensive than driving, birds will stop flying south for the winter.

35. In Chicago, every elevated train line comprises about thirty stations. So in Chicago, the elevated train system comprises about thirty stations.

36. No person who has only $1 in the bank is rich. If so, no person who has only $2 in the bank is rich. This line of reasoning suggests that ultimately we'd have to say that a person with $10 billion in the bank is not rich.

*37. The importance of the airline industry to the nation's economy cannot be underestimated. If the major airlines fail, America itself will fail. If America fails, then Western civilization is doomed. Thus we must act now to save the major airlines from bankruptcy.

38. Each part of this motorcycle weighs very little. Therefore, this motorcycle weighs very little.

39. You can drink as much coffee as you wish without getting jumpy. For clearly, one cup of coffee will not make you jumpy, and if that's so, then a cup and a half won't make you jumpy. And if a cup and a half won't make you jumpy, then neither will two cups. There is no way to draw the line.

*40. Each college in the university is semi-autonomous. Therefore, the university is semi-autonomous.

VI. YOUR OWN THINKING LAB

1. Are coffee mugs cups? Discuss what sort of semantic unclarity is involved in expressions containing the word 'mug.' Is it vagueness, ambiguity, or both? Provide sentences that illustrate the sort of semantic unclarity that may affect the uses of this word.

2. Identify the fallacy committed by the following arguments and explain what has gone wrong in each.

  A. If euthanasia were made legal, then people would use it to get rid of ailing relatives. But if people used it to get rid of ailing relatives, then there would be no difference between what we do in our society and what totalitarian regimes have done with firing squads and death camps. Therefore, euthanasia must not be made legal.

  B. If execution is rejected as cruel and unusual punishment, then life in prison without parole will be, too. But this line of reasoning leads eventually to proposing that dangerous criminals go free. That would create social chaos. It follows that execution should not be rejected as cruel and unusual punishment.

■ Writing Project

Some might contend that abortion is wrong because no clear line can be drawn to distinguish morally between the killing of fetuses and the killing of adults in death camps—so that if we permit the former, it follows that we must also permit the latter. Reconstruct the argument in defense of that conclusion. Then criticize it by objecting that it commits a slippery-slope fallacy. This will require arguing that a line *could* after all be drawn between the killing of fetuses and the mass killing of people in death camps (think of an important feature that distinguishes these acts of killing). But opponents of abortion can offer arguments for their view that don't commit the slippery-slope fallacy. Can you give an example?

■ Chapter Summary

Linguistic unclarity may be caused by:

1. **The *vagueness* of one or more words.** When a word is vague to a significant degree, its reference is unclear. When a statement is vague to a significant degree, it is neither determinately true nor determinately false.

2. **The *ambiguity* of one or more words.** When an expression is ambiguous, it has more than one meaning or referent, and it is unclear which meaning is intended by the speaker.

3. **Confused predication.** A fallacy of composition or of division (see below).

The Heap Paradox: An argument that trades on the vagueness of some term, so that although it appears a valid inference, from premises that are seemingly true it draws a conclusion that is plainly false. The argument creates a paradox or puzzle—which is a problem without obvious solution.

Fallacies of Unclear Language:

  Slippery slope, committed by any argument that moves through a continuum of cases, from a premise that appears true, to a claim about a catastrophic result or the flouting of a rule, either of which is presented as an unavoidable result from the initial premises. But its premises offer no good reason for the conclusion.

  Equivocation, committed by any argument in which some crucial expression occurs with more than one meaning.

Amphiboly, committed by any argument in which an awkward grammatical construction, word order, or phrasing of the premise creates ambiguity and makes it possible to draw the wrong conclusion.

Composition, committed by any argument that concludes that a whole (class, group) itself has a certain property, given that each of its parts or members has that property individually.

Division, committed by any argument that concludes that each part of a whole (class, group) has a certain property, given that the whole has that property.

■ Key Words

Semantic unclarity	Predicate
Vagueness	Meaning
Borderline case	Confused predication
Indeterminacy	Composition
Slippery-slope fallacy	Paradox
Ambiguity	Division
Equivocation	Reference
Amphiboly	Heap paradox

CHAPTER 10

Avoiding Irrelevant Premises

This chapter is devoted to the fallacies of relevance. You'll learn about six different ways in which premises may be irrelevant to the conclusion they're supposedly supporting. There is also a discussion of how logical thinkers can take account of emotion in reasoning. The topics include

- Appeal to pity.
- Appeal to force.
- Appeal to emotion.
- Ad hominem.
- Beside the point.
- Straw-man arguments.
- Non-fallacious appeals to emotion in everyday reasoning.

10.1 Fallacies of Relevance

Another source of error in reasoning that can cause an argument to be misleading is the failure of premises to be relevant to the conclusion they are offered to support. Even if a premise is plainly true, if it is also irrelevant to the conclusion it is supposedly backing up, then it cannot count as a reason for it, and the argument fails. Arguments that are fallacious by virtue of having irrelevant premises often rely on distractions that draw attention away from what truly matters for the conclusions at hand, and thus are sometimes employed as rhetorical tricks by artful persuaders who aim to influence us by psychologically effective but logically defective means. There are several types of informal fallacy that manifest this form of error, often known as 'fallacies of relevance.' We'll consider six of them here.

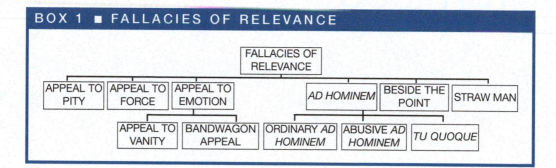

10.2 Appeal to Pity

One type of fallacy of relevance is the appeal to pity (also called *ad misericordiam*).

> An argument commits the fallacy of appeal to pity if and only if its premises attempt to arouse feelings of sympathy as a means of supporting its conclusion.

Consider, for example, an argument that was once made on behalf of clemency for Rudolf Hess, a close associate of Hitler arrested in Britain during World War II and later sentenced to life imprisonment for war crimes. In 1982, when Hess was old and in poor health, some people argued that he should be freed from prison. The argument went this way:

1
1. Hess has already spent more than forty years in prison.
2. He is in his eighties now and his health is failing.
3. This elderly man should be permitted to spend his last years with his family.
4. Hess should be granted clemency.

But Hess's age and failing health were irrelevant to the real issue: his guilt as one of the founders of a regime that had terrorized Europe. Many Russians, whose country had suffered millions of deaths at the hands of the German invaders, recognized this argument as an appeal to pity and objected vigorously. As a result, Hess's sentence was never commuted and he died in prison.

A similar argument was offered recently by the mother of a sea pirate, who begged the president of the United States for leniency in her son's case on the grounds that he was "lured into piracy by older friends." According to a report in the Associated Press, the pirate himself expressed contrition. "I am very, very sorry about what we did," he said through an interpreter. "All of this was about the problems in Somalia." But even if we do feel sorry for him, in view of his wretched existence in a war-torn, lawless land, that is hardly enough to justify the murder of innocent merchant seamen on foreign-flag ships. The argument is plainly an appeal to pity.

It's worth noting, however, that it's not only on behalf of scoundrels and criminals that people resort to the appeal to pity. We find it in everyday life in many guises, including some uses we may (wrongly) think free of this fallacy—for example, when a student argues,

2 You gave me a B in this course, but ... can't you give me an A? If I don't have an A, then it'll mean that my grade average will fall, and I won't be able to get into law school! And I've been working hard all semester.

The argument in fact is:

2' 1. I've been working hard in this course.

2. Any grade below an A would adversely affect my chances for law school.

3. I should get an A in this course.

This argument commits the fallacy of appeal to pity. But not because of premise 1: plainly, how hard the student has been working is not relevant to its conclusion, but that is the fallacy known as 'beside the point' (more on this later). What's making the argument count as an appeal to pity is premise 2: that premise shows that the argument attempts to support its conclusion by making the professor feel sorry for the student. It might succeed in doing that, but it fails to make its conclusion rationally acceptable.

More generally, an appeal to pity is a fallacious argument trading on the fact that feeling sorry for someone is often psychologically motivating. Yet that is not a good reason for the argument's conclusion. Logical thinkers would want to be able to recognize and avoid this fallacy. For some tips on this, see Box 2.

BOX 2 ■ HOW TO AVOID APPEAL TO PITY

1. An argument whose premises attempt to provoke feelings of sympathy that might move an audience to accept its conclusion commits the fallacy of appeal to pity.
2. Any such argument should be rejected, since it provides no reason relevant to its conclusion—that is, it provides no rational support for it.

10.3 Appeal to Force

Another informal fallacy trading on feelings, though in an entirely different way, is the appeal to force (sometimes called *ad baculum*, literally, 'to the stick').

> An argument commits the fallacy of appeal to force if and only if it resorts to a threat as a means of supporting its conclusion.

In any argument that commits this fallacy, the arguer attempts to arouse feelings of fear in someone as a way of getting her to accept a conclusion (it's as if he were saying, 'Agree with me or else!'). At the end of World War II, when Allied leaders met at Potsdam, Germany, to decide how Europe would be divided, Stalin's armored divisions already held Eastern Europe in an iron grip guaranteeing Soviet influence there. Told that the Pope had suggested a political settlement less accommodating to Soviet aims, Stalin harrumphed, "How many divisions does the Pope have?"

Of course, the threat voiced in an appeal to force need not be a physical threat. It might merely hint darkly of unfortunate consequences awaiting those who disagree with the arguer. To detect (and avoid) the fallacy of appeal to force in arguments, the rule is to check their premises as suggested in Box 3.

When Richard J. Daley was mayor of Chicago, from 1955 until his death in 1976, he exercised near-autocratic control over the Cook County Democratic Party organization. Public officials were well aware that they served at the pleasure of Mayor Daley and that any evidence of their disloyalty could have adverse consequences. Every time Daley would run for reelection, the word would go out to senior public officials serving in his administration:

3   We think it might be a good idea for you to get out and campaign for Mayor Daley in this election, Mr. Parks Commissioner [Street Commissioner, Fire Commissioner, etc.], because if you don't, and Mayor Daley wins ... well ... you might be out of a job! And ... you know ... we'd hate to see you lose your job! So, really, we're just giving you a little bit of friendly advice here ... that's all. We're looking out for you!

This may sound innocuous, but it's really a thinly veiled threat:

3'   1. If you don't campaign for Mayor Daley's reelection, you'll lose your job.

       2. You ought to campaign for Mayor Daley's reelection.

(3') qualifies as an appeal to force. After all, the reason it offers (what'll happen to the addressee if she or he doesn't campaign for Mayor Daley), although no doubt psychologically powerful as a motivator of enthusiastic campaigning, is not relevant to the conclusion that the addressee should campaign for Mayor Daley. In itself, it gives no reason why Daley deserves to be re-elected, so that people can campaign for him with a good conscience. Notice that it would have been possible to give an entirely different argument for the same conclusion that would commit no fallacy: campaigners could simply have said,

4   You ought to get out and campaign for Mayor Daley in this election because of all the great things the Daley administration has done for the city of Chicago,

and then listed the accomplishments of the Daley administration. (In fact, there were many.) Thus completed, (4)'s premises would be relevant to the argument's conclusion and might very well support it. By contrast, (3')'s premise is completely irrelevant to the argument's conclusion.

BOX 3 ■ HOW TO AVOID APPEAL TO FORCE

1. An argument whose premises merely express a threat of unpleasant consequences for those who refuse to accept the argument's conclusion commits the fallacy of appeal to force.
2. Any such argument should be rejected, since its premises provide only a "reason" that is irrelevant to the argument's conclusion—thus falling short of rationally supporting it.

10.4 Appeal to Emotion

So far, we've seen two ways in which fallacies of relevance might be committed by arguments that offer premises appealing to our emotions in ways utterly irrelevant to supporting their conclusions. A third variation on this common sort of mistake is found in the fallacy of appeal to emotion.

> An argument commits the fallacy of appeal to emotion if and only if it attempts to support its conclusions by appealing to people's feelings rather than to their reason.

This fallacy is sometimes called *ad populum*—literally, 'to the people.' In any argument that commits it, emotively charged language is used to try to persuade someone to accept a certain conclusion. In some cases, the language employed for this purpose may include images that carry emotive force, as can be seen from the immense popularity of this fallacy in television commercials and other advertising media. But often appeals to emotion are made by using words carefully chosen for maximum emotional impact. To detect and avoid this fallacy, follow the rules in Box 4.

Appeal to emotion is, of course, a medium much beloved by stem-winding political orators. In 1896, populist Democrat William Jennings Bryan drew upon biblical allusions to argue that the gold standard in U.S. monetary policy was bad for working people:

5   You shall not press down upon the brow of labor this crown of thorns; you shall not crucify mankind upon a cross of gold.

And forty years later, in the depths of the Great Depression, President Franklin D. Roosevelt attempted to rally support for his reforms with emotive language of stirring intensity:

6   This generation of Americans has a rendezvous with destiny.

Notice that each of these examples amounts to a premise offered in support of a conclusion to the effect: 'Therefore you should support my programs!' They are both arguments with implicit conclusions. And both try to move their audiences through the psychological power of emotively charged phrases such as 'crucify mankind,' 'crown of thorns,' 'rendezvous,' 'cross,' and 'destiny.' As these examples show, the fallacy of appeal to emotion is as likely to be committed by mainstream politicians as it is by demagogues and despots (such as Adolf Hitler, who used it constantly). But it is a fallacious form of argument, whoever indulges in it.

Sometimes reasoning that commits the fallacy of appeal to emotion rests on a clever use of images that provoke a strong emotional response. When President Lyndon Johnson was running for reelection in 1964, his campaign sought to capitalize on prevalent voter fears about the alleged recklessness of his opponent, Senator Barry Goldwater. In a charged, Cold War era, some feared that Goldwater might be too quick to resort to nuclear weapons, and Johnson's campaigners wanted to exploit this uneasiness. So the Democratic Party ran a television commercial that opened with a view a of sunny meadow and a little girl picking flowers, then cut to a dark screen with the fiery mushroom cloud of a nuclear explosion billowing up into the night sky. Across a black screen the message then flashed: 'VOTE FOR PRESIDENT JOHNSON.' One of the most notorious examples of emotively charged images in the history of political advertising, the commercial was widely denounced as tasteless, prompting Democrats to withdraw it.

BOX 4 ■ HOW TO AVOID APPEAL TO EMOTION

1. Be on guard for arguments that attempt, through the use of emotively charged words or images, to elicit a strong psychological response conducive to the acceptance of its conclusion.
2. Any such argument commits the fallacy of appeal to emotion and should be rejected. Why? Because its premises offer only "reasons" that are irrelevant, in the way suggested in (1), to the argument's conclusion. No such argument can provide rational support for its conclusion.

The Bandwagon Appeal

Some forms of emotional appeal are intended to take advantage of common feelings that seem to be part of human nature, such as the desire not to miss out on the latest trends—for example, when books are marketed as 'best sellers' or a film is touted as 'the Number One Hit Movie of the Summer!' This so-called bandwagon appeal exploits our desire to join in with the common experiences of others and not be left out. But the reasons offered for buying the book or seeing the movie merely note their popular appeal, not their quality. A best seller might be only a shallow entertainment, a hit movie little more than a television sitcom. That they're widely sought does nothing to support the claim that they're worth seeking.

Appeal to Vanity

Appeal to vanity (sometimes called 'snob appeal') is another of the varieties of *ad populum*—this time trying to exploit people's unspoken fears about self-esteem. When a car is advertised as in (7), the advertiser attempts to persuade prospective buyers to buy the car by making an appeal to their vanity.

7   Not for everyone—this is the car that tells the world who you are!

In another example of this argumentation tactic, Virgin Atlantic Airways has decided to attract customers to its premium-class service by calling it, not 'first class,' but 'Upper Class.' Can you see what is going on here?

10.5 Ad Hominem

Another way arguments can fail because of irrelevant premises is the very common fallacy of *ad hominem* (literally, 'to the man'), which has less to do with emotion than with personal attack. It is sometimes called 'argument against the person,' but we'll call it by its Latin name, since that has now come to be familiar in everyday usage.

> An argument commits the fallacy of ad hominem if and only if it attempts to discredit someone's—or some group's—argument, point of view, or achievement by means of personal attack.

That is, the fallacious *ad hominem* rests on some personal consideration strictly irrelevant to the matter at hand, which is intended to undermine someone's credibility, as a means of indirectly attacking the person's position or argument. The problem with such an *ad hominem*, of course, is that in this way the question of the real merit of that person's position is evaded. Instead, the *ad hominem* offers only a cheap shot aimed at the person herself. Before turning to some specific arguments of this sort, notice that they all fail to support their conclusions—yet they can be recognized easily and avoided in the way suggested in Box 5.

Examples of *ad hominem* are, unfortunately, easy to find—sometimes committed by people you'd not expect to be committing fallacies. Planned Parenthood recently ran a series of advertisements on buses and subways that featured a photo of several grumpy-looking men in suits. Across the photo was mounted the ad copy, which read, "79% of abortion opponents are men. 100% of them will never be pregnant." We may smile at this rhetorically clever juxtaposition of image and slogan, but, make no mistake, this is an *ad hominem* against male opponents of abortion. Instead of focusing on *what those men's objections to abortion may be*, the effect of the ad is simply to dismiss the objections as *men's views*. But the views of men—on abortion or any other topic—cannot be legitimately rejected solely on the basis of their provenance (that they are "men's views"). Rather, the question is: Are these views well supported? It's not *whose views they are* that matters, but do the proponents have good or bad arguments for their claims?

Suppose a new political scandal erupts in Washington. Senator Dunster has been caught using public funds to pay for expensive luxury vacations for himself and his family, and another legislator, Senator Brewster, has taken to the Senate floor to denounce this impropriety. But Dunster is a Harvard man and cannot resist pointing out that Brewster's college days were spent at Yale. In a speech, Dunster loudly responds,

8   These charges are all false! And these unfounded accusations are coming from exactly the place we would expect. Apparently Senator Brewster, like all Yalies, cannot resist the temptation to besmirch the reputation of a Harvard man!

Here Senator Dunster's argument is an *ad hominem* that attempts to discredit Brewster's statements, not by speaking to their content (the accusations of impropriety), but by pointing to Brewster's personal background—the fact that he is a Yale graduate. Its clear assumptions are that all Yalies are naturally prejudiced against Harvard graduates, and that that is why Brewster is saying these things! But Dunster's argument simply engages in personal attack:

it introduces an irrelevant consideration that has no power to actually discredit the opponent's claim (though it may appear to do so).

The thing to keep in mind, again, is that it's not *who says it* that makes a claim well supported or not, but rather whether there are in fact good reasons to back it up. Those reasons should be judged on their own merits: either they provide some support for the claim, or they don't. In our example, we would of course need to hear Senator Brewster's argument—presumably citing facts in support of the conclusion that Dunster had behaved inappropriately—in order to determine this.

BOX 5 ■ HOW TO AVOID A FALLACIOUS AD HOMINEM

1. Beware of any argument that appeals to some personal facts (or alleged facts) that are irrelevant to its conclusion.
2. Any such argument commits the fallacy of *ad hominem* and should be rejected, for its premises are irrelevant to its conclusion—that is, they are offered as a means of attempting to discredit an argument or point of view by discrediting the person who presents it.

The Abusive Ad Hominem

Sometimes *ad hominem* arguments attack a person's character. Suppose a moviegoer announces,

9 I have no desire to see Woody Allen's latest movie. I'm sure it's worthless, and I wouldn't waste my money on it—not after what I know about him now! He betrayed Mia Farrow and broke her heart when he became romantically involved with Mia's adopted daughter, Soon-Yi Previn. So his movies are without artistic merit, as far as I'm concerned.

Now, (9) plainly commits the fallacy of *ad hominem*, since it seeks to discredit Woody Allen as a film director not by invoking evidence that his movies are artistically questionable, but by a personal attack that refers to his relationship to Soon-Yi Previn (whom he later married). But this *ad hominem* is of a more abusive sort, since it attacks Allen's character—he is denounced on moral grounds as a 'betrayer,' which is, of course, a term of contempt. But, whatever we may think of Allen's personal qualities, does any of that prove that his films are bad? Isn't all of that simply irrelevant to an assessment of his art?

Tu Quoque

Finally, the fallacy of *ad hominem* is also committed when one tries to refute someone's point of view by calling attention to the person's hypocrisy regarding that very point of view. This is sometimes called 'tu quoque' (literally, 'you also'). For example, consider how Thomas Jefferson's writings must have sounded to the British in his day. Jefferson famously wrote, in the *Declaration of Independence*, "We hold these truths to be self-evident, that all men are created equal, that they are endowed by their Creator with certain unalienable Rights, that among these are Life, Liberty, and the pursuit of Happiness." But one can easily imagine how this must have been received in conservative circles in Britain in 1776. Tories certainly regarded this lofty language as risible political rhetoric, since they knew very well that Jefferson was himself a prominent slave holder. In London, Dr. Samuel Johnson scoffed,

"How is it that we hear the loudest yelps for 'liberty' among the drivers of Negroes?" Johnson's remark could be expanded into an extended argument that looks like this:

10 1. Jefferson claims that all men are created equal and have rights to liberty.

2. But Jefferson himself is a slave owner.

3. He preaches lofty principles for others that he does not practice himself.

4. Jefferson's claims about liberty and equality are false.

Yet if any did actually offer such an argument, it would have committed the fallacy of *tu quoque*, a form of *ad hominem*. The imagined argument, after all, tries to bring a personal matter—Jefferson's real-life hypocrisy about race and human nature—into the discussion to cast doubt on his assertions about human equality and rights. Now, it is of course true that the Sage of Monticello did not permit his own black slaves to enjoy the very liberty and equality he so forcefully advocated for himself and his fellow white men. But did that personal failure go any way at all toward showing that Jefferson's claims about liberty and equality were false? Naturally, we all think that people should not be hypocrites. People should practice what they preach. Yet if someone fails to heed this moral maxim, and we point out his hypocrisy, we have not thereby proved that what he preaches is false. In fact, we are only indulging in a form of *ad hominem*, a *tu quoque*.

Nonfallacious Ad Hominem

Before we leave the discussion of *ad hominem*, there remains one important clarification that should be added. Some uses of argument against the person are not fallacious, for there are contexts in which such an argument may be in order. In public life, for instance, the moral character of a politician may be a highly relevant issue to raise during a campaign, since we do very reasonably expect our elected leaders to be trustworthy. In the second example given above, Senator Brewster's speech calling Senator Dunster's personal rectitude into question amounts to a kind of personal attack, but it commits no fallacy (as does Dunster's reply), since conduct that is unethical (or illegal!) would not be irrelevant to an assessment of a person's fitness to serve as a senator. Brewster's remarks, then, could justifiably be seen as an *ad hominem* argument but not a fallacious one, for they commit no fallacy of irrelevant premises.

Similarly, in the Anglo-American system of justice, which employs an adversarial model in court—with attorneys on opposing sides each presenting an argument for their client's case and trying to undermine their opponent's position—some of what happens in the courtroom may appear to be *ad hominem*. Here, after all, attorneys might try to discredit a witness by presenting evidence about his personal life.

But in fact this does not amount to a fallacious *ad hominem* at all, since in the courtroom, the reliability of a witness is not irrelevant. Given that the purpose of a witness just is to give testimony, it is highly relevant to know whether the person can be believed or not. Thus an attorney does not commit a fallacy of *ad hominem* when she appeals to relevant personal matters in an attempt to discredit the claims made by a witness. An attorney's job is to defend her client's interest by aggressively pressing his case, and part of that may include presenting facts about a witness's background and personal life in an effort to undermine his credibility. This is a kind of personal attack, but it commits no fallacy.

Logical thinkers must bear in mind that courtroom procedure is a specialized subject in the law, and that we're not attempting here to venture into its complexities. When one is called to serve on a jury, one should follow the instructions of the judge. The important thing to notice now, however, is simply that there can be some uses of *ad hominem* that are not fallacious, and that it is the context that determines when this is so.

10.6 Beside the Point

An argument might commit a fallacy of relevance by offering premises that simply have little or nothing to do with its conclusion. Maybe they support some conclusion, but they don't support the one given by the argument. When this happens, the argument commits a beside-the-point fallacy (also known as *ignoratio elenchi*).

> An argument commits the fallacy of beside the point if and only if its premises fail to support its conclusion by failing to be logically related to its conclusion, though they may support some *other* conclusion.

Faced with an argument of this sort, we may at first find ourselves unable to identify the source of the confusion. For example, imagine that opponents of cruelty to animals introduce legislation to ban the mistreatment of chickens, pigs, and cows in certain 'factory farms.' But suppose the corporations who own the farms respond,

11 These farms are not cruel to animals. After all, the farms provide the food that most consumers want, and they do so in a manner that is cost-effective; moreover, these poultry, pork, and beef products are nourishing and contribute to the overall health of American families.

The odd thing about (11) is that nothing in its premises contributes toward providing support for the conclusion, 'These farms are not cruel to animals.' Perhaps the premises support *some* conclusion. But they don't support that one, since they offer no reason to think that the factory farms in question are not cruel. As a result, (11) commits the beside the point fallacy.

Here's another example that does so as well. Early in Barack Obama's administration, a state dinner at the White House was attended by a local couple who had not been invited and had no authorization to enter the White House. They were, in effect, party crashers. Threatened with prosecution under federal law for having breached White House security, they responded that they should not be prosecuted because they had "made a sacrifice in time

> ### BOX 6 ■ HOW TO AVOID THE BESIDE-THE-POINT FALLACY
>
> Logical thinkers should be on guard for
>
> 1. Arguments whose premises are simply irrelevant to proving the conclusion.
> 2. Any such argument is defective, even if nothing else is wrong with it; it commits a beside-the-point fallacy and should be rejected.

and money to get ready for the party." Now, let us suppose that it's *true* that they had made such a sacrifice. Even so, how is that relevant to their claim that they do not deserve prosecution for breaking the law? The proposed "reason" why they should not be prosecuted (namely, the alleged "sacrifice in time and money") is not a reason that supports the conclusion. This argument is plainly an instance of the beside-the-point fallacy.

Yet another example of this type of mistake was inadvertently provided by a radio listener who responded to a BBC program predicting a crisis of overpopulation in the United Kingdom by 2051. "We can meet this challenge," the listener confidently asserted, "because we all stood together as one people when we were fighting the Nazis." But there is more than one problem in this argument, not least of them the fact that none of the Britons who fought the Germans in World War II are likely to be alive in 2051. So, whatever the coping skills of those who prevailed in Britain's Finest Hour, their application in the envisaged crisis to come at mid-century seems unlikely. Moreover, it is not at all clear how a nation's possessing the military skills necessary to defeat Hitler proves anything at all about their ability to overcome an entirely different sort of problem in the foreseen population crisis. Thus the argument is only a beside-the-point fallacy. Its premise, though manifestly true, provides no support for the conclusion.

> **12** 1. We all stood together as one people when we were fighting the Nazis.
>
> 2. We can meet the coming challenge of overpopulation.

10.7 Straw Man

Finally, let us consider a type of informal fallacy committed by any argument where the view of an opponent is misrepresented so that it becomes vulnerable to certain objections. The distorted view may consist of a statement or a group of related statements (i.e., a position or a theory). Typically ignored in such distortions are charity and faithfulness, the principles of argument reconstruction discussed in Chapter 4. Given the principle of charity, interpreting someone else's view requires that we maximize the truth of each of its parts (in the case of an argument, premises and conclusion) and the strength of the logical relation between them. Given the principle of faithfulness, such interpretation requires that we strive for maximum fidelity to the author's intentions. It is precisely the lack of charity, faithfulness, or both, in the interpretation of the views of others with whom the arguer disagrees that results in straw man.

> An argument commits the fallacy of straw man if and only if its premises attempt to undermine some view through misrepresenting what that view actually is.

Situations where this type of informal fallacy often occurs include deliberations, such as debates and controversies. Straw man is (regrettably) a common tactic in public life, often heard in the rhetoric of political campaigns. Typically, the straw-man argument ascribes to an opponent some views that are in fact a distortion of his actual views. These misrepresentations may be extreme, irresponsible, or even silly views that are easy to defeat. The opponent's position, then, becomes a 'straw figure' that can be easily blown away. But to refute that position is of

1. A straw-man argument attempts to raise an objection O against a certain view—call it 'V.'
2. But the argument misrepresents V as being in fact W—where W is vulnerable to the objection O.
3. The argument concludes by rejecting V on the basis of O.

But does O really undermine V? It seems not. After all, O is an objection only to W, a distorted rendering of V, not to V itself.

course not at all to disprove the person's actual position. This can be seen in Box 7, which outlines what's going on in straw-man arguments.

It is not difficult to find examples of this fallacy in political debates. Imagine two rival political candidates who disagree about foreign policy: Barton declares that the nation should not act unilaterally in using military force but do so only with the support of traditional allies. But Burton tries to undermine Barton's credibility by arguing as follows:

13 1. My opponent's international policy is: Wait for foreign permission before acting.

2. Waiting for foreign permission before acting is inconsistent with promoting our national security and our right to act in our own self-interest.

3. Both promoting our national security and our right to act in our own self-interest are reasonable.

4. My opponent's international policy is unreasonable.

But suppose there is in fact no evidence that Barton does actually hold the view ascribed to her in the first premise—then what? In that case, (13) is a straw-man argument. Seeking the support of traditional allies before undertaking a potentially dangerous step is hardly the same thing as "waiting for foreign permission before acting." Burton is misrepresenting Barton's argument.

Consider another example: some members of Congress announce that they favor trials in civilian criminal courts for Guantanamo detainees. Their opponents then charge,

14 1. Those who favor such civilian trials are pro-terrorist.

2. To be pro-terrorist is to be against our country.

3. Those who favor such civilian trials are against our country.

To detect (and avoid) a fallacy of this sort, the rule is to check whether an argument's reasons against a certain view can really count as reasons against that view. Always ask yourself whether the target view has been reconstructed according to the principles of charity and faithfulness.

When objecting to a view V, if the argument goes, "View V is wrong because it faces objection O," keep in mind that, whether or not O is *actually* an objection to V depends on whether V has been construed in accordance with faithfulness and charity. An obviously false view may be a view nobody holds!

10.8 Is the Appeal to Emotion Always Fallacious?

Earlier in this chapter, the appeal to emotion was identified as one of the Fallacies of Relevance. But, it will be objected, it simply cannot be that a logical thinker's only appropriate attitude toward emotion is a wary distrust. Given the large role of emotion in human life—indeed, if we consider that life would surely be impoverished without it—philosophers can ill afford to ignore emotion, and logical thinking ought to have a way of accommodating the many benign manifestations of it that commit no fallacies.

What, then, are some of these? First, emotions plainly have an important role in motivating our actions. Feelings, sentiments, desires, and ordinary inclinations and aversions of many sorts all move us to act in everyday life in ways that involve no fallacious inferences. We need not go so far as holding that reason "is and ought to be the slave of the passions" to recognize that our feelings and desires motivate our actions. And actions motivated by feelings may be guided by reason (e.g., "don't do to others what you'd not like done to you").

Second, being alert to the personal emotional commitments of our loved ones, friends, and co-workers can give us reasons for action, or for forbearance. If we know what others care about—especially what matters to them in deep and important ways—then we'll know how to avoid saying things that will hurt their feelings. This is a concern about emotion (theirs!) that commits no fallacy. Similarly, if we know that mentioning certain subjects will cause a certain person to become enraged, then it's not fallacious to conclude that we should take his feelings into account and try to avoid such talk in his presence unless it's necessary.

Third, emotions may appropriately move us to take action for the sake of strangers who are suffering or in peril. When reports of famine, war, epidemics, and natural disasters motivate us to contribute to relief programs, we are following our feelings of compassion for our fellow human beings and commit no fallacy. Likewise, when our instincts of fairness move us to speak out on behalf of minorities subjected to prejudice or discrimination, there is no fallacy in acting on these feelings. And when we read of outrageous acts of brutality and violence, or criminal acts of an especially nefarious sort, there is no fallacy in concluding that such acts ought to be punished, or prevented if possible. Finally, we may, of course, appropriately and rationally respond to emotion in our desire to aid needy individuals, as when a doctor acts to relieve her patient's suffering, or when we give our pocket change to a homeless person begging in the street.

What all of the above examples have in common is this: they are appeals to emotion that are not irrelevant as reasons for our conclusions. That is, they represent types of situation in which one may rationally be moved by emotion. In the fallacy of appeal to emotion (*ad populum*), by contrast, the use of emotion always represents a diversion from the matter at hand, often a subtle attempt at manipulating one's feelings for the sake of some strictly irrelevant consideration that does not actually contribute to supporting the argument's conclusion (though it may appear to do so). Logical thinkers are advised to beware of such trickery, as it amounts to an abuse of reason.

But the purpose of logical thinking is not to turn people into coldly rational beings without emotions, like *Star Trek's* Mr. Spock. (Of course, since Spock is half-Vulcan and only half-human, he may be inclined to overestimate the value of rigidly rational behavior and to underrate the value of ordinary affections.) There are, after all, many occasions in life when it would be inappropriate, even crazy, to be too rational. Think of falling in love, for instance, or expressing affection toward one's parents, or toward one's children. Sentiments and desires are essential to any life that is recognizably human, and logical thinkers commit no fallacy when they are moved in appropriate ways by emotion.

Exercises

I. Review Questions

1. What does it mean to say that an argument's premises are 'irrelevant' to its conclusion?
2. How is the fallacy of appeal to pity a fallacy of 'irrelevant premises'?
3. What is the fallacy of appeal to force?
4. What is the fallacy of appeal to emotion?
5. What is the bandwagon appeal? How does it differ from an appeal to vanity?
6. What is an *ad hominem* argument?
7. Do all *ad hominems* involve an attack on someone's character?
8. Are all *ad hominem* arguments fallacious? What is a *tu quoque* argument?
9. What is the beside-the-point fallacy?
10. What is a straw-man argument? And how does it amount to a fallacy?

II. For each of the following arguments, identify the fallacy of relevance it commits.

1. CBS News is trying to make people believe that there are unsafe working conditions in this factory. But I tell you this: anyone who plans to continue working for me should not talk to reporters.

   SAMPLE ANSWER: Appeal to force

*2. I deserve the highest grade, Professor Arroyo, because I studied harder than anyone else.

3. You cannot say that divorce is immoral. After all, you yourself are divorced.

*4. A Princeton student found guilty of plagiarism admitted that the work was not her own but argued that the university ought not to penalize her for this infraction, since she had been 'under enormous pressure at the time, having to meet a deadline for her senior thesis with only one day left to write the paper.'—*The New York Times*, May 7, 1982

5. If Einstein's theory is right, then everything is relative. But 9-11 really happened, and that's a fact. So not everything is relative. Therefore Einstein's theory is wrong.

6. We needn't take seriously what the Reverend Brimstone says when he tells us that people should always be honest in their dealings with others. Just yesterday the Billy Brimstone Evangelistic Association was found guilty of soliciting funds for missionary work and then using them to buy the Reverend Brimstone a new Cadillac.

*7. Everywhere, people are increasingly getting rid of their iPods and instead listening to music on their cell phones. That's the way to listen to music on the move! So, if you're up-to-date and in touch with the latest things, you'll get rid of your iPod and use the phone to listen to music.

8. I know you're the coach of this baseball team, and you're entitled to your opinion. But I'm the owner of this ball club, and you work for me. If you really want Scooter Wilensky to play third base, you can put him there. Of course, I can always find another coach.

9. Everybody visits the Art Institute of Chicago. Therefore, you should, too.

*10. It's true that Knut Hamsun, the early twentieth-century Norwegian novelist, won the Nobel Prize for Literature, but as far as I am concerned his works are worthless. Anyone who collaborated with the Nazis, as Hamsun did during World War II, was not capable of producing works with literary merit.

11. A protestor demonstrating against the new president said, 'A recount of the ballots is needed in this presidential election. If not, we will blockade airports and highways, we'll take over embassies, and we'll bring traffic to a halt all over the country.'

12. People often point out that Richard Wagner, the nineteenth-century German composer of operas, wrote some of the most beautiful and powerful music ever written. But I say all of his music is worthless junk and should never be performed! It's well known that Wagner was a raving anti-Semite. And decades after his death, his biggest fan turned out to be Hitler.

*13. In Britain, the president of the Royal Society has suggested that scientific research on how to protect the environment should be supported by 'carbon taxes,' levied on countries producing the most air and water pollution. But this is nonsense, for his own country would be near the top of the list, and he himself drives a pollution-producing car!

14. The governor shouldn't be blamed for his staff members lying under oath to the grand jury. After all, he was under tremendous pressure at the time.

15. Humans are capable of creativity. Therefore, creativity is a value.

*16. Many contemporary physicists accept Heisenberg's indeterminacy principle, which implies that everything is indeterminate. But this cannot possibly be correct, as shown by the fact that mathematical truths are determinate.

17. Professor Nathan's history of the Catholic Church is a classic. But she is a Protestant, so we cannot expect her treatment of Catholicism to be fair.

18. In his dialogue *Meno*, Plato describes an exchange between Socrates and Anytus, a powerful and influential Athenian politician. Socrates suggests that the reason why the sons of prominent Athenian families often turn out badly is that their parents do not know how to educate them. To this, Anytus replies, 'Socrates, I think that you are too ready to speak evil of men; and, if you will take my advice, I would advise you to be careful. Perhaps there is no city in which it is not easier to do men harm than to do them good, and this is certainly the case at Athens, as I believe you know.'

*19. Over two million people die in the United States every year. Therefore, the United States is a dangerous place to visit, and we should take our vacation elsewhere.

20. Reverend Armstrong urges us not to support the war, saying that violence is barbaric in all forms and only breeds more violence in return. But his view should be rejected, since it amounts to arguing that our nation's enemies are not bad guys at all, and that we should just surrender to them.

21. Paul Robeson's accomplishments as an actor and singer are overrated. Really, he was not good at either. After all, he was well known to be pro-Communist and an admirer of Stalin.

*22. Global war is inevitable, for the cultures of East and West are radically different.

23. My opponent, Senator Snort, endorses the Supreme Court's view that prayer in public schools is a violation of the First Amendment. But I say to you, what is this but an endorsement of atheism? Senator Snort clearly thinks that people of faith have no place in today's America.

24. I know I've failed to pay my rent for the past three months, but if you evict me I'll have no place to go. How can you throw me, an eighty-year-old grandmother, out onto the street?

*25. Mafioso to shopkeeper: 'You got a nice business here. It'd be a shame if somethin' were to happen to it.'

26. Advertisement: 'You've always known that Mercedes-Benz was the car for you. It's not a car for everybody. But then, you're not just anybody. When you've truly achieved a place of distinction in life, you know you're ready. Mercedes-Benz.'

27. According to contemporary biology, species evolve over time. But I have never seen any animals evolving. Have you? Has anyone ever seen animals evolving? So, contemporary biology is false.

*28. "Everything that today we admire on earth—science and art, technique and innovations—is only the creative product of a few peoples and perhaps originally of one race. [Therefore, on the Germans] now depends also the existence of this entire culture. If they perish, then the beauty of this earth sinks into the grave with them . . . The man who misjudges and disdains the laws of race actually forfeits the happiness that seems destined to be his. He prevents the victorious march of the best race and with it also the presumption for all human progress . . . All that is not race in this world is trash."—Adolf Hitler, *Mein Kampf*.

29. Dear State Senator: Our organization believes that protecting the environment is an issue of paramount importance. Unless your legislature passes the Clean Air and Water Act, we will urge all business meetings, conventions, and tourists to boycott your state indefinitely.

*30. Darwin's theory of evolution cannot be correct. It holds that we all evolved from monkeys! But monkeys do not evolve into people. And we are too different to have evolved from them. Thus Darwin's theory of evolution has to be false.

31. Los Angeles has twenty or thirty downtowns. There is no conventional pattern of people commuting to work in one direction in the morning and the reverse in the evening. So it seems there is no central authority in organizing the city or its government.

32. French actress Brigitte Bardot insists that cruelty to animals is a serious crime and that we should treat our dogs and cats humanely. But we cannot take this seriously. She is well known for expressions of bigotry toward ethnic and religious minority immigrants in France.

*33. We in the industrialized world would suffer terribly if our government imposed energy-restricting policies. Thus the government should refrain from making energy restrictions in our country.

34. My opponent, Representative Smith, says she favors abolishing the death penalty. But what she is really saying is that it's just fine for murderers to be housed and fed for years at taxpayer expense, and that it's OK with her if they are ultimately released to prey on our citizens again.

*35. In the Gospel of St. John, Nathaniel expresses doubt, on first hearing of Jesus' teachings, that there could be a truly wise man from such an obscure, small town: "Nazareth! Can anything good come out of Nazareth?" —John 1:46:

36. President Gerald Ford granted his predecessor, Richard Nixon, a presidential pardon that spared Nixon from a possible prison sentence for his involvement in illegal activities in the Watergate scandal of 1972–74. Ford's advisers argued, "The humiliation of having to resign the presidency in disgrace is punishment enough for poor Nixon."

37. Liberal economic theories and the policies that have sprung from them cannot be good for this nation's economy over the long run, for these very theories and policies are now opposed by the great majority of Americans.

38. You'd better be careful not to mention the chairman Mr. Grace's friend Lulu around Mrs. Grace. If you mention her, I'll see to it that you're never promoted!

*39. State College should require basic computer literacy of all its students, since colleges everywhere are introducing a requirement of this kind into their curricula.

40. The UN should not sanction India for selling weapons to Myanmar. After all, India is still a developing country with millions of poor people in need of humanitarian aid.

III. Some of the following arguments commit a fallacy of appeal to emotion, and some don't. Determine which commits which.

1. Cousin Ed is always getting into scrapes with the law and can't seem to stay out of jail. But Aunt Betty and Uncle Jake love him nonetheless. So I ought not to make jokes about Ed in their presence.

   SAMPLE ANSWER: Not a fallacy of appeal to emotion

*2. As your representative in Congress, I have sworn upon the altar of God to uphold the sacred freedoms of our mighty democracy! Despite the scurrilous attacks of my yelping-dog opponents who accuse me of tax evasion, I have always defended the American way! Thus I ought to be reelected.

3. News reports from Zambia describe a nation devastated by an epidemic of AIDS. When I read of people dying for lack medical care, I feel horrible about this. Therefore, I'm contributing to relief efforts to send doctors to Zambia.

4. "I feel very bad for the couple next door," said Mary Ellen. "Jack and Harry have been told that gay couples are not welcome at their church. So I'm going to invite them to mine."

*5. Jurors in the Enron case were infuriated by the lies and deceptions perpetrated by the company's executives. "We were appalled," one juror said later, "and therefore we asked for the stiffest sentences possible."

6. In a famous television advertisement for an aftershave lotion, a commercial aired during televised sports events and aimed at men, a woman in a revealing dress purrs, "There's *something* about an Aqua Velva man."

7. *The Da Vinci Code* is the number-one best-selling book in America. So I really ought to read it.

8. I know she misses me. I miss her, too. So I'm going to e-mail her some photos of me that were taken just yesterday. I know she'll like that.

*9. Dear Membership Committee: When I heard that the Davis family's application for membership in the Country Club was rejected because some members did not like their religion, I was shocked. I was furious. So I have decided to resign from the Country Club as of today.

*10. Now all the guys at school are driving pickup trucks. The bigger the better! Everybody in our school has got one, and I feel that I've got to be part of this. So I am going to buy a pickup truck.

IV. YOUR OWN THINKING LAB

1. For each of the following claims, construct an argument that attempts to support it but fails by virtue of committing at least one of the fallacies discussed in this chapter.

   A. Members of the Board, I think it's time now for me to be promoted.

B. This is a case in which the Supreme Court ought to commute the death sentence.

C. Al Gore's views on global warming are wrong.

D. Football is a great entertainment.

E. Evolutionary theory contradicts the facts.

2. What's the matter with the following arguments?

A. Abortion is offensive to many people. Therefore, abortion is wrong.

B. Former president Bill Clinton was found to have lied about his affair with a White House intern. This suggests that his foreign policy was unacceptable.

C. As long as I get a cut from your profits, nobody gets hurt. Understand?

■ Writing Project

Read the Letters to the Editor section of your local daily newspaper every day for one week. Collect as many examples as you can find of fallacies of relevance committed by letter writers, and then write a short paper in which you report on these fallacious arguments. In each case, identify the fallacy committed and explain precisely how that fallacy is committed by that particular argument. Describe in this way all of the examples of fallacies you've found. (If your search also turns up examples of other types of fallacy besides fallacies of relevance, include your analyses of those arguments in your discussion, too.)

■ Chapter Summary

The fallacies of relevance are committed by arguments whose premises offer irrelevant reasons for their conclusions. They include arguments that attempt to get someone to accept a conclusion by means of:

1. **Appeal to Pity:** the premises are offered to arouse feelings of sympathy.

2. **Appeal to Force:** the premises resort to a threat.

3. **Appeal to Emotion:** the premises use emotively-charged language that appeals people's feelings.

4. **Ad Hominem:** the premises amount to a personal attack.

5. **Beside the Point:** the premises have nothing at all to do with the conclusion.

6. **Straw Man:** the premises are offered to undermine a misrepresented view.

■ Key Words

Irrelevant premise	Appeal to vanity
Appeal to pity	*Ad hominem*
Appeal to force	*Tu quoque*
Appeal to emotion	Beside the point
Bandwagon argument	Straw-man argument

More on Deductive Reasoning

Compound Propositions

This chapter examines the building blocks of propositional arguments. Its topics include

- A review of propositional arguments, first introduced in Chapter 5.
- The distinction between simple and compound propositions.
- Five types of compound proposition: negation, conjunction, disjunction, material conditional, and material biconditional.
- Translation of propositions into symbolic notation.
- Truth tables for defining propositional connectives and identifying contingencies, tautologies, and contradictions.

11.1 Argument as a Relation between Propositions

In this chapter and the next, we'll return to a topic briefly addressed in Chapter 5: propositional arguments. Here we'll have a close look at propositions, the building blocks of propositional arguments. Consider

1   1. If the Earth is a planet, then it moves.
      2. If the Earth does not move, then it is not a planet.

(1) is a propositional argument because it consists entirely in the relation between the propositions that make it up. Its premise and conclusion are compound propositions, which result from logical connections established between two simple propositions: 'The Earth is a planet' and 'The Earth moves.' The connections 'if . . . then . . .' and 'not' are among the five types of *truth-functional connectives* (or simply 'connectives') that we'll study here—namely,

Truth-Functional Connectives	Standard English Expression
negation*	not P
conjunction	P and Q
disjunction	either P or Q
conditional	if P, then Q
biconditional	P if and only if Q

* As we'll see, negation is called a 'connective' by courtesy.

Here we are using capital letters such as 'P,' 'Q,' and 'R' as symbols or "dummies" for any proposition. We'll use other capital letters from 'A' to 'O' to translate propositions in English into symbols, reserving P through W to represent non-specific propositions. Whenever possible, we'll pick the first letter of a word inside the proposition that we are to represent in symbols, preferably a noun if available. For example, 'If the Earth is a planet, then it moves' may be represented as 'If E, then M'—where

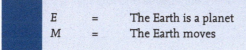

E	=	The Earth is a planet
M	=	The Earth moves

We'll resort to the same chosen symbol every time the proposition it symbolizes occurs again. And if we have already used a certain letter to stand for a different proposition, then a letter of another word, preferably a noun, in the proposition in question will serve. The argument form of example (1) may now be represented by replacing each proposition occurring in its premise and conclusion with a propositional symbol in this way, while momentarily retaining the connective 'if . . . then . . .' in English. The resulting translation is

1'   1. If E, then M
      2. If not M, then not E

Let's now consider the following arguments with an eye toward translating their propositions into symbols:

2　　1. Ottawa is the capital of Canada.
　　　2. It is not the case that Ottawa is not the capital of Canada.

3　　1. Either Fido is in the house or he's at the vet.
　　　2. Fido is not in the house.
　　　3. Fido is at the vet.

4　　1. Jane works at the post office and Bob at the supermarket.
　　　2. Bob works at the supermarket.

5　　1. TV is amusing if and only if it features good comedies.
　　　2. TV does not feature good comedies.
　　　3. TV is not amusing.

Once we have translated the propositions into symbols, we obtain

2'　1. O
　　　2. It is not the case that not O

3'　1. Either F or E
　　　2. Not F
　　　3. E

4'　1. J and B
　　　2. B

5'　1. A if and only if C
　　　2. Not C
　　　3. Not A

Although (2') through (5') feature connectives, not all propositional argument forms do: (6) doesn't.

6　　1. P
　　　2. P

In (6), the propositional symbol 'P' stands for exactly the same proposition in the premise and in the conclusion. Known as 'identity,' any argument with this form would of course be valid, since if its premise were true, its conclusion could not be false. But this is not our present concern. Rather, in this section we've considered propositional arguments and discovered that their premises and conclusions often feature truth-functional connectives. So let's now look more closely at these.

11.2 Simple and Compound Propositions

Any proposition that has at least one truth-functional connective is compound; otherwise, it is simple. Consider

7 Celine Dion is a singer and Russell Crowe is an actor.

This is a compound proposition, made up of the conjunction of two simple propositions,

8 Celine Dion is a singer.

9 Russell Crowe is an actor.

Conjunction is one of the five truth-functional connectives that we'll consider here—together with negation, disjunction, material conditional, and material biconditional. For each connective, we'll introduce a symbol and provide a truth-value rule that will be used to determine the truth value of whatever compound proposition is created by applying that connective. Since the truth-value rule associated with each connective defines the connective, each of them is a 'truth-functional connective.' But for the most part, we'll refer to them simply as 'connectives.' Here is the picture that will emerge:

BOX 1 ■ TRUTH-FUNCTIONAL CONNECTIVES

Connective	In English	In Symbols	Symbol's Name
negation	not P	~P	tilde
conjunction	P and Q	$P \cdot Q$	dot
disjunction	P or Q	$P \vee Q$	wedge
conditional	if P then Q	$P \supset Q$	horseshoe
biconditional	P if and only if Q	$P \equiv Q$	triple bar

Before turning to each of these connectives, notice that there is always one connective governing a compound proposition, called 'main connective.' By identifying the main connective, we determine *what kind* of compound proposition a given proposition is: a conjunction, a negation, a disjunction, etc. Obviously, in cases where a compound proposition contains more than one connective, it is crucial to be able to determine which connective is the main one.

Negation

Negation is a truth-functional connective standardly expressed in English by 'not,' and symbolized by '~', the tilde. Negation can affect one proposition by itself. Even so, we'll refer to it as a 'connective' by courtesy. In ordinary English, the expression for a negation may occur in any part of a statement. When a negation is added to a simple proposition, that proposition becomes compound. (10), which may be represented as (10') exemplifies this:

10 Russell Crowe is not an actor.

10' ~C

Here the simple proposition that has become compound by adding a negation is 'Russell Crow is an actor.' In (10'), we've used the tilde to represent negation, and C for the simple proposition affected by it. When possible, we'll use the first letter of an important word occurring in the proposition we wish to represent in symbolic notation.

Propositions affected by negation could also be themselves compound. For example,

11 It is false that both Mars and Jupiter have water.

12 It is not the case that Mary is not at the library.

To represent propositions that are negations, the symbol for negation always precedes what is negated. (12) is the negation of 'Mary is not at the library,' which is already a negation. So we have a double negation: the negation of a proposition that's itself a negation, which we can represent by the propositional formula

12' ~ ~ L

Since the two negations cancel each other out, (12') is logically the same as

12" L

Any proposition or propositional formula affected by a negation is a compound proposition. The 'truth-value rule' that defines negation, and can be used to determine the truth value of a proposition (or propositional formula) that's affected by that connective, is:

> A negation is true whenever the negated proposition is false.
> A negation is false whenever the negated proposition is true.

When a proposition is the logical negation of another, the two could not both have the same truth value: where 'P' is true, '~ P' is false; where 'P' is false, '~ P' is true. For example, (11) above, which is true, is the negation of 'both Mars and Jupiter have water,' which is false. But (14) below is not the negation of (13), since both propositions are false.

13 All orthodontists are tall.

14 No orthodontists are tall.

Now consider these:

15 Some orthodontists are not tall.

16 Some orthodontists are tall.

(15) is the negation of (13), and (16) is the negation of (14), for those pairs could not have the same truth value. But propositions that are logically the same would have the same truth value. For example, if (17) is true, (18) is also true.

17 Lincoln was assassinated.

18 It is not the case that Lincoln was not assassinated.

(18) is a case of double negation: it is the negation of 'Lincoln was not assassinated.'

Notice that propositions featuring expressions such as 'it is not true that,' 'it is false that,' 'it never happened that' are commonly negations—as are some propositions containing prefixes such as 'in-,' 'un-,' and 'non-.' For example,

19 My right to vote is inalienable.

Here 'inalienable' means 'not alienable.' (19) is logically the same as

19' My right to vote is not alienable.

Similarly, since 'unmarried' means 'not married,' (20) and (20') are also logically the same:

20 Condoleezza Rice is unmarried.

20' It is not the case that Condoleezza Rice is married.

But (21) is not a negation:

21 Unmarried couples are also eligible for the prize.

Here 'unmarried' is not being used to deny the whole proposition. It affects only the word 'couples.'

Finally, notice that although verbs such as 'miss,' 'violate,' 'fail,' and the like have a negative meaning, they need not be taken to express negations.

Conjunction

Conjunction is a compound proposition created by a truth-functional connective standardly expressed in English by 'and,' and in symbols by '·', the dot. The connective for conjunction is always placed between two propositions, each of which called a 'conjunct.' Conjuncts may themselves be simple or compound propositions. Let's consider the conjunctions of some simple propositions:

22 Mount Everest is in Tibet and Mont Blanc is in France.

23 Mars and Jupiter have water.

In symbols, these are

22' $E \cdot B$

23' $M \cdot J$

Recall (11) above:

11 It is false that both Mars and Jupiter have water.

The formula that represents this proposition is (11'), which has parentheses to indicate that both M and J are under the scope of the negation.

11' $\sim (M \cdot J)$

We'll have more to say on the use of parentheses and other punctuation signs later. Now let's consider why conjunction is a truth-functional connective: because it determines the truth value of the compound proposition affected by it, given the values of its members and this truth-value rule:

> A conjunction is true if and only if its conjuncts are both true. Otherwise, a conjunction is false.

(22) is true since both its conjuncts are in fact true. But if one conjunct is false and the other true, or both are false, then a conjunction is false. Thus (23) is false, since for all we know, both of its conjuncts are false. The following are also false:

24 Mount Everest is in Tibet and Mont Blanc is not in France.

25 Mount Everest is not in Tibet and Mont Blanc is not in France.

Since Mont Blanc is in France, the second disjunct in (24) is false, which makes the conjunction false. In a conjunction, then, falsity is like an infection: if there's any at all, it corrupts the whole compound. (Logical thinkers who are contemplating a career in politics should keep this in mind!) In (25), both conjuncts are false, since each is the negation of a true proposition. In symbols:

24' E • ~B

25' ~E • ~B

Note also that, like (23), many conjunctions in ordinary language are abbreviated. For instance,

26 Rottweilers and Dobermans are fierce dogs.

This is just a shortened way of saying

27 Rottweilers are fierce dogs and Dobermans are fierce dogs.

Yet (28) is not short for a conjunction of two simple propositions, but is rather a single proposition about a certain relation between some such dogs.

28 Some Rottweilers and Dobermans are barking at each other.

Another thing to notice is that conjunction, as a truth-functional connective, is *commutative*—that is, the order of the conjuncts doesn't affect the truth value of the compound. Assuming that (26) is true, the facts that make it true are exactly the same as those that make 'Dobermans are fierce dogs and Rottweilers are fierce dogs' true, which are also the same that make (27) true. However, we must be careful about this, since sometimes order matters. When it does, the conjunction is not a truth-functional connective: for example,

29 He took off his shoes and got into bed.

The facts that make (29) true do not seem to be the same as those that make (30) true:

30 He got into bed and took off his shoes.

The order of events, and therefore of the conjuncts, does matter in these non-truth-functional conjunctions—as it also does in (31) and (32).

31 He saw her and said 'hello.'

32 He said 'hello' and saw her.

Finally, note that besides 'and,' there are a number of English expressions for conjunction, including 'but,' 'however,' 'also', 'moreover,' 'yet,' 'while,' 'nevertheless,' 'even though,' and 'although.'

Disjunction

Disjunction, also a commutative connective, is a type of compound proposition created by the truth-functional connective standardly expressed in English by 'or,' and in symbols by 'v', the wedge. In representing a disjunction, the connective is placed between two propositions called 'disjuncts,' which may themselves be simple or compound propositions. Here are two disjunctions, first in English and then in symbols:

33 Rome is in Italy or Rome is in Finland.

33' I v F

34 Rome is not in Italy or Paris is not in France.

34' ~I v ~F

(33) and (34) are disjunctions and thus compound propositions. Disjunction is a truth-functional connective because it determines the truth value of the compound proposition it creates on the basis of the values of its members and this truth-value rule:

> A disjunction is false if and only if its disjuncts are both false. Otherwise, a disjunction is true.

Given the above rule, at least one of the disjuncts must be true for the disjunction to be true. So (33) is true, but (34) is false. (35) is also false, for both its disjuncts, both of them compound propositions, are false:

35 Either snow tires are useful in the tropics and air conditioners are popular in Iceland, or it is not the case that Penguins thrive in cold temperatures.

35' (S • A) v ~ P

Clearly, the conjunction (S · A) is false because both conjuncts are false, and ~ P is false because it is the negation of P, which is true. Since both disjuncts in (35) are false, given the truth-value rule for disjunction, (35) is false.

In addition to 'or,' disjunction can be expressed by 'either … or …' and 'unless,' and other locutions of our language. It is also sometimes found embedded in a negation in 'neither … nor …' (where negation is the main connective). Thus these are also disjunctions:

36 She is the director of the project, unless the catalog is wrong.

36' Either she is the director of the project, or the catalog is wrong.

(37) is a shortened version of (37'):

37 Neither the CIA nor the FBI tolerates terrorists.

37' Neither the CIA tolerates terrorists nor the FBI tolerates terrorists.

Since 'neither . . . nor . . .' is a common way to express the negation of a disjunction, (37) is logically the same as (or equivalent to)

38 It is false that either the CIA tolerates terrorists or the FBI tolerates terrorists.

Thus both (37) and (38) may be symbolized as the negation of a disjunction:

38' $\sim (C \vee F)$

Note that here the main connective is negation, not disjunction. Furthermore, (37) and (38) are logically equivalent to (39), which may be symbolized as

39 The CIA doesn't tolerate terrorists and the FBI doesn't tolerate terrorists.

39' $\sim C \cdot \sim F$

Finally, a truth-functional disjunction may be inclusive, when both disjuncts could be true ('either P or Q or both'), or exclusive, when only one could be ('either P or Q but not both'). This book focuses on inclusive disjunction, whose truth-value rule is given above.

Material Conditional

Material conditional, a type of compound proposition also called 'material implication' or simply 'conditional,' is created by a truth-functional logical connective, standardly expressed in English by 'if . . . then . . . ,' and in symbols by '$\supset$', the horseshoe. For example,

40 If Maria is a practicing attorney, then she has passed the bar exam.

A conditional has two members: the proposition standardly preceded by 'if' is its *antecedent*, and the one that follows 'then,' its *consequent*.

The conditional is a truth-functional connective because the value of the compound proposition it creates is determined by the truth value of the antecedent and consequent, together with this truth-value rule:

> A material conditional is false if and only if its antecedent is true and its consequent false. Otherwise, it is true.

Thus any conditional with a true consequent is true, and any conditional with a false antecedent is true.

The two propositions in a conditional, which may themselves be either simple or compound, stand in a hypothetical relationship, where neither antecedent nor consequent is being asserted independently. Does (40) assert that Maria is a practicing attorney? No. Does it claim that she has passed the bar exam? No. Rather, in any conditional, 'If *P*, then *Q*,' *P* and *Q* stand in a hypothetical relationship such that *P*'s being true implies that *Q* is also true. To challenge a conditional, one has to show that its antecedent is true and its consequent false at once.

Notice that sometimes the 'then' that often introduces the consequent of a conditional sentence may be left out. Moreover, besides 'if . . . then . . . ,' many other linguistic expressions can be used in English to introduce one or the other part of a conditional sentence. Such expressions may precede that sentence's consequent, its antecedent, or both—as shown in the examples below, where double underlines mark the antecedent and single underlines the consequent:

> Maria has passed the bar exam, provided <u>she is a practicing attorney</u>.
> Supposing that <u><u>Maria is a practicing attorney</u></u>, <u>she has passed the bar exam</u>.
> On the assumption that <u><u>Maria is a practicing attorney</u></u>, <u>she has passed the bar exam</u>.
> <u><u>Maria is a practicing attorney</u></u> only if <u>she has passed the bar exam</u>.
> That <u><u>Maria is a practicing attorney</u></u> implies that <u>she has passed the bar exam</u>.

We'll now translate these conditional sentences into our symbolic language, using '*M*' to stand for 'Maria is a practicing attorney' and '*E*' for 'Maria has passed the bar exam.' Our formula representing any of these propositions has '*M*' for the antecedent and '*E*' for the consequent. It lists '*M*' first, then the horseshoe symbol, and '*E*' last:

40' M ⊃ E

Here the rule is:

> To translate a conditional sentence into the symbolic language, we must list its antecedent first and its consequent last, whether or not these two parts occur in the English sentence in that order.

Let's now translate the conditionals below into the symbolic language using this glossary:

> N = The United States is a superpower
> I = China is a superpower
> C = China has agents operating in other countries
> O = The United States has agents operating in other countries

41 If China is a superpower, then China and the United States have agents operating in other countries.

41' I ⊃ (C • O)

42 It is not the case that if the United States has agents operating in other countries, then it is a superpower.

42' $\sim (O \supset N)$

43 China has agents operating in other countries provided that the United States and China are superpowers.

43' $(N \cdot I) \supset C$

44 If the United States doesn't have agents operating in other countries, then it is not a superpower.

44' $\sim O \supset \sim N$

45 That China has agents operating in other countries implies that either it is a superpower or the United States is not a superpower.

45' $C \supset (I \lor \sim N)$

46 If either the United States or China has agents operating in other countries, then neither the United States nor China is a superpower.

46' $(O \lor C) \supset \sim (N \lor I)$

47 If the United States is not a superpower, then it either has or doesn't have agents operating in other countries.

47' $\sim N \supset (O \lor \sim O)$

Note that 'P unless Q' could also be translated as 'if not P, then Q.' Thus 'China is a member of the UN unless it rejects the UN Charter' is equivalent to 'If China is not a member of the UN, then it rejects the UN Charter.'

Necessary and Sufficient Conditions. In any material conditional, the antecedent expresses a sufficient condition for the consequent, and the consequent a necessary condition for the antecedent. Thus another way of saying 'If P, then Q' is to say that P is sufficient for Q, and Q is necessary for P. A necessary condition of some proposition P's being true is some state of affairs without which P could not be true, but which is not enough all by itself to make P true. In (40), Maria's having passed the bar exam is a necessary condition of her being a practicing attorney (she could not be a practicing attorney if she had not passed it, though merely having passed doesn't guarantee that she's practicing). A sufficient condition of some proposition Q's being true is some state of affairs that is enough all by itself to make Q true, but which may not be the only way to make Q true. In (40), Maria's being a practicing attorney is sufficient for her having passed the bar exam (in the sense that the former guarantees the latter).

In a material conditional

- Its consequent is a necessary (but not sufficient) condition for the truth of its antecedent.
- Its antecedent is a sufficient (though not a necessary) condition for the truth of its consequent.

Material Biconditional

A material biconditional is a type of compound proposition, also called 'material equivalence,' or simply 'biconditional,' created by the truth-functional connective standardly expressed in English by 'if and only if,' and in symbols by '≡', the triple bar. Some other English expressions for the biconditional connective are 'just in case,' 'is equivalent to,' 'when and only when,' and the abbreviation 'iff.' Each of the two members of a biconditional could be either simple or compound. Here is a biconditional, in both English and symbols, made up of simple propositions:

48 Dr. Baxter is the college's president if and only if she is the college's chief executive officer.

48' $B \equiv O$

The truth value of the compound proposition the biconditional creates is determined by the truth value of its members, together with this truth-value rule:

> A material biconditional is true whenever its members have the same truth value—that is, they are either both true or both false. Otherwise, a biconditional is false.

Given this rule, for a biconditional proposition to be true, the propositions making it up must have the same truth value—that is, be both true or both false. When a biconditional's members have different truth values, the biconditional is false. (49) through (51) are false, for each features propositions with different truth values.

49 The Himalayas are a chain of mountains if and only if the Pope is the leader of the Anglican Church.

50 London is in England just in case Boston is in Bosnia.

51 Parrots are mammals if and only if cats are mammals.

By contrast, the following biconditionals are all true because in each case its members have the same truth value:

52 Lincoln was assassinated if and only if Kennedy was assassinated.

53 Beijing is the capital of France just in case Bill Gates is poor.

54 That oaks are trees and tigers are felines are logically equivalent.

In any biconditional, each member is both a necessary and a sufficient condition of the other. Thus in (48), Baxter's being the college's CEO is both a necessary and sufficient condition for her being the college's president, and her being the college's president is both a necessary and sufficient condition for her being the college's CEO. So a biconditional can be understood as a conjunction of two conditionals. Thus we can represent (52) in either of these ways:

52' $L \equiv K$

52" $(L \supset K) \cdot (K \supset L)$

(52'') is the conjunction of two conditionals whose antecedent and consequent imply each other. That is why the material equivalence relation is called a 'biconditional,' and, obviously, this connective is commutative.

BOX 2 ■ SUMMARY: COMPOUND PROPOSITIONS

- Any proposition that is affected by a truth-functional connective is *compound*. Otherwise, it is *simple*.
- The truth value of a compound proposition is determined by factoring in: (1) the truth values of its members, and (2) the truth-value rules associated with each connective affecting that proposition.
- Negation is the only connective that can affect a single proposition.

Exercises

I. Review Questions

1. What is a compound proposition?
2. What are the five logical connectives? And what does it mean to say that they are truth-functional?
3. Besides 'and,' what are some other words used to express a conjunction?
4. Besides 'either . . . or . . . ,' what are some other words used to express a disjunction?
5. Besides 'if . . . then . . . ,' what are some other words used to express a conditional?
6. Besides 'if and only if,' what are some other words used to express a biconditional?
7. In a material conditional, which part is understood to present a necessary condition of the other? Which part is understood to present a sufficient condition of the other?
8. How could the biconditional be rephrased using other truth-functional connectives?

II. For each of the following propositions, determine whether or not its main connective is a negation. Indicate double negation whenever appropriate.

1. Either London's air pollution is not at dangerous levels or San Francisco's isn't.

   SAMPLE ANSWER: Not a negation

2. It is false that London's air pollution is at dangerous levels.

*3. San Francisco's air pollution is unhealthy.

4. It is not the case that Mexico City's air pollution is not harmful.

5. Non-dangerous levels of air pollution are rare in big cities.

6. Dangerous levels of air pollution are illegal.

*7. Dangerous levels of air pollution violate the Kyoto Protocol.

8. It is not the case that dangerous levels of air pollution violate the Kyoto Protocol.

9. Dangerous levels of air pollution are not illegal.

*10. Cleveland's air quality now reaches non-dangerous levels of pollution.

III. For each of the following propositions, determine whether or not its main connective is a conjunction.

1. Mexico City's air pollution is not harmful, but Houston's is.

   SAMPLE ANSWER: Conjunction

2. Dangerous levels of air pollution are illegal and unhealthy.

3. Chicago's air is polluted; however, Washington's is worse.

*4. Rome's air is as unpolluted as Cleveland's.

5. In Toronto, air pollution is a fact of life; moreover, people are resigned to it in the summer.

6. New York's polluted air is often blown out to sea by westerly winds.

*7. The Kyoto Protocol mandates steps to reduce air pollution, but the United States has not complied.

8. London's air pollution is not at dangerous levels; however, that's not the case in San Francisco.

*9. Either Vancouver has low levels of air pollution or Montreal has dangerous levels of air pollution.

10. It is not the case that Canada is not a signatory of the Kyoto Protocol.

IV. For each of the following propositions, determine whether or not its main connective is a disjunction.

1. Neither China nor North Korea is a signatory of the Kyoto Protocol.

   SAMPLE ANSWER: Not a disjunction

*2. China and North Korea are not signatories of the Kyoto Protocol.

3. Either the United States complies with the Kyoto Protocol or it doesn't.

4. It is not the case that Mexico City's air pollution is either harmful or unhealthy.

5. Mexico City's air pollution is neither harmful nor unhealthy.

*6. New York's polluted air blows either out to sea or north to Canada.

7. Dangerous levels of air pollution violate health laws as well as the Kyoto Protocol.

*8. Dangerous levels of air pollution violate either the Kyoto Protocol or internal regulations.

*9. San Francisco's air pollution is at dangerous levels unless there is fresh air blowing from the sea.

10. It is false that neither China nor North Korea is a signatory of the Kyoto Protocol.

V. For each of the following propositions, determine whether or not its main connective is a material conditional.

1. If the United States and China sign the Kyoto Protocol, then the biggest polluters agree to comply.

   SAMPLE ANSWER: Conditional

2. That London's air pollution is not at dangerous levels implies that London is complying with the Kyoto Protocol.

*3. Either Montreal has dangerous levels of air pollution or Rome does.

4. Mexico City's air is not harmful provided that Houston's air is healthy.

*5. Chicago's air is unhealthy only if it has dangerous levels of pollutants.

6. Washington's air pollution is not a fact of life unless people are resigned to it.

7. That Canada has signed the Kyoto Protocol implies that Canada is willing to comply.

*8. It is not the case that if London has dangerous levels of air pollution, the United Kingdom has not signed the Kyoto Protocol.

9. Either Mexico City has air pollution or if Houston has it, so does Vancouver.

*10. That China has not signed the Kyoto Protocol implies that neither Canada nor the United Kingdom has signed it.

VI. For each proposition in Exercise V that is a conditional, mark its antecedent with double underline and its consequent with single underline (*4, *7, and *10).

1. SAMPLE ANSWER: If The USA and China sign the Kyoto Protocol, then the biggest polluters agree to comply.

VII. For each of the following propositions, determine whether or not its main connective is a material biconditional.

1. Only if Chicago has dangerous levels of air pollutants is its air unhealthy.

   SAMPLE ANSWER: Not a biconditional

*2. China has signed the Kyoto Protocol if and only if North Korea has.

3. Washington's air pollution is a fact of life just in case people are resigned to it.

4. If London's air pollution is not at dangerous levels, the United Kingdom has signed the Kyoto Protocol.

*5. Montreal has dangerous levels of air pollution if Rome does.

*6. London's air pollution is at dangerous levels if and only if its air is unhealthy.

7. It is false both that Houston's air is harmful and that it is unhealthy when and only when it reaches dangerous levels of pollution.

*8. Chicago's air is unhealthy just in case it has pollutants that are either dangerous or otherwise unhealthy.

9. Dangerous levels of air pollution violate the Kyoto Protocol if and only if they violate UN environmental regulations.

10. New York's air does not reach dangerous levels of pollution only if it is either blown out to sea by westerly winds or dispersed by thunderstorms.

VIII. YOUR OWN THINKING LAB

In each of the following, a proposition is taken either to be or not to be a condition that's necessary, sufficient, or both for the truth of another proposition. Provide the correct representation of each using the propositional symbols in parentheses and connectives as needed.

1. 'The potato has nutrients' (O) is necessary and sufficient for 'The potato is nutritious' (N).

   SAMPLE ANSWER: (O ⊃ N) · (N ⊃ O) or O ≡ N

2. 'John hunts' (J) is necessary for 'John is a hunter' (H).

*3. 'This figure is an isosceles triangle' (I) is a sufficient for 'This figure is a triangle' (F).

4. 'Fluffy is a cat' (C) is not a sufficient condition for 'Fluffy is a feline' (F).

5. 'Mary is a sister' (A) is necessary and sufficient for 'Mary is a female sibling' (F).

*6. 'Laurence is not British' (B) is not necessary for 'Laurence is not European' (E).

11.3 Propositional Formulas for Compound Propositions

Punctuation Signs

As we have seen in some examples above, parentheses, brackets, and braces can be used to remove ambiguity in formulas by indicating the scope of their logical connectives. When a compound proposition is joined to a simple proposition or to another compound proposition by a logical connective, parentheses are the first recourse for determining the scope of occurring connectives if necessary. When the compound proposition is more complex, brackets may be needed, and for even more complex compound propositions, braces. Thus parentheses are introduced first, then brackets, and finally braces. For examples illustrating their correct use, see Box 3.

The compound proposition (P • Q) ⊃ R is a conditional, while P • (Q ⊃ R) is a conjunction. Without brackets, the proposition (P • Q) ⊃ R v ~ S is ambiguous, since it is unclear which connective is its main connective: it admits of two different interpretations, one as a conditional, the other as a disjunction. Finally, the main connective in ~ {[(P • Q) ⊃ R] v ~ S} is the negation in the far left of this formula, which affects the whole formula. Compare ~ [(P • Q) ⊃ R] v ~ S. Now, without braces, the scope of that negation is the conditional marked by brackets, and the whole formula is not a negation but a disjunction.

Well-Formed Formulas

A formula representing a proposition, whether simple or compound, is well formed when it is acceptable within the symbolic notation that we are now using. To determine whether a compound formula is well formed, the *scope* (or range) of its truth-functional connectives matters.

BOX 3 ■ PUNCTUATION SIGNS		
parentheses	'( )' as in:	(P • Q) ⊃ R
brackets	'[ ]' as in	[(P • Q) ⊃ R] v ~ S
braces	'{ }' as in:	~ {[(P • Q) ⊃ R] v ~ S}

Within the scope of negation falls the simple or compound proposition that follows it. Negation is the only connective that has a single formula, simple or compound, within its scope. For the other connectives, each has two formulas (simple or compound) within its scope. Well-formed formulas (WFFs) often require punctuation signs to mark the scope of their connectives.

Recall (52'') above, $(L \supset K) \cdot (K \supset L)$, which is a well-formed formula with two conditionals set inside parentheses to eliminate ambiguity: parentheses are needed here to indicate that the compound proposition is a conjunction of two conditionals.

A different arrangement of punctuation signs could yield a different proposition even when all propositional symbols remain the same, as shown by $L \supset [K \cdot (K \supset L)]$. This is a conditional featuring a simple proposition as antecedent and a compound consequent that's a conjunction of a simple proposition with another conditional (one made up of simple propositions). If that conditional is false, we can say that by introducing negation and braces in this way: $\sim \{L \supset [K \cdot (K \supset L)]\}$. These are all WFFs, but the formulas in Box 4 are not.

BOX 4 ■ SOME FORMULAS NOT WELL FORMED

$P \sim Q$

$P \sim$

$P \lor Q \cdot P$

Symbolizing Compound Propositions

We'll now have a closer look at some compound propositions. But first, consider

55 Fox News is on television.

Since there is no connective here, (55) is a simple proposition that we may symbolize as

55' F

By contrast, (56), symbolized below as (56'), has a negation and is therefore compound.

56 CBS News is not on television.

56' $\sim$ C

Now consider (57), an abbreviated version of the longer proposition (57'):

57 Fox News is on television but CBS News is not.

57' Fox News is on television but CBS News is not on television.

Either way, we have a compound proposition featuring two connectives: conjunction and negation. The main connective, however, is the conjunction, whose scope is the entire compound proposition. The scope of negation is only the second proposition. The underlying principle for determining this is

> The scope of negation is always the proposition represented as immediately following the tilde. That proposition may be either simple or compound. In some cases, a correct symbolic representation would require that we use punctuation signs to remove ambiguity about *which* compound proposition falls within the scope of the negation.

Since in (57) the scope of the negation is clear, the formula symbolizing it requires no parentheses:

57″ F • ~C

What's the truth value of this formula if we know that the F and C are true? By applying the truth-value rule for negation, we can learn that '~ C' is false, and then, by applying the truth-value rule for the conjunction, that (57) is false, too.

Let's now try to identify the main connective in (58).

58 If both Harry and Miguel are on the team, then Bill is not on the team.

(58) is a conditional with an antecedent and a consequent that are compound propositions themselves—in symbols,

58′ (H • M) ⊃ ~B

(58′)'s antecedent is the conjunction H • M, and its consequent is the negation ~B. To indicate that the main connective is the conditional, (58′) needs parentheses in its antecedent. No parentheses are needed in the consequent, since the scope of the negation is clear: namely, B.

Let's now calculate the truth value of that formula, assuming that H and B are true and M is false. Given this assumption, (58′) is true, since its antecedent is false. In this case, it doesn't matter at all that its consequent, ~B, is false. Why? Because given the truth-value rule for the conditional, having a false antecedent is enough to make it true. And (58′)'s antecedent is false because one of the conjuncts, M, is false. Recall that according to the truth-value rule for conjunction, having a false conjunct is sufficient to make a conjunction false. Since a conditional with a false antecedent is itself true, (58′) comes out true under the present assumptions—as does the English sentence represented by it, (58) above.

Let's now try another:

59 Bats are nocturnal if and only if either goldfish are mammals or chipmunks are rodents.

We can represent 'Bats are nocturnal' as 'B,' 'Goldfish are mammals' as 'G,' and 'Chipmunks are rodents' as 'C.' The main connective is the conditional that appears flanked by a simple proposition on the left and by a disjunction on the right. In symbols, (59) becomes,

59′ B ≡ (G v C)

Let B and C be true and G false. Since we know the value of B, to determine the truth value of the biconditional we need to know the truth value of G v C, which is true: this disjunction has at least one true disjunct—namely, A. (59') is therefore true, given that both of its members have the same truth value (namely, true).

Using the same symbols, we can now represent two other propositions, (60) and (61).

60 It is not the case that either chipmunks are rodents or they are not rodents.

60′ $\sim (C \lor \sim C)$

61 It is false that bats are nocturnal just in case if goldfish are mammals, then chipmunks are, and they are not, rodents.

61′ $\sim \{B \equiv [G \supset (C \cdot \sim C)]\}$

With the same assignation of truth values for propositions C, B, and G, we can calculate that (60') is false, since it's the negation of a disjunction that's true given that C is true. But (61') is false, since it's the negation of a true biconditional whose members have the same truth value. Since $[G \supset (C \cdot \sim C)]$'s antecedent is false and its consequent false, the conditional is true. $C \cdot \sim C$ is false because the conjunction has a false conjunct, $\sim C$.

Here is a suggestion. To calculate the truth value of a compound proposition if you first know the truth values of its component simple propositions, proceed as follows:

1. Post the truth value of each component proposition under the corresponding propositional letter.
2. Identify the main connective. That's where the final result will be posted.
3. Begin calculating the truth value of smaller compounds within the larger proposition by using the truth-value rules for the connectives, and work outward toward the larger units.
4. Suppose you wish to calculate the truth value of $\sim [(E \cdot L) \supset (M \lor \sim F)]$, and you know that E and L are true and M and F are false. You can calculate that truth value by construing a diagram in this way, following steps (1) through (3):

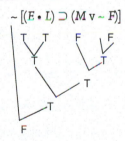

Exercises

IX. Review Questions

1. Why are punctuation signs part of the symbolic notation for propositions?
2. What's the scope of a negation?
3. When P is false and Q is true, what's the value of $P \supset Q$?
4. Define $P \equiv Q$ using only material conditional and conjunction.

11.3 PROPOSITIONAL FORMULAS FOR COMPOUND PROPOSITIONS

247

X. Which of these formulas are WFFs, and which aren't? For each WFF, determine whether it's simple or compound. If compound, identify the main connective.

1. $\sim D \sim (C \bullet B)$

   SAMPLE ANSWER: Not a WFF

2. $(\equiv F \vee \sim E)$

*3. $F \equiv \sim F$

4. $(\sim A \bullet \sim E) \vee A$

*5. $\sim (A \supset \sim A) \supset (F \sim B)$

6. $E \equiv F \vee C$

*7. $B \bullet (D \vee C)$

8. $(A \supset F) \bullet \sim (C \supset \sim B)$

*9. $\sim \{E \equiv B\} \vee \sim F$

10. $\sim (A \supset \sim C) \supset \sim (F \supset E)$

XI. For each of the following propositions, determine whether it is simple or compound, and, if compound, identify its main connective.

1. Franklin D. Roosevelt was not a senator.

   SAMPLE ANSWER: Compound. Negation.

2. Warren G. Harding did not finish his term in office.

*3. Ronald Reagan was reelected if and only if Mondale was defeated.

4. If Lyndon Johnson was born in Texas, then so was Eisenhower.

5. Either Arnold Schwarzenegger was a popular actor or Richard Nixon resigned.

*6. William McKinley was assassinated.

7. Nixon visited China only if Nixon traveled in Asia.

8. Woodrow Wilson will be remembered, unless the League of Nations was a folly.

*9. Theodore Roosevelt was a war hero, but he also built the Panama Canal.

10. Theodore Roosevelt was born into a wealthy family of prominent New Yorkers.

11. It is not the case that John F. Kennedy was from Colorado.

*12. John F. Kennedy was assassinated in 1963 while on a visit to Dallas.

13. Either Calvin Coolidge was a conservative or he was from New England.

14. Franklin D. Roosevelt went to Yalta in 1945 for a meeting with Allied leaders.

*15. Neither Eisenhower nor Kennedy was a pacifist.

16. It is false that Thomas Jefferson was not a Virginian.

17. Lyndon Johnson liked to entertain, but he did not like his Texas ranch.

*18. Millard Fillmore signed the Fugitive Slave Act.

19. It is not the case that James Madison was from Pennsylvania.

20. Franklin D. Roosevelt was a New Yorker if and only if Martin Van Buren was, too.

XII. Symbolize each proposition in the exercise above (*3, *6, *12, *15).

1. SAMPLE ANSWER: ~ F

XIII. Some of the following propositions involve more than one connective. For each of them, identify the main connective and provide the correct propositional formula.

1. It is false that Gus Hall was not a Communist.

   SAMPLE ANSWER: Negation   ~ ~ H

2. If Lincoln was the tallest president, then either Theodore Roosevelt or John F. Kennedy was the youngest.

*3. Either Franklin Roosevelt did not like Stalin at all, or he admired both that Stalin was unyielding against Hitler and that he stuck by his decisions.

4. Ronald Reagan was from Illinois just in case Gerald Ford was from Michigan and served in the House of Representatives.

5. If Harry Truman was a skillful politician but very plain-spoken, then he was not an unskillful politician.

*6. Herbert Hoover either was president during the stock market crash of 1929 or he wasn't.

7. It is not the case that Dirksen was from Ohio and had a mustache if and only if Taft was from Ohio.

8. Either both Taft and McKinley were Republicans or Dirksen was from Ohio.

*9. That Taft was a conservative Republican implies that neither Harding nor Dirksen were conservative Republicans.

10. Richard Nixon and Harry Truman both played the piano provided that Dirksen was not from Ohio.

11. It is not the case that both Truman did not play the piano and his daughter Margaret was not serious about music.

*12. It is not the case that Gerald Ford was a football star at the University of Minnesota just in case Truman played the piano and his daughter Margaret was serious about music.

13. John F. Kennedy and George H. W. Bush both served in the navy in World War II only if Gerald Ford did, too.

14. If that Bill Clinton is a moderate Democrat implies that Lyndon Johnson was a liberal, then that Taft was a conservative Republican implies that both Harding and Goldwater were conservative Republicans.

*15. If it is true that Bill Clinton smoked marijuana but he did not inhale, then it is false that Dirksen was from Ohio if and only if he had a mustache.

XIV. For each of the following propositional formulas, identify its main connective.

1. ~ {K v [(L v P) • O]}

   SAMPLE ANSWER: Negation

2. ~ (W v Z)

*3. $T \equiv (U \cdot R)$

4. $A \vee \sim (R \vee T)$

5. $(H \supset S) \cdot (L \equiv M)$

*6. $(J \vee R) \cdot (D \supset P)$

7. $\sim W \cdot Q$

*8. $\sim \{S \supset [P \cdot \sim (T \equiv U)]\}$

9. $\sim \sim H \equiv K$

10. $\sim A \equiv \sim [(R \supset T) \supset (U \cdot R)]$

XV. Describe each of the formulas in the exercise above.

1. SAMPLE ANSWER: $\sim \{K \vee [(L \vee P) \cdot O]\}$

Negation of a disjunction with a simple proposition and a conjunction as disjuncts. The conjunction itself has a disjunction of simple propositions, and a simple proposition as its conjuncts.

XVI. Assuming that 'A' and 'B' are true, and 'C' and 'D' are false, what's the truth value of each of the following formulas?

1. $\sim B \vee \sim A$

    SAMPLE ANSWER: false

2. $A \cdot D$

*3. $\sim B \supset A$

4. $\sim (A \supset \sim A)$

5. $C \supset B$

*6. $B \vee D$

7. $C \equiv D$

8. $\sim C$

*9. $\sim B \vee D$

10. $A \supset C$

11. $C \vee \sim A$

*12. $D \supset \sim B$

13. $\sim (B \vee C)$

14. $\sim (A \vee \sim D)$

*15. $O \equiv A$

16. $\sim D \vee C$

17. $B \equiv \sim A$

*18. $D \cdot \sim D$

19. $\sim (A \cdot D)$

20. $\sim C \supset \sim B$

XVII. For each of the following formulas, determine its truth value. Assume the following truth values: A, B, and C are true; D, E, and F are false.

1. $A \cdot E$

    SAMPLE ANSWER: False

2. $\sim C \vee F$

3. $B \supset \sim D$

*4. $B \cdot C$

5. $F \equiv D$

6. $\sim B \equiv \sim A$

*7. $B \vee F$

8. $E \cdot F$

9. $B \cdot E$

*10. $B \vee C$

11. $\sim B \vee C$

12. $A \supset (E \cdot C)$

*13. $\sim (C \cdot A)$

14. $\sim (\sim F \supset D)$

15. $(E \vee B) \supset \sim A$

*16. $\sim D$

17. $(F \lor {\sim} E) \equiv {\sim} (C \bullet B)$ 20. ${\sim} (D \supset {\sim} A) \supset (F \lor B)$ 23. $(A \supset F) \bullet {\sim} (C \supset {\sim} B)$

18. $B \equiv {\sim} F$ 21. $E \equiv (F \lor C)$ 24. ${\sim} (E \equiv B) \lor {\sim} F$

*19. $({\sim} B \bullet {\sim} F) \lor A$ *22. $B \bullet (D \lor C)$ *25. ${\sim} [(A \supset {\sim} C) \supset {\sim} (F \supset E)]$

XVIII. YOUR OWN THINKING LAB

1. For each of the formulas above, construct a statement whose truth value is as determined by the truth values assigned to it in that exercise.

   SAMPLE ANSWER: Either the Eiffel Tower is not in Paris or the Coliseum is not in Rome.

2. Describe each of the formulas in the above exercise.

   SAMPLE ANSWER: A disjunction whose disjuncts are negations.

11.4 Defining Connectives with Truth Tables

We're ready now to move on to truth tables, a procedure that will, in the next section, allow us to determine mechanically the truth value of compound propositions. But before turning to this, let's first use that procedure to define the above discussed truth-functional connectives.

Negation.   To define negation with a truth table, keep in mind that

---

BOX 5 ■ TRUTH-VALUE RULE FOR NEGATION

A negation is true if and only if the proposition denied is false. Otherwise, a negation is false.

A truth table defines negation by showing when ${\sim} P$, the negation of a simple proposition P, is true and when it is false:

To construct this truth table, we first write down P on the top, without a negation on the left, and with a negation on the right. We then write a vertical column on the left, under P, listing all the possible truth values of P, which are T (true) and F (false), since

Each proposition is either true or false.

In the column on the right, under ${\sim} P$, we apply the truth-value rule for negation to each row of the left column, and write down the truth value that we obtain on the right. An application of the rule given in Box 5 to each row in the column on the left yields the results, recorded in the column inside the box on the truth table's right-hand side. They are as follows:

First row: ~P is false when P is true
Second row: ~P is true when P is false

Other Truth-Functional Connectives.   To define the other truth-functional connectives, first we keep in mind that they involve two propositions, each of which could be T (true) or F (false). This determines the number of Ts and Fs that we'll write on the column on the left-hand side of the truth table. To calculate the total number of Ts and Fs in each column, we use the formula 2^n, where 2 stands for the two truth values a proposition may have (true or false) and n for the number of propositions of different types that occur in the formula to which we'd apply the procedure. In the definition of negation, there is only one proposition, so n is 1 and the formula 2^n produces two truth values: one T and one F. But, for conjunction, disjunction, conditional, and biconditional, each definition features two propositions, represented by P and Q. So the formula is 2^2 and yields four places for the truth values of occurring propositions: two Ts and two Fs. In the first column on the left, we assign half Ts followed by half Fs: that is, two Ts, and two Fs (see truth tables below). In the other column on the same side of the truth table, we assign four values in this way: T, F, T, F. On the top right-hand side of the table, have the formula whose truth value we wish to determine, and below it, the truth value resulting from the application of the corresponding truth-value rule to each row of assigned values on the left. The final result is marked by putting it inside a box and is obtained by applying the truth value rule of each occurring connective to the values on the left-hand side of the truth table. Let's now construct truth tables for each of the remaining types of compound propositions.

Conjunction.   To define this connective with a truth table, keep in mind that

BOX 6 ■ TRUTH-VALUE RULE FOR CONJUNCTION

A conjunction is true if and only if its conjuncts are both true. Otherwise, a conjunction is false.

The truth table has two columns on the left, each of which assigns four truth values, two Ts and two Fs, to each of its conjuncts. Its four horizontal rows are obtained by calculating the possible combinations of those values while applying the rule in Box 6. The result, in a box on the right, shows that a conjunction is true just in case the two conjuncts are true.

P Q	P • Q
T T	T
T F	F
F T	F
F F	F

Disjunction. To define this connective with a truth table, keep in mind that

> ### BOX 7 ■ TRUTH-VALUE RULE FOR DISJUNCTION
>
> A disjunction is true if and only if at least one disjunct is true. Otherwise, a disjunction is false.

The truth table for disjunction has two columns on the left, each assigning four truth values, two Ts and two Fs, to each of the disjuncts. Its four horizontal rows are the result of reading the possible combinations of those values while applying the rule in Box 7. The final result, inside the box in the right-hand column, amounts to a definition of disjunction: it shows that a disjunction is true just in case at least one of its disjuncts is true. Equivalently, it defines disjunction as a compound proposition that is false just in case both of its disjuncts are false.

P Q	*P* v *Q*
T T	T
T F	T
F T	T
F F	F

Material Conditional. To define this connective with a truth table, keep in mind that

> ### BOX 8 ■ TRUTH-VALUE RULE FOR MATERIAL CONDITIONAL
>
> A material conditional is false if and only if its antecedent is true and its consequent false. Otherwise, a conditional is true.

As before, it has two columns on the left, each assigning four truth values, two Ts and two Fs, to its antecedent and its consequent. Its four horizontal rows are obtained by calculating the possible combinations of those values and applying the rule in Box 8. The result, inside the box on the right-hand side, amounts to a definition of the material conditional. It shows that it is true in all cases except when its antecedent is true and its consequent false.

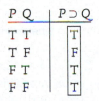

P Q	*P* ⊃ *Q*
T T	T
T F	F
F T	T
F F	T

Material Biconditional. To define this connective with a truth table, keep in mind that

> ### BOX 9 ■ TRUTH-VALUE RULE FOR MATERIAL BICONDITIONAL
>
> A material biconditional is true if and only if both members have the same truth value. Otherwise, a biconditional is false.

This truth table has two columns on the left, each assigning four truth values (two Ts and two Fs) to each simple proposition in the formula. Its four horizontal rows are obtained by calculating the possible combinations of those values and applying the rule in Box 9. The truth table's result appears inside the box on the right, and the truth table amounts to a definition of the material biconditional. It shows that it is true just in case its two members have exactly the same truth value: that is, they are either both true or both false.

P Q	P ≡ Q
T T	T
T F	F
F T	F
F F	T

The five truth tables we've now constructed provide truth-functional definitions for each of the five logical connectives. We can now use a similar procedure to determine the truth values of other compound propositions.

11.5 Truth Tables for Compound Propositions

The truth value of compound propositions can be determined with truth tables. To construct a truth table for a compound proposition, first identify the simple propositions in the formula whose value you wish to check. Once you have written them down on the top of the left-hand side of the truth table in the order that they appear in the formula, assign Ts and Fs in the way outlined above, using 2^n to calculate the total number of rows. For example, the truth table for F • ~ C is:

62	F C	F • ~ C
	T T	F F
	T F	T T
	F T	F F
	F F	F T

The formula on the right-hand side of this truth table is a conjunction of F, whose values we read in the first column on the left, and ~ C, whose values we need to determine first. We do this by applying the truth-value rule for negation to each row in the second column on the left. Once we determine ~ C's values, we enter them under the tilde on the right. We then determine the truth value of the conjunction by applying the truth-value rule for conjunction to F's values (available on the left-hand side of the truth table) and ~ C's values (under the tilde). We enter the values thus obtained under the dot, marking the resulting column with a box. This column under the main connective is the most important one, because it provides information about the truth values of the compound proposition F • ~ C. It tells us that this compound proposition is true only when 'F' and '~ C' are true (as shown in the second horizontal row). On all other assignments of values, that proposition is false.

Now let's construct a truth table for

58' (H • M) ⊃ ~ B

The truth table for (58') is:

63	H M B	(H • M) ⊃ ~ B
	T T T	T F F
	T T F	T T T
	T F T	F T F
	T F F	F T T
	F T T	F T F
	F T F	F T T
	F F T	F T F
	F F F	F T T

On its left-hand side, this truth table shows all possible combinations of truth values for the three members of the compound proposition represented by the formula on its right-hand side. That formula, whose truth value we want to determine, has three different simple propositions symbolized by H, M, and B. As before, to calculate the number of rows needed, we use the algorithm 2^n, here 2^3, which reveals that eight rows are needed. Accordingly, we assign Ts and Fs to the three columns on the left—beginning with the one farthest to the left (the one under H), which has the top half Ts and the bottom half Fs—and continue to divide that pattern in half as we move across to each of the two other columns to the right (under M and B). This convention guarantees that we do get all possible combinations of truth values. On the top line, it's all Ts, on the bottom line, it's all Fs, and in between are all other possible arrangements.

Once we have entered these values, we look at the compound proposition formula on the top right. It is a conditional, so the main connective is '⊃', under which we place the final result (inside the box). But we can determine the possible truth values of the conditional only after we first find the possible truth values of the antecedent, H • M, and the consequent, ~ B. Those truth values make up the column under '•' and the column under '~'. The final step consists in applying the rule for the truth value of the conditional to those two columns.

BOX 10 ■ TRUTH TABLES FOR COMPOUND PROPOSITIONS

As we've seen, in a truth table, the number of truth values assigned to each simple proposition on the left-hand side depends on how many different propositions occur in the formula at the top of the right-hand side, whose truth value we wish to determine. For any simple proposition there are only two possible truth values (true and false); therefore, for a compound proposition such as ~ P, only two rows are needed. But with more propositions, the number of truth values would increase according to the formula 2^n: with two, it's four lines; with three, it's eight lines; with four, it's sixteen lines; and so on. In the case of (62), then, we need four lines. And, just to make sure that we get all possible combinations of truth values, we'll adopt this convention: in the column under whatever letter symbol is farthest to the left, we put T in the top half of the rows and F in the bottom half; and in the column under the other letter symbol to the right of that, we put a sequence of alternating Ts and Fs.

11.6 Logically Necessary and Logically Contingent Propositions

Contingencies

What, then, have we learned about the truth values of the compound propositions on the right-hand side of truth tables (62) and (63)? Just this: that each is neither necessarily true nor necessarily false, but instead sometimes true and sometimes false, depending on the truth values of the component simple propositions and the logical connectives. Propositions that yield such truth values are contingencies. A compound proposition is a contingency if its truth table displays at least one T and at least one F in the column under the main connective. In (63), there is at least one T and at least one F under the '⊃'—and in (62), under the '·'. In light of those results, each of these compound propositions is a contingency.

Contradictions

Contradictions are compound propositions that are always false, simply by virtue of their form (and regardless of the actual truth values of their component simple propositions). In a truth table for a contradiction, the column under the main connective symbol is all Fs. Consider

64 $B \equiv {\sim}B$

Since (64) contains no proposition other than B, which occurs twice, the algorithm 2^1 yields two places for truth values, one for T and the other for F. Accordingly, the truth table runs:

65

B	B	≡	~ B
T		F	F
F		F	T

This truth table reveals (64) to be a contradiction.

Tautologies

Some propositions are tautologies: they are always true, simply by virtue of their form (and regardless of the actual truth values of their component propositions). The truth table of a tautology would have all Ts under the formula's main connective. The negation of (64) above is a tautology, which reads,

66 ${\sim}(B \equiv {\sim}B)$

The truth table for this proposition shows all Ts under the formula's main connective:

67

B	~	(B	≡	~ B)
T	T		F	F
F	T		F	T

(67) gives the truth value of (66), thus confirming that it is a tautology. Among well-known tautologies in logic are the so-called principles of *excluded middle*, P v ~ P, and *non-contradiction*, ~(P • ~P). For further practice, check that these are tautologies by constructing a truth table for each. Keep in mind that

---

BOX 11 ■ CONTRADICTIONS, TAUTOLOGIES, AND NEGATION

The negation of a contradiction is a tautology, and the negation of a tautology is a contradiction.

Exercises

XIX. Review Questions

1. How are truth tables used to define the five propositional connectives?
2. In a truth table for a compound proposition, how do we know how many horizontal rows are required? What is the rationale for this?
3. In a truth table for a compound proposition, which column is the most important? And what does that column tell us?
4. What is a tautology?
5. What is a contradiction?
6. What is a contingency?

XX. For each of the following formulas, construct a truth table to determine whether it is a contingency, tautology, or contradiction.

1. $W \supset \sim K$

   SAMPLE ANSWER: Contingency

W K	$W \supset \sim K$
T T	F F
T F	T T
F T	T F
F F	T T

2. $(L \lor N) \lor A$

*3. $B \supset (M \supset B)$

4. $\sim J \bullet (G \lor N)$

*5. $\sim [(A \bullet B) \supset (B \bullet A)]$

6. $D \lor (\sim M \supset \sim D)$

7. $\sim [\sim (A \bullet B) \equiv (\sim A \lor \sim B)]$

*8. $(\sim A \lor \sim B) \supset (B \bullet A)$

9. $(F \supset \sim N) \bullet \sim (F \supset \sim N)$

*10. $\sim A \equiv \sim (\sim K \lor \sim H)$

11. $(D \lor M) \supset (M \lor D)$

*12. $\sim [(\sim A \bullet H) \lor \sim (H \supset \sim I)]$

13. $(E \bullet \sim G) \supset G$

14. $A \equiv \sim \sim A$

15. $\sim (A \equiv B) \equiv \sim L$

*16. $\sim \{[A \bullet (B \bullet C)] \equiv [(A \bullet B) \bullet C]\}$

17. $\sim \{[(A \bullet B) \lor (\sim B \supset A)] \supset B\}$

*18. $(A \bullet B) \equiv (B \bullet A)$

19. $(\sim B \supset A) \equiv [(B \lor \sim D) \supset C]$

*20. $(A \equiv B) \equiv [(A \supset B) \bullet (B \supset A)]$

XXI. For each of the following propositions, first translate it into a propositional formula using the symbols provided in parentheses at the end, and then determine with a truth table whether it is a contingency, tautology, or contradiction.

1. If Earth is the center of the universe, then our planet is special. (E, O)

SAMPLE ANSWER: Contingency

E O	E ⊃ O
T T	T
T F	F
F T	T
F F	T

*2. Earth is not the center of the universe or our planet is special. (E, O)

3. Either our planet is special or it isn't. (O)

*4. Earth is not the center of the universe just in case there is something special about our planet. (E, O)

5. There is something special about our planet; however, Earth is not the center of the universe. (O, E)

6. It is false that either our planet is special or it isn't. (O)

*7. If Earth is the center of the universe and there is something special about our planet, then there is something special about our planet. (E, O)

8. It is not the case that human life has value if and only if human life has value. (H)

9. Human life has a purpose, but it is not the case that it has value. (L, H)

10. Human life has value only if it has a purpose. (H, L)

*11. Human life has value and a purpose if and only if it is not false that human life does have value and a purpose. (H, L)

*12. It is not the case that both Earth is the center of the universe and there is something special about our planet just in case it is false that human life has value and a purpose. (E, O, H, L)

13. Neither is Earth the center of the universe nor is there something special about our planet. (E, O)

*14. Neither is Earth the center of the universe nor is there something special about our planet if and only if both Earth is not the center of the universe and it is not the case that there is something special about our planet. (E, O)

15. Either human life has both value and a purpose or if it is false that there is something special about our planet, then Earth is the center of the universe. (H, L, O, E)

XXII. YOUR OWN THINKING LAB

Write down ordinary English sentences for each of the formulas below following this glossary: 'F' = Fred is at the library; 'M' = Mary is at the library; 'L' = The library is open; 'I' = I have Internet access; 'E' = The essay is due on Thursday.

1. M • ~ L

SAMPLE ANSWER: 1. Mary is at the library but the library is not open.

2. $F \equiv (L \cdot M)$

*3. $F \equiv (L \lor \sim M)$

4. $(L \cdot I) \supset (F \lor M)$

*5. $E \equiv (L \supset I)$

6. $(E \cdot L) \supset (M \lor F)$

*7. $\sim [\sim F \supset (\sim L \lor M)]$

8. $(M \cdot F) \equiv (E \cdot L)$

■ Writing Project

Find five compound propositions in English where the words used to translate the logical connectives *don't* accord with the truth-value rules for those connectives. Write a short piece arguing that the connectives in your examples are not truth-functional. Suggestions: look for conjunctions that are not commutative, or 'if . . . then . . .' sentences where the consequent appears *not* to be a necessary condition of the antecedent (e.g., 'If I have money for bus fare then I'll take the bus').

BOX 12 ■ SYMBOLIC NOTATION FOR PROPOSITIONS

Propositional Letters	Connectives	Punctuation Signs
From A to O for specific propositions	~ negation	( ) parentheses
	• conjuction	[ ] square brackets
From P to W for unspecific ones	v disjunction	{ } braces
	⊃ Conditional	
	≡ Biconditional	

■ Chapter Summary

Propositions: the building blocks of propositional arguments. Each proposition is either true or false, and either simple or compound.

Compound proposition: any proposition whose truth value is in part determined by the truth-value rule of one of the truth-functional connectives. It falls into one or another of these categories:

1. *Tautology.* Always true, by virtue of its form. Its truth table shows only Ts under the main connective.

2. *Contradiction.* Always false, by virtue of its form. Its truth table shows only Fs under the main connective.

3. *Contingency.* Neither always true nor always false. Its truth table shows at least one T and one F under the main connective.

Five Connectives and their truth-value rules:

1. *Negation.* True if and only if the proposition denied is false.

2. *Conjunction.* True if and only if its conjuncts are both true.

3. *Disjunction.* True if and only if at least one disjunct is true.

4. *Conditional.* False if and only if its antecedent is true and its consequent false.

5. *Biconditional.* True if and only if both members have the same truth value.

Truth Tables for the Connectives

Negation

P	~P
T	F
F	T

Conjunction

P	Q	P • Q
T	T	T
T	F	F
F	T	F
F	F	F

Disjunction

P	Q	P v Q
T	T	T
T	F	T
F	T	T
F	F	F

Conditional

P	Q	P ⊃ Q
T	T	T
T	F	F
F	T	T
F	F	T

Biconditional

P	Q	P ≡ Q
T	T	T
T	F	F
F	T	F
F	F	T

■ Key Words

Compound proposition
Negation
Conjunction
Disjunction
Material conditional
Antecedent

Consequent
Material biconditional
Tautology
Contradiction
Contingency

CHAPTER 12

Checking the Validity of Propositional Arguments

In this chapter you'll learn some ways to determine whether propositional arguments are valid or invalid. The topics will include

- The use of truth tables in checking argument forms for validity.
- Some standard valid argument forms in propositional logic: *modus ponens, modus tollens,* contraposition, hypothetical syllogism, and disjunctive syllogism.
- The formal fallacies of affirming the consequent, denying the antecedent, and affirming a disjunct.
- An introduction to proofs of validity.

12.1 Checking Validity with Truth Tables

As we have seen, truth tables provide a procedure for determining whether a compound proposition is a tautology, contradiction, or contingency. Moreover, they generate that outcome in a mechanical way, applying certain rules that yield a result in a finite number of steps. But they have another use that we'll explore at length here: they allow us to determine mechanically whether an argument is valid or not. Consider, for example, this argument:

1   1. Either buffalo are prairie animals or coyotes are.

    2. Buffalo are prairie animals.

    3. Coyotes are not prairie animals.

To determine whether (1) is valid or not requires that we first obtain its argument form. We translate (1)'s premises and conclusion into our standard symbolic notation and obtain:

1'   1. B v C

    2. B

    3. ~ C

Our next step is to transform this vertical listing of premises and conclusion into a horizontal one, using commas to separate premises and writing the symbol '∴', which reads 'therefore,' in front of the conclusion. This gives us

1'   B v C, B ∴ ~C

We can now test this argument form for validity with a truth table. We enter the formula at the top of the truth table on its right-hand side, and each different simple proposition that occurs in that formula on the left-hand side. Next, we assign truth values to those simple propositions, following the algorithm 2^n, which for the formula under consideration is 2^2 (since the simple propositions occurring in it are two, B and C). Once this is done, we focus on the smaller formulas that represent the argument's premises and conclusion, calculating their truth values one at a time. These calculations are performed in the standard way described in Chapter 11. In the final step, we check (in a way we'll presently explain) to see whether the argument is valid or not. Our truth table for checking the validity of (1) above looks like this:

2   B C | B v C, B ∴ ~C

B C	B v C	B	~C	
T T	T	T	F	←
T F	T	T	T	
F T	T	F	F	
F F	F	F	T	

In (2), a value has been calculated for each formula representing the argument's premises and conclusion. How? By reasoning as follows: the first premise is a disjunction, so its truth value is calculated by applying the truth-value rule for disjunction to B and C, whose values have been assigned on the left-hand side. The first column on the right, placed under the wedge, shows the result of this calculation. Since the second premise, B, is a simple proposition, we cannot calculate its values by using any of the truth-value rules for connectives. So we assign to B the same values that we have assigned it in the first column on the left-hand side of the table. That is, we simply transfer those values to the second column on the right-hand side of the table (this step can be omitted, since B's values are readily available in the first column on the left, and could be read directly from there). We then proceed to calculate the truth value of ~C by applying the truth-value rule for negation to the values of C, which are displayed in the second column on the left. We write down the results of this calculation under the tilde, as shown by the truth table's third column on the right. We're ready now to check whether the formula on its top right-hand side is a valid argument form. To determine this, we scan horizontally each row displaying the values of B v C, B, and ~ C (ignoring all vertical columns). We are looking for a row where the premises B v C and B are both true and the conclusion ~ C false. And we do find precisely that in the first row. This shows the argument represented by the formula to be invalid, since

> If a truth table devised to test the validity of an argument displays at least one row where premises are all true and conclusion false, that proves the invalidity of the argument form tested.

BOX 1 ■ WHAT DO TRUTH TABLES HAVE TO DO WITH VALIDITY?

The relation between validity and truth tables is simply this:

1. If it is possible for an argument to have all of its premises true and its conclusion false at once—that is, if this occurs on one or more horizontal rows in its truth table—then the form is invalid (as is any argument with that form).
2. But if this is not possible—that is, if its truth table shows no such row—then the form is valid.

(Recall that if an argument's form is such that it is possible for all of its premises to be true and its conclusion false at once, then its premises do not entail its conclusion.)

The first row (indicated by an arrow) in the above truth table demonstrates the invalidity of the form being tested (see rationale in Box 1). In this way we show that (1) is invalid. Similar truth tables could be constructed to demonstrate the invalidity of any argument of the same form. For example,

3   Either the media foster public awareness, or public opinion leads to public policy.
    Since the media foster public awareness, it is not the case that public opinion leads to public policy.

Since this argument has the same form as (1) above, the results of any correct truth table for checking its validity would be exactly the same as those displayed in (2). (You should construct such a truth table for your own practice.)

Let's now use a truth table to check the validity of another argument:

4   1. If Sally voted in the presidential election, then she is a citizen.
    2. Sally is not a citizen.
    _____
    3. Sally did not vote in the presidential election.

This has the form

4' M ⊃ C, ~C ∴ ~M

First, notice that there are only two different simple propositions in this argument form, M and C, each of which occurs twice. Thus we need only four assignments of values (two Ts and two Fs) on the left-hand side of the truth table, and four horizontal rows. The next step is to calculate the truth value of (4')'s premises and conclusion. Each of these is a compound proposition, for which we'll write the truth value in the column under its connective symbol: in the first premise, under '⊃', and in the second premise and conclusion under '~'. In this argument there are no simple propositions; to test for validity, therefore, we scan only the rows in columns under the connectives: in the premises, these are the columns under the horseshoe '⊃' and the tilde '~', and in the conclusion, it's the column under the tilde '~'. We're looking for a row in which all the premises are true and the conclusion false, which would indicate invalidity. But the scan shows that there is no such row in this truth table.

5 | M | C | M ⊃ C, | ~C | ∴ | ~M |
|---|---|---|---|---|---|
| T | T | T | F | | F |
| T | F | F | T | | F |
| F | T | T | F | | T |
| F | F | T | T | | T |

The absence of such a row means that (4'), and therefore also (4), is valid. This test proves validity because the truth table gives an exhaustive list of all possible combinations of truth values of the premises and conclusion, and no horizontal row shows that the former can be true and the latter false at once. Thus in all arguments with (4')'s form, the premises entail the conclusion. Consider these arguments:

6 If Professor Tina Hare is at the University of Liverpool, then she works in England. Professor Tina Hare doesn't work in England. Thus Professor Tina Hare is not at the University of Liverpool.

7 If the Earth is not a planet, then Mars is not a planet. But Mars is a planet. Hence, the Earth is a planet.

For your own practice, construct a truth table for these arguments to check their validity. You'll see that their final result will be exactly like that in (5) above.

Let's try one more argument, this time more complex.

8 Since France is not a member of the union, it follows that Britain is not. For if France is not a member, then either the Netherlands is or Britain is.

We can reconstruct (8) as

8' 1. France is not a member of the union.
    2. If France is not a member of the union, then either the Netherlands is a member
       of the union or Britain is a member of the union.
    3. Britain is not a member of the union.

which has the form

8" ~F, ~F ⊃ (N v B) ∴ ~B

To test (8") for validity, we first note that since three different simple propositions occur in it, the truth table will need eight horizontal lines. Once we write down all possible combinations of truth values for these simple propositions on the left-hand side of the truth table, we then calculate the truth values of premises and conclusion and enter the results under each connective symbol on the right-hand side. Here is the truth table, with the rows showing the argument's invalidity indicated by an arrow:

9	F N B	~F,	~F	⊃	(N v B)	∴ ~B	
	T T T	F	F	T	T	F	
	T T F	F	F	T	T	T	
	T F T	F	F	T	T	F	
	T F F	F	F	T	F	T	
	F T T	T	T	T	T	F	←
	F T F	T	T	T	T	T	
	F F T	T	T	T	T	F	←
	F F F	T	T	F	F	T	

The more complex formula on (9)'s right-hand side is the one representing the argument's second premise: it's got three connectives in it. How do we determine which is the most important? We do this by reading carefully and looking at the parentheses: they tell us that it is the horseshoe placed between ~ F and (N v B). But in order to determine the truth values in the column under the horseshoe, we first have to know the possible truth values of its antecedent, ~F, and its consequent, (N v B). Once we have the value of ~ F, which can be obtained by applying the rule for the truth value of negation to F on the left-hand side of the truth table, we enter those values under ~ F, the first premise of the argument (so they don't need to be written twice if desired). The value of (N v B) can be obtained by applying to the values of N and B the rule for the truth value of the disjunction on the left-hand side of the truth table. To calculate the value of ~ B, we proceed in a manner similar to that in which we calculated the values of ~ F. Once this is done, then, ignoring all the other columns, we scan each horizontal row showing the truth value for each premise and conclusion on the right-hand side of the truth table. We ask ourselves: is there any horizontal row in which both premises are true and the conclusion false? And the answer is Yes! It happens twice: on rows 5 and 7. Thus the argument form (8") has been proved invalid, and so any argument that has that argument form, such as (8) above, is invalid.

BOX 2 ■ HOW TO CHECK VALIDITY WITH TRUTH TABLES

- When we use a truth table to check an argument's validity, we first write the formula capturing the argument's form at the top on the right.
- Each different type of proposition that occurs in that formula goes at the top on the left.
- The rows under the formula itself offer an exhaustive list of possible combinations of truth values for premises and conclusion.
- To decide whether an argument form is valid or not, we scan each row under the formula.
- Any row showing that there is a configuration of truth values in which premises are true and the conclusion false proves that the argument form is invalid.
- If there is no such row, then the argument form is valid.

Exercises

I. Review Questions

1. How do we construct a truth table to check the validity of a propositional argument?
2. How do we tell by a truth table whether an argument is valid or not?
3. Why is the truth-table technique a mechanical procedure for checking the validity of an argument?
4. If at least one row of a truth table for an argument shows all false premises and a true conclusion, is that relevant to determining the argument's validity?

II. Use truth tables to determine whether each of these formulas represents a valid or an invalid argument.

1. H ⊃ ~K , ~K ∴ H

   SAMPLE ANSWER: Invalid

H K	H ⊃ ~K, ~K ∴ H
T T	F F F
T F	T T T
F T	T F F
F F	T T T

2. L v N, ~N ∴ L

3. R ⊃ (M ⊃ R) ∴ M v R

*4. J, J v N ∴ ~N

5. ~(B ≡ A) ⊃ ~L ∴ L ⊃ (B ≡ A)

6. D v (~M ⊃ ~D) ∴ M ⊃ D

7. ~(G • E), ~G ∴ E • ~G

*8. ~C v ~B, ~(B • A) ∴ A v C

9. (F ⊃ ~N) • ~(F ⊃ ~N) ∴ ~N

*10. ~B, ~(~K ≡ ~H) ∴ K ⊃ ~H

11. (D v M) ⊃ (M v D) ∴ M v D

12. ~ [(~A • H) v (H ⊃ ~B)] ∴ ~A • ~H

*13. K • (~E v O), ~E ⊃ ~K ∴ O

*14. E ⊃ A, ~~A ∴ ~E v ~A

15. A ⊃ B ∴ ~(~B ⊃ ~A)

16. ~M v O, M ∴ O

17. A • B ∴ ~A

18. C ⊃ D ∴ D ⊃ C

19. C ⊃ D ∴ ~C v D

20. C ⊃ D, ~C ∴ ~D

21. A ≡ B ∴ (A ⊃ B) • (B ⊃ A)

*22. H • (~I v J), J ⊃ ~H ∴ J

*23. ~ O, A ⊃ B ∴ ~O • B

24. C ⊃ D, D ∴ C

25. C ∴ C v D

III. Translate each of the following arguments into symbolic notation. Then construct a truth table to determine whether it is valid or invalid.

1. Henry's running for mayor implies that Bart will not move to Cleveland, for if Henry runs for mayor then Jill will resign, and Jill's resigning implies that Bart will not move to Cleveland. (H, J, B)

SAMPLE ANSWER: Valid

H J B	H ⊃ J,	J ⊃ ~B	∴ H ⊃ ~B
T T T	T	F F	F F
T T F	T	T T	T T
T F T	F	T F	F F
T F F	F	T T	T T
F T T	T	F F	T F
F T F	T	T T	T T
F F T	T	T F	T F
F F F	T	T T	T T

2. If Quebec is a part of Canada, then some Canadians are voters. If Ontario is a part of Canada, then some Canadians are voters. Hence, if Quebec is a part of Canada, then Ontario is a part of Canada. (B, C, O)

*3. Algeria will not intervene politically if and only if Britain will not send economic aid. Thus Algeria will intervene politically unless France will not veto the treaty, for Britain will not send economic aid only if France will veto the treaty. (A, B, F)

4. Neither Detroit nor Ann Arbor has cold weather in February. If Michigan sometimes has snow in winter, then either Detroit or Ann Arbor has cold weather in February. Therefore, it is not the case that Michigan sometimes has snow in winter. (D, A, M)

5. Either the examinations in this course are too easy or the students are extremely bright. In fact, the students are extremely bright. From this it follows that the examinations in this course are not too easy. (E, B)

*6. If John is a member of the Elks lodge, then either Sam used to work in Texas or Timothy is a police officer. But it is not the case that Sam used to work in Texas, and Timothy is not a police officer. Therefore, John is not a member of the Elks lodge. (J, A, I)

*7. Both antelopes and Rotarians are found in North America. But Rotarians are found in North America if and only if French police rarely drink gin. It follows that if it is not the case that French police rarely drink gin, then antelopes are not found in North America. (A, O, F)

8. Dogs are not always loyal. For rattlesnakes are always to be avoided unless either dogs are always loyal or cats sometimes behave strangely. (D, A, C)

9. If either Romans are not fast drivers or Nigeria does have a large population, then it is not the case that both Nigeria does have a large population and Argentineans are coffee drinkers. Hence, Romans are fast drivers, for Argentineans are coffee drinkers only if Nigeria does not have a large population. (F, N, A)

*10. We may infer that mandolins are easy to play but French horns are difficult instruments. For mandolins are easy to play if and only if either didgeridoos are played only by men or French horns are difficult instruments. But if French horns being difficult instruments implies that didgeridoos are not played only by men, then it is not the case that mandolins are easy to play. (M, F, D)

11. If both Ellen is good at math and Mary is good at writing, then Cecil is a pest. It follows that Mary is good at writing. For either Cecil is not a pest unless Mary is not good at writing, or both Ellen is not good at math and Cecil is a pest. But Cecil is a pest if and only if Ellen is good at math. (E, M, C)

*12. Penguins are not commonly found in Arabia. For manatees like being underwater unless penguins being commonly found in Arabia implies that alligators do not like being underwater. But penguins are commonly found in Arabia if and only if neither alligators nor manatees like being underwater. (E, M, A)

13. If Jupiter is a moon, then it orbits a planet. It is not the case that Jupiter orbits a planet. Therefore, Jupiter is not a moon. (J, O)

14. Aluminum in antiperspirants is not safe. For it is safe provided it is not absorbed into the bloodstream, but it is absorbed into the bloodstream. (A, F)

15. If tree leaves change their color, then chlorophyll is broken down. But chlorophyll is broken down if and only if both red pigments begin to fill the cells and tree leaves change their color. Thus either chlorophyll is broken down or both red pigments begin to fill the cells and tree leaves change their color. (L, C, E)

12.2 Some Standard Valid Argument Forms

As we saw in Chapter 5, any argument that has one valid form (or more) is itself valid and counts as a substitution instance or example of that form (or forms). And any argument that's a substitution instance of an invalid form is itself invalid. There are, however, numerous valid and invalid forms that propositional arguments may have. As a result, it is not always possible to learn about the validity or invalidity of a propositional argument just by recognizing that it's an instance of a valid or an invalid form. But being able to recognize at least some of the most common valid and invalid forms can nonetheless be very helpful. Here we'll revisit five such forms that we've already encountered briefly in Chapter 5 and learn more about how to spot arguments that instantiate them.

Modus Ponens

A common valid argument has a conditional premise, another premise affirming that conditional's antecedent, and a conclusion affirming its consequent. For example,

> 10 1. If José is a firefighter, then he works for the fire department.
>
> 2. José is a firefighter.
> _____
>
> 3. José works for the fire department.

This argument exemplifies the valid argument form called 'modus ponens' (literally, 'mode of putting or affirming'), which in symbols is

> 10' 1. P ⊃ Q
>
> 2. P
> _____
>
> 3. Q

Because the antecedent in a material conditional expresses a sufficient condition for the truth of the consequent, and the antecedent is asserted as being true in a *modus ponens*, any argument with this form is valid. In other words, if it's true that P implies Q, and also true that P, then Q's truth follows necessarily. The validity of arguments with this form is demonstrated by truth table (11).

11 P Q	P ⊃ Q, P ∴ Q		
T T	T	T	T
T F	F	T	F
F T	T	F	T
F F	T	F	F

As you can see, there is no horizontal row in this truth table on which both premises are true and the conclusion false.

Modus Tollens

Another very common valid argument form is *modus tollens* (literally, 'mode of negating'). An argument is an instance of this form when it has two premises, one of which is a conditional and the other a negation of that conditional's consequent. Its conclusion is a negation of the conditional's antecedent. For example,

12 1. If copper is a precious metal, then it is expensive.

    2. But copper is not expensive. _____

    3. Copper is not a precious metal.

The form of this argument is *modus tollens*, which runs

12' 1. P ⊃ Q

    2. ~Q

    3. ~P

Recall that, in a material conditional, the consequent expresses a necessary condition for the truth of the antecedent. If Q is necessary for P, then if it is not the case that Q, it is not the case that P. That is, denying the consequent of the conditional premise entails the denial of its antecedent. Any argument that is a substitution instance of *modus tollens* is valid, as shown by this truth table:

13 P Q	P ⊃ Q, ~Q ∴ ~P		
T T	T	F	F
T F	F	T	F
F T	T	F	T
F F	T	T	T

Contraposition

Contraposition is an argument form consisting of a single premise that is a conditional and a conclusion that switches the premise's antecedent and consequent and makes each fall under the scope of negation. For example,

14 1. If Anna is a revolutionary, then Anna is opposed to the established order. _____

    2. If Anna is not opposed to the established order, then Anna is not a revolutionary.

(14)'s form mirrors that of contraposition, since it is

14' 1. $P \supset Q$

   2. $\sim Q \supset \sim P$

(14') helps us to see that (14) is a valid argument given that it has a valid argument form. Why is that form valid? For similar reasons *modus tollens* is: since in the premise Q is the consequent of a material conditional, it is a necessary condition for the truth of the conditional's antecedent P. Thus if Q is false, then P must be false, too. The validity of contraposition is shown by this truth table:

15	P	Q		$P \supset Q$	$\therefore$	$\sim Q$	$\supset$	$\sim P$
	T	T		T		F	T	F
	T	F		F		T	F	F
	F	T		T		F	T	T
	F	F		T		T	T	T

Hypothetical Syllogism

Hypothetical syllogism is labeled this way because it has two premises (that's the 'syllogism' part) and because its premises (as well as its conclusion) are hypothetical or conditional statements. Consider

16 1. If Elaine is a newspaper reporter, then she is a journalist.

   2. If Elaine is a journalist, then she knows how to write.

   3. If Elaine is a newspaper reporter, then she knows how to write.

This argument has the form

16' 1. $P \supset Q$

   2. $Q \supset R$

   3. $P \supset R$

(16') allows us to see that (16) mirrors hypothetical syllogism, which is a valid argument form.

   A closer look at this form reveals that premise 1's consequent is premise 2's antecedent, and premise 1's antecedent together with premise 2's consequent are, respectively, the antecedent and consequent of the conclusion. Obviously, since the antecedent of a conditional expresses a sufficient condition for the truth of its consequent, when P is a sufficient condition for Q, and Q a sufficient condition for R, it follows that P is a sufficient condition for R. (16) is a substitution instance of this form and is therefore valid. The following truth table shows the validity of hypothetical syllogism:

17	P	Q	R		$P \supset Q$	$Q \supset R$	$\therefore$	$P \supset R$
	T	T	T		T	T		T
	T	T	F		T	F		F
	T	F	T		F	T		T
	T	F	F		F	T		F
	F	T	T		T	T		T
	F	T	F		T	F		T
	F	F	T		T	T		T
	F	F	F		T	T		T

Disjunctive Syllogism

Finally, in our sample of valid argument forms, there is one that does not use conditionals at all: disjunctive syllogism. The form is labeled this way because it has two premises (that's the 'syllogism' part) and because one of its premises is a disjunction. Here, one premise presents a disjunction, and the other denies one of the two disjuncts, from which the affirmation of the other disjunct then follows as the conclusion. For example,

18 1. Either my car was towed away by the police or it was stolen.

    2. My car was not towed away by the police.

    3. My car was stolen.

(18) is a substitution instance of disjunctive syllogism, and as such may be correctly represented in one of the two possible arrangements for the premises of that argument form, depending on which disjunct is denied:

18a 1. P v Q
    2. ~P
    3. Q

18b 1. P v Q
    2. ~Q
    3. P

In the case of (18), since the negation affects the first disjunct of the disjunctive premise, the correct representation is (18a). But the principle underlying either version of disjunctive syllogism is: given the truth-functional definition of inclusive disjunction, if a premise that is an inclusive disjunction is true but one of its disjuncts false, it follows that the other disjunct must be true. Thus any argument mirroring (18a) or (18b) is valid—as demonstrated by this truth table:

19

P Q	P v Q,	~P ∴	Q
T T	T	F	T
T F	T	F	F
F T	T	T	T
F F	F	T	F

More Complex Instances of Valid Forms

When we set about trying to analyze propositional arguments, it's immensely helpful to be able to recognize these five basic valid argument forms, because any time you find an argument that has one, you thereby know that it's valid! No further procedure is required. For the argument to be valid, it is enough that the general form of the argument's premises and conclusion mirror that of a valid form. This means that the premises and conclusion of a valid argument could feature connectives other than those featured in the valid form mirrored by that argument. That's fine, provided that *main* connectives are exactly the same. Let's make a list including this and other considerations to keep in mind when deciding about the form of propositional arguments:

#1. The order of the premises does not matter for an argument to have the form of a *modus ponens, modus tollens,* hypothetical syllogism, or disjunctive syllogism.

#2. The English expression for a connective may be other than the standard one.

#3. Pairs of negations cancel each other out. Thus any proposition without negation could be construed as having double negation.

#4. In addition to matching main connectives, a valid argument could feature connectives other than those in the corresponding basic valid form.

The following argument illustrates points #1 and #3:

20 If fleas are micro-organisms, then it is not the case that fleas are visible to the naked eye. But fleas are visible to the naked eye. Hence, fleas are not micro-organisms.

(20)'s argument form reveals it to be an instance of *modus tollens*:

20' 1. E
    2. M ⊃ ~E
    3. ~M

Given #3, E in premise 1 is logically equivalent to ~~E, which is the negation of premise 2's consequent, ~E. And conclusion 3 negates its antecedent. But given #1, that is exactly the form of a *modus tollens*!

Here is an argument illustrating point #2:

21 1. The cruise is on its way only if the strike is over.
   2. But the strike is not over.
   3. The cruise is not on its way.

Once we've replaced 'only if' by the standard 'if . . . then . . . ,' then it is clear that (21) is an instance of *modus tollens*, which can be represented as

21' 1. C ⊃ O
    2. ~O
    3. ~C

Why is (21)'s premise 1 represented as C ⊃ O? Because 'only if' is just another way to express a conditional in ordinary English. In such cases, the conditional's antecedent is what comes before 'only if' and its consequent what comes after it. To brush up your knowledge of alternative ways to express each of the truth-functional connectives, we suggest that you review the section on compound propositions in Chapter 11. But here is another example of point #1 above, this time involving a disjunction expressed using 'unless' instead of the standard 'either . . . or' locution in English. Once we know that that's what 'unless' amounts to, we can recognize (22) as a disjunctive syllogism of the form (22').

22 1. George is watching *The Simpsons* tonight unless he is playing football.
   2. He is not playing football tonight.
   3. George is watching *The Simpsons* tonight.

22' 1. G v F
    2. ~F
    3. G

Another example of points #1 and #3 above is

   23 1. That Ed is a bank employee implies that he has a job.

      2. Ed is a bank teller only if he is a bank employee.

      3. That Ed is a bank teller implies that he has a job.

Neither the order of the premises (inverted here), nor the use of 'implies' and 'only if' for the material conditional, should matter in recognizing (23) as an instance of hypothetical syllogism. This becomes clear once we've put the premises in logical order and written down the argument in symbols—as (23'), where E stands for 'Ed is a bank teller,' B for 'Ed is a bank employee,' and J for 'Ed has a job.'

   23' 1. E ⊃ B

      2. B ⊃ J

      3. E ⊃ J

Now consider the following arguments, together with their correct representations:

   24 1. Costa Rica is a peaceful country and doesn't have an army.

      2. Costa Rica is a peaceful country and doesn't have an army only if it doesn't have public unrest.

      3. Costa Rica doesn't have public unrest.

   24' 1. C • ~A

      2. (C • ~A) ⊃ ~N

      3. ~N

   25 1. Joey was either tried in Europe or extradited to the United States.

      2. That Joey was either tried in Europe or extradited to the United States implies that his defense failed and he is not free.

      3. Joey's defense failed and he is not free.

   25' 1. J v E

      2. (J v E) ⊃ (D • ~F)

      3. D • ~F

If we focus strictly on the main connective in premises and conclusions, then it's clear that both arguments turn out to be substitution instances of *modus ponens*. This is so because each consists of a conditional premise (which happens to come second) and another premise that asserts the antecedent of that conditional (which happens to come first). Neither the order of these premises nor the fact that they themselves are compound propositions made up of several connectives affects the status of the arguments as instances of *modus ponens*.

Exercises

IV. Review Questions

  1. Explain the validity of *modus ponens* by reference to the necessary and sufficient conditions in a material conditional.

2. Which sense of disjunction is required for disjunctive syllogism to be valid? Which of the valid forms employs disjunction?

3. Suppose the order of the premises in a valid propositional argument is changed. Does that affect the validity of the argument?

4. When you have established that an argument is a formal fallacy, what have you discovered about that argument?

V. The following formulas are instances of *modus ponens*, *modus tollens*, contraposition, hypothetical syllogism, or disjunctive syllogism. Say which is which.

1. A ⊃ ~B

  A

  ~ B

SAMPLE ANSWER: *Modus ponens*

2. (K v N) v A

  ~A

  K v N

*3. L ⊃ ~M

  B ⊃ L

  B ⊃ ~M

4. ~(F • H)

  A ⊃ (F • H)

  ~A

*5. ~E ⊃ ~D

  ~E

  ~D

*6. (A v L) ⊃ (B • C)

  ~(B • C) ⊃ ~(A v L)

7. ~C v ~A

  A

  ~C

*8. (A • ~F) ⊃ ~G

  G

  ~(A • ~F)

9. J ⊃ A

  A ⊃ ~C

  J ⊃ ~C

10. ~H ⊃ ~(E v A)

  (E v A) ⊃ H

11. ~B ≡ C

  (~B ≡ C) ⊃ ~A

  ~A

*12. A ∨ (G ∨ F)
   ~ (G ∨ F)
   ‾‾‾‾‾‾‾‾‾
   A

13. A ⊃ O
  ‾‾‾‾‾‾‾
  ~ O ⊃ ~ A

14. C ∨ O
  ~ C
  ‾‾‾‾‾
  O

15. (G ∨ F) ⊃ A
  (A ⊃ O) ⊃ (G ∨ F)
  ‾‾‾‾‾‾‾‾‾‾‾‾‾‾‾‾‾
  (A ⊃ O) ⊃ A

VI. The following arguments are instances of the valid forms discussed above. Symbolize each and identify its form.

1. Wynton Marsalis is an authority on music, for he is a famous jazz trumpeter who is equally well known as a performer of classical music. But if he is a famous jazz trumpeter who is equally well known as a performer of classical music, then Wynton Marsalis is an authority on music. (F, A)

   SAMPLE ANSWER: F ⊃ A, F ∴ A *Modus ponens*

2. Ernie is a liar or Ronald is not a liar. It is not the case that Ronald is not a liar. Therefore, Ernie is a liar. (E, L)

*3. If Staten Islanders are not Mets fans, then Manhattan's being full of fast talkers implies that Queens is not the home of sober taxpayers. Thus if it is not the case that Manhattan's being full of fast talkers implies that Queens is not the home of sober taxpayers, then it is not the case that Staten Islanders are not Mets fans. (I, M, H)

4. Penelope is not a registered Democrat. For Penelope is a registered Democrat only if she is eligible to vote in the United States. But she is not eligible to vote in the United States. (D, E)

*5. If Democrats are always compassionate, then Republicans are always honest. For if Democrats are always compassionate, then they sometimes vote for candidates who are moderates. But if they sometimes vote for candidates who are moderates, then Republicans are always honest. (D, M, H)

*6. If Emma is a true pacifist, then she is not a supporter of war. Emma is a true pacifist. It follows that she is not a supporter of war. (E, A)

7. If this cheese was not made in Switzerland, then it's not real Emmentaler. Therefore, if it is real Emmentaler, then it was made in Switzerland. (C, E)

*8. Either gulls sometimes fly inland or hyenas are not dangerous. But hyenas are dangerous. So, gulls sometimes fly inland. (G, H)

9. If both Enriquez enters the race and Warshawsky resigns, then Bosworth will win the election. But if Bosworth will win the election, then Mendes will not win the election. Thus if both Enriquez enters the race and Warshawsky resigns, then Mendes will not win the election. (E, A, B, M)

*10. Microbes are not creating chronic diseases such as diabetes, multiple sclerosis, and even schizophrenia. Hospitals need to improve their cleaning practices only if it is the case that microbes are creating many chronic diseases such as diabetes, multiple sclerosis, and even schizophrenia. It follows that hospitals need not improve their cleaning practices. (M, H)

11. California farmers grow either vegetables that thrive in warm weather or citrus fruits and bananas. Since they don't grow citrus fruits and bananas, they must grow vegetables that thrive in warm weather. (A, C, B)

12. Steve's attacker was not a great white shark. An attack of the sort he suffered last week must be by either a great white shark or by a shark of another type that felt threatened in the presence of a swimmer unknowingly wading into its feeding area. Therefore, Steve was attacked by a shark of another type that felt threatened in the presence of a swimmer unknowingly wading into its feeding area. (G, A)

13. Calcium is good for healthy bones. Either vitamin D is good for healthy bones or calcium is not good. Therefore, vitamin D is good for healthy bones. (C, D)

14. If herons wade either in mud holes or lagoons, then they catch bacterial infections. But they don't catch bacterial infections. Thus herons wade in neither mud holes nor lagoons. (H, L, I)

15. If she has a tune stuck in her head, she is either happy or annoyed. Therefore, if she is neither happy nor annoyed, then she doesn't have a tune stuck in her head. (H, A, N)

VII. YOUR OWN THINKING LAB

1. Construct an argument of your own for each of the argument forms listed in exercise (V).

2. Construct truth tables for each of the argument forms listed in exercise (VI).

12.3 Some Standard Invalid Argument Forms

Already we have seen that arguments may have defects of various kinds that cause them to fail. Types of defects that undermine arguments constitute the so-called fallacies, among which, as we have already seen at some length, the informal fallacies figure prominently. Now we must consider their analogues in propositional logic, which include some of the formal fallacies.

All formal fallacies have in common that they occur in an argument that has a superficial similarity to some valid form but departs from that form in some specifiable way. They are therefore instances of failed deductive arguments. Recall that an argument is invalid if it is possible that an argument with the same form could have true premises and a false conclusion. To prove the invalidity of an argument, then, it is enough to find a single case of an argument with exactly the same logical form whose premises are true and conclusion false. Consider the following argument:

26 1. If the messenger came, then the bell rang about noon.

2. The bell rang about noon.
   _____

3. The messenger came.

This argument is invalid because it is possible for its premises to be true and its conclusion false. Even if the premises and conclusion all happen to be true in a certain case, there are other scenarios in which arguments with an identical form could have true premises and

BOX 3 ■ INVALID ARGUMENT FORMS

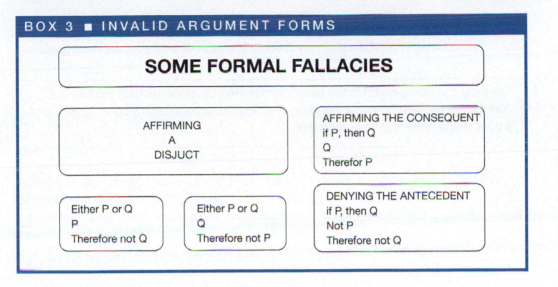

SOME FORMAL FALLACIES

| AFFIRMING
A
DISJUCT | AFFIRMING THE CONSEQUENT
if P, then Q
Q
Therefor P |

| Either P or Q
P
Therefore not Q | Either P or Q
Q
Therefore not P | DENYING THE ANTECEDENT
if P, then Q
Not P
Therefore not Q |

a false conclusion. Suppose that the messenger didn't come, but the bell did ring about noon, though it was a neighbor who rang it. In this scenario, (26)'s premises are true and its conclusion false. Thus the scenario amounts to a counterexample that shows the invalidity of (26).

It is often possible to find real-life counterexamples that prove the invalidity of certain arguments. Yet we could do without such counterexamples, since to show that an argument is invalid, it is sufficient to describe a 'possible world' (which may or may not be the actual world—it's simply a scenario involving no internal contradiction) where an argument with the same form would have true premises and a false conclusion.

Thus the invalidity of an argument can be proved in the way just shown: one tries to describe a scenario where the premises of the argument in question are true and its conclusion is false. If such a scenario is not forthcoming, we may first extract the argument form—which, in the case of (26), is

26' 1. P ⊃ Q

   2. Q

   3. P

Then we try to find an example of an argument with the same form that in some possible scenario would have true premises and a false conclusion. For example,

27 1. If Barack Obama is a Republican, then he is a member of a political party.

   2. Barack Obama is a member of a political party.

   3. Barack Obama is a Republican.

(27) shows that, in a scenario where the possible world is the actual world, an argument with the same form as (27) has true premises and a false conclusion. By the definition of invalidity, (27) is invalid. At the same time, it amounts to a counterexample to any argument with the same form.

Affirming the Consequent

The above notoriously invalid arguments are both instances of affirming the consequent.

> Affirming the consequent is the fallacy committed by any argument featuring a conditional premise, another premise affirming that conditional's consequent, and a conclusion affirming its antecedent.

Affirming a proposition amounts to saying that it is true. In arguments that commit this fallacy, what is affirmed is the consequent of a material conditional. This always expresses only a necessary, but not a sufficient, condition for the truth of the conditional's antecedent. As a result, the truth of the consequent never guarantees that of the antecedent (which is the conclusion in affirming the consequent). Here is a more complex example of affirming the consequent:

28 1. If the Olsons are deer hunters, then, if they hunt, they do not hunt pheasants.

   2. If the Olsons hunt, then they do not hunt pheasants.

   3. The Olsons are deer hunters.

28' 1. $O \supset (H \supset \sim A)$

   2. $H \supset \sim A$

   3. O

As with any instance of affirming the consequent, (28) is invalid. The invalidity of the form is shown by this truth table:

29
P Q	$P \supset Q$,	Q	∴	P	
T T	T	T		T	
T F	F	F		T	
F T	T	T		F	←
F F	T	F		F	

As you can see, there *is* a horizontal row in this truth table on which both premises are true and the conclusion false.

BOX 4 ■ HOW TO AVOID AFFIRMING THE CONSEQUENT

In a *modus ponens*, a premise affirms the antecedent (not the consequent) of the other premise (while the conclusion affirms the consequent).

■ Thus watch out for any argument that appears to be a *modus ponens* but is not, since its conditional premise's consequent is affirmed by the other premise (while its antecedent is affirmed by the argument's conclusion).

Denying the Antecedent

Another formal fallacy that may undermine propositional arguments is denying the antecedent.

> Denying the antecedent is the fallacy committed by any argument featuring a conditional premise, another premise denying that conditional's antecedent, and a conclusion denying its consequent.

Suppose we run across an argument of this sort:

30 1. If Oscar is a violinist with the Boston Symphony, then he can read music.

2. In fact, Oscar is not a violinist with the Boston Symphony.

3. He cannot read music.

Clearly, this argument is invalid. Oscar's being a violinist with the Boston Symphony Orchestra is a sufficient condition of his being able to read music (if he's in the BSO, that guarantees that he can read music). But it's not a necessary condition, since lots of people can read music who are not in the Boston Symphony! Thus the conclusion, 'Oscar cannot read music,' does not follow with necessity. In brief, (30) is invalid because it commits the fallacy of denying the antecedent. More generally, any argument that instantiates this fallacy is invalid because denying the antecedent of the conditional premise amounts to saying that that antecedent is false. But the antecedent of a material conditional expresses a sufficient (though not a necessary) condition for the truth of the consequent: so the antecedent could be false and the consequent true. Thus from a denial of the antecedent of a conditional, it does not follow that its consequent is also to be denied. The argument is an instance of denying the antecedent. Any argument that commits this fallacy has this invalid form:

30' 1. $P \supset Q$

2. $\sim P$

3. $\sim Q$

The invalidity of denying the antecedent can be shown by truth table (31):

31

P Q	$P \supset Q$,	$\sim P$	$\therefore \sim Q$	
T T	T	F	F	
T F	F	F	T	
F T	T	T	F	←
F F	T	T	T	

BOX 5 ■ HOW TO AVOID DENYING THE ANTECEDENT

In a *modus tollens*, the consequent of the conditional premise is denied by the other premise (while its antecedent is denied by the conclusion).

■ Thus watch out for any argument that appears to be a *modus tollens* but is not, since its conditional premise's antecedent is denied by the other premise (while its consequent is denied by the argument's conclusion).

Affirming a Disjunct

Another formal fallacy is affirming a disjunct:

> Affirming a disjunct is the fallacy committed by any argument featuring a premise that is an inclusive disjunction, another premise affirming one of the disjuncts, and a conclusion denying the other disjunct.

Affirming a disjunct is an invalid form because, as we saw earlier in our discussion of the truth-functional connectives, 'or' is to be understood in the inclusive sense (i.e., either P or Q or both)—not the exclusive sense (i.e., either P or Q but not both). The inclusive disjunction is true in all cases except where both disjuncts are false. Thus assuming that a certain inclusive disjunction is true, denying one disjunct (which amounts to saying that it is false) entails that the other disjunct must be true. But affirming one of its disjuncts (which amounts to saying that it is true) does not entail the denial of the other—that is, does not entail that the other is false. (In the case of an exclusive disjunction, what we are calling 'affirming a disjunct' would not be a fallacy.) Consider the following example:

32 1. Either my car was towed away by the police or was stolen.

2. My car was in fact towed away by the police.

3. My car was not stolen.

Is there any way this conclusion could be false if both premises were true? Yes! A possible scenario is that thieves came in the night and broke into my car, then drove it to an illegal parking space, from which the police towed it! If that were the case, then both of (32)'s premises would be true and its conclusion false at once. Thus the conclusion does not follow necessarily from the premises—it is not entailed by them. So the argument is invalid. But the thing to notice is that (32) instantiates version (a) of the invalid form affirming a disjunct. This fallacy is committed by any argument of one of these forms:

32' a 1. P v Q   b 1. P v Q
     2. P   2. Q
     ──────   ──────
     3. ~ Q   3. ~ P

Since, here, the 'either . . . or . . . ' connective in (32) is inclusive, to affirm one of the two alternatives does not entail a denial of the other. In any case where the disjunction is inclusive, an argument with either of (32')'s forms is invalid. The invalidity of affirming a disjunct is clearly shown by this truth table:

33 P Q	P v Q,	P ∴ ~Q		
T T	T	T	F	←
T F	T	T	T	
F T	T	F	F	
F F	F	F	T	

We have identified three invalid argument forms that correspond to three types of formal fallacy. Whenever you find an argument that has one, a truth table is not required. All you need to do to prove invalidity is simply to show that the argument has one of these forms: affirming the consequent, denying the antecedent, or affirming a disjunct. If you can keep separate in your mind these three invalid forms and the five valid forms discussed earlier, you should find it much easier to distinguish valid and invalid propositional arguments.

BOX 6 ■ HOW TO AVOID AFFIRMING A DISJUNCT

Note that in a disjunctive syllogism, a premise denies one of the disjuncts of the other premise, and the conclusion asserts the other.

■ Thus, watch out for any argument that appears to be a disjunctive syllogism but it is not, since one of its premises asserts a disjunct of the other premise, while its conclusion denies the other.

Exercises

VIII. Review Questions

1. How does the type of disjunction at work in disjunctive syllogism bear on the fallacy of affirming a disjunct?
2. How does affirming a disjunct differ from disjunctive syllogism?
3. How does affirming the consequent differ from *modus ponens*?
4. How does denying the antecedent differ from *modus tollens*?
5. What's the cash value of recognizing that an argument commits a formal fallacy?

IX. Some of the following arguments commit formal fallacies, and some don't. Indicate which do and which don't, identifying formal fallacies and valid argument forms by name.

1. If the defendant's 2007 Toyota sedan was used as the getaway car in the robbery, then it was not in the mechanic's garage with a cracked engine block on the date of the crime. But it was in the mechanic's garage with a cracked engine block on that date! From this it follows that the defendant's 2007 Toyota sedan was not used as the getaway car in the robbery.

   SAMPLE ANSWER: *Modus tollens*. Valid.

2. If this car has faulty brakes, then it's dangerous to drive. But this car does not have faulty brakes. Therefore it's not dangerous to drive.

*3. If our public officials take bribes, then there is corruption in our government. But if the mayor and several City Council members were paid to support the appropriations bill, then our public officials take bribes. So, if the mayor and several City Council members were paid to support the appropriations bill, then there is corruption in our government.

4. Barry is a union member, for he will not cross the picket line. And if he were a union member, then he would not cross the picket line.

*5. Ireland does not allow abortion. Either Ireland allows abortion or Ireland is a conservative country. Hence, Ireland is a conservative country.

6. Either we'll stop polluting the environment or life on Earth will eventually die out. But in fact we will stop polluting the environment. Thus life on Earth will not eventually die out.

*7. If Desmond is a successful film critic, then he is a good writer. But Desmond is not a successful film critic. Therefore, he is not a good writer.

8. These sculptures are expensive only if they're rare. So it must be that they are rare, since they're very expensive.

*9. If cardiac surgeons are Mercedes-Benz drivers, then they have driver's licenses, so if cardiac surgeons don't have driver's licenses, then they are not Mercedes-Benz drivers.

10. If Bob has no record of military service, then he is not a combat veteran. It follows that Bob has no record of military service, since he is not a combat veteran.

*11. Either Darwin's theory provides a roughly accurate account of the origin of the human species or the method of carbon-14 dating that has been used to establish the age of hominid fossils is not reliable. But that method is reliable. Therefore, Darwin's theory provides a roughly accurate account of the origin of the human species.

12. Atkinson will run for reelection unless Hernandez does. Accordingly, Atkinson will not run, because Hernandez will run for reelection.

*13. Zebras are mammals. But if zebras are mammals, then they are warm-blooded creatures. From this we may infer that zebras are warm-blooded creatures.

14. Since clams are not mammals, they are shellfish. For if clams are shellfish, then they are not mammals.

*15. If Frank Sinatra was born in Brooklyn, then he was a New Yorker. But Sinatra was not a New Yorker, so he was not born in Brooklyn.

16. Jack will buy either a bulldog or a Labrador retriever. But in fact Jack will buy a Labrador retriever. Therefore, Jack will not buy a bulldog.

*17. If Tom's barbecued steaks are tender, then they weren't overcooked. Since Tom's barbecued steaks weren't overcooked, we may conclude that they are tender.

18. If this scarf isn't too colorful, then Anne will like it. But this scarf is too colorful. Therefore, Anne will not like it.

*19. Barbados is sunny; however, London often has rain. But if it is not the case that both Barbados is sunny and London often has rain, then Nebraska is densely populated. Therefore, Nebraska is not densely populated.

20. If tortillas or tamales are Japanese dishes, then burgers and pizza are Mexican dishes. Therefore, if it is not the case that then burgers and pizza are Mexican dishes, then neither tortillas nor tamales are Japanese dishes.

X. **The following arguments exemplify valid or invalid forms of the sort discussed above. For each of them, provide the correct symbolic notation, name the argument form it exemplifies, and say whether it's valid or invalid.**

1. Ankara is the capital of Turkey. Consequently, Turkey's capital is in Asia Minor, for if Ankara is the capital of Turkey, then Turkey's capital is in Asia Minor. (A, C)

SAMPLE ANSWER: A ⊃ C, A∴C. *Modus ponens;* valid.

2. Either Big Joey will finally get whacked or his family will become more powerful. But Big Joey will not get whacked. So his family will become more powerful. (J, O)

3. Bengal tigers are not seen anywhere in the world today only if they are extinct. But Bengal tigers are not extinct; hence, they are sometimes seen in the world today. (B, E)

*4. If Eminem is a hip-hop artist, then he is a musician. But Eminem is not a hip-hop artist. We can infer that he is not a musician. (E, M)

5. If belief in evolution is not prevalent in America, then high school science education is ineffective. It follows that if high school science education is effective, then belief in evolution is prevalent in America. (B, E)

*6. Homer Simpson will vote in the election unless he decides that all the candidates are crooks. Since he has in fact decided that all the candidates are crooks, Homer will not vote in the election. (H, D)

*7. That fruit bats sleep in the daytime implies that they fly only at night, for if fruit bats sleep in the daytime then they are nocturnal creatures, and if they are nocturnal creatures then they fly only at night. (B, N, F)

8. Plutonium is radioactive. For either plutonium is radioactive or both argon and cobalt are, too, but it is not the case that both argon and cobalt are radioactive. (F, A, C)

9. If Christina Aguilera is a big star, then her songs are featured on MTV. It follows that Christina Aguilera's songs are featured on MTV, since she is a big star. (C, H)

10. That Eric is a NASCAR fan implies that he doesn't mind loud noise. Thus if Eric does mind loud noise, then he is not a NASCAR fan. (E, H)

*11. If Boris is a member of the Communist Party, then he is not an enthusiastic supporter of big business. But Boris is an enthusiastic supporter of big business, so he is not a member of the Communist Party. (M, E)

*12. Jason would buy a house in Acapulco only if he won the lottery. Since he did win the lottery, it follows that he will buy a house in Acapulco. (J, L)

13. Tigers thrive in either Africa or East Asia provided that either Africa or East Asia has warm weather. Either Africa or East Asia does have warm weather. Hence, tigers thrive in either Africa or East Asia. (A, E, F, I)

14. If I have a pickup truck and drive long distances, then I'm contributing to greenhouse gases. And I'm contributing to greenhouse gases. Therefore, I have a pickup truck and drive long distances. (I, D, G)

15. If working adults spend a lot of time online, they don't get enough information. If they don't get enough information, they're badly informed. Thus if working adults spend a lot of time online, they're badly informed. (O, I, B)

XI. YOUR OWN THINKING LAB

1. Give two examples of your own illustrating the following: affirming the consequent, denying the antecedent, and affirming a disjunct.

2. Use the method of counterexample discussed above in connection with the formal fallacies to explain why those two examples are invalid.

3. For each of the propositional arguments below, give its form and standard name (if any), use a truth table to decide whether it is valid or not, and propose an argument of your own with exactly the same form.

A. If the cold front is here, then we don't go to the beach. Thus if we go the beach, then the cold front is not here.

B. Either the small apples or the ripe ones are on sale. The ripe apples are on sale. Therefore, the small apples are not on sale.

C. She is at Lalo's if her class is over. She is at Lalo's. Therefore, her class is over.

D. I don't see my glasses there. If I don't see them there, then they are not there. Hence, they are not there.

E. If Ptolemy was right, then the Sun and planets orbit the Earth. But it is not the case that the Sun and planets orbit the Earth. Therefore, Ptolemy was not right.

F. The ring is made of either gold or silver. In fact, it is not made of silver. Therefore, it is made of gold.

G. If the pool doesn't have chlorine, then it is not safe to swim in it. Since it is not safe to swim in it, it follows that the pool doesn't have chlorine.

H. Irving is either a bachelor or he is a Dodgers fan. He is not a Dodgers fan. Therefore, he is a bachelor.

I. If magnets cure rheumatism, then there is a market for them. But since it is not the case that magnets cure rheumatism, there isn't a market for them.

J. There is a storm outside. If there is a storm outside, I'd better stay indoors. So, I'd better stay indoors.

K. If Mary knows Juan, then she knows Jennifer. She knows Jennifer. Therefore she knows Juan.

L. Tokyo is the capital of either Japan or Bangladesh. Tokyo is not the capital of Japan. So Tokyo is the capital of Bangladesh.

M. Customer Services handles complaints about merchandise that is either damaged or imperfect. Customer Services handles complaints about merchandise that is damaged. Therefore, Customer Services doesn't handle complaints about merchandise that is imperfect.

N. If the 'Big Bang' theory is not wrong, then the universe is expanding. The 'Big Bang' theory is not wrong. Therefore the universe is expanding.

O. Either students who got As or those who have missed no class are eligible for the prize. Students who have missed no class are eligible for the prize. So students who got As are not eligible for the prize.

12.4 A Simplified Approach to Proofs of Validity

Some valid argument forms such as those discussed above are often used as basic rules of inference in the so-called proofs of validity. This is a procedure designed to show the steps by which the conclusion of a valid propositional argument follows from its premises. In constructing a proof for an argument, we assume that it is in fact valid, and we try to show that it is. Before we can proceed to construct some such proofs, we'll add other basic valid argument forms and rules of replacement to our list so that we can have enough rules of inference to prove the conclusions of a great number of valid propositional arguments.

The Basic Rules

In constructing our proofs of validity, then, we'll need some valid argument forms and some logical equivalences between compound propositions. The former will serve as rules of inference, which will permit us to draw a conclusion from a premise or premises. The latter will serve as rules of replacement, which will permit us to substitute one expression for another that is logically equivalent to it. Our list of rules includes the following:

Basic Rules of Inference

1. *Modus Ponens* (MP) $P \supset Q, P \therefore Q$
2. *Modus Tollens* (MT) $P \supset Q, {\sim}Q \therefore {\sim}P$
3. Hypothetical Syllogism (HS) $P \supset Q, Q \supset R \therefore P \supset R$
4. Disjunctive Syllogism (DS) $P \vee Q, {\sim}P \therefore Q$
5. Simplification (Simp) $P \cdot Q \therefore P$
6. Conjunction (Conj) $P, Q \therefore P \cdot Q$
7. Addition (Add) $P \therefore P \vee Q$

Basic Rules of Replacement

8. Contraposition (Contr) $(P \supset Q) \equiv ({\sim}Q \supset {\sim}P)$
9. Double Negation (DN) $P \equiv {\sim}{\sim}P$
10. De Morgan's Theorem (DeM) $\sim(P \cdot Q) \equiv ({\sim}P \vee {\sim}Q)$
    $\sim(P \vee Q) \equiv ({\sim}P \cdot {\sim}Q)$
11. Commutation (Com) $(P \vee Q) \equiv (Q \vee P)$
    $(P \cdot Q) \equiv (Q \cdot P)$
12. Definition of Material Conditional (Cond) $(P \supset Q) \equiv ({\sim}P \vee Q)$
13. Definitions of Material Biconditional (Bicond) $(P \equiv Q) \equiv [(P \supset Q) \cdot (Q \supset P)]$
    $(P \equiv Q) \equiv [(P \cdot Q) \vee ({\sim}P \cdot {\sim}Q)]$

What Is a Proof of Validity?

Proofs of validity may be formal or informal. In a formal proof, the relation of entailment is taken to obtain strictly between certain well-formed formulas of a system of logic that need have no interpretation in a natural language (such as English, Portuguese, Mandarin). Furthermore, the basic rules of inference and replacement used in formal proofs are such that they could be used to prove the conclusion of any valid propositional argument from its premises. On the other hand, in the informal proofs proposed here, entailment is taken to be a relation that obtains between certain propositions that are expressible in a natural language. When a proof is offered as involving only formulas, it is assumed in the informal approach that these have an interpretation in a natural language. Moreover, the basic rules offered in our informal approach fall short of allowing proofs of validity for *any* valid propositional argument.

We'll construct proofs to check the validity of certain arguments and assume that those arguments have an interpretation in English—even though for convenience's sake they may be offered only in the symbolic notation. For valid arguments that are expressed in English, we'll first translate them into the symbolic notation. Then we'll proceed to prove their validity by using the rules listed above in a way that we'll explain shortly. These rules can be used to demonstrate the validity of many propositional arguments, and we'll next see just how this is done.

Whether in a formal or informal approach, all proofs of validity require that we assume that, for any valid argument, it must in principle be possible to show its validity by the proof procedure, which shows that a valid argument's conclusion follows from its premises once we apply to those premises one or more basic rules of inference and/or replacement. Such rules are 'basic' in the sense of being accepted without a proof. (Since any proof at all within this system would assume at least some of them, there are basic rules that cannot be proved within the system.)

How to Construct a Proof of Validity

Let's now put our basic rules to work and demonstrate the validity of the following argument:

34 Both Alice and Caroline will graduate next year. But if Caroline will graduate next year, then Giselle will win a scholarship if and only if Alice will graduate next year. So, either Giselle will win a scholarship if and only if Alice will graduate next year, or Helen will be valedictorian.

First, we translate the argument into the symbolic notation as follows:

34' A • C, C ⊃ (G ≡ A) ∴ (G ≡ A) v H

We can now prove that this argument's conclusion, (G ≡ A) v H, follows from its premises. How? By showing that such a conclusion can be deduced from (34')'s premises by applying to them only basic rules of inference and replacement. Our proof, whose four steps (numbered 3, 4, 5, and 6) aim at deducing the intended conclusion from (34')'s premises, runs

34'' 1. A • C
    2. C ⊃ (G ≡ A)   ∴ (G ≡ A) v H
    3. C • A   from 1 by Com
    4. C   from 3 by Simp
    5. G ≡ A   from 2 and 4 by MP
    6. (G ≡ A) v H   from 5 by Add

In line 3, we deduce C•A by applying commutation (see Com in the rules above) to premise 1. Any time we deduce a formula, we justify what we've done on the right-hand side of the proof. In this example, the justification includes expressions such as 'from,' 'and,' and 'by' that we'll later omit ('from') or replace by punctuation marks ('and' and 'by'). Note that a proof's justification requires two things: (a) that we state the premise number to which a certain rule was applied (if more than one, we write down the premises' numbers in the order in which the rule was applied to them), and (b) that we state the name of the rule applied. After justifying how a formula was deduced from the premise/s of an argument, that formula can be counted as a new premise listed with its own line number. Since C • A in line 3 has been deduced from the argument's premises, it is now a premise that can be used in further steps of the proof. In fact, it is used in line 4 to deduce C in the way indicated on the right-hand side of that line. Premises 2 and 4 allow us to deduce G ≡ A in line 5, which follows from them by *modus ponens* (MP). In line 6, addition (Add) allows us to deduce the formula that proves (34)'s validity: namely, the conclusion of that argument. We have thus shown that its conclusion follows from its premises, and we have done so by showing that it can be obtained by applying only basic rules of inference and replacement to those premises. Thus (34) has been proved valid.

Proofs vs. Truth Tables

As we've seen, in the case of truth tables, the truth values of an argument's premises and conclusion are assigned according to rules associated with the truth-functional connectives involved in that argument. Although here we've defined only five such connectives, their total number is in fact sixteen. This is a fixed number. By contrast, the actual number of valid argument forms and logically equivalent expressions that could be used to construct proofs of validity may vary from one deductive system to another. Furthermore, the proof procedure allows for *no* fixed number of steps to correctly deduce an argument's conclusion from its premises: it often depends on which premises and basic rules we decide to use.

Since in these respects proofs permit a certain degree of flexibility, it is sometimes possible, within a single system of basic rules, to construct more than one correct proof to demonstrate the validity of a certain argument. That is, unlike a truth table, a proof is not a mechanical procedure that always yields a result in the same way in a fixed number of steps. Moreover, it might happen that, in constructing a proof for a certain valid argument, we err in our assessment of its validity. We might simply "fail to see" at the moment that certain rules can be put at the service of deducing that argument's conclusion from its premises and mistakenly conclude that the argument is invalid. That's why we say that, for any valid argument, one could 'in principle' construct a proof of its validity. It must be admitted, however, that proofs do have one big advantage over truth tables: namely, that the latter tend to be very long and unwieldy when an argument features propositions of many different types. Proofs face no such problem.

Exercises

XII. Review Questions

1. In what does the method of proof consist?
2. Do proofs offer any advantage over truth tables?
3. What is a rule of inference?
4. How are rules of inference used in a proof?
5. What are rules of replacement?
6. In this section, a distinction has been drawn between a formal and an informal approach to proofs. What is that distinction?

XIII. **Justify the steps in each of the following proofs of validity using the rules of inference and replacement given in this section.**

1. 1. A ⊃ B
   2. ~B   /∴ ~A • (~B v C)
   3. ~A   1, 2 MT   SAMPLE   ANSWER
   4. ~B v C   2 Add
   5. ~A • (~B v C)   3, 4 Conj

2. 1. ~D ⊃ ~E
   2. E v ~(I ⊃ D)
   3. I ⊃ D   /∴ E • D
   4. ~~(I ⊃ D)
   5. E
   6. ~~E
   7. ~~D
   8. D
   9. E • D

*3. 1. ~D • C
   2. F ⊃ ~C
   3. ~F ⊃ (E v D)   /∴ D v E
   4. ~~C ⊃ ~F
   5. C ⊃ ~F
   6. C ⊃ (E v D)
   7. C • ~D
   8. C
   9. E v D
   10. D v E

4. 1. ~ A • (A v E)   /∴ E v ~E
   2. ~A
   3. (A v E) • ~A
   4. A v E
   5. E
   6. E v ~E

*5. 1. (G ⊃ D) ⊃ ~F
   2. D ⊃ F
   3. D • C   /∴ ~(G ⊃ D)
   4. ~ F ⊃ ~D
   5. (G ⊃ D) ⊃ ~D
   6. D
   7. ~~D
   8. ~(G ⊃ D)

6. 1. A ⊃ ~(B ⊃ ~D)
   2. ~(B ⊃ ~D) ⊃ ~D

3. D

4. A ⊃ ~D

5. ~~D

6. ~A

/∴ ~A

*7. 1. (D ⊃ C) v ~(A v B)

2. A

3. ~(A v B) v (D ⊃ C)

4. A v B

5. ~~(A v B)

6. D ⊃ C

7. ~ D v C

/∴ ~D v C

8. 1. (~D • C) • H

2. ~D • C

3. ~D

4. ~D v ~H

5. ~H v ~D

/∴ ~H v ~D

*9. 1. (E v A) ⊃ C

2. [(E v A) ⊃ C] ⊃ (E • G)

3. E • G

4. E

5. E v A

6. C

/∴ C

10. 1. (D ⊃ C) ⊃ ~(A • B)

2. ~ D ⊃ (A • B)

3. ~(A • B) ⊃ ~~D

4. (D ⊃ C) ⊃ ~~D

5. (D ⊃ C) ⊃ D

6. ~(D ⊃ C) v D

7. D v ~(D ⊃ C)

/∴ D v ~(D ⊃ C)

*11. 1. (~H v L) ⊃ ~(I • G)

2. G • I

3. I • G

4. ~~(I • G)

5. ~(~H v L)

6. ~~H • ~L

7. H • ~L

8. ~L • H

/∴ ~L • H

12. 1. (B ⊃ C) v ~A

2. ~(B ⊃ C) v A

3. (B ⊃ C) ⊃ A

4. ~A v (B ⊃ C)

5. A ⊃ (B ⊃ C)

6. [A ⊃ (B ⊃ C)] • [(B ⊃ C) ⊃ A]

7. A ≡ (B ⊃ C)

/∴ A ≡ (B ⊃ C)

13. 1. ~A ⊃ (I v ~D)
   2. ~A • ~I   /∴ ~D
   3. ~A
   4. I v ~D
   5. ~I • ~A
   6. ~I
   7. ~D

14. 1. E • [~I • (~D v I)]   /∴ ~D v F
   2. [~I • (~D v I)] • E
   3. ~I • (~D v I)
   4. ~I
   5. (~D v I) • ~I
   6. ~D v I
   7. ~D
   8. ~D v F

15. 1. E   /∴ C v (E v D)
   2. E v D
   3. (E v D) v C
   4. C v (E v D)

XIV. Translate each of the following arguments into symbolic notation using the propositional symbols within parentheses and construct a correct proof of validity for it.

1. The Bensons and the Nelsons will be at the party. But if the Nelsons are at the party, then the Finnegans will not be there. The Finnegans will be at the party only if the Bensons will not be there. It follows that the Finnegans will not be at the party. (B, N, F)

SAMPLE ANSWER:
1. B • N
2. N ⊃ ~F
3. F ⊃ ~B   /∴ ~F
4. N • B   1 Com
5. N   4 Simp
6. ~F   2, 5 MP

2. If elephants are mammals, then they are not warm-blooded creatures. It is not the case that elephants are not warm-blooded creatures. From this we may infer that either elephants are not mammals or they are not warm-blooded creatures. (E, C)

3. Either municipal bonds will not continue to be a good investment or stocks will be a wise choice for the small investor at the present time. Municipal bonds will continue to be a good investment. Therefore, stocks will be a wise choice for the small investor at the present time. (M, C)

*4. If Romania establishes a democracy, then Bulgaria will, too. Either Mongolia will not remain independent or Romania will not establish a democracy. Bulgaria will not establish a democracy, but Romania will. Thus Mongolia will not remain independent. (D, B, M)

5. Zoe will not resign next week. For Keith will serve on the committee, and either Zoe will not resign next week or Oliver will. But if Zoe does resign next week, then Keith will not serve on the committee. (K, E, O)

*6. Honduras will support the treaty, but it is clear that either Russia will not support it or Japan will support it. Japan supporting the treaty implies that Honduras will not support it. Therefore, Japan will not support the treaty. (H, I, J)

7. If Macedonians and the Danes were polytheists, then most ancient Europeans also were. The Romans' not being polytheists implies that both the Macedonians and the Danes were polytheists. It follows that if most ancient Europeans were not polytheists, then the Romans were polytheists. (M, D, E, O)

*8. Railroads are safe investments, but oil companies are not. It follows that oil companies are not safe investments but public utilities are, because railroads are safe investments only if public utilities are, too. (I, C, B)

9. Dramatists are not opinionated or historians are not disputatious. For if dramatists are opinionated, then musicians are not good at math. But musicians are good at math. (D, M, H)

*10. Sicily is an island. Besides, if Italy is the home of famous soccer players, then Egypt is not the birthplace of Caesar. In addition, if Italy is not the home of famous soccer players, then Norway being full of tourists implies that Egypt is not the birthplace of Caesar. It follows that Sicily is an island, and Egypt's being the birthplace of Caesar implies that if Norway is full of tourists, then Egypt is not the birthplace of Caesar. (I, H, E, N)

■ Writing Project

Provide a hypothetical syllogism for the conclusion that if globalization is promoted, products will be cheaper. Then offer a *modus ponens* for the conclusion that globalization entails fewer American jobs. Compare the relative strength of these two arguments by discussing the support for their premises. At the end of this discussion, reconstruct both arguments, marking in each case premises and conclusion.

■ Chapter Summary

Procedures for determining whether an argument is valid:

1. **Truth Tables:** a mechanical technique that shows an argument form to be invalid if there is a row where all premises are true and the conclusion false. Otherwise, it is valid.

2. **Proofs:** a nonmechanical technique that shows an argument to be valid if its conclusion can be deduced by applying only valid rules of inference and replacement to the argument's premises.

Some valid forms. When an argument has any of these forms, it is valid:

1. *Modus ponens* $P \supset Q, P \therefore Q$
2. *Modus tollens* $P \supset Q, \sim Q \therefore \sim P$
3. Hypothetical Syllogism $P \supset Q, Q \supset R \therefore P \supset R$
4. Disjunctive Syllogism $P \lor Q, \sim P \therefore Q$
5. Contraposition $P \supset Q \therefore \sim Q \supset \sim P$
                    $\sim Q \supset \sim P \therefore P \supset Q$

Some invalid forms. When an argument has any of these forms, it commits a formal fallacy and is invalid:

1. Affirming the Consequent $P \supset Q, Q \therefore P$
2. Denying the Antecedent $P \supset Q, \sim P \therefore \sim Q$
3. Affirming a Disjunct $P \vee Q, P \therefore \sim Q$

■ Key Words

Truth table for arguments
Modus ponens
Modus tollens
Contraposition
Hypothetical syllogism
Disjunctive syllogism

Formal fallacy
Affirming the consequent
Denying the antecedent
Affirming a disjunct
Counterexample
Proof of validity

CHAPTER 13

Categorical Propositions and Immediate Inferences

In this chapter you'll read about logical relations between categorical propositions, which are the building blocks of syllogistic arguments. The topics include

- Standard categorical propositions and the class relationships they represent.
- Non-standard categorical propositions and their translation into standard categorical propositions.
- How to represent categorical propositions in Venn diagrams and in traditional logic.
- The Square of Opposition, both traditional and modern versions.
- The problem of existential import.
- Other immediate inferences from categorical propositions.

13.1 What Is a Categorical Proposition?

Categorical Propositions

Categorical propositions are propositions that represent relations of inclusion or exclusion between classes of things, such as

    1   All philosophers are wise persons.

    2   No philosophers are wise persons.

Or between partial classes, such as

    3   Some philosophers are wise persons.

Or between partial classes and whole classes, such as

    4   Some philosophers are not wise persons.

The relationships between classes that matter for categorical propositions are, then, these four:

- Whole inclusion of one class inside another
- Mutual, total exclusion between two classes
- Partial inclusion, whereby part of one class is included inside another.
- Partial exclusion, whereby part of one class is wholly excluded from another

In the above examples of categorical propositions, 'philosophers' is the subject term and 'wise persons' the predicate term. These terms are the logical, rather than syntactical, subject and predicate of a categorical proposition. Each of them denotes a class of entities: that made up by all and only the entities to which the term applies. Thus 'philosophers' denotes the class of philosophers and 'wise persons' the class of persons who are wise.

Categorical propositions (1) through (4) illustrate four ways in which the class of philosophers and the class of wise persons can stand in relationships of inclusion or exclusion. Each of these relationships may be represented in one of the following ways:

    1' All philosophers are wise persons.

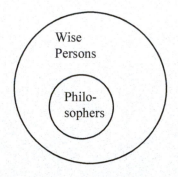

2' No philosophers are wise persons.

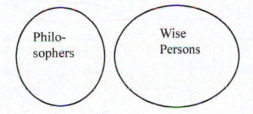

3' Some philosophers are wise persons.

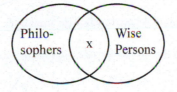

4' Some philosophers are not wise persons.

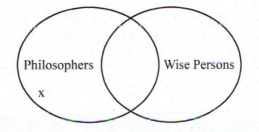

In traditional logic, first developed in antiquity by Aristotle (384–322 BCE), the standard notation to represent the logical form of categorical propositions is to use 'S' as a symbol for any subject term, and 'P' for any predicate term. In that notation, then, the logical form of the above categorical propositions is, respectively,

1. All S are P
2. No S are P
3. Some S are P
4. Some S are not P

In traditional logic, only statements that can be shown to have these logical forms qualify as expressing a categorical proposition. Any such proposition always represents one of the four relationships between classes mentioned above, which can now be described by using the symbols 'S' and 'P,' which stand for the classes denoted by the proposition's subject and predicate. Those relationships are as in Box 1. But we can also represent them by circle diagrams, in which case we'd have

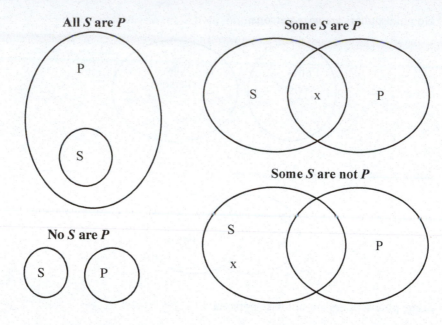

Note that in the first two diagrams the terms '*S*' and '*P*' stand for classes, while in the other two the symbol '*x*' is introduced to stand for at least one member of the class denoted by '*S*.' If at least one member of that class is included in the class denoted by '*P*,' that's logically equivalent to saying that some *S* are *P*. If at least one member of the class *S* is not included in the class denoted by '*P*,' that's logically equivalent to saying that some *S* are not *P*.

BOX 1 ■ CLASS RELATIONS IN CATEGORICAL PROPOSITIONS

- In (1), the entire class of Ss is included inside the class of Ps.
- In (2) the classes of Ss and Ps wholly exclude each other.
- In (3), part of the class of Ss is included in the class of Ps.
- In (4), part of the class of Ss is wholly excluded from the class of Ps.

Standard Form

Statements (1) through (4) above illustrate standard form categorical propositions. They are all composed of certain basic elements. Among these are, of course, the subject and predicate terms (which are not the grammatical but rather the logical subject and predicate of the proposition). Another basic element of standard categorical propositions is its so-called quantity, marked by a quantifier: an expression indicating whether the proposition's relation of inclusion or exclusion involves whole or partial classes. In (1) and (2), this is done by means of the universal quantifiers 'all' and 'no' (the latter combining the universal quantifier with negation), in (3) and (4) by 'some,' which is a particular (in the sense of non-universal) quantifier. Standard categorical propositions are also said to have quality: each categorical proposition is either affirmative or negative, depending on whether it lacks or contains negation. Statements (1) and (3) are affirmative, while (2) and (4) negative. Finally, there is the copula or verb of being, that may occur in singular ('is'/'is not') or plural ('are'/'are not'). These, then, are the basic elements of any categorical proposition in standard form.

Any standard-form categorical proposition has
- A quantity (it is either universal or particular)
- A quality (it is either affirmative or negative)
- A subject term and a predicate term
- A copula connecting those terms

In any given categorical proposition, it is the combination of quantifier and the presence or absence of negation that determines its type. As shown in Box 2, there are four types of standard categorical propositions, each with its characteristic logical form—namely, universal affirmative, universal negative, particular affirmative, and particular negative.

In traditional logic, the capital letters 'A,' 'E,' 'I,' and 'O' are used as names of the four types of categorical proposition. Each letter is a shorthand way of referring to propositions falling under one of the four types. The use of these letters is a mnemonic device invented by traditional logicians from the Latin words *affirmo* ('I affirm') and *nego* ('I deny'). The first vowel of each word stands for the universal categorical propositions—'A' for universal affirmative and 'E' for universal negative—and the second vowel for particular propositions—'I' for particular affirmative and 'O' for particular negative. Hereafter, we'll refer to each of the four types of categorical proposition by using these letter names. Thus consider again our previous examples:

1 All philosophers are wise persons.
2 No philosophers are wise persons.
3 Some philosophers are wise persons.
4 Some philosophers are not wise persons.

These illustrate, respectively, an *A* proposition, an *E* proposition, an *I* proposition, and an *O* proposition.

BOX 2 ■ STANDARD CATEGORICAL PROPOSITIONS		
NAME	**TYPE**	**FORM**
A	Universal Affirmative	All S are P
E	Universal Negative	No S are P
I	Particular Affirmative	Some S are P
O	Particular Negative	Some S are not P

Non-Standard Categorical Propositions

Of course, very few propositions are already in the standard form—that is, only some have explicitly all the elements found in an *A*, *E*, *I*, or *O* proposition. However, it seems possible to translate many non-standard categorical propositions into one of these forms by making some changes. For example, (5) is a categorical proposition that can be translated into the *A* proposition (5'):

5 Cobras are dangerous.

5' All cobras are dangerous.

Quantifiers such as 'each,' 'every,' 'any,' 'everything,' 'everyone,' and the like are universal, and therefore logically equivalent to 'all.' Note that they are often omitted in propositions such as (5). When that happens, the quantifier must be made explicit if the proposition is to be in standard form. Furthermore, certain conditionals can also be translated into *A* propositions: to say that all cobras are dangerous is logically equivalent to saying that

5" If something is a cobra, then it is dangerous.

Therefore, when you encounter conditionals such as (5"), you must translate them as *A* propositions. Keep in mind that the default quantifier for any seemingly universal affirmative proposition is 'all,' except when careful reading of the proposition suggests a non-universal quantifier. For example,

6 The dogs bark at night.

This does not translate into an *A* proposition in standard form, but rather into an *I* proposition, such as

6' Some dogs are nighttime barkers.

Although (6') sounds odd in English, what matters here is logical form: translating a proposition into standard categorical form often has that linguistic side-effect.

What about non-standard universal negative propositions? Consider

7 No one in my class plays Scrabble.

Since (7) is an *E* proposition, we'll make the necessary changes to obtain one in the standard form. For example,

7' No classmates of mine are Scrabble players.

Here again, a conditional can be translated into an *E* proposition: to say 'No classmates of mine are Scrabble players' is to say

7" If someone is my classmate, then that person is not a Scrabble player.

Note that a conditional that can be adequately translated into an *E* proposition must have a negation in its consequent. Now consider

8 There are classmates of mine who play Scrabble.

This translates into the *I* proposition

> 8'   Some classmates of mine are Scrabble players,

as does

> 8"   Classmates of mine who play Scrabble exist.

That is, any proposition about what exists or "what there is" translates into an *I* proposition, provided it doesn't have negation. When such a proposition does have negation, as in

> 9   There are classmates of mine who do not play Scrabble,

it translates into an *O* proposition, such as

> 9'   Some classmates of mine are not Scrabble players.

We'll have more to say on translation under "Existential Import" below. But in the next section we'll first consider some inferences that can be drawn from categorical propositions.

Exercises

I. Review Questions

1. What are categorical propositions? Describe their parts and types.
2. For each type of categorical proposition, give an example in non-standard form, and then translate it into standard form.
3. In a standard-form categorical proposition, what are the functions of the copula and the quantifier?
4. What do *A* and *I* propositions have in common? And what about *E* and *O*?
5. What do *A* and *E* propositions have in common? And what about *I* and *O*?

II. In the following categorical propositions, mark subject terms with one line and predicate terms with two lines, and determine their quantity and quality.

1. SAMPLE ANSWER: Some newspapers are sound sources of information. Particular affirmative.

2. All natives of Mars are aliens.

*3. No political scandals are situations sought by city officials.

4. All police officers are persons who get the facts.

5. Some psychological studies are not rigorous studies.

*6. Some railroad engineers who are not car owners are train users.

7. All human rights that concern freedom are self-evident rights recognized by the UN.

*8. Some single-celled organisms that thrive in the summer are bacteria that are not harmful.

9. Some bananas that grow in non-tropical countries are not Central American fruits.

10. No daisies observed so far by experts and non-experts alike are flowers that can be found at the North Pole.

III. For each categorical proposition above, determine whether it is of type *A*, *E*, *I*, or *O*.

SAMPLE ANSWER: I proposition.

IV. In the following categorical propositions, mark subject terms with one line, predicate terms with two lines, and determine their quantity, quality, and type.

1. No poodle is a dangerous dog.

SAMPLE ANSWER: No poodle is a dangerous dog. Universal negative, E.

2. Some chemicals are acids.

*3. Some firefighters are not men.

4. No vegetarians are fond of mutton.

*5. Some precious metals were not available in Africa.

6. No vehicle that has no flashing light on top is an emergency vehicle.

*7. Some historians are persons who are interested in the future.

8. Some blizzards that produce no ice are not road hazards.

*9. All spies are persons who cannot avoid taking risks.

10. Some universities that are not very selective are institutions that charge high tuition.

V. Select four categorical propositions from exercise above, one for each of the four types, and represent each of them with a diagram of the sort suggested at the beginning of this section.

SAMPLE ANSWER: 1. No poodle is a dangerous dog.

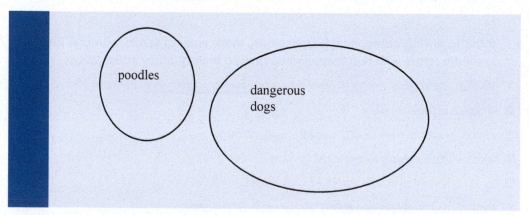

VI. Match each of the following sentences with a type of categorical proposition and rewrite it in standard form:

1. There are Bostonians who are not Red Sox fans.

SAMPLE ANSWER: O. Some Bostonians are not Red Sox fans.

*2. No movie star loves being ignored by the media.

3. Every mollusk is a shellfish.

*4. No member of Congress who's being investigated can leave the country.

5. If someone is a mayor, then she is a politician.

*6. There are mathematical equations that do not amount to headaches.

7. A college with a high out-of-state tuition is not within my budget.

*8. There are dogs that don't bark.

9. Precious metals are still available in many parts of Africa.

*10. Speedy vehicles that don't put their occupants at risk exist.

VII. YOUR OWN THINKING LAB

For each of the following diagrams, write down two categorical propositions that could be represented by it, one in the standard form and the other in some non-standard form.

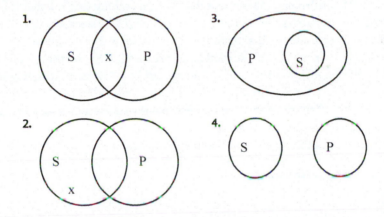

13.2 Venn Diagrams for Categorical Propositions

We may now represent the four types of categorical propositions by means of standard Venn diagrams (devised by the English logician John Venn, 1834–1923). A Venn diagram for a categorical proposition employs two intersecting circles, the one on the left representing the class denoted by its subject term, the one on the right the class denoted by its predicate. Let's first consider a Venn diagram and some equivalent notations for a universal affirmative proposition, such as

10 All U.S. citizens are voters.

Boolean Notation:

$S\overline{P} = 0,$

A Proposition:

All S are P

The Venn diagram representing (10) consists of two intersecting circles, one for the subject term ('U.S. citizens') and the other for the predicate ('voters').

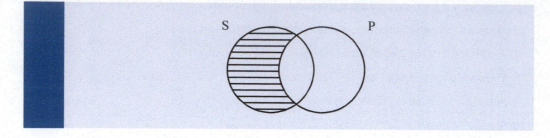

Since, according to (10), all members of the class denoted by its subject term are members of the class denoted by its predicate term, the crescent-shaped part of S that has no members (i.e., that representing U.S. citizens who are not voters) has been shaded out in the diagram. With the Venn-diagram technique, shading a space means that that space is empty. Thus, in the above diagram, S non-P is shaded out, to represent that there is nothing that is S that is non-P. This is consistent with reading (10) as saying that the subclass of U.S. citizens who are not voters is an empty subclass—or, equivalently, that there are no U.S. citizens who are not voters.

On the previous page, (10)'s translation is provided, first, in the algebraic notation introduced by the English mathematician George Boole (1815–1864), which reads, 'S non-P equals o,' and then in the notation of traditional logic, reading 'All S are P.' What both say is captured by the Venn diagram in the box: namely, that the subclass of S non-P (represented by the shaded portion of the diagram) is empty.

Now let's look at (11), an instance of the universal negative.

11 No U.S. citizens are voters.

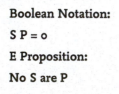

Boolean Notation:

S P = o

E Proposition:

No S are P

Since (11) is a universal proposition, its Venn diagram shows an empty subclass that has been shaded out: the football-shaped center area, the intersection of 'S' and 'P,' which represents the U.S. citizens who are voters. The diagram thus captures that (11) denies that there are any such voters: in other words, asserting (11) amounts to saying that the class of voting U.S. citizens has no members. To the left of the diagram, (11)'s Boolean notation '$S\,P = 0$' tells us that the sub-class '$S\,P$' is empty. Immediately below, we find (11)'s notation and type in traditional logic. Keep in mind that, for any universal categorical proposition (whether affirmative or negative), there will be a part of the circles shaded out, to indicate that that part has no members.

Next, consider the particular affirmative

12 Some U.S. citizens are voters.

Boolean Notation:

$S\,P \neq 0$

I Proposition:

Some S are P

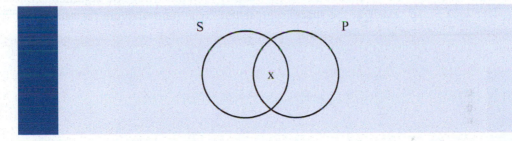

This time, no universal claim is being made, but rather a particular one: a claim about part of a class. As a result, the diagram shows no shading at all, but an 'x' instead, in the area where there are some members. Since 'some' logically amounts to 'at least one,' (12) is equivalent to

12' There is at least one U.S. citizen who is a voter.

Putting an 'x' in the football-shaped center space indicates that that space, '$S\,P$,' is not empty—in effect, that it has some members (at least one). To the left of the diagram, we find (12)'s Boolean translation '$S\,P \neq 0$,' which tells us that the subclass '$S\,P$' (i.e., the football-shaped area in the center) is not empty—together with its type and notation in traditional logic.

Finally, what about a particular negative? Consider

13 Some U.S. citizens are not voters.

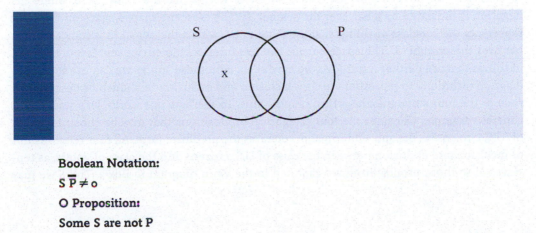

Boolean Notation:

$S\,\overline{P} \neq 0$

O Proposition:

Some S are not P

Because (13) is also a particular proposition, there's no shading in its Venn diagram. And, again, if 'some' means 'at least one,' then (13) is logically equivalent to

13' There is at least one U.S. citizen who is not a voter.

That the class of U.S. citizens who are not voters (the crescent-shaped space on the left side of the diagram) is not empty—that is, that it has at least one member—is represented in that subclass, '*S* non-*P*,' with an 'x.' The same is expressed both by the Boolean translation to the left of the diagram, which tells us that '*S* non-*P*' is not empty, and by the notation in traditional logic that follows.

With these four diagrams, then, we can represent all of the different types of class relationship featured in the four types of categorical propositions. In the next chapter, we'll see how Venn diagrams can be used to check the validity of some syllogistic arguments. But first, let's look more closely at the spaces represented by a Venn diagram for categorical propositions. These are as follows:

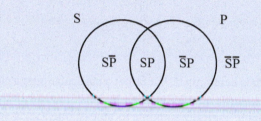

The two intersecting circles represent the two classes of things related in a categorical proposition—the one on the left, the class denoted by its subject, the one on the right, the class denoted by its predicate. The circles also determine four subclasses that we may identify with the spaces drawn. The space in the center, where they overlap, represents the subclass of things that are both *S* and *P* at once (i.e., the subclass of things that are simultaneously members of both classes), which is indicated by the notation '*SP*.' The crescent-shaped space on the left represents the subclass of things that are *S* but not *P*, where the negation is indicated by a bar over the symbol '*P*.' The crescent-shaped space on the right represents the subclass of things that are *P* but not *S*, where the negation is indicated by a bar over the symbol '*S*.' The space outside the two interlocking circles represents the class of things that are neither *S* nor *P*. As we have seen, with these spaces we can use the Venn-diagram technique to represent the class inclusion and exclusion relationships described in each of the four standard categorical propositions. To see how this works, let's start with a concrete example. Consider the four categorical propositions that may be constructed out of 'U.S. citizens' as the subject term and 'voters' as the predicate term. All four relationships of inclusion and exclusion between the class of U.S. citizens and the class of voters, as represented in those propositions, are captured in the Venn diagram in Box 3. There we may

BOX 3 ■ VENN DIAGRAMS FOR CATEGORICAL PROPOSITIONS

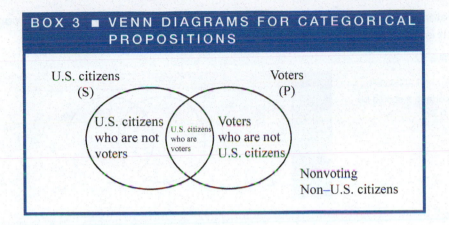

identify the following subclasses: (1) U.S. citizens who are voters, (2) U.S. citizens who are not voters, (3) voters who are not U.S. citizens (which would include, for instance, those who vote in other countries), and (4) non-U.S. citizen who are non-voters (which would include, for instance, not only current citizens of other countries who do not vote, but also Henry VIII, Julius Caesar, and even things like the Eiffel Tower, the Magna Carta, and the Grand Canyon—in fact *everything* we can think of belongs to one or the other of these four possible subclasses).

For each categorical proposition, then, there is a Venn diagram that shows the relationship of inclusion or exclusion that it involves. The bottom line is:

- The areas displayed by a Venn diagram relevant to representing a categorical proposition are three: those inside each intersecting circle and their intersection itself.
- A Venn diagram for an *A* or *E* proposition shows a shaded area where there are no members. No 'x' occurs in this diagram.
- A Venn diagram for an *I* or *O* proposition shows an 'x' in the area where there are members. No area is shaded in this diagram.

Exercises

VIII. Review Questions

1. In the previous section, Venn diagrams were used to represent categorical propositions. Explain how this technique works.
2. What do Venn diagrams for universal propositions have in common? What about those for particular propositions?
3. What does it mean when spaces are shaded out in Venn diagrams for categorical propositions? And what's the meaning of an 'x' placed in one of the circles?
4. What do the two circles stand for in a Venn diagram for a categorical proposition?

IX. **Determine whether each Boolean notation for the diagram on the right is correct. If it isn't, provide the correct one.**

1. $S\,\overline{P} = 0$

SAMPLE ANSWER:
Incorrect. It should be:
$S\,\overline{P} \neq 0$

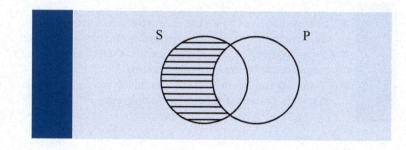

2. $S\,P \neq 0$

*3. $S\,\overline{P} \neq 0$

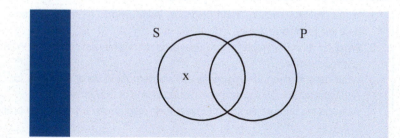

4. $S\,\overline{P} \neq 0$

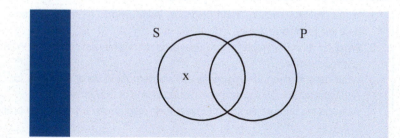

X. For each categorical proposition below, first identify its letter name and traditional notation. Then select the correct Venn diagram and Boolean notation for it from the following menu:

Venn Diagram

1

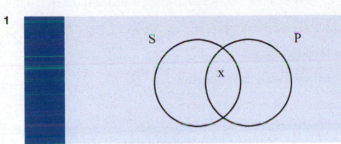

2

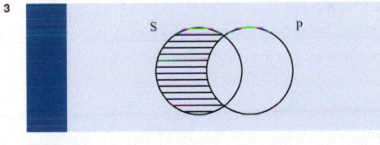

3

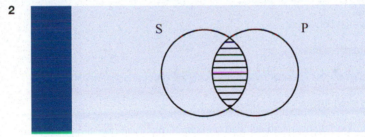

4

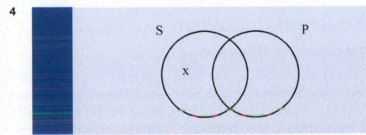

(1) $SP = 0$ (2) $S\overline{P} = 0$ (3) $S\overline{P} \neq 0$ (4) $SP \neq 0$

1. No Sumo wrestlers are men who wear small-size shirts.

   SAMPLE ANSWER: E proposition; no S are P. Venn Diagram 2, Boolean notation 1.

2. Some sports cars are very expensive machines.

*3. All llamas are bad-tempered animals.

4. Some grocers are not members of the Rotary Club.

5. All waterfalls are places people in kayaks should avoid.

*6. No spiders are insects.

7. Some advertisers are artful deceivers.

8. Some cowboys are not rodeo riders.

*9. No atheists are churchgoers.

10. All oranges are citrus fruits.

11. Some rivers that do not flow northward are not South American rivers.

*12. If a number is even, then it is not odd.

13. There are marathon runners who eat fried chicken.

14. Some accountants who are graduates of Ohio State are not owners of bicycles.

*15. Not all oils are good for you.

16. Some reference works are books that are not in the library.

17. If an architect is well known, then that architect has good taste.

*18. Nothing written by superstitious people is a reliable source.

19. Chiropractors who do not have a serious degree exist.

*20. Some resorts that are not in the Caribbean are popular tourist destinations.

13.3 The Square of Opposition

The Traditional Square of Opposition

Categorical propositions of the above four types were traditionally thought to bear logical relations to each other that enable us to draw certain immediate inferences. These are single-premise arguments, to some of which we'll turn now. We'll first look at the immediate inferences represented in the Traditional Square of Opposition, a figure that looks like this:

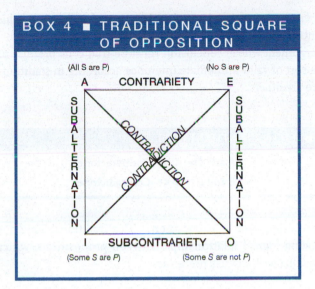

BOX 4 ■ TRADITIONAL SQUARE OF OPPOSITION

The relations represented in the Traditional Square of Opposition, which involve two categorical propositions at a time, are as follows:

Relation	Established Between	Name of Related Propositions
Contradiction	A and O; E and I	Contradictories
Contrariety	A and E	Contraries
Subcontrariety	I and O	Subcontraries
Subalternation	A and I; E and O	Superalterns: A and E
		Subalterns: I and O

Let's now take up each of these relations in turn.

Contradiction. Propositions of the types in diagonally opposite corners of the Square are contradictories. Propositions that stand in the relation of contradiction cannot have the same truth value: if one is true, then the other is false, and vice versa. Thus A and O propositions will always have opposite truth values if their subjects and predicates are the same, as will propositions of types E and I. Thus if (1) is true, (4) is false:

1   All philosophers are wise persons.

4   Some philosophers are not wise persons.

On the other hand, if (1) is false, then that's logically the same as saying that (4) is true. Similarly, if it's true that

3   Some philosophers are wise persons,

(that is, there is at least one philosopher who is a wise person), then it is false that

2   No philosophers are wise persons.

And conversely, if (3) is false, then (2) is true. When we infer the truth value of a proposition from that of its contradictory, as we've been doing here, we make a valid immediate inference: a single-premise argument whose conclusion must be true if its premise also is. But contradiction is only one sort of valid immediate inference according to traditional logicians; as we shall see next, there are others.

BOX 5 ■ CONTRADICTION	
A and O ⇨⇦	Contradictories
E and I ⇨⇦	Contradictories

Contrariety, Subcontrariety, and Subalternation.   The Traditional Square of Opposition also includes the following logical relationships between propositions, which are valid given certain assumptions that we'll discuss presently:

A and *E*   ⇨   Contrariety
I and *O*   ⇨   Subcontrariety
A and *I*   ⇨   Subalternation
E and *O*   ⇨   Subalternation

Contrary propositions cannot both be true at once, but can both be false. For instance, by contrariety, if (14) is true we can infer that (15) is false:

14 All bankers are cautious investors.

15 No bankers are cautious investors.

That's because these categorical propositions cannot both be true. Yet they could both be false (as in fact they are).

But contrariety differs from subcontrariety, and neither of these is the same as contradiction. Subcontrary propositions can both be true at once but cannot both be false. By subcontrariety, if (16) is false, then (17) is true:

16 Some students are vegetarians.

17 Some students are not vegetarians.

These categorical propositions cannot both be false but could both be true (as in fact they are).

Finally, there is the relationship of subalternation, which is a little more complex, since the correct inference of truth values varies depending on whether we go from the universal proposition to the corresponding particular, or the other way around. Logically speaking, to say that an *A* proposition and the corresponding *I* proposition are in the relation of subalternation is to say that if the *A* proposition is true, then the *I* proposition must be true, as well, but also that if the *I* proposition is false, then the *A* must be false. And similarly, for an *E* proposition and the corresponding *O*, to say that they are in the relation of subalternation means that if the *E* proposition is true, then necessarily the *O* proposition is true, but also that if the *O* is false, then the *E* must be false as well. In either case, the universal proposition is called 'superaltern,' and the particular of the same quality 'subaltern.' So

> Subalternation is a logical relation between:
>
> - *A* and *I* (*A* superaltern, *I* subaltern)
> - *E* and *O* (*E* superaltern, *O* subaltern)
>
> In this relation:
>
> - Truth transmits downward (from superaltern to subaltern)
> - Falsity transmits upward (from subaltern to superaltern)

Let's reason by subalternation as traditional logicians would. Suppose it's true that

18 All trombone players are musicians.

Then it must also be true that

19 Some trombone players are musicians.

This suggests that truth transmits downward. At the same time, since it is false that some trombone players are not musicians, it follows that it is also false that no trombone players are musicians—and this suggests that falsity transmits upward. But a false superaltern such as (14) clearly fails to entail a false subaltern, since that some bankers are cautious investors is true.

14 All bankers are cautious investors.

And a true subaltern such as (17) fails to entail a true superaltern, since that no students are vegetarians is false.

17 Some students are not vegetarians.

Truth-Value Rules and the Traditional Square of Opposition   Let's now summarize all relationships represented in the Traditional Square of Opposition, together with the rules to be used for drawing immediate inferences from it:

Contradiction: Contradictory propositions cannot have the same truth value (if one is true, the other must be false, and vice versa).

Contrariety: Contrary propositions cannot both be true at once, but can both be false.

Subcontrariety: Subcontrary propositions cannot both be false at once, but can both be true.
Subalternation from the superaltern to subaltern (i.e., from the universal proposition to the particular proposition of the same quality):

> If the superaltern is true, then the subaltern must be true.

> If the superaltern is false, then the subaltern is undetermined

Subalternation from the subaltern to superaltern (i.e., from the particular proposition to the universal proposition of the same quality):

> If the subaltern is true, then the superaltern is undetermined.
> If the subaltern is false, then the superaltern must be false.

Given the relationships of contradiction, contrariety, subcontrariety, and subalternation represented in the Traditional Square of Opposition, then assuming the truth values listed on the left, we can infer the values listed on the right.

If *A* is true	⇨	*E* is false, *O* is false, and *I* is true.
If *A* is false	⇨	*E* is undetermined, *O* is true, and *I* is undetermined.
If *E* is true	⇨	*A* is false, *I* is false, and *O* is true.
If *E* is false	⇨	*A* is undetermined, *I* is true, and *O* is undetermined.
If *I* is true	⇨	*A* is undetermined, *E* is false, and *O* is undetermined.
If *I* is false	⇨	*A* is false, *E* is true, and *O* is true.
If *O* is true	⇨	*A* is false, *E* is undetermined, and *I* is undetermined.
If *O* is false	⇨	*A* is true, *E* is false, and *I* is true.

Existential Import

Although inferences by contrariety, subcontrariety, and subalternation are all licensed as valid by the Traditional Square of Opposition, our ability to draw such inferences is undermined by a significant difference between universal propositions, on the one hand, and particular propositions, on the other: namely, that the latter (*I* and *O*) have existential import while the former (*A* and *E*) do not. That is, *I* and *O* propositions implicitly assume the existence of the entities denoted by their subject terms. Since 'some' is logically the same as 'at least one,' therefore an I proposition such as (20) is logically equivalent to (20'):

20 Some cats are felines.

20' There is at least one cat that is a feline.

Note that 'there is at least one cat . . .' amounts to 'cats exist.' Similarly, an O proposition such as (21) is logically the same as (21'), which likewise presupposes that some cats exist:

21 Some cats are not felines.

21' There is at least one cat that is not a feline.

On the other hand, A and E propositions are logically the same as conditionals: (22) is equivalent to (22') and (23) to (23').

22 All cats are felines.

22' If anything is a cat, then it is a feline.

23 No cats are felines.

23' If anything is a cat, then it is not a feline.

Understood in this way, a universal categorical proposition doesn't have existential import, since it is equivalent to a conditional, a compound proposition that is false if and only if its antecedent is true and its consequent false. So (22') would be false if and only if there are cats but they are not felines, as would (23') if there are cats but they are felines. If cats did not exist, the antecedents of these conditionals would be false, and those conditionals true (independent of the truth value of their consequents).

Thus the inference by contrariety is undermined: given this understanding of universal propositions, contrary propositions could both be true in cases where their subjects are empty (i.e., have no referents). Consider (24), which is equivalent to (24'):

24 All unicorns are shy creatures.

24' If anything is a unicorn, then it is a shy creature.

Since nothing is a unicorn, (24')'s antecedent is false, and the whole conditional therefore true. Now consider its contrary, (25), which is equivalent to (25'):

25 No unicorns are shy creatures.

25' If anything is a unicorn, then it is not a shy creature.

Here again, since nothing is a unicorn, (25')'s antecedent is false, and the whole conditional therefore true. Clearly, then, (24) and (25) could both be true! It follows that, unless we assume that the subject term of a true universal proposition is non-empty, we cannot infer that its contrary is false.

Now, what about subcontrariety? This involves *I* and *O* propositions—which, in the modern understanding, do have existential import. Although, given the Traditional Square of Opposition, subcontraries cannot both be false, in the modern understanding they can. Consider now

26 Some unicorns are shy creatures.

This is equivalent to

26' There are unicorns and they are shy creatures.

Thus understood, (26) is false, since there are no unicorns. Compare

27 Some unicorns are not shy creatures.

This is equivalent to

27' There are unicorns and they are not shy creatures.

Since there are no unicorns, (27) turns out to be false as well. Thus (26) and (27) could both be false at once. It follows that we cannot draw valid inferences by subcontrariety.

Finally, consider subalternation. From what we have just seen, this relation also begins to look suspicious. How can one validly infer, for example, from an *A* proposition that has no existential import, an *I* proposition that does? Of course, *I*-from-*A* and *O*-from-*E* inferences might seem unproblematic at first, whenever the things denoted by their subject terms exist—for example, trombone players, accountants, and tigers. But when we're talking about entities whose existence is questionable, inference by subalternation leads to absurdities, such as

28 1. All unicorns are shy creatures.
    2. Some unicorns are shy creatures.

Since the conclusion in (28) is equivalent to (26') above, the argument appears to have "proved" that unicorns exist! This attempt to draw a conclusion by subalternation fails because it ignores the fact that the premise has no existential import, while the conclusion (its subaltern) does have it.

The Modern Square of Opposition

Some qualifications of the allowable valid inferences according to the Square of Opposition are needed to restrict the range of valid inferences involving categorical propositions. As shown in Box 6, the Modern Square modifies the traditional one so that it leaves out the relationships of subalternation, contrariety, and subcontrariety, retaining only contradiction as a relation sanctioning valid immediate inferences. Contradiction holds between A and O and between E and I propositions, which are in opposite corners of the Square, marked by the two diagonals, as shown in Box 6.

From this Modern Square, we can see two things about a proposition and the negation of its contradictory. First, they are logically equivalent: if the proposition in one corner is true, then the negation of its contradictory must be true; and if the proposition in one corner is false, then the negation of its contradictory must be false. Second, they entail each other: any

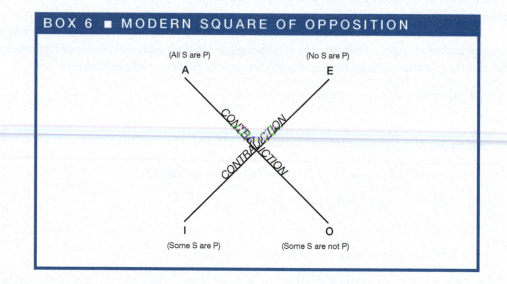

BOX 6 ■ MODERN SQUARE OF OPPOSITION

(All S are P) — A
(No S are P) — E
(Some S are P) — I
(Some S are not P) — O
CONTRADICTION

inference from a proposition to the negation of its contradictory preserves truth value and is therefore valid.

Here, then, is a complete list of the equivalences (and entailment relations) between a proposition of one of the four standard types and the negation of its contradictory sanctioned by the Modern Square of Opposition:

1. $A = \text{not } O$
2. $E = \text{not } I$
3. $I = \text{not } E$
4. $O = \text{not } A$

So, given (1), if 'All oranges are citrus fruits' is true, then 'It is not the case that some oranges are not citrus fruits' must be true; and vice versa. But given (4), if 'Some oranges are not citrus fruits' is true, then 'All oranges are citrus fruits' must be false while 'It is not the case that all oranges are citrus fruits' must be true. You should try, as an exercise, to run an example for each of these equivalences. The bottom line is that for the listed propositions, each pair have the same truth value: if one is true, the other must also be true; and if one is false, the other must likewise be false. The former yields validity, the two combined logical equivalence. Venn diagrams are consistent with the modern view of the Square of Opposition. After all, it is only for particular propositions that we're required to use an 'x' to indicate where there are members of the subject class (if they exist at all). Universal propositions never require us to indicate where there are members, but only where there aren't any (i.e., by shading).

BOX 7 ■ LOGICAL EQUIVALENCE AND VALIDITY

Logical Equivalence

When two propositions are logically equivalent, if one is true, then the other is also true; and if one is false, then the other must be false as well. This is because the conditions under which they are true or false are the same. Thus logically equivalent propositions have the same truth values: they are either both true or both false. As a result, one of them could be substituted for the other while preserving the truth value of the larger expression in which they occur, provided that neither occurs in a special context that could not allow such substitutions. For example, a proposition 'P' is logically equivalent to 'It is not the case that not P'; therefore, one can be replaced by the other while preserving the truth value of the larger expression in which one of them occurs, provided that, for instance, the expression does not occur inside quotation marks.

Validity

When two propositions are logically equivalent, if one is true, the other is true as well. This satisfies the definition of entailment or valid argument: logically equivalent propositions entail each other. Any argument from one to the other is valid.

Exercises

XI. Review Questions

1. What is an immediate inference?
2. Which immediate inferences are valid according to the Traditional Square of Opposition, and which according to the Modern Square of Opposition? Support your answer with examples.
3. Subalternation works differently depending on whether it is an inference from superaltern to subaltern or vice versa. Explain.
4. What does it mean to say that certain propositions have existential import? Which categorical propositions have it, according to the modern interpretation of the Square of Opposition?

XII. For each of the following, first name the type of the proposition related to it by contrariety or subcontrariety, as the case may be, and state that proposition. Then assume that the proposition given is true and determine the truth value of its contrary or subcontrary.

1. All Icelanders are believers in elves.

   SAMPLE ANSWER: *E.* Contrary. No Icelanders are believers in elves. False.

2. No epidemics are dangerous.

*3. Some humans are not mortal.

4. No riverboat gamblers are honest men.

*5. All labor unions are organizations dominated by politicians.

6. Some conservatory gardens are not places open to the public.

*7. Some lions are harmless.

8. No used-car dealers are people who can be trusted.

*9. Some bats are not nocturnal creatures.

10. Some historians are interested in the past.

XIII. For each of the propositions above, assume that it is false and determine the truth value of its contrary or subcontrary. (*4, *6, *10)

   SAMPLE ANSWER: 1. *E.* Contrary. Undetermined.

XIV. For each of the following, give the letter name of its contradictory and state that proposition.

1. All bankers are fiscal conservatives.

   SAMPLE ANSWER: *O.* Some bankers are not fiscal conservatives.

*2. No Democrats are opponents of legalized abortion.

3. Some SUVs are vehicles that get good gas mileage.

*4. All professional athletes are highly paid sports heroes.

5. Some tropical parrots are not birds that are noisy and talkative.

*6. Some chipmunks are shy rodents.

7. No captains of industry are cheerful taxpayers.

*8. Some cartographers are amateur musicians.

9. All anarchists are opponents of civil authority.

*10. Some airlines are not profitable corporations.

XV. First suppose each categorical proposition listed in the previous exercise is true. What could you then know about the truth value of its contradictory? Second, suppose each proposition in the list is false. What could you then know about the truth value of its contradictory?

XVI. For each of the following, first name the type of the proposition related to it by subalternation and state that proposition. Then assume that the proposition given is true and determine the truth value of its superaltern or subaltern.

1. Some westerns are not good movies.

   SAMPLE ANSWER: E. Superaltern. No westerns are good movies. Undetermined.

2. Some string quartets are works by modern composers.

*3. No butterflies are vertebrates.

4. No parakeets are philosophy majors.

*5. Some comets are not frequent celestial events.

6. All Internal Revenue agents are hard workers.

*7. Some porcupines are not nocturnal animals.

8. Some Rotarians are pharmacists.

*9. No extraterrestrials are Republicans.

10. All amoebas are primitive creatures.

XVII. For each of the propositions above, assume that it is false and determine the truth value of its superaltern or subaltern. (*4, *8, *10)

   SAMPLE ANSWER: 1. E. Superaltern. False.

XVIII. For each proposition below, first give the letter names of all propositions related to it according to the Traditional Square of Opposition, specify those relationships, and state those propositions. Then, assuming that each proposition listed below is true, what would be the truth values of the given propositions? (Tip for in-class correction: Move clockwise through the relations in the Square.)

1. All tables are pieces of furniture.

   SAMPLE ANSWER: E. Contrary. No tables are pieces of furniture. False.
   O. Contradictory. Some tables are not pieces of furniture. False.
   I. Subaltern. Some tables are pieces of furniture. True.

2. Some griffins are mythological beasts.

3. No liars are reliable sources.

*4. Some bassoonists are anarchists.

5. All trombone players are musicians.

*6. No Americans are people who care about global warming.

7. All white horses are horses.

*8. All acts of cheating are acts that are wrong.

9. Some cyclists are not welcome in the Tour de France.

*10. Some things are things that are observable with the naked eye.

XIX. Assuming that the propositions listed in the previous exercise are false, what is the truth value of each proposition related to them by the Traditional Square of Opposition? (*3, *5, *7)

SAMPLE ANSWER: E. Contrary. No tables are pieces of furniture. Undetermined.

O. Contradictory. Some tables are not pieces of furniture. True.

I. Subaltern. Some tables are pieces of furniture. Undetermined.

XX. YOUR OWN THINKING LAB

1. Assuming that the propositions listed in (XVIII) above are true, use the Modern Square of Opposition to draw a valid inference from each of them.

SAMPLE ANSWER: All tables are pieces of furniture.

It is false that some tables are not pieces of furniture.

2. Consider propositions such as 'No centaur is a Freemason,' 'All hobbits live underground,' and 'Some Cyclops are nearsighted.' What's the matter with them according to modern logicians? Explain.

*3. Determine which logical relation among those represented in the Traditional Square of Opposition holds between premise and conclusion in each of the following arguments. Is the argument valid according to the Modern Square of Opposition? Discuss.

A. All automobiles that are purchased from used-car dealers are good investments. Therefore, some automobiles that are purchased from used-car dealers are good investments.

SAMPLE ANSWER: Subalternation. Invalid by the Modern Square.

B. Some residents of New York are dentists. Therefore, it is not true that no resident of New York is a dentist.

*C. No boa constrictors are animals that are easy to carry on a bicycle. Therefore, it is false that boa constrictors are animals that are easy to carry on a bicycle.

D. Some motorcycles that are made in Europe are not vehicles that are inexpensive to repair. Therefore, it is not the case that all motorcycles that are made in Europe are vehicles that are inexpensive to repair.

*E. It is false that some restaurants located in bus stations are places where one is likely to be poisoned. Therefore, some restaurants located in bus stations are not places where one is likely to be poisoned.

F. It is not the case that some politicians are not anarchists. Therefore, no politicians are anarchists.

*G. No pacifists are war supporters. Therefore, it is not true that some pacifists are war supporters.

13.4 Other Immediate Inferences

We'll now turn to three more types of immediate inference that can be validly drawn from categorical propositions: conversion, obversion, and contraposition. In some cases, conversion and contraposition allow an inference from a universal to a particular proposition, but the validity of those inferences requires the assumption that the subject terms in the universal premises do not refer to empty classes such as mermaids and square circles.

Conversion

Conversion allows us to infer, from a categorical proposition called the 'convertend,' another proposition called its 'converse' by switching the former's subject and predicate terms while retaining its original quantity and quality. Thus from an E proposition such as

29 No SUV is a sports car,

we can infer by conversion

29' No sports car is an SUV.

Here the convertend's subject and predicate terms have been switched, but its quantity and quality remain the same: universal negative. The inference from (29) to (29') is valid: if (29) is true, then (29') must be true as well (and vice versa). Similarly, by conversion, an I proposition yields an I converse when the subject and predicates terms of the convertend are switched. For example, the converse of (30) is (30'):

30 Some Republicans are journalists.

30' Some journalists are Republicans.

If (30) is true, then (30') must also be true and vice versa—so the inference is valid and the two propositions are logically equivalent.

For A propositions, however, an inference by conversion in this straightforward way would not be valid. For, clearly, (31') does not follow from (31):

31 All pigs are mammals.

31' All mammals are pigs.

Rather, an A proposition can be validly converted only 'by limitation'—for (31") does follow from (31)

31" Some mammals are pigs.

In such a case of conversion by limitation, the convertend's quantity has been limited in the converse: the valid converse of an A proposition is an I proposition where the subject and predicate terms have been switched and the universal quantifier 'all' replaced by the non-universal quantifier 'some.'

Finally, note that in the case of O propositions, there is no valid conversion at all. If we tried to convert the true proposition (32), we'd get the false proposition (32').

32 Some precious stones are not emeralds.

32 Some emeralds are not precious stones.

This proves the invalidity of the inference from (32) to (32'). For any O proposition, an immediate inference by 'conversion' commits the fallacy of illicit conversion, and the same fallacy is committed when an A proposition is inferred by 'conversion' from another A proposition. To sum up, here are the rules for conversion:

BOX 8 ■ CONVERSION

	Convertend	Converse	Inference
A	All *S* are *P*	Some *P* are *S*	(Valid by limitation only)
E	No *S* are *P*	No *P* are *S*	VALID
I	Some *S* are *P*	Some *P* are *S*	VALID
O	Some *S* are not *P*		(No valid conversion)

Obversion

A categorical proposition's obverse is inferred by changing the proposition's quality (i.e., from affirmative to negative, or negative to affirmative) and adding to its predicate the prefix 'non.' The proposition deduced by obversion is called the 'obverse,' and that from which it was deduced, the 'obvertend.' The inference is valid across the board. Thus from the A proposition (33) it follows by obversion (33'):

33 All eagles are birds.

33' No eagles are non-birds.

From the E proposition (34), obversion yields (34'):

34 No cell phones are elephants.

34' All cell phones are non-elephants.

The obverse of *I* proposition (35) is (35'):

35 Some Californians are surfers.

35' Some Californians are not non-surfers.

The obverse of O proposition (36) is (36'):

36 Some epidemics are not catastrophes.

36' Some epidemics are non-catastrophes.

In each of these, the obvertend's predicate has been replaced in the obverse proposition by the predicate for its class complement, which is the class made up of everything outside of the class in question. For instance, for the class of senators, the class complement is the class of non-senators, which includes mayors, doctors, bricklayers, airplanes, butterflies, planets, postage stamps, inert gases, and so forth . . . in fact, everything that is not a senator. The class complement of the class of horses is non-horses, a similarly vast and diverse class of things. For the class of diseases, the class complement is non-diseases. And so on. The expression that denotes any such complement is a term complement.

BOX 9 ■ EQUIVALENCES AND NON-EQUIVALENCES BY CONVERSION

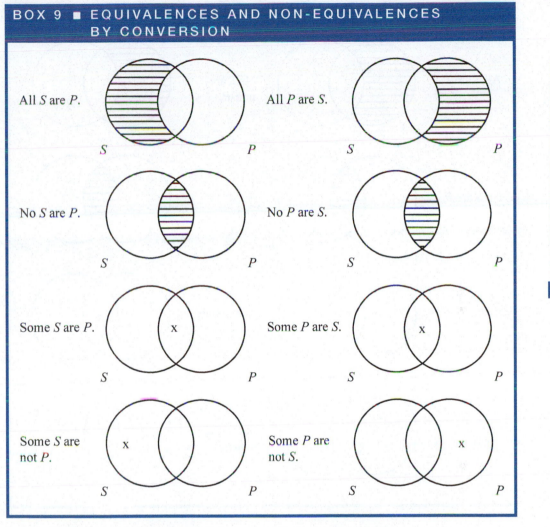

All *S* are *P*.

All *P* are *S*.

No *S* are *P*.

No *P* are *S*.

Some *S* are *P*.

Some *P* are *S*.

Some *S* are not *P*.

Some *P* are not *S*.

Unlike conversion, obversion is a valid immediate inference for all four types of categorical proposition. For each of the four pairs of categorical propositions listed below, an immediate inference from obvertend to obverse would be valid: if the obvertend is true, the obverse would be true too. The following table summarizes how to draw such inferences correctly:

BOX 10 ■ OBVERSION

	Obvertend	Obverse	Inference
A	All *S* are *P*	No *S* are non-*P*	VALID
E	No *S* are *P*	All *S* are non-*P*	VALID
I	Some *S* are *P*	Some *S* are not non-*P*	VALID
O	Some *S* are not *P*	Some *S* are non-*P*	VALID

BOX 11 ■ EQUIVALENCES BY OBVERSION

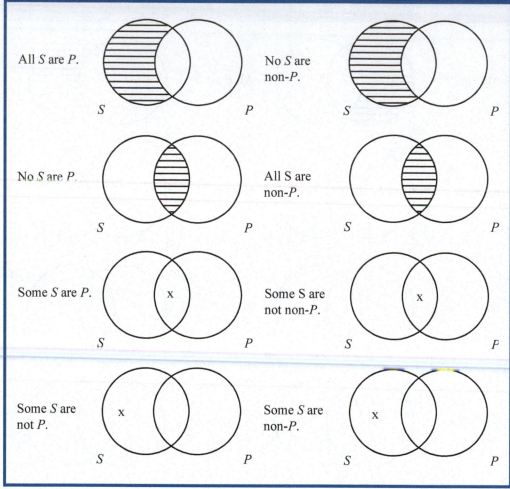

All *S* are *P*.   No *S* are non-*P*.

No *S* are *P*.   All S are non-*P*.

Some *S* are *P*.   Some S are not non-*P*.

Some *S* are not *P*.   Some *S* are non-*P*.

Contraposition

Contraposition allows us to infer a conclusion, the contrapositive, from another proposition by preserving the latter's quality and quantity while switching its subject and predicate terms, each preceded by the prefix 'non.' Thus the contrapositive of (37) is (37'):

37 All croissants are pastries.

37' All non-pastries are non-croissants.

Given contraposition, an *A* proposition of the form 'All *S* are *P*' is logically equivalent to another *A* proposition of the form 'All non-*P* are non-*S*.' Recall that whenever two propositions are logically equivalent, they have exactly the same truth value: if (37) is true, (37') is also true, and if (37) is false, (37') must be false. And, as noted in Box 7 in the previous section, whenever two propositions are logically equivalent, we may infer the one from the other: any such inference would be valid. To visualize this relationship between (37) and (37′), you may want to have a look at the corresponding Venn diagrams in Box 12 (think of '*S*' in the diagram as standing for 'croissants' and '*P*' for 'pastries').

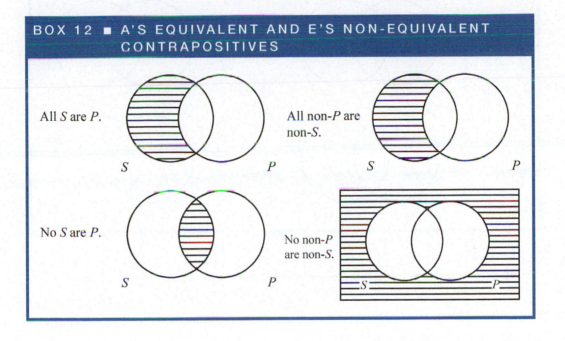

BOX 12 ■ A'S EQUIVALENT AND E'S NON-EQUIVALENT CONTRAPOSITIVES

All *S* are *P*.

All non-*P* are non-*S*.

No *S* are *P*.

No non-*P* are non-*S*.

The contrapositive of an *I* proposition is another proposition of exactly the same quality and quantity (that is, another *I* proposition), where the subject and predicate terms have been switched and prefixed by 'non.' The contrapositive of (38) is (38′):

38 Some croissants are pastries.

38′ Some non-pastries are non-croissants.

But (38) and (38′) are not logically equivalent, as can be seen in the corresponding Venn diagram in Box 12. Thus any inference drawn from one to the other by contraposition would be invalid, an instance of the fallacy of illicit contraposition.

With *E* propositions there is also a danger of committing the fallacy of illicit contraposition. But the fallacy can be avoided by limiting the quantity of the original *E* proposition in its contrapositive. That is, an *E* proposition's valid contrapositive is an *O* proposition in which subject and predicate have been switched and pre-fixed by 'non.' Thus consider

39 No leopards are reptiles.

The correct contrapositive, one that limits the quantity of (39) while preserving its quality, is (39′), which is also true.

39′ Some non-reptiles are not non-leopards.

(40) is inferred from (39) by contraposition without limitation, which makes the inference invalid.

BOX 13 ■ I'S NONEQUIVALENT AND O'S EQUIVALENT CONTRAPOSITIVES

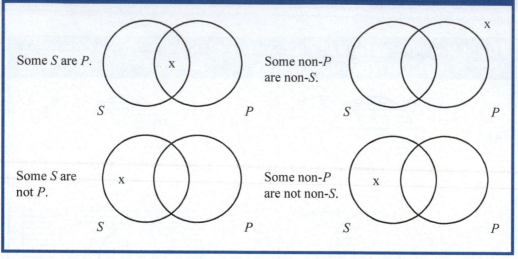

Some *S* are *P*.

Some non-*P* are non-*S*.

Some *S* are not *P*.

Some non-*P* are not non-*S*.

40 No leopards are reptiles; therefore, no non-reptiles are non-leopards.

Contraposition of an *O* proposition yields a logically equivalent *O* proposition; thus inferences from one to the other are always valid. Thus from (41) we can validly infer (42) by contraposition:

41 Some athletes are not runners.

42 Some non-runners are not non-athletes.

BOX 14 ■ SECTION SUMMARY

CONVERSION: Switch *S* and *P*, keep the same quality and quantity (exceptions: *A* and *O*)

	Convertend	Converse	Inference
A	All *S* are *P*	Some *P* are *S*	(Valid by limitation only)
E	No *S* are *P*	No *P* are *S*	VALID
I	Some *S* are *P*	Some *P* are *S*	VALID
O	Some *S* are not *P*		Not valid

OBVERSION: Change quality and add prefix 'non' to *P*

	Obvertend	Obverse	Inference
A	All *S* are *P*	No *S* are non-*P*	VALID
E	No *S* are *P*	All *S* are non-*P*	VALID
I	Some *S* are *P*	Some *S* are not non-*P*	VALID
O	Some *S* are not *P*	Some *S* are non-*P*	VALID

BOX 14 ■ Continued

CONTRAPOSITION: Switch *S* and *P* and add prefix 'non' to each (exceptions: *E* and *I*)

	Premise	Contrapositive	Inference
A	All *S* are *P*	All non-*P* are non-*S*	VALID
E	No *S* are *P*	Some non-*P* are not non-*S*	(Valid by limitation only)
I	Some *S* are *P*		Not valid
O	Some *S* are not *P*	Some non-*P* are not non-*S*	VALID

Exercises

XXI. Use each of the following categorical propositions as a premise in an inference by conversion, indicating when any such inference is not valid or has restrictions.

1. No accountants are spendthrifts.

   SAMPLE ANSWER: No accountants are spendthrifts.
   No spendthrifts are accountants.

2. All beagles are dogs.

*3. Some candidates are not incumbents.

4. Some trees are conifers.

*5. All amateurs are non-professionals.

6. Some contrabassoons are antiques.

*7. No quarks are molecules.

8. Some union workers are not clerks.

*9. All owls are nocturnal creatures.

10. No podiatrists are assassins.

XXII. Use each of the following categorical propositions as a premise in an inference by obversion.

1. Some octogenarians are regular voters.

   SAMPLE ANSWER: Some octogenarians are regular voters.
   Some octogenarians are not non-regular voters.

2. All streetcars are public conveyances.

*3. Some popular songs are hits.

4. All alloys are metals.

*5. Some psychotherapists are not Democrats.

6. Some robberies are violent crimes.

*7. All hexagons are plane figures.

8. No provosts are alligator wrestlers.

*9. Some Labrador retrievers are affectionate pets.

10. No office buildings are abstract objects.

XXIII. Use each of the following categorical propositions as a premise in an inference by contraposition, indicating when any such inference is not valid or has restrictions.

1. All infectious diseases are illnesses.

   SAMPLE ANSWER: All infectious diseases are illnesses.
   All non-illnesses are non-infectious diseases.

*2. Some used-car salesmen are not fast talkers.

3. No non-assassins are violent persons.

*4. Some citizens are non-voters.

5. Some ethicists are not non-vegetarians.

*6. No musicians are non–concert goers.

7. Some non-aligned nations are not non-signers of the recent UN agreement.

*8. Some police officers are cigar smokers.

9. All turkeys are native American wildfowls.

*10. Some pickup trucks are not non-expensive vehicles.

XXIV. For each of the following categorical propositions, give its valid converse, obverse, and contrapositive (when possible). Indicate any exceptions and inferences that are valid by limitation only.

1. Some non-angular figures are not non-circles.

   SAMPLE ANSWER:

   Converse; not valid.

   Obverse; some non-angular figures are circles.

   Contrapositive; some circles are not angular figures.

2. Some non-popular magazines are tabloids.

3. No UN members are non-polluters.

*4. All airports are non-crowded places.

5. Some non-surgeons are medical doctors.

6. All non-airplanes are non-flying objects.

*7. Some non-eagles are not non-friendly birds.

 8. No non-musicians are guitar players.

*9. No sanitation workers are non–city employees.

10. All non-blogs are non-sound sources of information.

XXV. YOUR OWN THINKING LAB

1. Explain the notions of conversion and contraposition by limitation by appealing to *logical equivalence* and *valid inference*. Support your explanation with examples.

*2. The following inferences are drawn by conversion, obversion, or contraposition. First, determine which is drawn by which, and whether each inference is valid. If not, could the inference be made valid? Explain.

 *A. Some students of the social sciences are not psychology majors. Therefore, some psychology majors are not students of the social sciences.

 *B. No movies starring Jennifer Lopez are non-suitable films for viewing by adults. Therefore, all movies starring Jennifer Lopez are suitable films for viewing by adults.

 C. All dolphins are whales. Therefore, all non-whales are non-dolphins.

 *D. Some tigers are non-Bengali felines. Therefore, some Bengali felines are non-tigers.

 E. Some government officials are not persons who have taken bribes. Therefore, some persons who have taken bribes are not government officials.

 F. All news reports are pieces of writing done with word processors. Therefore, some pieces of writing done with word processors are news reports.

 *G. No warmongers are pacifists. Therefore, no non-pacifists are non-warmongers.

*3. The following immediate inferences are drawn by one of the relations in the Traditional Square of Opposition, or by conversion, obversion, or contraposition. Determine which is drawn by which, and whether the inference is valid.

 A. Some non-pacifists are not non-conscientious objectors. Therefore, some conscientious objectors are not pacifists.

  SAMPLE ANSWER: Contraposition, valid.

 B. No animals that are avoided by letter carriers are lap dogs. Therefore, it is not the case that some animals that are avoided by letter carriers are lap dogs.

 *C. Some candidates for public office are not persons who are well known. Therefore, no candidates for public office are persons who are well known.

 D. All carpenters are non-union members. Therefore, no carpenters are union members.

 *E. Some hallucinations are not mirages. Therefore, some mirages are not hallucinations.

 F. No non-dangerous animals are creatures that are kept in zoos. Therefore, no non-creatures that are kept in zoos are dangerous animals.

*G. All astronauts are motorcycle riders. Therefore, it is not the case that no astronauts are motorcycle riders.

H. Some naval ships are submarines. Therefore, some naval ships are not submarines.

*I. All fanatics are political zealots. Therefore, no fanatics are non–political zealots.

J. All generals are non-amateurs. Therefore, all amateurs are non-generals.

■ Writing Project

Write a short paper in which you discuss five universal generalizations of pop culture that you find questionable. First, write these generalizations down as propositions of either type A or E, and then offer counterexamples to each of them.

■ Chapter Summary

Categorical proposition: proposition that's an instance of one of these forms:

1. All S are P (universal affirmative, type A)
2. No S are P (universal negative, type E)
3. Some S are P (particular affirmative, type I)
4. Some S are not P (particular negative, type O)

Venn diagrams for categorical propositions: graphic representations of the relationships between the subject and predicate terms of a categorical proposition. For universal propositions, shaded-out areas signify classes with no members. For particular propositions, an 'x' signifies where there is at least one member.

Immediate inference: a deductive argument with a single premise.

The Traditional Square of Opposition: visual outline of immediate inferences based on these relationships among categorical propositions:

1. *Contradiction.* It holds between A and O, and between E and I. Contradictory propositions cannot have the same truth value: if one is true, then the other must be false, and vice versa).

2. *Contrariety.* It holds between A and E. Contrary propositions cannot both be true at once, but can both be false.

3. *Subcontrariety.* It holds between I and O. Subcontrary propositions cannot both be false at once, but can both be true.

4. *Subalternation.* It holds between A and I, and between E and O.

   a. From A to I and E to O: if the superaltern is true, then its subaltern is true. If the superaltern is false, then its subaltern is undetermined.

   b. From I to A and O to E: if the subaltern is true, then its superaltern is undetermined. If the subaltern is false, then its superaltern is false.

The Modern Square of Opposition: the only valid immediate inferences by opposition are those based on contradiction. Since only particular propositions have existential import, inferences by contrariety, subcontrariety, and subalternation are not valid.

Other immediate inferences include:

CONVERSION. *S* and *P* switch. Valid for *E* and *I*, but not *A* and *O*, propositions.

	Convertend	Converse	Inference
A	All *S* are *P*	Some *P* are *S*	(Valid by limitation only)
E	No *S* are *P*	No *P* are *S*	VALID
I	Some *S* are *P*	Some *P* are *S*	VALID
O	Some *S* are not *P*		Not valid

OBVERSION. Quality changes, *P* takes prefix 'non.' Valid for *A*, *E*, *O* and *I* propositions.

	Obvertend	Obverse	
A	All *S* are *P*	No *S* are non-*P*	VALID
E	No *S* are *P*	All *S* are non-*P*	VALID
I	Some *S* are *P*	Some *S* are not non-*P*	VALID
O	Some *S* are not *P*	Some *S* are non-*P*	VALID

CONTRAPOSITION. *S* and *P* switch, each taking prefix 'non.' Valid for *A* and *O*, but not for *E* and *I* propositions.

	Premise	Contrapositive	
A	All *S* are *P*	All non-*P* are non-*S*	VALID
E	No *S* are *P*	Some non-*P* are not non-*S*	(Valid by limitation only)
I	Some *S* are *P*		Not valid
O	Some *S* are not *P*	Some non-*P* are not non-*S*	VALID

■ Key Words

Categorical proposition
Immediate inference
Existential import
Obversion
Conversion
Square of opposition
Illicit contraposition

Illicit conversion
Contraposition
Subcontrariety
Subalternation
Contradiction
Contrariety

Categorical Syllogisms

Here you'll read more about traditional logic. This chapter is entirely devoted to syllogistic arguments. It first explains what categorical syllogisms are and then examines two methods of checking them for validity. The topics include

- Recognizing categorical syllogisms.
- How to determine the form of a syllogism on the basis of its mood and figure.
- Testing syllogism forms for validity using Venn diagrams.
- Distribution of terms.
- Testing syllogism forms for validity using traditional logic's rules of validity.
- Some patterns of failed syllogism.

14.1 What Is a Categorical Syllogism?

Beginning in antiquity with Aristotelian logic, and continuing for many centuries in other schools of logic, a number of methods have been proposed for analyzing deductive arguments of the sort we have broadly called 'syllogistic.' A syllogism is a deductive argument with two premises. A categorical syllogism is a syllogism made up entirely of categorical propositions. Thus there are several different kinds of syllogistic argument, some of which were considered in Chapters 5 and 12. In this chapter, we'll look closely at categorical syllogisms, which, for our purposes here, we'll refer to simply as 'syllogisms.' For example,

1
1. All rectangles are polygons.
2. All squares are rectangles.
3. All squares are polygons.

Argument (1) is a syllogism, since it has two premises and a conclusion, all of which are categorical propositions. A closer look at (1)'s premises and conclusion reveals that it has exactly three terms in the position of subject or predicate: 'rectangle,' 'polygon,' and 'square.' Each of these denotes a category (or class) of things, and these categories are related in such a way that the argument's conclusion follows validly from its premises. According to that conclusion, the class of squares is wholly included in the class of polygons, which must be true provided that (1)'s premises are true. This is a valid deductive argument: its conclusion is entailed by its premises. But other syllogisms might be invalid. When a syllogism meets the deductive standard of validity, entailment hinges on relations among the terms of three different types that occur as subject or predicate of the categorical propositions that make up the syllogism. Since the validity of an argument depends on its having a valid form, several methods have been proposed for determining when syllogisms have such forms. But before turning to these, more needs to be said about the structure of standard syllogisms.

The Terms of a Syllogism

A standard syllogism consists of three categorical propositions, two of which function as premises and one as a conclusion. Each of these has a subject term and a predicate term denoting two classes of things, with the proposition as a whole representing a certain relation of exclusion or inclusion among the classes denoted by its subject and predicate terms. Our inspection of each of the categorical propositions making up (1) above showed that its component propositions feature subject and predicate terms of three different types: namely, 'polygon,' 'square,' and 'rectangle.' In fact, this is something all standard syllogisms have in common, since they all feature terms of three different types: the so-called major, minor, and middle terms. The major term is the predicate of the conclusion. The minor term is the subject of the conclusion, and the middle term is the term that occurs only in the premises. Consider (1) again,

1
1. All rectangles are polygons.
2. All squares are rectangles.
3. All squares are polygons.

By looking at the predicate and subject of (1)'s conclusion, we can identify this syllogism's major and minor terms respectively: 'polygons' (the conclusion's predicate) and 'squares' (its subject). Notice that each of these terms occurs also in the premises, but that does not bear on their status as major and minor terms, which is determined solely by their functions as predicate and subject of the conclusion. But in (1), there is also the term 'rectangles,' which occurs in the subject and predicate positions in the premises. It is the 'middle term,' so called because its function is to mediate between the two premises—to connect them, so that they're both talking about the same thing. In any syllogism, the middle term occurs in both premises but not in the conclusion. Another thing to notice is this: that although each of the three terms of argument (1) is a single word, this is not so in all syllogisms—since sometimes phrases can function as subject and predicate of a categorical proposition.

Let's now identify the major, minor, and middle terms in

2 1. No military officers are pacifists.
   2. All lieutenant colonels are military officers.
   3. No lieutenant colonels are pacifists.

By using the rule just suggested, we can determine that the major term here is 'pacifists,' the minor term 'lieutenant colonels,' and middle term 'military officers.'

BOX 1 ■ A SYLLOGISM'S TERMS

The important thing to keep in mind is that in order to identify the three words or phrases that are to count as the terms of a syllogism, we look first to the syllogism's conclusion. The major term is whatever word or phrase turns up in the predicate place (i.e., after the copula) in the conclusion. The minor term is whatever word or phrase turns up in the subject place (i.e., between the quantifier and the copula) in the conclusion. And the middle term is the term that does not occur in the conclusion at all but occurs in both premises—whether it be a single word, as in (1), or a more complex expression, as in (2).

The Premises of a Syllogism

The conclusion of (1) above is the proposition

> 3. All squares are polygons.

In the notation of traditional logic, this is symbolized as

> 3'. All S are P

It is common practice to represent the minor and major terms of a syllogism as 'S' and 'P' respectively, and its middle term as 'M.' We'll adopt that practice and represent any syllogism by replacing its three terms by those symbols, keeping logical words such as quantifiers and negation. In the case of (1) above, we thus obtain

1' 1 All *M* are *P*
   2 All *S* are *M*
   3 All *S* are *P*

In a standard syllogism, the minor and the major terms occur in different premises. That containing the major term is the 'major premise.' Since (1)'s major term is 'polygons,' its major premise is

> 1. All rectangles are polygons.

In symbols this becomes

> 1'. All *M* are *P*

The premise that contains the minor term is the minor premise. Since (1)'s minor term is 'squares,' its minor premise is

> 2. All squares are rectangles.

In symbols this becomes

> 2'. All *S* are *M*

You may have noticed that, in both examples of syllogism considered thus far, each has been arranged with its major premise first, its minor premise second, and its conclusion last. This is standard order for a reconstructed syllogism. Although in ordinary speech and writing a syllogism's premises and conclusion might be jumbled in any order whatsoever, when we reconstruct it, its premises must be put into standard order (this will become especially important later). We can now determine which premise is which in (1) above:

1' 1. All *M* are *P*   ↩   MAJOR PREMISE
   2. All *S* are *M*   ↩   MINOR PREMISE
   3. All *S* are *P*

Recognizing Syllogisms

However jumbled they may be in their real-life occurrences, syllogisms can be recognized by first identifying their conclusions. Once we've identified the conclusion of a putative syllogism, we can check whether it is indeed a syllogism: the conclusion's predicate gives us the major term, its subject the minor term. Once we've identified these terms, we can then look at the argument's premises and ask: Which premise contains the major term? (That's the major premise.) Which contains the minor term? (That's the minor premise.) After listing these in the standard order, as premises 1 and 2 respectively, and replacing its relevant terms

BOX 2 ■ CATEGORICAL SYLLOGISMS

To qualify as a categorical syllogism, an argument must have three categorical propositions and exactly three terms in the positions of subject or predicate, each occurring twice.

with symbols, we are in a position to determine whether the argument is a syllogism. How? By applying to it the rule in Box 2.

Consider the following argument:

3 All governors are public officials. Therefore, some public officials are governors.

(3) is not a syllogism, for it lacks the number of terms and premises needed to qualify. Compare

4 Since no salamanders are nocturnal animals, no salamanders are bats. For all bats are nocturnal animals.

Is (4) a syllogism? (4) consists of two sentences, and to qualify as a syllogism it must have, among other things, two premises and a conclusion. But a careful look at those two sentences reveals that they do actually express three categorical propositions. We must now determine which of them is the conclusion. Although there is no conclusion indicator here, some premise indicators, such as 'since' and 'for,' preceding the first and third propositions respectively, will help us to identify the argument's premises and thereby also its conclusion—which is

No salamanders are bats.

From this conclusion, we can see immediately that 'bats' (its predicate) is '*P*,' the major term, and 'salamanders' (its subject) is '*S*,' the minor term. This in turn enables us to identify the major premise, which is the one that contains the major term, 'bats':

All bats are nocturnal animals.

The minor premise is the one that contains the minor term, 'salamanders':

No salamanders are nocturnal animals.

Clearly, then, the middle term is 'nocturnal animals,' since it is the only term of the relevant kind that occurs in both premises. We can then reconstruct the argument in standard order:

4' 1. All bats are nocturnal animals.
2. No salamanders are nocturnal animals.
3. No salamanders are bats.

BOX 3 ■ THE BUILDING BLOCKS OF CATEGORICAL SYLLOGISMS

A categorical syllogism (or, simply, syllogism)

- Is made up of three categorical propositions.
- Has three terms, each of which occurs exactly twice in the argument.

The three terms of a syllogism are

NAME		LOGICAL FUNCTION	SYMBOL
Major term	⇨	Predicate of conclusion	P
Minor term	⇨	Subject of conclusion	S
Middle term	⇨	Occurs only in both premises	M

- The occurrence of the major and minor terms in the premises determines the names of the premises and their order.
- The two premises of a syllogism are

Major premise	⇨	(Listed first)
Minor premise	⇨	(Listed second)

When the minor term, major term, and middle term are replaced by 'S,' 'P,' and 'M,' as before, we find this pattern:

4" 1. All *P* are *M*
2. No *S* are *M*
3. No *S* are *P*

This is one among the many possible patterns of syllogisms. Some such patterns are valid, others invalid. Before we turn to some methods for determining which is which, let's have a closer look at argument patterns of this syllogistic sort.

14.2 Syllogistic Argument Forms

Traditionally, syllogisms are said to have forms, which are determined by their figures and moods. We'll consider these one at a time, beginning with figure.

Figure

Since a syllogism has three terms (major, minor, and middle), each of which occurs twice in either subject or predicate position, there are the four possible "figures" or configurations of these terms for any such argument:

1st Figure	2nd Figure	3rd Figure	4th Figure
M P	*P M*	*M P*	*P M*
S M	*S M*	*M S*	*M S*
S P	*S P*	*S P*	*S P*

Each of these represents a syllogism's premises and conclusion in standard order without quantifiers and copulas. The only feature that differs substantially among them is the arrangement of the two occurrences of the middle term in the premises. So it's the configuration of the middle term in the premises that determines for any syllogism what its figure is. We can emphasize that by representing the position of this term alone in each figure:

1st Figure	2nd Figure	3rd Figure	4th Figure
M	M	M	
	M	M	M
M	M	M	M

Thus it will be a simple matter to identify the figure of any syllogism: once we have identified its middle term, we note whether it occurs in the subject or predicate place accordingly, and then check which figure that amounts to. In this way, we can determine that arguments (1) and (2) are in the first figure and (4), in the second figure. Using this method, we can determine the figure of any proposed syllogism.

Consider this one:

5 Because some sharks are saltwater fish and no animals that can survive in a river are saltwater fish, some sharks are not animals that can survive in a river.

First, we identify the conclusion of the argument—namely,

> Some sharks are not animals that can survive in a river.

Since we now know that 'sharks' is the minor term and 'animals that can survive in a river' the major, we can proceed to identify this syllogism's minor and major premises and reconstruct it as follows:

5' 1. No animals that can survive in a river are saltwater fish.
    2. Some sharks are saltwater fish.
    _____
    3. Some sharks are not animals that can survive in a river.

By replacing the relevant terms with the symbols used above, (5')'s argument form is revealed as

5" 1. No P are M
    2. Some S are M
    _____
    3. Some S are not P

Disregarding the quantifiers and copulas, we note the location of the middle term in each of the premises and can easily determine that the syllogism is in the second figure.

Mood

What about mood? As we've seen, a syllogism is made up of three categorical propositions: two make up its premises and one its conclusion. And any categorical proposition must be one or

BOX 4 ■ HOW TO DETERMINE A SYLLOGISM'S FIGURE

- Focus only on the occurrences of the middle term in the premises as either a subject or a predicate.
- The conclusion always has the minor term as its subject and the major term as its predicate. The predicate and subject of the conclusion determine what are to count as the major and minor terms in any syllogism.
- 'P' stands for the major term and occurs in premise 1, which is the major premise (i.e., the premise containing the major term).
- 'S' stands for the minor term and occurs in premise 2, which is the minor premise (i.e., the premise containing the minor term).

the other of four types: universal affirmative, universal negative, particular affirmative, or particular negative—whose names (as we saw in Chapter 13) are, respectively, A, E, I, and O.

> The mood of a syllogism consists in a list of the names of its three component propositions.

In (5") above, the major premise is type E, the minor premise is I, and the conclusion is O; thus its mood is EIO. In the other examples above, the mood is (1) AAA, (2) EAE, and (4) AEE. Now consider this argument form:

6   1. Some P are M
   2. Some M are S
   3. Some S are not P

In (6), both premises are type I, and the conclusion is type O. Hence, (6)'s mood is IIO (and its figure, the fourth). How about this one?

7   1. No P are M
   2. No S are M
   3. Some S are P

Since (7)'s premises are both type E and its conclusion type I, its mood is EEI. At the same time, given the position of (7)'s middle term, the argument form exemplifies the second figure.

Determining a Syllogism's Form

So (7)'s mood and figure together are EEI-2. Since the mood and figure of a syllogism constitute its form, we may equivalently say that (7)'s form is EEI-2.—as (6)'s form is IIO-4, and so on. The form of a syllogism, then, is given by the combination of its mood and figure.

In traditional logic, determining the forms of syllogisms was crucial to establishing their validity, for it is the form that can reveal whether a syllogism follows or flouts certain rules of validity that we'll consider later. Before we do that, however, let's review the steps described so far.

mood + figure = form

Let's try the whole process of finding a syllogism's form, starting at the beginning. Consider this argument:

8   No campus residence halls without wi-fi are good places to live. After all, some campus residence halls without wi-fi are old buildings, but some old buildings are not good places to live.

Argument (8)'s conclusion is

> No campus residence halls without wi-fi are good places to live.

How do we know? Because we have read the argument carefully and asked ourselves: What claim is being made? (In addition, the premises are introduced by an indicator, 'after all'). Having found the conclusion, we then look for its predicate and subject, which are the major and minor terms, respectively:

> *P* = 'good places to live'
> *S* = 'campus residence halls without wi-fi'

We can now identify the syllogism's major and minor premises. Since the major premise must contain the major term, it must be

> Some old buildings are not good places to live.

We can therefore put this as the first premise. Similarly, the minor premise must contain the minor term, so it must be

> Some campus residence halls without wi-fi are old buildings.

That is the second premise. Thus the reconstructed syllogism is

9   1. Some old buildings are not good places to live.
     2. Some campus residence halls without wi-fi are old buildings.
     3. No campus residence halls without wi-fi are good places to live.

Argument (9) illustrates a pattern that may be represented as

9'   1. Some *M* are not *P*
     2. Some *S* are *M*
     3. No *S* are *P*

Any syllogism illustrating this pattern would be of the form OIE-1. For example,

10   1. Some CIA operatives are not FBI agents.
     2. Some women are CIA operatives.
     3. No women are FBI agents.

Now something has gone wrong with (10) and any other syllogism along the same pattern—that of (9') above. Clearly, any such syllogism may have true premises and a false conclusion. Next we'll consider which syllogistic patterns are valid and which are not.

Exercises

I. Review Questions

1. What is generally understood by 'syllogism' and 'categorical syllogism'?
2. How do we identify the major term, minor term, and middle term of a syllogism?
3. What is meant by 'major premise'?
4. What is meant by 'minor premise'?
5. When is a syllogism in standard order?
6. How do we identify the mood of a syllogism?
7. How do we identify the figure of a syllogism?
8. How do we determine the form of a syllogism?

II. For each of the following arguments, determine whether it is a syllogism. If it isn't, indicate why, and move on to the next argument. If it is, put the syllogism into standard order, and replace its major, minor, and middle terms with the appropriate symbol 'P,' 'S,' or 'M.'

1. Some dinosaurs are not members of the reptile family. For no members of the reptile family are mammals and some dinosaurs are mammals.

   SAMPLE ANSWER:

1. No members of the reptile family are mammals.	1. No P are M
2 Some dinosaurs are mammals.	2. Some S are M
3 Some dinosaurs are not members of the reptile family.	3. Some S are not P

2. Some Japanese car manufacturers make fuel-efficient cars, but no fuel-efficient cars are pickup trucks. Since all pickup trucks are expensive vehicles, therefore no Japanese car manufacturers make expensive vehicles.

*3. All North American rivers are navigable. It follows that no North American rivers are non-navigable.

4. Some summer tourists are mountain climbers. For some risk takers are summer tourists and all mountain climbers are risk takers.

*5. No Sinatra songs are popular with first graders, since all Sinatra songs are romantic songs and no romantic songs are popular with first graders.

*6. Some men are Oscar winners but no Oscar winners are talk-show hosts. Thus some men are not talk-show hosts.

7. Some persons knowledgeable about heart disease are not members of the American Heart Association. For one thing, although some cardiologists are members of the American Heart Association, some aren't. In addition, all cardiologists are persons knowledgeable about heart disease.

8. No eye doctors are optometrists but some eye doctors are professionals with MD degrees. It follows that some professionals with MD degrees are not optometrists.

*9. All metals are substances that expand under heat. Therefore, it is not the case that some metals are not substances that expand under heat.

10. No conservatives are supporters of gay marriage. Hence, some supporters of gay marriage are persons who favor abortion rights, since no conservatives are persons who favor abortion rights.

*11. All computer scientists are programmers, and some programmers are pool players. It follows that some computer scientists are pool players.

12. No movie reviewers are mathematicians. Since all mathematicians are experts in geometry and some mathematicians are experts in geometry, it follows that no movie reviewers are experts in geometry.

III. For each of the following syllogistic forms, identify its mood and figure.

1. 1. Some *M* are *P*
   2. Some *M* are *S*
   3. Some *S* are not *P*

   SAMPLE ANSWER: IIO-3

2. 1. No *M* are *P*
   2. No *S* are *M*
   3. No *S* are *P*

3. 1. Some *P* are not *M*
   2. Some *S* are not *M*
   3. All *S* are *P*

*4. 1. All *M* are *P*
   2. Some *S* are *M*
   3. All *S* are *P*

5. 1. Some *P* are *M*
   2. Some *S* are *M*
   3. Some *S* are *P*

*6. 1. No *P* are *M*
   2. All *M* are *S*
   3. All *S* are *P*

7. 1. Some *M* are *P*
   2. All *M* are *S*
   3. No *S* are *P*

*8. 1. Some *M* are not *P*
   2. Some *S* are not *M*
   3. No *S* are *P*

9. 1. Some *P* are *M*
   2. All *S* are *M*
   3. All *S* are *P*

*10. 1. Some *M* are not *P*
   2. Some *S* are *M*
   3. Some *S* are *P*

11. **1.** Some *P* are not *M*
    2. Some *M* are not *S*
    3. Some *S* are *P*

*12. **1.** No *M* are *P*
    2. No *M* are *S*
    3. All *S* are *P*

IV. Reconstruct each of the following syllogisms and give its form:

1. Since all Italian sports cars are fast cars, it follows that no fast cars are inexpensive machines, because no inexpensive machines are Italian sports cars.

   SAMPLE ANSWER: EAE-4

1. No inexpensive machines are Italian sports cars.	1. No *P* are *M*
2. All Italian sports cars are fast cars.	2. All *M* are *S*
3. No fast cars are inexpensive machines.	3. No *S* are *P*

2. Because no airlines that fly to Uzbekistan are airlines that offer discount fares, some airlines that offer discount fares are carriers that are not known for their safety records. For some carriers that are not known for their safety records are airlines that fly to Uzbekistan.

*3. Since some residents of California are people who are not Lawrence Welk fans, and all people who listen to reggae music are people who are not Lawrence Welk fans, we may infer that some residents of California are people who listen to reggae music.

4. No members of the Committee for Freedom are people who admire dictators. For all members of the Committee for Freedom are libertarians, and no libertarians are people who admire dictators.

*5. All loyal Americans are people who are willing taxpayers. Hence, all people who are willing taxpayers are supporters of the president in his desire to trim the federal budget, for all loyal Americans are supporters of the president in his desire to trim the federal budget.

6. All Rottweilers that are easily annoyed are animals that are avoided by letter carriers; for some lap dogs are not Rottweilers that are easily annoyed, but no animals that are avoided by letter carriers are lap dogs.

*7. No reptiles weighing over eighty pounds are animals that are convenient house pets. After all, all animals that are convenient house pets are creatures your Aunt Sophie would like, but no creatures your Aunt Sophie would like are reptiles weighing over eighty pounds.

8. Since some senators are people who will not take bribes, and all people who will not take bribes are honest people, it follows that some senators are honest people.

*9. No explosives are safe things to carry in the trunk of your car. For some explosives are devices that contain dynamite, and some devices that contain dynamite are not safe things to carry in the trunk of your car.

10. No chiropractors are surgeons. Hence, some chiropractors are not persons who are licensed to perform a coronary bypass, since some persons who are licensed to perform a coronary bypass are surgeons.

*11. No pacifists are persons who favor the use of military force. Hence, some persons who favor the use of military force are not conscientious objectors, for some pacifists are not conscientious objectors.

12. Some rhinos are not dangerous animals, because all dangerous animals are creatures that are kept in zoos, and some rhinos are not creatures that are kept in zoos.

1. For each of the following syllogistic forms, provide a syllogism that is an instance of it:

1 AAA-1

2 AEE-2

3 OAO-3

4 EIO-4

5 AII-3

6 EAE-1

7 EAE-2

8 AEE-4

9 IAI-3

10 IAI-4

2. All of the above syllogistic forms are valid. What do you now know about the conclusion of a syllogism that exemplifies any of them? And what would you know about any such syllogism if its premises were in fact true?

14.3 Testing for Validity with Venn Diagrams

Syllogisms can have configurations that make up 256 different forms. Since some of these are valid and some are not, it is essential that there be some dependable way of determining, for any given syllogistic form, whether it is valid. In fact, there are several different ways of doing this, but we shall focus here on one very widely accepted technique, based on Venn diagrams, the rudiments of which we examined in Chapter 13.

How to Diagram a Standard Syllogism

In using Venn diagrams to check the validity of syllogisms, we adapt that system of two-circle diagrams for categorical propositions to a larger diagram with three interlocking circles.

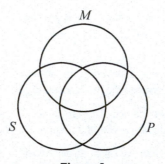

Figure 1

Here the circles represent the three distinct classes of things denoted by the three terms of a syllogism. The two bottom circles, labeled *S* and *P*, represent the classes denoted by the syllogism's minor and major terms.

BOX 5 ■ VALIDITY AND VENN DIAGRAMS

Any syllogism could be tested for validity by means of a Venn diagram, which would begin with three intersecting circles as in Figure 1. Once the Venn diagram is completed, it shows whether the syllogism is valid or invalid.

The top circle, labeled '*M*,' represents the class denoted by the syllogism's middle term. Now notice another thing about this diagram: we can find within it subclass spaces of two important shapes that will be crucial to our diagrams. We've already encountered these in the two-circle diagrams discussed in the last chapter. They are the American football shape (Figure 2) and the crescent (Figure 3):

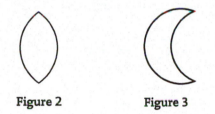

Figure 2   **Figure 3**

On the three-circle Venn diagram, the football shape can be found in three places. Can you see where? The crescent can be found in six places. Can you locate these? For the purpose of putting shading or xs on the three-circle Venn diagram, the only subclass spaces we'll be concerned with are those in the shape of either a football or a crescent. If you try to shade or put an x in any other shape, you'll not be using the Venn system.

Finally, notice that on the three-circle diagram, there are three different ways of grouping the circles together into pairs.

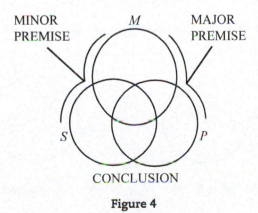

Figure 4

These three groupings mark the areas where each of a syllogism's three propositions are represented: *M* and *P* are used to diagram its major premise, *M* and *S* its minor premise, and *S* and *P* its conclusion. Again, the purpose of drawing this sort of three-circle Venn diagram is to test the validity of a syllogism. But the test requires that we diagram propositions across two circles at a time, using what we have learned in Chapter 13 about Venn diagrams for each of the four types of categorical proposition. To do this, we take into account, one at a time, pairs of circles representing the major premise, minor premise, and the conclusion, in each case ignoring the circle that is irrelevant to the task at hand. To see how this works, let's test a syllogism.

11 1. No poets are cynics.
2. All police detectives are poets.
3. No police detectives are cynics.

A quick look reveals that this syllogism is already in standard order, so the first step in argument analysis has been done. We can then see that the major term is 'cynics,' the minor term 'police detectives,' and the middle term 'poets'—so that the argument is an instance of the form EAE-1, which we could spell out in this standard way:

11' 1. No *M* are *P*
2. All *S* are *M*
3. No *S* are *P*

Now, are syllogisms of this form valid or invalid? A Venn diagram can test this. The first rule to follow in implementing this test is:

Diagram only the syllogism's premises. Do not try to diagram the conclusion.

So we are concerned at this stage only with two sets of two circles each. One set will be used to represent the major premise (Figure 5), the other to represent the minor premise (Figure 6):

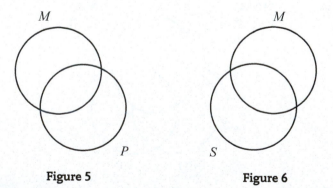

M *P*

Figure 5

M *S*

Figure 6

Now, which premise shall we diagram first? Here the rule, whose rationale will soon become apparent, is

If one premise is universal and the other particular, you must diagram the universal premise first, whichever it is. But if both premises are universal, or both particular, it doesn't matter which is diagrammed first.

In (11')'s case, both premises are universal, so it's a matter of indifference which one we choose to diagram first. Let's arbitrarily choose the major premise, an E proposition of the form 'No *S* are *P*' that we earlier learned to diagram this way:

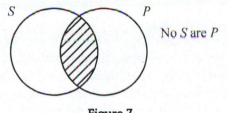

No *S* are *P*

Figure 7

When drawn directly on the pair of circles in the larger diagram, the diagram looks like this:

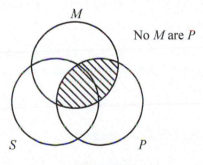

No *M* are *P*

Figure 8

So much for the major premise. Now what about the minor? In (11') the minor premise is an A proposition, and the two-circle Venn diagram that represents it, you'll recall, is

All *S* are *P*

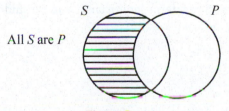

Figure 9

If we represent the minor premise in this way, the larger diagram will then look like this:

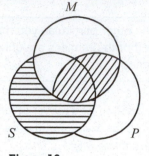

Figure 10

Here we have both premises in the diagram: at this point, the diagram is complete. We'll put no more marks on it. Now for the final step: We simply ignore the circle for the middle term altogether and look at the circles representing the syllogism's conclusion, asking ourselves, do we have there a two-circle Venn diagram symbolizing the type of categorical proposition exemplified by the argument's conclusion? If yes, then the diagram shows its form to be valid. If no, then the diagram shows it to be invalid. Since the conclusion in (11') is 'No S are P,' and that is an E proposition, whose diagram is the same as in Figure 7 above; and since a glance at Figure 10 reveals that the football-shaped space where S and P overlap has indeed gotten shaded out, the diagram proves (11')'s form, EAE-1, to be valid. This means, then, that any syllogism whatsoever having that form will also be valid. The principle here is simple:

If in diagramming both premises of a syllogism, we've *automatically* diagrammed its conclusion, the argument is valid. Any time this fails to happen, the syllogism is invalid.

Now let's test another syllogism with a Venn diagram:

12 1. Some conservatives are public figures.
2. All politicians are public figures.
3. Some politicians are conservatives.

Here again we find a syllogism that is already in standard order, so that the first step in the analysis has been done. With the argument arranged in this order, it's then clear that its major term is 'conservatives,' its minor term 'politicians,' and its middle term 'public figures.' Argument (12)'s pattern is

12' 1. Some P are M
2. All S are M
3. Some S are P

This pattern is IAI-2. To check the validity of a syllogism with this pattern, we'll construct a Venn diagram. Recall that only the premises are diagrammed (not the conclusion), and notice that, in this argument, the order in which the premises are diagrammed does matter. That's because, here, one premise is universal and the other particular. The universal premise must be diagrammed first and the particular second. For this syllogism, then, we have no choice but to diagram the minor premise first and the major premise second. The minor premise is an A proposition represented in the Venn diagram in this way:

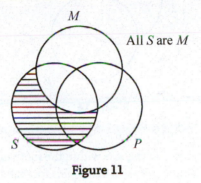

All S are M

Figure 11

Next we add to the diagram the syllogism's major premise, an I proposition that, once incorporated in the diagram, makes it look like this:

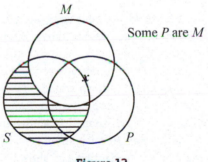

Some P are M

Figure 12

Recall that the Venn diagram for any I proposition is

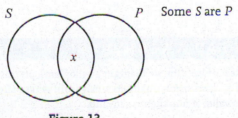

Some S are P

Figure 13

Similarly, the diagram of the major premise in the syllogistic form we are representing now, is

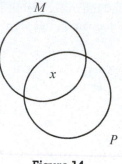

Figure 14

But why does the 'x' in Figure 12 fall on the line within the football-shaped space where M and P intersect? Clearly, if we're going to put an 'x' inside this football to indicate that at least some M are P, we have to decide which side of the line in that space the 'x' goes on. Had one or the other half of the football been shaded, the 'x' would have gone in the unshaded part. But here there's no shading, so we have no justification for choosing one side of the line over the other—all we know is that the 'x' goes somewhere inside the football, and we express this non-committal position by putting the 'x' on the line dividing the football-shaped space ('xs' don't always go on lines like this, but here it does).

Now let's look at Figure 12 and see what it tells us about the validity or invalidity of the form IAI-2, which is that of syllogisms such as (12) above. Because the conclusion of this argument is 'Some S are P,' the form will be shown valid only if the process of diagramming the two premises as we've described has automatically produced a correct diagram for that conclusion. Since that is an I proposition, the form would be valid only if the pair of circles representing the conclusion shows an 'x' in the space where S and P overlap. But in fact we do not find that at all. In Figure 12, the football-shaped space where S and P overlap is partly shaded, and there is an 'x' on its outer edge. Because there is no 'x' clearly inside this football, however, we must conclude that the Venn diagram has shown IAI-2 to be an invalid form. Here the process of diagramming the two premises failed to produce automatically a diagram for the conclusion in the bottom pair of circles. Thus IAI-2 is invalid, and argument (12), which has this form, is an invalid syllogism. We've proved that, whatever the truth values of its component propositions (in this case, they're all true), its conclusion does not follow validly from its premises.

BOX 6 ■ HOW TO READ A VENN DIAGRAM'S RESULT

In using a Venn diagram as a test of validity, we diagram a syllogism's premises first and then check whether we can read off its conclusion unambiguously from what's already in the diagram. If we can, then the syllogism is valid. If not, then it's invalid.

Finally, let's use a Venn diagram to test the validity of syllogisms of the form OIE-1. For example, (9) above, whose form we spelled out as

9' 1. Some *M* are not *P*
  2. Some *S* are *M*
  3. No *S* are *P*

Because both premises are particular, it doesn't matter which one is diagrammed first. We choose to diagram the minor premise first, which we represent in this way:

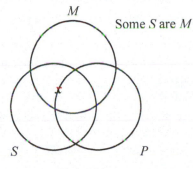

Some *S* are *M*

Figure 15

On the larger diagram, the diagram for that premise looks like this:

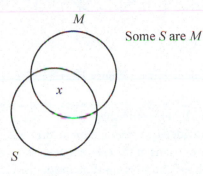

Some *S* are *M*

Figure 16

The diagram for the major premise shows an 'x' in the part of M that is outside of P.

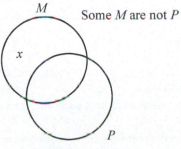

Some *M* are not *P*

Figure 17

When we represent that premise in the three-circle diagram, we get this:

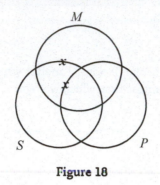

Figure 18

Why? Because in Figure 18, the crescent-shaped space where the 'x' goes in representing "Some M are not P" is itself divided by a line, and on neither side of it do we find shading. Had one or the other of these two portions of the crescent been shaded out, the 'x' would have gone in the other part. But here, there's no shading at all inside the crescent; therefore, if we are to put an 'x' inside it, we have no choice but to put the 'x' on the line dividing the crescent—to indicate that we're non-committal about precisely which side of the line it goes on. Given that the crescent, "M that are non-P," is divided by a line, it is simply not decidable on which side of it the 'x' goes.

Now we're finished with the diagramming and ready to check for validity. We compare the conclusion of the argument with the part of the diagram that represents it. Do they match up? Clearly, in this case they do not. For the conclusion of the argument is the *E* proposition 'No S are *P*.' A correct Venn diagram for any such proposition shows the intersection between S and P shaded out (see Figure 7 above). But that is not what Figure 18 represents. So here's an instance where the process of diagramming the premises did not automatically produce in the bottom pair of circles a diagram that represents the conclusion as given. Thus the Venn diagram proves the form OIE-1 to be invalid. We conclude that argument (9) is invalid.

BOX 7 ■ SECTION SUMMARY

How to test the validity of a syllogism with a Venn diagram:

- Draw three intersecting circles.
- Diagram only the premises.
  - If one premise is universal and the other particular, you must diagram the universal premise first, whichever it is.
  - But if both premises are universal or both particular, then it doesn't matter which is diagrammed first.
- Once you have diagrammed the premises, if the conclusion is already unequivocally diagrammed too, the argument is valid. Otherwise, the argument is invalid.

Exercises

VI. Review Questions

1. In using a Venn diagram to represent an argument form, what are the only two shapes in which shading or an 'x' can go?
2. In a three-circle Venn diagram, what is represented by each of the circles?
3. Which part of a Venn diagram represents the major premise of a syllogism?
4. Which part of a Venn diagram represents the minor premise of a syllogism?
5. In diagramming a syllogism with a Venn diagram, which premise is diagrammed first?
6. How do we tell, using a Venn diagram, whether a syllogism is valid or not?

VII. Reconstruct each of the following syllogisms, identify its form, and test it for validity with a Venn diagram.

1. Since all logicians are philosophers, and some philosophers are not vegetarians, it follows that some logicians are not vegetarians.

   SAMPLE ANSWER: 1 Some philosophers are not vegetarians.
   2 All logicians are philosophers.
   _____
   3 Some logicians are not vegetarians.

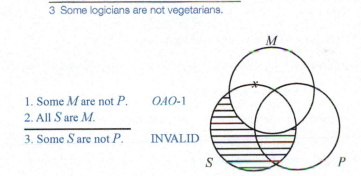

   1. Some *M* are not *P*.   *OAO*-1
   2. All *S* are *M*.
   _____
   3. Some *S* are not *P*.   INVALID

2. No dictators are humanitarians, because no tyrants are humanitarians, and some dictators are tyrants.

3. Some medical conditions that are not treatable by conventional means are causes of death. Hence, some causes of death are not things related to eating pizza, for no medical conditions that are not treatable by conventional means are things related to eating pizza.

*4. Some taxi drivers are people who never run red lights, because all taxi drivers are people who are not elitists, and some people who never run red lights are people who are not elitists.

5. Some economists who are members of the faculty at the University of Chicago are not monetarists; therefore, no monetarists are White Sox fans, for all economists who are members of the faculty at the University of Chicago are White Sox fans.

6. Since all readers of poetry are benevolent people, it follows that no fanatics are benevolent people, for no fanatics are readers of poetry.

*7. No armadillos are intelligent creatures, for all intelligent creatures are things that will stay out of the middle of the highway, but no armadillos are things that will stay out of the middle of the highway.

8. No newspaper columnists are motorcycle racers; however, some motorcycle racers are attorneys. Therefore, some attorneys are not newspaper columnists.

9. Some candidates for public office are not persons who are well known. After all, some citizens who are listed on the ballot are not persons who are well known, and all citizens who are listed on the ballot are candidates for public office.

*10. Because some axolotls are creatures that are not often seen in the city, we may infer that some mud lizards that are found in the jungles of southern Mexico are creatures that are not often seen in the city, since all axolotls are mud lizards that are found in the jungles of southern Mexico.

11. Since some members of Congress are not senators, it follows that some members of Congress are not experienced politicians, for all senators are experienced politicians.

12. Some historical developments are not entirely explainable. After all, all historical developments are contingent things, and no contingent things are entirely explainable.

*13. All orthodontists are dentists who have done extensive post-doctoral study, but no impoverished persons are dentists who have done extensive post-doctoral study. Thus no orthodontists are impoverished persons.

14. All people who ride bicycles in rush-hour traffic are courageous people, for some courageous people are professors who are not tenured members of the faculty, and no professors who are not tenured members of the faculty are people who ride bicycles in rush-hour traffic.

15. Some investment brokers are not Harvard graduates. So some financiers are not investment brokers, since some financiers are not Harvard graduates.

*16. All philosophy majors are rational beings, but no parakeets are rational beings. Therefore, no parakeets are philosophy majors.

17. Since some wars are inevitable occurrences, and no inevitable occurrences are things that can be prevented, it follows that some wars are not things that can be prevented.

18. All factory workers are union members, for some union members are not persons who are easy to convince, and some factory workers are not persons who are easy to convince.

*19. Since no hallucinations are optical illusions, we may infer that some misunderstandings that are not avoidable are optical illusions, for some misunderstandings that are not avoidable are hallucinations.

20. Some senators who are not opponents of foreign aid are friends of the president. But all friends of the president are influential people who are well informed about world events; hence, some senators who are not opponents of foreign aid are influential people who are well informed about world events.

21. Some fantastic creatures that are not found anywhere in nature are not dogfish. So we may infer that no dogfish are fish that bark, since some fantastic creatures that are not found anywhere in nature are fish that bark.

*22. Some college presidents are not benevolent despots, for no benevolent despots are defenders of faculty autonomy, and no defenders of faculty autonomy are college presidents.

23. Since some elderly professors who are not bald are respected scholars, it follows that some classical philologists are respected scholars. For no elderly professors who are not bald are classical philologists.

24. Some people who have quit smoking are people who are not enthusiastic sports fans, but no soccer players are people who are not enthusiastic sports fans. So some people who have quit smoking are soccer players.

*25. All philanderers are habitual prevaricators. Therefore, no preachers who are well-known television personalities are philanderers, because no habitual prevaricators are preachers who are well-known television personalities.

26. Some pinchpennies are not alumni who are immensely wealthy. For no pinchpennies are generous contributors to their alma mater, and some alumni who are immensely wealthy are generous contributors to their alma mater.

27. All persons employed by the state government are civil servants, for no persons employed by the state government are persons who are eligible to participate in the state lottery, and no civil servants are persons who are eligible to participate in the state lottery.

*28. Since all great music is uplifting, it follows that some jazz is great music, for some jazz is uplifting.

29. No Muscovites are country bumpkins, but some Russians who are veterans of World War II are not Muscovites. Hence, some country bumpkins are not Russians who are veterans of World War II.

*30. Some interest-bearing bank accounts are not an effective means of increasing one's wealth. After all, some investments that are insured by the federal government are not an effective means of increasing one's wealth, and all investments that are insured by the federal government are interest-bearing bank accounts.

VIII. YOUR OWN THINKING LAB

1. It is sometimes said that the conclusion of a valid syllogism is already contained in its premises. How could this be explained in connection with Venn diagrams for testing the validity of syllogisms?

2. For each form represented below, give two syllogisms of your own:

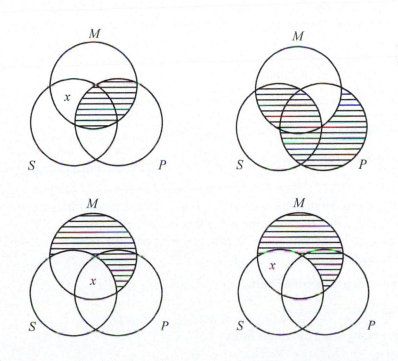

14.4 Distribution of Terms

Although Venn Diagrams provide a reliable way of checking syllogistic forms for validity, they are not the only way of doing so. Another method relies on a short list of rules of validity that any indisputably valid syllogism must follow and a list of fallacies that any such syllogism necessarily avoids. We'll devote the remainder of this chapter to a look at some details of this technique, which is based on one of the traditional parts of Aristotelian logic, To use this method, it's first necessary to understand the notion of distribution of terms.

Earlier, we saw that one use of the word 'term' is to refer to the substantive parts of a categorical proposition: its subject and predicate are its terms. To describe a term as 'distributed' is to say that it's referring to an entire class. In a proposition that is universal affirmative, the pattern of distribution is:

A proposition = subject distributed, predicate undistributed

Thus in

13 All oranges are citrus fruits,

the subject term, 'oranges,' is distributed, since, preceded by 'all,' it's plainly referring to the whole class of oranges. But its predicate term, 'citrus fruits,' is not distributed, since no universal claim of any kind is being made here about all members of the class of things to which it refers—namely, citrus fruits.

In a proposition that is universal negative, the pattern of distribution is

---
E proposition: subject distributed, predicate distributed.

Consider

14 No apples are citrus fruits,

which is true, and, as we saw in Chapter 13, logically equivalent to

14' No citrus fruits are apples.

Either way, these propositions deny of the whole class of apples that it includes citrus fruits, and of the whole class of citrus fruits that it includes apples. Put a different way, (14) is asserting that there is total, mutual exclusion between the whole classes of apples and citrus fruits. So it's clear that in (14) both the subject term and the predicate term are distributed. Here something is being said about entire classes (namely, that they exclude each other).

Let's now turn to the patterns of distribution for particular propositions, which include particular affirmatives such as

15 Some oranges are edible fruits,

and particular negatives, such as

16 Some oranges are not edible fruits.

The pattern of distribution for any particular affirmative proposition is

> *I* proposition: subject undistributed, predicate undistributed

and for any particular negative proposition it is

> *O* proposition: subject undistributed, predicate distributed

(15) amounts to the proposition that there is at least one orange that is an edible fruit. This proposition's subject is undistributed because this term doesn't refer to the whole class of oranges, but only to 'some' of them. Similarly, its predicate term, 'edible fruits,' is equally undistributed, since this term doesn't refer to the whole class of edible fruits but only to those edible fruits that are oranges.

Finally, although the subject of (16) is not distributed for the reasons just provided for the subject of (15), its predicate term is. Why? Because it refers to the class of edible fruits as a whole, which becomes plain when (16) is recast as the proposition that there is at least one orange that is not in the class (taken as a whole) of edible fruits. (16) says that the *entire class* of edible fruits excludes at least one orange

To sum up, the four patterns of distribution are as follows:

A (universal affirmative)	All *S* are *P*	Subject distributed, predicate not
E (universal negative)	No *S* are *P*	Both terms distributed
I (particular affirmative)	Some *S* are *P*	Neither term distributed
O (particular negative)	Some *S* are not *P*	Predicate distributed, subject not

Keeping in mind the pattern of distribution outlined here (and also below) will make it easier for you to use the rules of validity to determine whether syllogistic argument forms are valid or invalid.

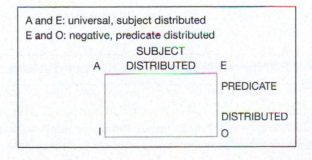

A and E: universal, subject distributed
E and O: negative, predicate distributed
SUBJECT
A   DISTRIBUTED   E
PREDICATE
DISTRIBUTED
I   O

14.5 Rules of Validity and Syllogistic Fallacies

Here we'll consider six rules that can be put at the service of testing the validity of any given categorical syllogism.

BOX 8 ■ DETERMINING VALIDITY WITH THE SIX RULES

- Any syllogism that obeys all six rules is valid.
- Any syllogism that breaks even one rule is invalid—though some syllogisms may break more than one.

We'll also look at the fallacies that are committed when these rules are broken. First proposed in Aristotelian logic, rules along the lines we'll discuss here represent an alternative to Venn diagrams as a procedure for determining the validity of syllogisms. Let's consider each of these rules one at a time, together with its rationale.

> **RULE 1: A syllogism must have exactly three terms.**

The conclusion of a syllogism is a categorical proposition where two terms are related in a certain way. But they could be so related only if there is a third term to which the subject and predicate of the conclusion are each independently related. That is, for a syllogism's conclusion to follow validly from its two premises, there must be precisely three terms, no more and no fewer, each occurring twice: the major term as the predicate of the conclusion and as either the subject or predicate of the major premise; the minor term as the subject of the conclusion and as either the subject or predicate of the minor premise; and the middle term once in each of the premises, where it may appear as either subject or predicate.

Syllogisms sometimes flout this rule of validity by having some term used with two different meanings in its two occurrences, so that the argument equivocates (see Chapter 9). Any such argument is said to commit the *fallacy of four terms* (or *Quaternio Terminorum*). For example, consider

17 1. All the members of that committee are snakes.
    2. All snakes are reptiles.
    _____
    3. All members of that committee are reptiles.

Here the term 'snakes' is plainly used with two different meanings. As a result, the syllogism commits the *fallacy of four terms* and is therefore invalid.

> **RULE 2: The middle term must be distributed at least once.**

A syllogism's middle term, you'll recall, is the term that occurs in both premises (and only in the premises). It functions to connect the minor and major terms, so that the relation among these could be as presented in the syllogism's conclusion. But the middle term can do that only if it's referring to a whole class in at least one of the premises, for if it refers to one class or part of a class in the major premise and another in the minor, then the minor and major terms would be connected to things that have nothing in common. As a result, the relation among these terms would not be as presented in the syllogism's conclusion. Any such syllogism commits the *fallacy of undistributed middle* and is invalid—as, for example, is this argument:

18   1. All feral pigeons are birds with feathers.
    2. Some birds with feathers are animals that distract attackers.
    3. Some animals that distract attackers are feral pigeons.

> **RULE 3:** If any term is distributed in the conclusion, it must be distributed also in the premise in which it occurs.

Recall that the mark of validity for an argument is that its conclusion must follow necessarily from its premises. But no argument can be valid in that sense if its conclusion says more than what is already said in the premises. Syllogisms, which are deductive arguments, fail to be valid when their conclusions go beyond what is supported by their premises. That is the case of a syllogism whose minor or major term is distributed in the conclusion (thus referring there to a whole class) but not in the premise in which it also occurs (referring there to only part of a class). Any such syllogism commits the *fallacy of illicit process*, which may involve either the minor or major term. Thus the fallacy has the following two versions:

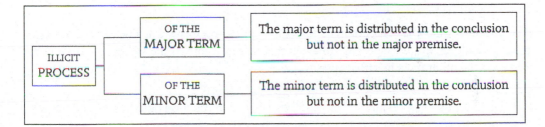

Consider

19   1. All tigers are felines.
    2. No lions are tigers.
    3. No lions are felines.

The term 'felines' in (19)'s conclusion involves the whole class of felines, which is said to be excluded from the whole class of lions. But premise 1 is not about the whole class of felines, since there the term 'felines' is not distributed. The fallacy committed by this argument is *illicit process of the major term* (for short, 'illicit major').
Now consider

20   1. All suicide bombers are persons willing to die.
    2. All suicide bombers are opponents of the status quo.
    3. All opponents of the status quo are persons willing to die.

The term 'opponents of the status quo' in (20)'s conclusion involves a whole class of people with a certain view, which is said to be included in the class denoted by the major term. But premise 2 is not about that whole class of people, since there the term 'opponents of the status quo' is the predicate of an A proposition and therefore not distributed. The fallacy committed by this argument is *illicit process of the minor term* (for short, 'illicit minor').

Finally, notice that it is also possible for an argument to commit both of these fallacies at once. One more thing: since there's no distribution in a type-I proposition, any syllogism with a type-I conclusion obeys rule 3 by default. But if the conclusion is an *A*, *E*, or *O* proposition, then it'll have some distributed term in it, and the logical thinker will want to make sure that any term distributed in the conclusion is also distributed in the appropriate premise.

> **RULE 4:** A valid syllogism cannot have two negative premises.

If a syllogism's major premise is negative, the classes denoted by its middle and major terms either wholly or partially exclude each other. And if its minor premise is also negative, the classes denoted by its middle and minor term also either wholly or partially exclude each other. From such premises no conclusion validly follows about the relation between the classes denoted by the minor and major terms. When this happens, the argument is said to commit the *fallacy of exclusive premises*—for example,

21 1. No ferns are trees.
    2. Some elms are not ferns.
    3. Some elms are not trees.

The upshot of rule 4 is that certain combinations in the premises will always render a syllogism invalid: EE, EO, OE, and OO. To avoid this fallacy, if one of the syllogism's premises is negative, the other must be affirmative.

> **RULE 5:** If there is a negative premise, the conclusion must be negative; and if there is a negative conclusion, there must be one negative premise.

Recall that affirmative categorical propositions represent class inclusion, either whole inclusion of one class in another (A proposition), or inclusion of part of a class within another class (I proposition). Thus the class inclusion represented in a syllogism's affirmative conclusion could be validly inferred only when both premises also represent class inclusion. On the other hand, a syllogism's negative conclusion, which would represent a relation of class exclusion, cannot follow validly from two affirmative premises (which assert only relations of *inclusion*).

When rule 5 is violated, a syllogism commits either the *fallacy of drawing an affirmative conclusion from a negative premise*, or that of *drawing a negative conclusion from two affirmative premises*. Either way, the syllogism is invalid. For example,

22 1. All humans are mammals.
    2. Some lizards are not humans.
    3. Some lizards are mammals.

This commits the *fallacy of drawing an affirmative conclusion from a negative premise;* while

23 1. All poets are creative writers.
    2. <u>All creative writers are authors.</u>
    3. No authors are poets.

commits the *fallacy of drawing a negative conclusion from two affirmative premises.* Syllogisms flouting rule 5 are so obviously invalid that it is rare to encounter them. Finally, note that any syllogism containing only affirmative propositions obeys rule 5 by default.

> RULE 6: If both premises are universal, the conclusion must be universal.

As we saw in the previous chapter, of the four types of standard categorical propositions, only I and O carry existential import; that is, only these presuppose the existence of the entities denoted by their subject terms. Thus there is no valid syllogism with two universal premises and a particular conclusion. Any such syllogism draws a conclusion with existential import on the basis of premises having no such import. Syllogisms of this sort violate rule 6, committing the so-called *existential fallacy.* For example,

24 1. All beings that breathe are mortal.
    2. <u>All mermaids are beings that breathe.</u>
    3. Some mermaids are mortal.

Here the conclusion is equivalent to *"There is* at least one mermaid that is mortal"—in effect endorsing the existence of mermaids. Finally, note that any syllogism in which one or more of its premises is particular (i.e., type I or O) obeys rule 6 by default.

Rules of Validity vs. Venn Diagrams

Each of the six rules of validity stipulates a necessary condition of validity in categorical syllogisms. Thus a syllogism that obeys any one of these rules meets a necessary condition of being valid. But that is of course not yet to meet a sufficient condition of validity. Only obeying all six rules together is a sufficient condition for the validity of a syllogism. This technique thus provides a method of checking for validity that is every bit as reliable as that of Venn diagrams. The rules could, then, be used together with the Venn diagrams, so that if we make a mistake in one method, the other method may catch it. Any syllogistic form that commits one or more of the above fallacies will show up as invalid on a Venn diagram, and any time the diagram shows a form to be invalid, it will be found to commit one or more fallacies. Likewise, any syllogistic form that obeys all six rules will be shown valid by a Venn diagram.

In order to use the method of rules and fallacies to check syllogism forms for validity, you'll want to do two things: (1) keep clearly in mind which rules and fallacies go together, and (2) remember that the rules and fallacies are *not* two different ways of saying the same thing! The rules are prescriptions about what should be kept in mind in assessing the validity of a syllogism. The fallacies are errors in the reasoning underlying those syllogisms that break the rules. Each fallacy can be associated with the flouting of one of the rules.

Again, the six rules collectively stipulate the necessary and sufficient conditions of validity for categorical syllogisms, but committing even one of the fallacies makes a syllogism invalid. Since it's valid syllogisms that preserve truth, the rules are to be obeyed and the fallacies to be avoided.

Let's now summarize the eight fallacies and the six rules of validity that they violate.

Fallacy		Rule Violated
Four terms	1	A syllogism must have exactly three terms.
Undistributed middle	2	The middle term must be distributed at least once.
Illicit process of the major/minor term	3	If any term is distributed in the conclusion, it must also be distributed in one of the premises.
Exclusive premises	4	A valid syllogism cannot have two negative premises.
Affirmative from a negative and Negative from two affirmatives	5	If there is a negative premise, the conclusion must be negative; and if there is a negative conclusion, one premise must be negative.
Existential fallacy	6	If both premises are universal, the conclusion must be universal.

Exercises

IX. Review Questions

1. What does it mean to say that a term in a categorical proposition is 'distributed'?
2. What are the patterns of distribution in the four different types of categorical proposition?
3. What are the six rules of validity in categorical syllogisms?
4. Can you name, for each of the six rules of validity, the fallacy (or fallacies) committed when the rule is broken?
5. Can you explain what has gone wrong in each of the eight fallacies that amount to violations of the rules of validity?
6. If you've drawn a Venn diagram that appears to show a certain syllogistic form valid, but you've also discovered that the form appears to commit a fallacy in violation of one of the rules of validity, what should you conclude?

X. The following categorical propositions are type A, E, I, or O. For each of them, say which type it is and whether its subject and predicate are distributed.

1. All wombats are marsupials.

   SAMPLE ANSWER: A. Subject distributed; predicate undistributed

2. Some alligator wrestlers are not emergency-room patients.

*3. Some rare coins are expensive things to insure.

4. No vampires are members of the Rotary Club.

5. Some citrus fruits are not things grown in Rhode Island.

*6. All chess players are patient strategists.

7. No interstate highways are good places to travel by bicycle.

8. Some politicians are not persons who have been indicted by the courts.

*9. Some motorcycles are collectors' items.

10. All movies starring Tom Hanks are films worth seeing.

*11. Some paintings by Rubens are not pictures in museums.

12. No Yorkshire terriers are guard dogs.

13. Some airlines are not transatlantic carriers.

*14. All professional astrologers are charlatans.

15. Some Texans are stockbrokers.

XI. Reconstruct each of the following syllogisms, identify its form, and determine whether it is valid or not by applying the rules of validity. For any syllogism that is invalid, name the fallacy (or fallacies) it commits.

1. Some astronauts are not musicians trained in classical music. So no members of the New York Philharmonic are astronauts, for all members of the New York Philharmonic are musicians trained in classical music.

   SAMPLE ANSWER:

   1 Some astronauts are not musicians trained in classical music.
   2 All members of the New York Philharmonic are musicians trained in classical music.
   3 No members of the New York Philharmonic are astronauts.

1 Some *P* are not *M*.	OAE-2	INVALID
2 All *S* are *M*.		Illicit Process of the Major Term
3 No *S* are *P*.		

2. Since all generals who are veterans of the Vietnam War are experienced soldiers, and all experienced soldiers are persons who are practiced in the art of planning battle strategies, it follows that some persons who are practiced in the art of planning battle strategies are generals who are veterans of the Vietnam War.

*3. Since no people who are truly objective are people who are likely to be mistaken, it follows that no people who ignore the facts are people who are truly objective, for all people who ignore the facts are people who are likely to be mistaken.

4. All submarines are warships, but some naval ships are not submarines. Hence, some naval ships are not warships.

*5. Some people who bet on horse races are people who can afford to lose, since some people who bet on horse races are people who expect to win, and no people who expect to win are people who can afford to lose.

6. All persons with utopian ideals are fanatics, because some fanatics are political zealots, even though some political zealots are not persons with utopian ideals.

*7. Some metals are copper alloys, but all copper alloys are good conductors of electricity. It follows that some good conductors of electricity are not metals.

8. Some Connecticut firms are corporations. After all, some Connecticut firms are insurance companies, and all insurance companies are corporations.

*9. No egalitarians are sympathetic dissidents; thus no sympathetic dissidents are rabble rousers, for some rabble rousers are egalitarians.

10. All passenger pigeons are birds. For some passenger pigeons are not intelligent creatures, but all birds are intelligent creatures.

*11. Since some coaches are not talent scouts, we may infer that no athletes are talent scouts. After all, some athletes are not coaches.

12. Some gangsters are criminals, and all gangsters are pedestrians, so no criminals are pedestrians.

*13. Some living things are pigs, for all college men are living things, and some college men are pigs.

14. Some fast vehicles are helicopters, because some fast vehicles are war planes, but some helicopters are not war planes.

*15. All postmodernists are admirers of Heidegger. No admirers of Heidegger are utilitarians. Hence, no postmodernists are utilitarians.

16. Since all good investments are smart purchases, no smart purchases are municipal bonds. After all, some municipal bonds are good investments.

*17. All paramecia are single-celled organisms, and all single-celled organisms are invertebrates; therefore, all paramecia are invertebrates.

18. Whereas some flash drives are handy devices, some handy devices are not DVDs, for no DVDs are flash drives.

*19. Because all good neighbors are well-intentioned zealots, no well-intentioned zealots are respectful people, for all good neighbors are respectful people.

20. No Scandinavian nations are tax havens. After all, some Scandinavian nations are countries in Europe, but some countries in Europe are tax havens.

*21. Since some traitors are not benefactors, it follows that all embezzlers are traitors, for no embezzlers are benefactors.

22. Some board games are not contests of strategy, but all contests of strategy are chess matches. Thus all chess matches are board games.

*23. No angora goats are hamsters. No angora goats are great white sharks. Therefore, no great white sharks are hamsters.

24. Some large natural disasters are tropical storms, for some hurricanes are large natural disasters, and all hurricanes are tropical storms.

*25. Some average people are not photogenic. Accordingly, some average people are not television news anchors, since all television news anchors are photogenic.

1. The six rules discussed in this section can be used to test the validity of syllogistic arguments such as those in (XI). For any argument with the same form, what would these rules show?

2. Provide syllogisms of your own whose forms illustrate each of the four figures and use Venn diagrams to check those forms for validity.

3. For each of the arguments in (2), check for validity using the rules of validity. If any argument is invalid, name the fallacy (or fallacies) it commits.

■ Writing Project

In the Writing Project at the end of Chapter 1, you were asked to write a short essay defending some claim about which you felt strongly. Go back to this essay now and write a second paper in which you offer a critical assessment of your original argument, appealing to the methods of argument analysis you've learned in this course.

■ Chapter Summary

Categorical syllogism: a deductive argument made up of three categorical propositions. It has three terms, each of which occurs exactly twice in the argument, with one of them occurring only in the premises.

The terms of a syllogism:

1. *Major term*. Symbolized by P, it's the predicate of the conclusion.
2. *Minor term*. Symbolized by S, it's the subject of the conclusion.
3. *Middle term*. Symbolized by M, it occurs only in the premises.

A syllogism's premises:

1. The *major premise* is the one that contains the major term ➔ Listed first
2. The *minor premise* is the one that contains the minor term ➔ Listed second

A syllogism's form: a combination of its mood and figure.

1. The *figure* is determined by the arrangement of the middle term as subject or predicate in a syllogism's premises.
2. The *mood* is determined by the arrangement of categorical proposition types in a syllogism's premises and conclusion.

How to test the validity of a syllogism with a Venn diagram:

1. Draw three intersecting circles.
2. Diagram only the premises.

3. If one premise is universal and the other particular, then you must diagram the universal premise first, whichever it is.

4. But if both premises are universal or both particular, then it doesn't matter which is diagrammed first.

5. The major premise is diagrammed across the 'M' and 'P' circles, the minor premise across the 'M' and 'S' circles.

6. Once you have diagrammed the premises, if the conclusion is thereby already unequivocally diagrammed across the 'S' and 'P' circles, then the argument is valid. Otherwise, the argument is invalid.

Syllogisms that violate any of the following rules are invalid:

- RULE 1: A syllogism must have exactly three terms. An argument that violates this rule commits the *fallacy of four terms*.
- RULE 2: The middle term must be distributed at least once. An argument that violates this rule commits the *fallacy of undistributed middle*.
- RULE 3: If any term is distributed in the conclusion, it must be distributed also in one of the premises. An argument that violates this rule commits either the *fallacy of illicit process of the major term* (where the major term is distributed in the conclusion but not in the major premise) or that of *illicit process of the minor term* (where the minor term is distributed in the conclusion but not in the minor premise). It is also possible for an argument to commit both of these fallacies at once.
- RULE 4: A valid syllogism cannot have two negative premises. An argument that violates this rule commits the *fallacy of exclusive premises*.
- RULE 5: If there is a negative premise, the conclusion must be negative; and if there is a negative conclusion, there must be one negative premise. An argument that violates this rule commits either the *fallacy of affirmative from a negative*, or the *fallacy of negative from two affirmatives*.
- RULE 6: If both premises are universal, the conclusion must be universal. An argument that violates this rule commits the *existential fallacy*.

■ Key Words

Categorical syllogism	Illicit process of the major term
Syllogism form	Exclusive premises
Rules of validity	Affirmative from a negative
Venn diagram	Negative from two affirmatives
Fallacy of four terms	Existential fallacy
Undistributed middle	Illicit process of the minor term

Solutions to Selected Exercises

SOLUTIONS TO CHAPTER 1

IV

3. premise **6.** neither **8.** neither **10.** premise **13.** conclusion

V

3. Badgers are native to southern Wisconsin. <After all,> (they are always spotted there). **6.** (In the past, every person who ever lived did eventually die.) [This suggests that] all human beings are mortal. **9.** Online education is a great option for working adults in general, regardless of their ethnic background. <For one thing,> (there is a large population of working adults who simply are not in a position to attend a traditional university). **12.** (There is evidence that galaxies are flying outward and apart from each other.) [So] the cosmos will grow darker and colder. **15.** Captain Binnacle will not desert his ship, even though it is about to go down, <for> (only a cowardly captain would desert a sinking ship), and (Captain Binnacle is no coward). **18.** The University of California at Berkeley is strong in math, <for> (many instructors in its Math Department have published breakthrough papers in the core areas of mathematics). **20.** (No one who knowingly and needlessly endangers his or her life is rational.) [Thus] college students who smoke are not rational, <because> (every college student who smokes is knowingly and unnecessarily endangering his or her life. **25.** <Given that> (all Athenians are Greeks) and that (Plato was an Athenian), [we may infer that] Plato was a Greek.

VII

4. no argument **10.** argument **13.** no argument **16.** argument **18.** no argument **20.** argument

IX

4. argument **6.** explanation **9.** argument **10.** explanation

SOLUTIONS TO CHAPTER 2

II

3. rhetorical power **5.** evidential support **8.** logical connectedness **10.** linguistic merit and rhetorical power **11.** rhetorical power **12.** evidential support and logical connectedness **15.** linguistic merit

III

2. rhetorical power **4.** evidential support **6.** logical connectedness **8.** evidential support **10.** logical connectedness **12.** rhetorical power

IV

3. weak logical connectedness **6.** strong logical connectedness **9.** failed logical connectedness

V

3. impossible. This scenario is ruled out by the definition of rational acceptability. **6.** possible. **8.** impossible. This scenario is ruled out by the definition of linguistic merit. **10.** impossible. This scenario is ruled out by the definition of rhetorical power. **13.** possible **15.** possible

VIII

3. expressive **5.** directive **7.** informative **10.** expressive **12.** directive **15.** expressive **18.** commissive **20.** commissive

IX

4. imperative **7.** declarative **10.** interrogative **13.** declarative **16.** exclamatory **19.** declarative

X

3. interrogative; (b) asking a question (directive); (c) expressing annoyance at the hearer's conduct toward Harry (expressive) **5.** exclamatory; (b) reporting that the dog bites (informative); (c) requesting that people refrain from entering a place (directive) **7.** interrogative; (b) asking a question (directive); (c). reporting that the person may be pretending to be sleeping (informative) **10.** declarative; (b) reporting a fact (informative); ((c). expressing hope that things will go better in the future (expressive)

XI

3. (A) Those players are automata resembling humans. (B) Those players act mechanically.
6. (A) We are coming near to a mountain that is a volcano. (B) We are about to have a crisis.
9. (A) Jim wears two different hats. (B) Jim plays two different roles, or has two different official responsibilities.
12. (A) That city is populated by insects. (B) That city is crowded, with many people in the street.
15. (A) He is a piece of burnt bread. (B) He's finished

XII

2. Indirect speech act. Recast: asserting that Abe is a person of no authority.
5. .Indirect speech act. Recast: requesting that we press criminal charges now.
7. Figurative language. Recast: For teenagers, flip-flops are fashionable items.

XV

3. small elephant =df. elephant that is smaller than most elephants
5. human being =df. featherless biped
7. horse =df. beast of burden with a flowing mane

XVI

3. contextual **5.** reportive **7.** contextual **9.** ostensive

XVII

3. too broad and too narrow **5.** too narrow **7.** too broad and too narrow **9.** too broad

SOLUTIONS TO CHAPTER 3

II

3. nonbelief **5.** belief **7.** nonbelief **9.** belief

III

4. The nonbelief about whether the Sun will rise tomorrow. **6.** The belief that the Earth is a planet.
8. The nonbelief about whether galaxies are flying outward. **10.** The belief that I am thinking.
12. The nonbelief about whether there is life after death. **14.** The nonbelief about whether humans have evolved or were created by God.

IV

1. Because under special circumstances (e.g., a threat) a person's behavior may not express his actual beliefs. The same could happen if he is insincere—that is, he intends to misrepresent his beliefs. **6.** The options are belief, disbelief, and nonbelief about whether there is life after death.

VI

3. inaccurate **5.** vague statement: "tallness" doesn't clearly apply or fail to apply to a person of that height.
7. evaluative statement: the statement uses 'better than' to evaluate two things. **10.** accurate **13.** accurate
15. evaluative statement: the statement evaluates something as being unjust.

VII

3. empirical statement **5.** empirical statement **7.** not an empirical statement **10.** empirical statement
13. empirical statement **15.** not an empirical statement.

VIII

2. Not true because that's only likely, not certain. **4.** Not true because there are no records to prove that they knew they were in America. **5.** Not true because it was *a* citizen of the U.S.S.R who did it. **7.** Not true because the shape of the country only resembles that of boot.

IX

3. inconsistent. The beliefs are contradictory. **5.**consistent. In a possible world, both beliefs could be true.
7. inconsistent. The beliefs are contradictory. **9.** inconsistent. The beliefs are contradictory. **11.** consistent. These beliefs are true in all possible worlds. **13.** inconsistent. The beliefs are contradictory. **15.** inconsistent. Both beliefs are necessarily false.

X

3. Conceptual **5.** Conceptual **7.** Other. The content features "inhumane" and is therefore evaluative. **8.** Empirical
11. Other. This content features "delicious" and is therefore evaluative. **13.** Empirical **15.** Empirical.

XI

3. nonconservative 5 .conservative 7. nonconservative 9. conservative 11. conservative 13. nonconservative 15. nonconservative

XII

3. irrational 5. irrational 7. rational 9. irrational

SOLUTIONS TO CHAPTER 4

II

3. Anyone born in Germany is a European. 6. Whatever the Federal Reserve Board says banks will do is probably what they will do. 9. She is not telling the truth. 12. Canadians are used to cold weather. 15. Jane is a cell-phone user. 17 Religious theories should not be taught in biology courses in public schools. 20. Pelicans are birds. 24. Planets with dry lake beds might have had life at some time.

III

3. No real vegetarian eats meat. Alicia is a real vegetarian. Thus she doesn't eat meat. Hence, there is no point in taking her to Tony Roma's Steak House. Extended argument. 5. If the ocean is rough here, then there will be no swimming. If there is no swimming, tourists will go to another beach. Thus if the ocean is rough here, then tourists will go to another beach. Simple argument. 7. No Democrat votes for Republicans. Since Keisha voted for Republicans, she is not a Democrat. Thus she won't be invited to Jamal's party, for only Democrats are invited to his party. Extended argument. 9. To understand most web pages, you have to read them. To read them requires a good amount of time. Thus to understand web pages requires a good amount of time. Since I don't have any time, I keep away from the web and as a result, I miss some news. Extended argument. 11. Because Jerome is an atheist and Cynthia's mother does not like him, it follows that Jerome will not be invited to the family picnic next month. We may also infer that Jerome will come to see Cynthia only when her mother is not around. Extended argument. 13. Professor Veebelfetzer will surely be expelled from the Academy of Sciences. For he admits using false data in his famous experiment on rat intelligence. As a result, his name will also be removed from the list of those invited to the Academy's annual banquet next fall. Extended argument. 15. Since books help to develop comprehension skills, web pages do that, too. After all, in both cases one must read carefully to understand what is presented. Simple argument.

IV

4. extended, with more than two conclusions 7. extended, with more than two conclusions 10. extended, with at most two conclusions

VII

3. inductive 6. inductive 8. deductive 10. deductive 12. inductive 15. inductive 18. inductive 20. deductive 23. inductive 25. deductive

XI

3. non-normative 5. non-normative 7. normative 9. non-normative 11. normative 13. non-normative 15. non-normative 17. non-normative 19. non-normative

XII

4. aesthetic and moral 6. prudential and moral 9. legal 10. prudential 13. moral and prudential 15.aesthetic and prudential 17. prudential 20. moral and prudential

XIII

3. Whatever is designed by Sir Norman Foster is beautiful. 6. Whatever takes you where you want to go faster is better. 9. Married people deal better with financial problems. 12. Hit songs are the best songs. 15. Soldiers ought to do whatever their commanding officer orders them to do. 18. Whatever is the appropriate punishment for murder is ethically justified. 20. You ought to obey the law.

SOLUTIONS TO CHAPTER 5

II

4. valid 7. valid 10. valid 13. valid 16. invalid 19. valid 22. invalid 25. invalid 28. valid

IV

3. logically possible 5. logically possible 8. logically impossible

VII

3. Either *M* or *B*
Not *M*
___
B

5. Either C or S
$$\frac{\text{Not } C}{S}$$

7. If M, then C
$$\frac{M}{C}$$

VIII

2. a is L
$$\frac{\text{No } L \text{ is } D}{a \text{ is not } D}$$

5. All A are P
$$\frac{\text{Some } P \text{ are } F}{\text{Some } A \text{ are } F}$$

8. No I is F
$$\frac{o \text{ is } I}{o \text{ is not } F}$$

IX

3. categorical argument **5.** propositional argument **7.** categorical argument **9.** propositional argument
11. propositional argument **13.** categorical argument **15.** categorical argument

X

4. All C are D
$$\frac{\text{No } T \text{ are } D}{\text{No } C \text{ are } T}$$ Categorical

6. If M, then L
$$\frac{\text{Not } L}{\text{Not } M}$$ Propositional

9. If O, then F
$$\frac{}{\text{If not } F, \text{ then not } O}$$ Propositional

11. All B are I
$$\frac{\text{Some } B \text{ are } C}{\text{Some } I \text{ are } C}$$ Categorical

13. No S are G
$$\frac{\text{All } G \text{ are } D}{\text{No } S \text{ are } D}$$ Categorical

15. No P is S
$$\frac{v \text{ is } P}{v \text{ is not } S}$$ Categorical

18. If O, then H
$$\frac{\text{Not } H}{\text{Not } O}$$ Propositional

20. Either M or not J
$$\frac{\text{Not } M}{\text{Not } J}$$ Propositional

XI

3. hypothetical syllogism **6.** *modus tollens* **9.** contraposition **18.** *modus tollens*
20. disjunctive syllogism

XII

3. true **5.** false **7.** false **9.** true

XIII

3. Most C are E
$$\frac{m \text{ is not } E}{m \text{ is not } C}$$

Counterexample: an argument in which C = American citizen, E = people permitted to vote
in the United States, and m = a two-year old American citizen.

5. No A are E
   Some A are H
   No H are E
      Counterexample: an argument in which A = fish , E = mammal, and H = aggressive animals.
7. ƒ is D
   Some D are B
   ƒ is B
      Counterexample: an argument in which ƒ = a certain mute dog, D = dog, and B = barking animal.

XVI
2. false **4.** false **6.** false **8.** true

XVII
2. Entailment does matter, since an argument can't be sound unless it has it. **4.** There is a relationship between validity and truth: in a valid argument, if the premises are true, the conclusion must be true.

XVIII
4. logically impossible **6.** logically possible **8.** logically possible **10.** logically impossible **12.** logically possible

SOLUTIONS TO CHAPTER 6

II
3. deductive **6.** inductive **9.** deductive **12.** deductive **15.** inductive

IV
2. causal argument **5.** analogy **8.** analogy **9.** statistical syllogism **11.** causal argument **14.** enumerative induction

VII
3. statistical syllogism, reliable **6.** enumerative induction, not reliable **9.** causal argument, reliable **12.** statistical syllogism, reliable **15.** enumerative induction, not reliable **18.** analogy, not reliable **21.** analogy, reliable
23. causal argument, undeterminable (the reliability of the argument depends on that of the cited source)
25. causal argument, reliable

SOLUTIONS TO CHAPTER 7

II
3. appeal to ignorance **6.** false cause **7.** weak analogy **9.** appeal to unqualified authority **12.** appeal to unqualified authority **15.** hasty generalization **18.** appeal to ignorance **19.** appeal to unqualified authority

III
3. false cause/hasty generalization **5.** false cause/appeal to unqualified authority **7.** hasty generalization/false cause **9.** false cause **11.** appeal to unqualified authority **12.** appeal to ignorance **15.** weak analogy/hasty generalization

V
2. fallacy **4.** not a fallacy **5.** fallacy **7.** fallacy **9.** not a fallacy

VI
1. Hasty generalization. Not a fallacy when the sample of tigers so far observed is very large, comprehensive, and randomly selected. **3.** Appeal to ignorance. Not a fallacy when the experts agree that the concept of 'centaur' is empty and plays no role in explaining anything.

SOLUTIONS TO CHAPTER 8

II
3. that the mind is different from the body **5.** that supernatural beings are only fictional **7.** that Aaron is a hunter **9.** that if a plane figure is a circle, then it is not a rectangle

III
3. both **5.** conceptual **7.** conceptual **9.** both

IV
3. begs the question **5.** begs the question **7.** both **10.** both **13.** begs the question against **16.** begs the question against **19.** begging the question

V
4. impossible **6.** impossible **8.** possible **10.** impossible

VI

4. *C* 6. *K* 8. *I*

VII

3. BURDEN OF PROOF on S. Since the argument has at least one false premise, its conclusion could be false.
5. BURDEN OF PROOF on O. S's argument is now rationally compelling. 7. BURDEN OF PROOF on O. The conclusion of her argument could be false (it has at least one false premise).

VIII

1. The argument begs the question, because in order to accept its premises you have to accept its conclusion. And it begs the question against those who argue that marriage is a union between two persons independent of their genders. 5. To be deductively cogent, the argument must: (1) be valid, and (2) have premises that are not only acceptable, but more clearly acceptable than its conclusion. 6. Such an argument could not be cogent, since it wouldn't be truth-preserving—and, as a result, its conclusion could be false (even with all premises true). But the argument need not be rejected on that ground, since it could be inductively strong, thus making its conclusion reasonable to believe. 10. The burden is on you. It means: it's your turn. You must offer an argument or accept defeat in the debate.

X

3. accident 6. false alternatives 9. complex question 12. false alternatives 13. accident 15. accident

XI

4. complex question 6. false alternatives 9. accident 12. begging the question against 15. complex question 17. begging the question / begging the question against 20. accident 22. begging the question 25. accident

SOLUTIONS TO CHAPTER 9

II

3. not plainly vague 5. not plainly vague 7. plainly vague 9. not plainly vague 12. plainly vague 15. plainly vague

V

3. composition 7. division 10. slippery slope
13. composition 17. slippery slope 20. composition 24. division 27. division 30. amphiboly 33. amphiboly 37. slippery slope 40 composition

SOLUTIONS TO CHAPTER 10

II

2. beside the point (NOT appeal to pity) 4. appeal to pity 7. appeal to emotion (bandwagon) 10. *ad hominem*
13. *ad hominem* (*tu quoque*) 16. straw man 19. beside the point 22. beside the point 25. appeal to force 28. appeal to emotion 30. straw man 33. appeal to pity 35. *ad hominem* 39. appeal to emotion (bandwagon)

III

2. fallacy of appeal to emotion 5. not a fallacy of appeal to emotion 9. not a fallacy of appeal to emotion
10. fallacy of appeal to emotion (bandwagon appeal)

SOLUTIONS TO CHAPTER 11

II

3. negation 7. not a negation 10. not a negation

III

4. not a conjunction 7. conjunction 8. not a conditional 9. not a conjunction

IV

2. not a disjunction 6. disjunction 8. disjunction 9. disjunction

V

3. not a conditional 5. conditional 8. not a conditional 10. conditional

VI

4. <u>Mexico City's air is not harmful</u> provided that <u>Houston's air pollution is healthy</u>. 7. <u>That Canada has signed the Kyoto Protocol</u> implies that <u>Canada is willing to comply</u>. 10. That <u>China has not signed the Kyoto Protocol</u> implies <u>that neither Canada nor the UK has signed it</u>.

VII

2. biconditional 5. not a Biconditional 6. biconditional 8. biconditional

VIII

3. $I \supset F$ **6.** $\sim(\sim E \supset \sim B)$

X

3. WFF **5.** not a WFF **7.** WFF **9.** not a WFF

XI

3. compound; biconditional **6.** simple **9.** compound; conjunction **12.** simple **15.** compound; negation of disjunction/conjunction of negations **18.** simple

XII

3. $E \equiv M$ **6.** M **12.** K **15.** $\sim(E \vee K)$

XIII

3. disjunction $\sim F \vee (A \cdot L)$ **6.** disjunction. $H \vee \sim H$ **9.** conditional. $C \supset \sim(H \vee D)$ **12.** negation. $\sim[F \equiv (P \cdot M)]$
15. conditional. $(C \cdot \sim I) \supset \sim(O \equiv M)$

XIV

3. biconditional **6.** conjunction **8.** negation

XVI

3. true **6.** true **9.** false **12.** true **15.** false **18.** false

XVII

4. true **7.** true **10.** true **13.** false **16.** true **19.** true **22.** true **25.** false

XX

3. Tautology

B M	B ⊃ (M ⊃ B)
T T	[T] T
T F	[T] T
F T	[T] F
F F	[T] T

5. Contradiction

A B	~ [(A • B) ⊃ (B • A)]
T T	[F] T T T
T F	[F] F T F
F T	[F] F T F
F F	[F] F T F

8. Contingency

A B	(~A v ~B) ⊃ (B • A)
T T	F F F [T] T
T F	F T T [F] F
F T	T T F [F] F
F F	T T T [F] F

10. Contingency

A K H	~A ≡ ~(~K v ~H)
T T T	F [F] T F F F
T T F	F [T] F F T T
T F T	F [T] F T T F
T F F	F [T] F T T T
F T T	T [T] T F F F
F T F	T [F] F F T T
F F T	T [F] F T T F
F F F	T [F] F T T T

12. Contingency

A H I	~	[(~A • H)	v	~	(H ⊃ ~I)]
T T T	F	F F	TT	F	F
T T F	T	F F	FF	T	T
T F T	T	F F	FF	T	F
T F F	T	F F	FF	T	T
F T T	F	T T	TT	F	F
F T F	F	T T	TF	T	T
F F T	T	T F	FF	T	F
F F F	T	T F	FF	T	T

16 Contradiction

A B C	~	{[A • (B • C)]	≡	[(A • B) • C]}
T T T	F	T T T	T	T T T
T T F	F	F F T	T	T F
T F T	F	F F T	F	F
T F F	F	F F T	F	F
F T T	F	F T T	F	F
F T F	F	F F T	F	F
F F T	F	F F T	F	F
F F F	F	F F T	F	F

18. Tautology

A B	(A • B)	≡	(B • A)
T T	T	T	T
T F	F	T	F
F T	F	T	F
F F	F	T	F

20. Tautology

A B	(A ≡ B)	≡	[(A ⊃ B) • (B ⊃ A)]
T T	T	T	T T T
T F	F	T	F F T
F T	F	T	T F F
F F	T	T	T T T

XXI

2. Contingency

E O	~E v O
T T	F T
T F	F F
F T	T T
F F	T T

4. Contingency

E O	~E ≡ O
T T	F F
T F	F T
F T	T T
F F	T F

7. Tautology

E O	(E • O) ⊃ O
T T	T **T**
T F	F T
F T	F T
F F	F T

11. Tautology

H L	(H • L) ≡ ~ ~ (H • L)
T T	T **T** T F T
T F	F T F T F
F T	F T F T F
F F	F T F T F

12. Contingency

E O H L	~ (E • O) ≡ ~ (H • L)
T T T T	F T **T** F T
T T T F	F T F T F
T T F T	F T F T F
T T F F	F T F T F
T F T T	T F F F T
T F T F	T F T T F
T F F T	T F T T F
T F F F	T F T T F
F T T T	T F F F T
F T T F	T F T T F
F T F T	T F T T F
F T F F	T F T T F
F F T T	T F F F T
F F T F	T F T T F
F F F T	T F T T F
F F F F	T F **T** T F

14. Tautology

E O	~ (E v O) ≡ (~E • ~O)
T T	F T **T** F F F
T F	F T T F F T
F T	F T T T F F
F F	T F T T T T

XXII

3. Fred is at the library if and only if either the library is open or Mary is not at the library. **5.** The essay is due on Thursday just in case the library being open implies that I have Internet access. **7.** It is not the case that if Fred is not at the library then either the library is not open or Mary is at the library.

SOLUTIONS TO CHAPTER 12

II

4. Invalid

J N	J, J v N ∴ ~N	
T T	**T**	F ←
T F	T	T
F T	T	F ←
F F	F	T

8. Invalid

C B A	~C	~C v ~B	•	~(B • A)	B • A	A v C
T T T	F	F	F	F	T	T
T T F	F	F	F	T	F	T
T F T	F	T	T	T	F	T
T F F	F	T	T	T	F	T
F T T	T	T	F	F	T	T
F T F	T	T	T	T	F	F	←
F F T	T	T	T	T	F	T
F F F	T	T	T	T	F	F

(Premise: ~C v ~B . ~(B • A) ∴ A v C — ← marks the F T F row)

10. Valid

B K H	~B	~	~K	≡	~H	⊃	~H
T T T	F	F	F	T	F	F	F
T T F	F	T	F	F	T	T	T
T F T	F	T	T	F	F	T	F
T F F	F	F	T	T	T	T	T
F T T	T	F	F	T	F	F	F
F T F	T	T	F	F	T	T	T
F F T	T	T	T	F	F	T	F
F F F	T	F	T	T	T	T	T

(Premise: ~B , ~(~K ≡ ~H) ∴ K ⊃ ~H)

13. Valid

K E O	•	~E	~E v O	~E	⊃	~K	O
T T T	T	F	T	F	T	F	T
T T F	F	F	F	F	T	F	F
T F T	T	T	T	T	F	F	T
T F F	T	T	T	T	F	F	F
F T T	F	F	T	F	T	T	T
F T F	F	F	F	F	T	T	F
F F T	F	T	T	T	T	T	T
F F F	F	T	T	T	T	T	F

(Premise: K • (~E v O) , ~E ⊃ ~K ∴ O)

14. Invalid

E A	E ⊃ A	~~A	~A	~E	v	~A
T T	T	T	F	F	F	F	←
T F	F	F	T	F	T	T
F T	T	T	F	T	T	F
F F	T	F	T	T	T	T

(Premise: E ⊃ A , ~~A ∴ ~E v ~A — ← marks the T T row)

22. Invalid

H I J	•	~I	~I v J	⊃	~H
T T T	T	F	T	F	F
T T F	F	F	F	T	F
T F T	T	T	T	F	F
T F F	T	T	T	T	F	←
F T T	F	F	T	T	T
F T F	F	F	F	T	T
F F T	F	T	T	T	T
F F F	F	T	T	T	T

(Premise: H • (~I v J) , J ⊃ ~H ∴ J — ← marks the T F F row)

23. Invalid

O	A	B	~O,	A ⊃ B	∴	~O • B
T	T	T	F	T		F F
T	T	F	F	F		F F
T	F	T	F	T		F F
T	F	F	F	T		F F
F	T	T	T	T		T T
F	T	F	T	F		T F
F	F	T	T	T		T T
F	F	F	T	T		T F	←

III

3. Invalid

A	B	F	~A ≡ ~B,	~B ⊃ F	∴	A v ~F
T	T	T	F T F	F T		T F
T	T	F	F T F	F T		T T
T	F	T	F F T	T T		T F
T	F	F	F F T	T F		T T
F	T	T	T F F	F T		F F
F	T	F	T F F	F T		T T
F	F	T	T T T	T T		F F
F	F	F	T T T	T F		T T	←

6. Valid

J	A	I	J ⊃ (A v I),	~A • ~I	∴	~J
T	T	T	T T	F F F		F
T	T	F	T T	F F T		F
T	F	T	T T	T F F		F
T	F	F	F F	T T T		F
F	T	T	T T	F F F		T
F	T	F	T T	F F T		T
F	F	T	T T	T F F		T
F	F	F	T F	T T T		T

7. Valid

A	O	F	A • O,	O ≡ F	∴	~F ⊃ ~A
T	T	T	T	T		F T F
T	T	F	T	F		T F F
T	F	T	F	F		F T F
T	F	F	F	T		T F F
F	T	T	F	T		F T T
F	T	F	F	F		T T T
F	F	T	F	F		F T T
F	F	F	F	T		T T T

10. Invalid

M	F	D	M ≡ (D v F),	(F ⊃ ~D) ⊃ ~M	∴	M • F
T	T	T	T T	F F T F		T
T	T	F	T T	T T F F		T
T	F	T	T T	T F F F		F
T	F	F	F F	T T F F		F
F	T	T	F T	F F T T		F
F	T	F	F T	T T T T		F
F	F	T	F T	T F T T		F
F	F	F	T F	T T T T		F	←

Invalid

E M A	M v (E ⊃ ~A),	E ≡ ~(A v M)	∴ ~E
T T T	T F F	F F T	F
T T F	T T T	F F T	F
T F T	F F F	F F T	F
T F F	T T T	T T F	F
F T T	T T F	T F T	T
F T F	T T T	T F T	T
F F T	T T F	T F T	T
F F F	T T T	F T F	T

←

V

3. hypothetical syllogism **5.** *modus ponens* **6.** contraposition **8.** *modus tollens* **12.** disjunctive syllogism

VI

3. $\sim I \supset (M \supset \sim H) \therefore \sim(M \supset \sim H) \supset \sim\sim I$ contraposition **5.** $D \supset M; M \supset H \therefore D \supset H$ hypothetical syllogism
6. $E \supset \sim A, E \therefore \sim A$ *modus ponens* **8.** $C \vee H, H \therefore G$ disjunctive syllogism **10.** $\sim M, H \supset M \therefore \sim H$ *modus tollens*

IX

3. hypothetical syllogism; valid **5.** disjunctive syllogism; valid **7.** denying the antecedent; invalid **9.** contraposition; valid **11.** disjunctive syllogism; valid **13.** *modus ponens*; valid **15.** *modus tollens*; valid **17.** affirming the consequent; invalid **19.** denying the antecedent; invalid

X

4. $E \supset M, \sim E \therefore \sim M$ denying the antecedent; invalid **6.** $H \vee D, D \therefore \sim H$ affirming a disjunct; invalid
7. $B \supset N, N \supset F \therefore B \supset F$ hypothetical syllogism; valid **11.** $M \supset \sim E, E \therefore \sim M$ *modus tollens*; valid
12. $J \supset L, L \therefore J$ affirming the consequent; invalid

XIII

3.
1. $\sim D \cdot C$	
2. $F \supset \sim C$	
3. $\sim F \supset (E \vee D)$	/ ∴ $D \vee E$
4. $\sim\sim C \supset \sim F$	2 Contr
5. $C \supset \sim F$	4 DN
6. $C \supset (E \vee D)$	5, 3 HS
7. $C \cdot \sim D$	1 Com
8. C	7 Simp
9. $E \vee D$	6, 8 MP
10. $D \vee E$	9 Com

5.
1. $(G \supset D) \supset \sim F$	
2. $D \supset F$	
3. $D \cdot C$	/ ∴ $\sim(G \supset D)$
4. $\sim F \supset \sim D$	2 Contr
5. $(G \supset D) \supset \sim D$	1, 4 HS
6. D	3 Simp
7. $\sim\sim D$	6 DN
8. $\sim(G \supset D)$	5, 7 MT

7.
1. $(D \supset C) \vee \sim(A \vee B)$	
2. A	/ ∴ $\sim D \vee C$
3. $\sim(A \vee B) \vee (D \supset C)$	1 Com.
4. $A \vee B$	2 Add
5. $\sim\sim(A \vee B)$	4 DN
6. $D \supset C$	3, 5 DS
7. $\sim D \vee C$	6 Cond

9.
1. $(E \vee A) \supset C$	
2. $[(E \vee A) \supset C] \supset (E \cdot G)$	/ ∴ C
3. $E \cdot G$	1, 2 MP
4. E	3 Simp
5. $E \vee A$	4 Add
6. C	1, 5 MP

11. 1. $(\sim H \lor L) \supset \sim(I \cdot G)$
   2. $G \cdot I$ /∴ $\sim L \cdot H$
   3. $I \cdot G$ 2 Com
   4. $\sim\sim(I \cdot G)$ 3 DN
   5. $\sim(\sim H \lor L)$ 1, 4 MT
   6. $\sim\sim H \cdot \sim L$ 5 DeM
   7. $H \cdot \sim L$ 6 DN
   8. $\sim L \cdot H$ 7 Com

XIV

4. 1. $D \supset B$
   2. $\sim M \lor \sim D$
   3. $\sim B \cdot D$ /∴ $\sim M$
   4. $D \cdot \sim B$ 3 Com.
   5. D 4 Simp
   6. $\sim\sim D$ 5 DN
   7. $\sim M$ 2, 6 DS

6. 1. $H \cdot (\sim I \lor J)$
   2. $J \supset \sim H$ /∴ $\sim J$
   3. H 1 Simp
   4. $\sim\sim H$ 3 DN
   5. $\sim J$ 2, 4 MT

8. 1. $I \cdot \sim C$
   2. $I \supset B$ /∴ $\sim C \cdot B$
   3. I 1 Simp
   4. B 2, 3 MP
   5. $\sim C \cdot I$ 1 Com
   6. $\sim C$ 5 Simp
   7. $\sim C \cdot B$ 6, 4 Conj

10. 1. I
   2. $H \supset \sim E$
   3. $\sim H \supset (N \supset \sim E)$ /∴ $I \cdot [E \supset (N \supset \sim E)]$
   4. $\sim\sim E \supset \sim H$ 2 Contr
   5. $\sim\sim E \supset (N \supset \sim E)$ 4, 3 HS
   6. $E \supset (N \supset \sim E)$ 5 DN
   7. $I \cdot [E \supset (N \supset \sim E)]$ 1, 6 Conj

Solutions to Chapter 13

II

3. No <u>political scandals</u> are <u>situations sought by city officials</u>. Universal negative. **6.** Some <u>railroad engineers who are not car owners</u> are <u>train users</u>. Particular affirmative. **8.** Some <u>single-celled organisms that thrive in the summer</u> are <u>bacteria that are not harmful</u>. Particular affirmative.

IV

3. Some <u>firefighters</u> are not <u>men</u>. Particular negative, O. **5.** Some <u>precious metals</u> are not <u>available in Africa</u>. Particular negative, O. **7.** Some <u>historians</u> are <u>persons who are interested in the future</u>. Particular affirmative, I. **9.** All <u>spies</u> are <u>persons who cannot avoid taking risks</u>. Universal affirmative, A.

VI

2. E: No movie stars are persons who love being ignored by the media. **4.** E: No member of Congress who's being investigated is a person who can leave the country. **6.** O: Some mathematical equations are not equations that amount to headaches. **8.** O: Some dogs are not dogs that bark. **10.** I: Some speedy vehicles are vehicles that don't put their occupants at risk.

IX

3. incorrect

X

3. A proposition, All S are P. Venn diagram 3, Boolean notation 2. **6.** E proposition, No S are P. Venn diagram 2, Boolean notation 1. **9.** E proposition, No S are P. Venn diagram 2, Boolean notation 1. **12.** E proposition, No S are P.

Venn Diagram 2, Boolean notation 1. **15.** *O* proposition, Some *S* are not *P*. Venn diagram 4, Boolean notation 3. **18.** *E* proposition, No *S* are *P*. Venn diagram 2, Boolean notation 1. **20.** *I* proposition, Some *S* are *P*. Venn diagram 1, Boolean notation 4.

XII

3. I. Subcontrary. Some humans are mortal. Undetermined. **5.** E. Contrary. No labor unions are organizations dominated by politicians. False. **7.** O. Subcontrary. Some lions are not harmless. Undetermined. **9.** I. Subcontrary. Some bats are nocturnal creatures. Undetermined.

XIII

4. A. Contrary. Undetermined. **6.** I. Subcontrary. True. **10.** O. Subcontrary. True.

XIV

2. I. Some Democrats are opponents of legalized abortion. **4.** O. Some professional athletes are not highly paid sports heroes. **6.** E. No chipmunks are shy rodents. **8.** E. No cartographers are amateur musicians. **10.** A. All airlines are profitable corporations.

XVI

3. O. Subaltern. Some butterflies are not vertebrates. True. **5.** E. Superaltern. No comets are frequent celestial events. Undetermined. **7.** E. Superaltern. No porcupines are nocturnal animals. Undetermined. **9.** O. Subaltern. Some extraterrestrials are not Republicans. True.

XVII

4. I. Subaltern. Undetermined. **8.** A. Superaltern. False. **10.** I. Subaltern. Undetermined.

XVIII

4. A. Superaltern. All bassoonists are anarchists. Undetermined.
   E. Contradictory. No bassoonists are anarchists. False.
   O. Subcontrary. Some bassoonists are not anarchists. Undetermined.
6. O. Subaltern. Some Americans are not people who care about global warming. True.
   I. Contradictory. Some Americans are people who care about global warming. False.
   A. Contrary. All Americans are people who care about global warming. False.
8. E. Contrary. No acts of cheating are acts that are wrong. False.
   O. Contradictory. Some acts of cheating are not acts that are wrong. False.
   I. Subaltern. Some acts of cheating are acts that are wrong. True.
10. A. Superaltern. All things are things that are observable with the naked eye. Undetermined.
   E. Contradictory. No things are things that are observable with the naked eye. False.
   O. Subcontrary. Some things are not things that are observable with the naked eye. Undetermined.

XIX

3. O. Subaltern. Some liars are not reliable sources. Undetermined.
   I. Contradictory. Some liars are reliable sources. True.
   A. Contrary. All liars are reliable sources. Undetermined.
5. E. Contrary. No trombone players are musicians. Undetermined.
   O. Contradictory. Some trombone players are not musicians. True.
   I. Subaltern. Some trombone players are musicians. Undetermined.
7. E. Contrary. No white horses are horses. Undetermined.
   O. Contradictory. Some white horses are not horses. True.
   I. Subaltern. Some white horses are horses. Undetermined.

XX

3. C. Contrariety, invalid according to the modern square.
   E. Subcontrariety, invalid according to the modern square.
   G. Contradiction, valid according to the modern square.

XXI

3. Some candidates are not incumbents.
   Some incumbents are not candidates. NOT VALID
5. All amateurs are nonprofessionals.
   Some nonprofessionals are amateurs. BY LIMITATION
7. No quarks are molecules.
   No molecules are quarks.

9. All owls are nocturnal creatures.
   Some nocturnal creatures are owls. BY LIMITATION

XXII

3. Some popular songs are hits.
   Some popular songs are not non-hits.
5. Some psychotherapists are not Democrats.
   Some psychotherapists are non-Democrats.
7. All hexagons are plane figures.
   No hexagons are non-plane figures.
9. Some Labrador retrievers are affectionate pets.
   Some Labrador retrievers are not non-affectionate pets.

XXIII

2. Some used car salesmen are not fast talkers.
   Some non–fast talkers are not non–used car salesmen.
4. Some citizens are non-voters.
   Some voters are non-citizens. NOT VALID
6. No musicians are non-concertgoers.
   Some concertgoers are not non-musicians. BY LIMITATION
8. Some police officers are cigar smokers.
   Some cigar smokers are non–police officers. NOT VALID
10. Some pickup trucks are not non-expensive vehicles.
   Some expensive vehicles are not non–pickup trucks.

XXIV

4. All airports are non-crowded places.
   Converse by limitation, Some non-crowded places are airports.
   Obverse, No airports are crowded places.
   Contrapositive, All crowded places are non-airports.
7. Some non-eagles are not non-friendly birds.
   Converse, not valid.
   Obverse, Some non-eagles are friendly birds.
   Contrapositive, Some friendly birds are not eagles.
9. No sanitation workers are non–city employees.
   Converse, No non–city employees are sanitation workers.
   Obverse, All sanitation workers are city employees.
   Contrapositive by limitation, Some city employees are not non–sanitation workers.

XXV

2. A. Conversion, not valid. The converse of an *O* premise is always invalid.
   B. Obversion, valid.
   D. Contraposition, not valid. The contrapositive of an *I* premise is always invalid.
   G. Contraposition, not valid. The argument could be made valid by limitation—that is, by making its conclusion particular negative.
3. C. Subalternation, invalid.
   E. Conversion, not valid.
   G. Contrariety, valid by the traditional square only.
   I. Obversion, valid.

SOLUTIONS TO CHAPTER 14

II

3. Not a syllogism: the argument has one premise.
5. No romantic songs are popular with first graders.　　　　1. No *M* are *P*
   All Sinatra songs are romantic songs.　　　　　　　　　　2. All *S* are *M*
   No Sinatra songs are popular with first graders.　　　　　3. No *S* are *P*
6. No Oscar winners are talk-show hosts.　　　　　　　　　1. No *M* are *P*
   Some men are Oscar winners.　　　　　　　　　　　　　　2. Some *S* are *M*
   Some men are not talk-show hosts.　　　　　　　　　　　3. Some *S* are not *P*

9. Not a syllogism: the argument has one premise.

11. Some programmers are pool players.
    All computer scientists are programmers.
    Some computer scientists are pool players.

1. Some M are P
2. All S are M
3. Some S are P

III

4. AIA-1 **6.** EAA-4 **8.** OOE-1 **10.** OII-1 **12.** EEA-3

IV

3. 1. All people who listen to reggae music are people who are not Lawrence Welk fans.
    2. Some residents of California are people who are not Lawrence Welk fans.
    3. Some residents of California are people who listen to reggae music.

    1. All P are M AII-2
    2. Some S are M
    3. Some S are P

5. 1. All loyal Americans are supporters of the president in his desire to trim the federal budget.
    2. All loyal Americans are people who are willing taxpayers.
    3. All people who are willing taxpayers are supporters of the president in hisdesire to trim the federal budget.

    1. All M are P AAA-3
    2. All M are S
    3. All S are P

7. 1. All animals that are convenient house pets are creatures your aunt Sophie would like.
    2. No creatures your Aunt Sophie would like are reptiles weighing over eighty pounds.
    3. No reptiles weighing over eighty pounds are animals that are convenient house pets.

    1. All P are M AEE-4
    2. No M are S
    3. No S are P

9. 1. Some devices that contain dynamite are not safe things to carry in the trunk of your car.
    2. Some explosives are devices that contain dynamite.
    3. No explosives are safe things to carry in the trunk of your car.

    1. Some M are not P OIE-1
    2. Some S are. M
    3. No S are P

11. 1. Some pacifists are not conscientious objectors.
    2. No pacifists are persons who favor the use of military force.
    3. Some persons who favor the use of military force are not conscientious objectors.

    1. Some M are not P OEO-3
    2. No M are S
    3. Some S are not P

VII

4. 1. Some people who never run red lights are people who are not elitists.
    2. All taxi drivers are people who are not elitists.
    3. Some taxi drivers are people who never run red lights.

    1. Some P are M IAI-2
    2. All S are M
    3. Some S are P INVALID

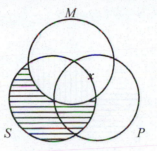

7. **1.** All intelligent creatures are things that will stay out of the middle of the highway.
2. No armadillos are things that will stay out of the middle of the highway.
3. No armadillos are intelligent creatures.

     1. All *P* are *M*   AEE-2
     2. No *S* are *M*
     3. No *S* are *P*   VALID

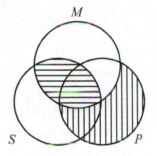

10. **1.** Some axolotls are creatures that are not often seen in the city.
2. All axolotls are mud lizards that are found in the jungles of southern Mexico.
3. Some mud lizards that are found in the jungles of southern Mexico are creatures that are not often seen in the city.

     1. Some *M* are *P*   IAI-3
     2. All *M* are *S*
     3. Some *S* are *P*   VALID

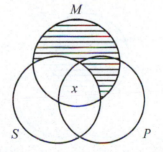

13. **1.** No impoverished persons are dentists who have done extensive postdoctoral study.
2. All orthodontists are dentists who have done extensive postdoctoral study.
3. No orthodontists are impoverished persons.

     1. No *P* are *M*   EAE-2
     2. All *S* are *M*
     3. No *S* are *P*   VALID

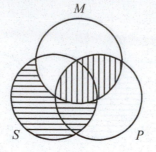

16. **1.** All philosophy majors are rational beings.
   2. No parakeets are rational beings.
   3. No parakeets are philosophy majors.

     1. All P are M AEE-2
     2. No S are M
     3. No S are P VALID

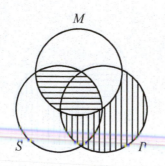

19. **1.** No hallucinations are optical illusions.
   2. Some misunderstandings that are not avoidable are hallucinations.
   3. Some misunderstandings that are not avoidable are optical illusions.

     1. No M are P EII-1
     2. Some S are M
     3. Some S are P INVALID

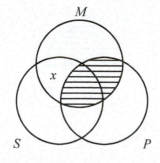

22. **1.** No benevolent despots are defenders of faculty autonomy.
   2. No defenders of faculty autonomy are college presidents.
   3. Some college presidents are not benevolent despots.

     1. No P are M EEO-4
     2. No M are S
     3. Some S are not P INVALID

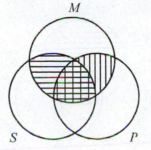

25. **1.** All philanderers are habitual prevaricators.
2. No habitual prevaricators are preachers who are well-known television personalities.
3. No preachers who are well-known television personalities are philanderers.

1. All *P* are *M*	AEE-4
2. No *M* are *S*	
3. No *S* are *P*	VALID

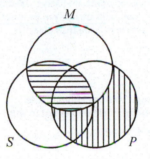

28. **1.** All great music is uplifting.
2. Some jazz is uplifting.
3. Some jazz is great music.

1. All *P* are *M*	AII-2
2. Some *S* are *M*	
3. Some *S* are *P*	INVALID

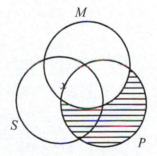

30. **1.** Some investments that are insured by the federal government are not an effective means of increasing one's wealth.
2. All investments that are insured by the federal government are interest-bearing bank accounts.
3. Some interest-bearing bank accounts are not an effective means of increasing one's wealth.

1. Some *M* are not *P*	OAO-3
2. All *M* are *S*	
3. Some *S* are not *P*	VALID

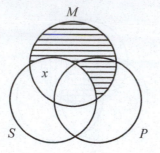

X

3. I. Subject undistributed; predicate undistributed. **6.** A. Subject distributed; predicate undistributed. **9.** I. Subject undistributed; predicate undistributed. **11.** O. Subject undistributed; predicate distributed. **14.** A. Subject distributed; predicate undistributed.

XI

3. 1. No people who are truly objective are people who are likely to be mistaken.
  2. All people who ignore the facts are people who are likely to be mistaken.
  3. No people who ignore the facts are people who are truly objective.

     1. No *P* are *M*   EAE-2   VALID
     2. All *S* are *M*
     3. No *S* are *P*

5. 1. No people who expect to win are people who can afford to lose.
  2. Some people who bet on horse races are people who expect to win.
  3. Some people who bet on horse races are people who can afford to lose.

     1. No *M* are *P*
     2. Some *S* are *M*
     3. Some *S* are *P*

     EII-1   INVALID   Affirmative from a negative

7. 1. Some metals are copper alloys.   1. Some *P* are *M*
  2. All copper alloys are good conductors of electricity. 2. All *M* are *S*
  3. Some good conductors of electricity are not metals. 3. Some *S* are not *P*

     IAO-4   INVALID   Illicit process of the major term and negative
                                from two affirmatives

9. 1. Some rabble-rousers are egalitarians.   1. Some *P* are *M*
  2. No egalitarians are sympathetic dissidents.   2. No *M* are *S*
  3. No sympathetic dissidents are rabble-rousers.   3. No *S* are *P*

     IEE-4   INVALID   Illicit process of the major term

11. 1. Some coaches are not talent scouts.   1. Some *M* are not *P*
  2. Some athletes are not coaches.   2. Some *S* are not *M*
  3. No athletes are talent scouts.   3. No *S* are *P*

     OOE-1   INVALID   Illicit process of the minor term and exclusive
                                premises

13. 1. Some college men are pigs (i.e., dirty).   1. Some *M* are *P*
  2. All college men are living things.   2. All *M* are *S*
  3. Some living things are pigs (i.e., animals).   3. Some *S* are *P*

     IAI-3   INVALID   Fallacy of four terms

15. 1. No admirers of Heidegger are utilitarians.
    2. All postmodernists are admirers of Heidegger.
    3. No postmodernists are utilitarians.

       1. No M are P
       2. All S are M
       3. No S are P

       EAE-1   VALID

17. 1. All single-celled organisms are invertebrates.
    2. All paramecia are single-celled organisms.
    3. All paramecia are invertebrates.

       1. All M are P
       2. All S are M
       3. All S are P

       AAA-1   VALID

19. 1. All good neighbors are respectful people.
    2. All good neighbors are well-intentioned zealots.
    3. No well-intentioned zealots are respectful people.

       1. All M are P
       2. All M are S
       3. No S are P

       AAE-3   INVALID   Illicit major and illicit minor. and negative
                              from two affirmatives

21. 1. Some traitors are not benefactors.
    2. No embezzlers are benefactors.
    3. All embezzlers are traitors.

       1. Some P are not M
       2. No S are M
       3. All S are P

       OEA-2   INVALID   Exclusive premises and affirmative from a negative

23. 1. No angora goats are hamsters.
    2. No angora goats are great white sharks.
    3. No great white sharks are hamsters.

       1. No M are P
       2. No M are S
       3. No S are P

       EEE-3   INVALID   Exclusive premises

25. 1. All television news anchors are photogenic.
    2. Some average people are not photogenic.
    3. Some average people are not television news anchors.

       1. All P are M
       2. Some S are not M
       3. Some S are not P

       AOO-2   VALID

Glossary/Index[1]

ACCIDENT   FALLACY OF PRESUMPTION committed by inferring that a certain generalization applies to a case that is clearly an exception to it, 143, 175–176, 378.

ACCURACY   VIRTUE of any BELIEF that is either true or approximately true 52ff.

AD BACULUM   See APPEAL TO FORCE.

ADDITION   The principle that, from P, "either P or Q" can be inferred. See RULE OF INFERENCE.

AD HOMINEM   Argument that attempts to undermine an ARGUMENT, BELIEF, or theory by discrediting those who propose it. Such personal attack often commits a FALLACY OF RELEVANCE. See also NON-FALLACIOUS AD HOMINEM, 143, 209–212, 378.

AD IGNORANTIAM   See APPEAL TO IGNORANCE.

AD MISERICORDIAM   See APPEAL TO PITY.

AD POPULUM   See APPEAL TO EMOTION.

AD VERECUNDIAM   See APPEAL TO UNQUALIFIED AUTHORITY.

AESTHETIC JUDGMENT   Judgment that concerns EVALUATIONS or NORMS involving matters of taste. 82–83, 378. See also NORMATIVE ARGUMENT.

AFFIRMATIVE FROM A NEGATIVE   In a CATEGORICAL SYLLOGISM, the FORMAL FALLACY of inferring an affirmative CONCLUSION from one or two negative PREMISES, 349.

AFFIRMING A DISJUNCT   FORMAL FALLACY of attempting to deduce the NEGATION of one DISJUNCT in an inclusive DISJUNCTION by asserting the other DISJUNCT, 270–271.

AFFIRMING THE CONSEQUENT   FORMAL FALLACY of attempting to deduce the ANTECEDENT of a MATERIAL CONDITIONAL by asserting its CONSEQUENT, 270, 378.

AGAINST THE PERSON   See AD HOMINEM.

AMBIGUITY   A problem of unclear language affecting any expression that could have more than one MEANING when the context makes unclear which meaning the speaker intends it to have, 182, 183ff, 189–190.

AMPHIBOLY   FALLACY OF UNCLEAR LANGUAGE committed by any ARGUMENT in which an awkward grammatical construction, word order, or phrasing may lead to the wrong CONCLUSION, 143, 191–193, 378.

ANALOGY   Type of INDUCTIVE ARGUMENT whereby a certain CONCLUSION about an individual or class of individuals is drawn on the basis of some similarities that individual or class has with other individuals or classes. See also WEAK ANALOGY, 129–130.

ANTECEDENT   The if-clause of a MATERIAL CONDITIONAL, 229–231.

APPEAL TO AUTHORITY   ARGUMENT that invokes expert opinion as a reason for its CONCLUSION. See also APPEAL TO UNQUALIFIED AUTHORITY.

APPEAL TO EMOTION   FALLACY OF RELEVANCE committed by an ARGUMENT that resorts to emotively charged language or images to support its CONCLUSION, 143, 207–208, 215–216, 378.

APPEAL TO FORCE   FALLACY OF RELEVANCE committed by an ARGUMENT that resorts to a threat as a way of trying to persuade someone to accept a CONCLUSION, 143, 205–206, 378.

APPEAL TO IGNORANCE   FALLACY OF FAILED INDUCTION committed by an ARGUMENT that draws a CONCLUSION on the basis of the absence of evidence against it, 150–151, 159, 378.

APPEAL TO PITY   FALLACY OF RELEVANCE committed by an ARGUMENT that attempts to arouse feelings of sympathy as a means of supporting its CONCLUSION, 143, 204–205, 378.

APPEAL TO UNQUALIFIED AUTHORITY   FALLACY OF FAILED INDUCTION committed by an ARGUMENT that invokes spurious expert opinion, 143, 152–154, 378.

APPEAL TO VANITY   A variation of the FALLACY of APPEAL TO EMOTION that invokes feelings of self-esteem as a way to support a certain CONCLUSION, 208, 378.

---

[1] Terms in CAPITALS are cross-listed in this glossary/index.

MATERIAL BICONDITIONAL (1) TRUTH- FUNC-TIONAL CONNECTIVE standardly expressed by 'if and only if'; (2) COMPOUND PROPOSITION that is true when both propositions joined have the same TRUTH VALUE and false when they have different truth values, 232–233, 236, 245.

MATERIAL CONDITIONAL (1) TRUTH-FUNC-TIONAL CONNECTIVE standardly expressed by 'if . . . then . . . '; (2) COMPOUND PROPOSI-TION that is true in all cases except when its ANTECEDENT is true and its CONSEQUENT false, 229–231, 236, 245.

MATERIAL EQUIVALENCE *See* MATERIAL BICONDITIONAL.

MEANING The content of an expression, 182.

METHOD OF AGREEMENT AND DIFFERENCE One of Mill's five methods for identifying causes, which holds that what different occurrences of a certain phenomenon have in common is proba-bly its cause, and that factors that are present only when some observed phenomenon occurs are probably its cause, 128–129.

METHOD OF CONCOMITANT VARIATION One of Mill's five methods for identifying causes, which holds that when variations in one phenomenon are highly correlated with those in another, one is likely the cause of the other, or both may be caused by some third factor, 129.

MIDDLE TERM In a CATEGORICAL SYLLOGISM, the TERM that occurs in both premises, 323ff.

MINOR PREMISE In a CATEGORICAL SYLLO-GISM, the premise that contains the MINOR TERM, 325ff.

MINOR TERM In a CATEGORICAL SYLLOGISM, the SUBJECT of the CONCLUSION, 323ff.

MISSING PREMISE Implicit PREMISE that must be made explicit in ARGUMENT RECONSTRUCTION, 72–73.

MODUS PONENS VALID ARGUMENT FORM with one CONDITIONAL premise, another that affirms that conditional's ANTECEDENT, and a CONCLUSION that asserts its CONSEQUENT. *See also* RULE OF INFERENCE, 99ff, 230–231, 277.

MODUS TOLLENS VALID ARGUMENT FORM with one CONDITIONAL premise, another that denies that conditional's CONSEQUENT, and a CONCLUSION that denies its ANTECEDENT, 99ff, 261, 277. *See also* RULE OF INFERENCE.

MOOD In a CATEGORICAL SYLLOGISM's FORM, the configuration of CATEGORICAL PROPOSI-TION types that make up its PREMISES and CONCLUSION, 328–330. *See also* FORM.

MORAL JUDGMENT Judgment that concerns EVALUATIONS or NORMS about what is good or bad, right or wrong, not because it's sanctioned by law or custom, but because it deserves praise or blame in itself, 82–83, 384. *See also* NORMATIVE JUDGMENT.

NATURAL LANGUAGE Language of a speech community. 4–5, 33–35, 184–185. *See also* FOR-MAL LANGUAGE.

NECESSARILY FALSE PROPOSITION PROPO-SITION that is false in all POSSIBLE WORLDS, 57–58, 248, 384. *See also* CONTRADICTION.

NECESSARILY TRUE PROPOSITION PROPO-SITION that is true in all POSSIBLE WORLDS, 248, 384. *See also* TAUTOLOGY.

NECESSARY AND SUFFICIENT CAUSE NECESSARY CAUSE that is the one and only possible cause of a certain event, 127–128, 231–232, 236, 384.

NECESSARY CAUSE Cause of an event without which that event could not occur, 127–128, 384.

NECESSARY CONDITION For any state of affairs, some other state of affairs without which the for-mer could not be the case. In a CONDITIONAL, its CONSEQUENT. 231ff, 261, 271. *See also* SUFFICIENT CONDITION.

NEGATION (1) TRUTH-FUNCTIONAL CON-NECTIVE standardly expressed by 'not'; (2) COMPOUND PROPOSITION whose TRUTH VALUE is the opposite of that of the same propo-sition unaffected by the connective, 224–226, 243.

NEGATIVE FROM TWO AFFIRMATIVES FORMAL FALLACY committed by a CATEGOR-ICAL SYLLOGISM that draws a NEGATIVE CONCLUSION from two AFFIRMATIVE premises, 350.

NON CAUSA PRO CAUSA A variation of the FALLACY of FALSE CAUSE committed by an argument that misidentifies some event contemporaneous with another as its cause, when in reality it's not, 149–150, 385.

NONBELIEF Having neither a BELIEF nor a DISBELIEF, 48ff.

NONCONCLUSIVE REASON PREMISE (or premises) that falls short of entailing a CON-CLUSION, 78. *See also* INDUCTIVE ARGU-MENT and CONCLUSIVE REASON.

NONCONTRADICTION Deductive rule that a proposition cannot be both true and false, 249, 385.

NON-FALLACIOUS *AD HOMINEM* Personal attack that, in context, is not irrelevant to the CONCLUSION of an ARGUMENT, 211–212, 385.

NON-LITERAL LANGUAGE Use of language whereby a sentence expresses a PROPOSITION different from the one it would express if the con-tents of its parts were taken at face value, 35, 40.

Index of Names